The Performing Arts

World Anthropology

General Editor

SOL TAX

Patrons

CLAUDE LÉVI-STRAUSS
MARGARET MEAD†
LAILA SHUKRY EL HAMAMSY
M. N. SRINIVAS

MOUTON PUBLISHERS · THE HAGUE · PARIS · NEW YORK

The Performing Arts

Music and Dance

Editors

JOHN BLACKING
JOANN W. KEALIINOHOMOKU

MOUTON PUBLISHERS · THE HAGUE · PARIS · NEW YORK

ISBN 90–279–7870–0 (Mouton)
Indexes by Society of Indexers, Great Britain
Jacket photo courtesy of UPI
Cover and jacket design by Jurriaan Schrofer
Phototypeset in V.I.P. Times by
Western Printing Services Ltd, Bristol
Printed in Great Britain

General Editor's Preface

Expressive behavior in the human species, which also provides aesthetic satisfaction, must have been important to human adaptation from earliest times, enabling us to posit that even then there existed "performing arts." Later came the attachment of the arts to specific cultural or symbolic patterns as described by Professor Blacking in his Introduction to this volume. He develops a theory of music which may indeed go beyond music and even the arts to all expressive behaviors which are socially disciplined. This book is the positive result of a venture originating with its senior editor in collaboration with Dr. Justine Cordwell, editor of a companion volume on *The visual arts*. Her book includes a full description of their joint conference on "Art and Anthropology." That conference preceded the IXth International Congress, which included a major segment on Affective Response in Man, which produced other books in this series on world views and cosmology, religion, shamanism, myths and folklore, and language as well as these on the visual and the performing arts. The Congress itself brought together people of cultures from all continents to look afresh at anthropology.

Like most contemporary sciences, anthropology is a product of the European tradition. Some argue that it is a product of colonialism, with one small and self-interested part of the species dominating the study of the whole. If we are to understand the species, our science needs substantial input from scholars who represent a variety of the world's cultures. It was a deliberate purpose of the IXth International Congress of Anthropological and Ethnological Sciences to provide impetus in this direction. The *World Anthropology* volumes, therefore offer a first glimpse of a human science which members from all societies have played an active role. Each of the books is designed to be self-contained; each is an attempt to update its particular sector of scientific knowledge and is written by specialists from all parts of the world. Each volume should be read and reviewed individually as a separate volume on its own given subject. The set as a whole will indicate what changes are in store for anthropology as scholars from the developing countries join in studying the species of which we are all a part.

The IXth Congress was planned from the beginning not only to include as many of the scholars from every part of the world as possible, but also with a view toward the eventual publication of the papers in high-quality volumes. At previous Congresses scholars were invited to bring papers which were then read out loud. They were necessarily limited in length; many were only summarized; there was little time for discussion; and the sparse discussion could only be in one language. The IXth Congress was an experiment aimed at changing this. Papers were written with the intention of exchanging them before the Congress, particularly in extensive pre-Congress sessions; they were not intended to be read aloud at the Congress, that time being devoted to discussions — discussions which were simultaneously and professionally translated into five languages. The method for eliciting the papers was structured to make as representative a sample as was allowable when scholarly creativity — hence self-selection — was critically important. Scholars were asked both to propose papers of their own and to suggest topics for sessions of the Congress which they might edit into volumes. All were then informed of the suggestions and encouraged to rethink their own papers and the topics. The process, therefore, was a continuous one of feedback and exchange and it has continued to be so even after the Congress. The some two thousand papers comprising *World Anthropology* certainly then offer a substantial sample of world anthropology. It has been said that anthropology is at a turning point; if this is so, these volumes will be the historical direction-markers.

As might have been foreseen in the first post-colonial generation, the large majority of the Congress papers (82 percent) are the work of scholars identified with the industrialized world which fathered our traditional discipline and the institution of the Congress itself: Eastern Europe (15 percent); Western Europe (16 percent); North America (47 percent); Japan, South Africa, Australia, and New Zealand (4 percent). Only 18 percent of the papers are from developing areas: Africa (4 percent); Asia-Oceania (9 percent); Latin America (5 percent). Aside from the substantial representation from the U.S.S.R. and the nations of Eastern Europe, a significant difference between this corpus of written material and that of other Congresses is the addition of the large proportion of contributions from Africa, Asia, and Latin America. "Only 18 percent" is two to four times as great a proportion as that of other Congresses; moreover, 18 percent of 2,000 papers is 360 papers, 10 times the number of 'Third World" papers presented at previous Congresses.

In fact, these 360 papers are more than the total of *all* papers published after the last International Congress of Anthropological and Ethnological Sciences which was held in the United States (Philadelphia, 1956).

The significance of the increase is not simply quantitative. The input of scholars from areas which have until recently been no more than subject matter for anthropology represents both feedback and also long-awaited theoretical contributions from the perspectives of very different cultural, social, and historical traditions. Many who attended the IXth Congress were convinced that anthropology would not be the same in the future. The fact that the Xth Congress (India, 1978) was our first in the "Third World" may be symbolic of the change. Meanwhile, sober consideration of the present set of books will show how much, and just where and how, our discipline is being revolutionized.

As indicated in the first paragraph above, there are in this series a number of books on human affective response which are likely to interest readers of this volume as well as its companion volume edited by Dr. Cordwell. Not mentioned above but also of relevance to the topics treated here are books bearing on primatological and archaeological beginnings as well as on descriptions of cultural forms in various parts of the world.

Chicago, Illinois   Sol Tax
July 7, 1979

Table of Contents

Introduction

JOHN BLACKING

The papers in this volume were submitted to the sessions on the performing arts at the IXth International Congress of Anthropological and Ethnological Sciences, held in Chicago in August-September 1973. Not all the papers were read and discussed, and not all authors were present. No attempt has been made to select papers which illustrate a particular theme or theoretical framework, because earlier plans to organize a gathering of scholars to discuss specific issues in theory and method had been thwarted when financial support proved meagre and several of those invited were unable to attend. Although I had been appointed editor of the proceedings, there were not even funds available for my own journey to the Congress! I have therefore had to rely upon the written versions of the papers and tape recordings of the meetings, in preparing this volume with Joann Kealiinohomoku.

Unfortunately, the tape recordings of the discussions neither provided a theme or themes with which to link the papers, nor were they sufficiently integrated to be published as part of the volume. Nevertheless, what the volume lacks in thematic unity it gains in diversity, as it reflects the different interests and approaches of twenty-four scholars from Austria, India, Ireland, Japan, Nigeria, Rumania, South Africa, USA, USSR, Vietnam, and Yugoslavia.

Some papers had to be translated into English, and in a number of cases authors could not be contacted or did not respond to editorial requests. The bulk of the copy editing has been done by Martin Bayley and Karen Tkach, with the dance papers initially edited by Joann Kealiinohomoku. I am most grateful for their assistance, but take responsibility for any errors or textual misinterpretations that may have crept in. I am also grateful to Barbara Krader for checking some of the East European place names and references.

In spite of the diversity of approach and content of the papers, there are some recurrent themes that transcend even the six general headings under which I have grouped them. For example, a common interest in the role of music and dance in society is expressed both in the content of theoretically oriented papers and case studies, and in the aim of several contributors to record traditions that provide evidence of popular creativity and ancient national cultural identity.

Most authors agree that the forms and meanings of the performing arts cannot be understood without referring to their social context and functions. Cong-Huyen-Ton-Nu Nha-Trang discusses the function of Vietnamese folk songs as a medium for communicating political, economic, and emotional issues. C.O. Okoreaffia describes the uses of music and dance by the Igbo of Nigeria to honor a dead person. The cost of the ritual ensures that the surplus material wealth of the deceased is consumed and a degree of equality is restored in a competitive society, while its display and commemorative aspects ensure that what is really important about the deceased, his spiritual essence and the record of his human career, are remembered. Whereas the Igbo *Igeri Ututu* music and dance ritual lays the dead person to rest, the Cumina cult of Jamaica uses music and dance to socialize trance and help call up the spirits of deceased ancestors, or zombies. Possession by zombies is manifested in the dance movements. Joseph Moore compares the Cumina cults, which are "African with New World negro inventions" (p. 305) with the Revival cults, which are syncretistic and blend African and European Christian elements and traditions. As might be expected, in Revival groups the bodies of the faithful are possessed by the Holy Ghost, the archangels and prophets, some of the disciples, and the spirits of former members of the Revival flock who have died.

Social context and function therefore illuminate the meaning of music and dance, but they do not explain their styles and forms, except in the very general sense that hoeing, weeding, threshing, pounding, and canoeing, songs must differ systematically according to the work that they are designed to accompany. Thus, although the function of rice-planting music and its technological correlates are the same in Chindo Island, off the southwestern Korean coast, and in the Chūgoku region of the Japanese mainland, as indeed they are in most other parts of eastern and southeastern Asia where rice planting ceremonies are held, Ruriko Uchida shows that their music differs considerably. Similarly, although the music and the movements of the Cumina and Revival cults vary according to the different purposes and agents of possession, the social uses and functions of the music and dance do not explain the different styles, any more than a sociological analysis of Vietnamese folksongs necessarily explains why particular modes and intervals are chosen.

Social context, and social use and function, are, like musical traditions, conventional frameworks for the play of social interaction, or, in the case of social function, the constructs of anthropologists. Indeed, if music is a cultural phenomenon and a social fact, as most authors seem to agree, musical and cultural forms should be homologous; and Midori Himeno observes that "considering the Taiwan aborigines as a whole . . . there are as many musical differences between the tribes as there are other cultural differences" (p. 157). But to say that musical and cultural forms are homologous does not explain musical variety any more than cultural variety. Nor are arguments about historical accretion or environmental influences convincing as explanations of cultural variety, because historical and environmental influences are effective only insofar as human beings choose to make them so in the course of their social interaction.

Explanations of differences in styles of music and dance must therefore begin with an account of the choices that musicians and dancers make in the course of performance—choices about patterns of sound and movement, that are inevitably related to decisions made in the course of social interaction in other fields. For the decisions that people make about musical and choreographic processes are made with the same minds as the decisions that are made about social interaction; and the decisions that actors make as human beings generally precede those that they make in their capacity as music-makers and dancers. In their paper, Bonnie Wade and Ann Pescatello show how the status of women in the performing arts in India and Iberia "is linked first to the status of women in general in those cultures, and second to the status of the particular art in which they perform" (p. 135).

There are, however, many problems that arise when the sources of cultural forms are sought in patterns of social relations, and nowhere is this more apparent than in analyses of music, dance, and other types of ritual activity. It comes out in some of the papers by East European and Russian authors, who show concern about a dilemma which faces any anthropologist who believes that new social relations should give rise to new cultural forms. On the one hand, they observe, as does Petrosian in his study of the totemic dances of Armenia, that cultural forms change with changing social conditions, or when they are transmitted from one area to another, as Olivera Mladenović and Madeleine Andjelić point out respectively in their accounts of the *Kolo na kolu* dance in Yugoslavia, and of Hungarian variants of South Slavic folksongs and tales. On the other hand, Putilov reports that there has been no change in the musical instruments of Bongu village in New Guinea, which was studied a century ago by the Russian anthropologist Muklukho-Maklai, although there have been social changes and most of their neighbors have adopted the modern instruments that are popular throughout Oceania. Petrosian also argues that "despite all the changes in the patterns and contents of dances, they have preserved their original roots" (p. 72).

Petrosian's notion of "original roots" also appears in Ksenia Sikharulidze's and Emilia Comişel's papers on Georgian rituals and songs of weather and the Rumanian folklore calendar. In other words, communities have a culture that can transcend changing social formations. Although culture exists only insofar as individuals invoke and reinvent it in the course of social interaction, some systems of significant symbols do persist over time (see my paper, p. 3), and although in the course of more than two thousand years of history, "complex customs" may "have lost at least some of their old meanings through conditions created by technical, economic, and social revolution, they remain as folk manifestations of great artistic value" (Comişel, p. 200). Thus analysis of the Rumanian folklore calendar helps Comişel to discover more about the ancient culture of the Rumanian people and to *prove* "the continuity of the Rumanians' presence in this region" (p. 200). An important aim of folklore research is therefore to gather material that may be used to enrich the education of the young and the recreation of adults, and to reinforce a sense of national identity.

The theoretical implications of this kind of use of traditional performing arts are briefly discussed for music on p. 4, and elaborated in Joann Kealiinohomoku's paper comparing the functions of traditional dances in Balinese and Hawai'ian societies. Her point is that the notion of culture as "original roots" is too vague: *it is not culture in general that can transcend changing social formations, but very specifically, affective culture* – which is, of course, the topic of this volume. Thus

If a society experiences radical changes, such as Hawai'ian society did, in its living patterns, in its social organization, there is little left of the original *unless* its affective culture can maintain its viability (p. 62).

"Hawai'ian affective culture is not viable through syncretism as Balinese affective culture is", because it was functionally interrelated to the old religion, the old technology, the old hierarchical political system, and many other features of precontact Hawai'i which Hawai'ians do not wish to revive. But it has become viable again through a reinterpretation of the hula which fulfils the Hawai'ian need to maintain a sense of cultural identity in the context of contemporary Hawai'ian society. Thus the affective culture of the Hawai'ians has transcended changing social formations, and although its forms are *not* a reflection of new needs, new functions and new social formations, its meanings and its social contexts have changed.

Affective culture can remain formally static while being socially and emotionally dynamic, so that there need not be a contradiction between the development (dynamic) of a nation and the preservation (static) of its artistic forms. Moreover, an unavoidable feature of music and dance is that no two performances can ever be the same in terms of their meanings to participants, even if they may sound or look identical to the ears of the tape recorder and sonagram and the eye of the camera. It is the combination of cultural continuity and social change in the performance event that helps to make affective culture a crucial element in the social life of communities; and, not surprisingly, it comes to have considerable relevance in countries where there are ethnic minorities. If Comişel's work on the Rumanian folklore calendar justifies Rumanians' claims to Rumanian territory, what is the status of American Indians in the USA or of Armenians and Yakuts in the USSR? Perhaps this problem partially accounts for the emphasis that Russian scholars seem to place on structural studies of dance and music, and the rich variety of dance notations that they have developed. M. Zhornitskaia acknowledges the importance of ethnic variations in Soviet affective culture, but argues that the relations between the dances of the Soviet people are greater than the differences:

The available data show that Russian, Belorussian, and Ukrainian folk dances have a common origin, and folk dances in the Transcaucasus have common stable specific elements. The same is true of folk dances in the extreme northeast of Siberia, and so on (p. 85).

Thus the uniqueness of the affective culture of any single Soviet ethnic group is explained by the specific geographical and historical conditions in which it exists; but at the same time no ethnic group stands alone outside any of the "choreographic complexes" that can be identified in the Soviet Union, and so any one group's sense of cultural identity must include cooperation and identification with other ethnic groups.

The concern for identifying clusters of features by which a music or dance style can be identified and related to others prompts several authors to call for greater uniformity in methods of recording and in terminology, so that exchange of experience and cross-cultural studies may be more easily undertaken (e.g. p. 86). Joseph Moore's diagrams of the characteristic movements of Cumina dances (pp. 301–304) are easier for the average anthropologist than Laban, Benesh, or Lisitsian notation, but I wonder if such gross distinctions of the subtleties of movement variation are adequate for effective analysis, and to what extent anthropologists must defer to people with years of experience in music or dance notation. The trouble is that experts in those fields are often rather deficient in their analyses of social relations, and so we are back in a position where the connections between social relations and music and dance forms cannot be precisely demonstrated.

One solution to the problem is for closer cooperation between anthropologists, musicologists, and choreologists, and for more rigorous anthropological training for the latter—since technical training in music and dance generally takes much longer. Another solution is that of Alan

Lomax, who has reduced the parameters of song and dance styles to terms that most anthropologists can manage, and has argued that these gross categories are adequate for identifying the salient features of a style: in fact, he claims that a sample of only ten songs is enough to establish a style. My worries about Lomax's important pioneering work in cantometrics and choreometrics are directed not so much at the generality of his variables and the fact that many of the societies studied have more music and dance styles than those selected for the cross-cultural survey, as at the usefulness of cross-cultural studies that examine the cultural products rather than the social and cognitive processes by which they are constituted. It can, of course, be argued in some cases that a particular musical result can only be obtained in one way, so that a description of the product is at the same time an analysis of the social and cognitive process. Hewitt Pantaleoni's comparison of rhythmic patterns in African and Afro-American music is one such case.

Because I am more concerned with "musical" processes than musical products, what interests me most about Seaton and Watson's paper is not the ordinal scaling and clustering of world song styles (p. 99 ff), which, as they say, corresponds to the culture regions of Murdock's *Ethnographic atlas*, and might therefore be described as a self-fulfilling prophecy generated by the evolutionary models of anthropology. Much more interesting is the ordinal scaling and clustering of cantometric variables: for even if this also fulfills Lomax's anthropological prophecy of "contrastive" models for song performance ("the highly individualized and group-dominating" Model A, and "the highly cohesive, group-involving" Model B), at least it draws attention to clusters of variables which constitute varieties of the musical *process*. And when we know what, if any, are the crucial parameters that make social interaction "musical" and which of these "musical" features tend to cluster, then we shall be in a better position to relate the "musical" processes to other social and cognitive processes of the people who make the music, and so go some way toward explaining the variety of music and dance styles in terms of the varieties of social relations and cognitive processes brought to bear on the invention and reinvention of culture.

In the circulated Congress draft of my own paper, I urged that the biological foundations of music should be established, as part of the goal of identifying a purely "musical" process and revealing the nature of music as a primary modeling system. I was particularly attracted by the evidence of right and left cerebral dominance for music and verbal language in cases of amusia and aphasia, and of early musical abilities of children, and I had recently written a paper in which I argued that the evolutionary sequence of human communication had been dance-music-verbal language (Blacking 1976). Since then I have come to the view that although music is, like verbal language, fundamentally a species-specific behavior and not a human invention, and that there is much to be gained from studying it as a unique code, or system of signs, the search for an innate "musical" process is more useful as a heuristic device than as a legitimate means to an attainable scientific goal. It concentrates attention on the clusters of elements that distinguish the essentially musical from other forms of communication; but it is most unlikely to reveal elements that are *purely* "musical." Similarly, Eric Lenneberg (1967) demonstrated that verbal language is not just a special adaptation of organs for eating and breathing, and that parts of the body evolved specifically for language; but at the same time other capabilities and behaviors are necessary for the development of language in individual organisms, such as hearing and social interaction at certain stages of growth. Again, in seeking to identify the basic, necessary components of any "dance" activity and construct a general model of the choreographic process, Judith Hanna points out that such activities must be studied in the context of the social relations of a specific community of dance participants and observers.

Okoreaffia's paper also reminds us that in most parts of Africa music and dance can never be isolated, since they are intelligible only as parts of multimedia events. Several other authors, such as Joseph Moore and Gertrude Kurath, explicitly or implicity maintain that music and dance are complementary modes of nonverbal communication that must be analyzed interdependently. Sithole's and Kurath's papers show specifically how performers and audiences conceive both musical expression and musical experience in multimedia terms, and Kubik presents more evidence to confirm a point that has been made by a number of writers on African music: namely, that there are close links between movement patterns and music-making in processes of enculturation and learning, of execution, of perception, and of aesthetic appreciation.

Although Kubik claims to be "treating the relevant processes exclusively in their musical context" and avoiding "extramusical implications or associations with sound complexes" (p. 221), it seems to me from what follows that he is doing nothing of the sort! He appears to be defining "music" in African terms as part of a multimedia event, and his paper is devoted to describing movement patterns, tuning systems, and the perception of "inherent patterns" of rhythm and melody through the perceptions and concepts used by practicing African musicians. This inevitably involves him in "extramusical" data, although the focus of his analysis is the sound complexes themselves, the products of the musical processes. I would go further and suggest that the appreciation of music as a multimedia event is present in European notions of "music", no less than in African. Most analyses of music sound, even those that claim to be phenomenological, are full of metaphors, similes, and general ideas that invoke extramusical associations. And those that explicitly seek to avoid extramusical associations, such as Hans Keller's wordless functional analyses, can hardly eliminate them altogether, since the perception and recognition of musical patterns by composer, performer, listener, and analyst, are always part of social processes within given cultural frameworks.

Another crucial point that arises from the evidence in Kubik's paper and in Kauffman's paper on the importance of tactility in African music, and refers back to the issue of biological capabilities, is: to what extent are the perceptive and performing abilities of musicians and audiences in Africa developed through enculturation and learning within particular musical traditions, and to what extent are they generally available, innate propensities that some music traditions have taken up and others neglected? For example, might Europeans pick out "inherent patterns" (see pp. 231–240) in music, if they had not been trained to do otherwise? Perhaps they do, in any case, and this might be an important factor in explaining people's different perceptions of the same work. (Contradictions in analyses of a Mozart piano concerto, for instance, might be due to perceptive flexibility, rather than right or wrong perceptions of musical structures. In many African musical systems, the diversity of "inherent patterns" available to performers and listeners would be taken as a measure of the aesthetic value of the piece, and not as evidence of ignorance or conceptual confusion). Was the potential development of children's musical expression inhibited by the available intervals and rhythms of the songs for children discussed by Ghizela Suliţeanu (pp. 205–219)? Were Venda children in South Africa in 1956–1958 more "advanced" musically (see Blacking 1967, especially pp. 28–30) because they were expected to use a wider range of intervals and scales at an earlier age than is considered normal in many European societies? My own research into the performances of small children suggests that they can perceive and sing more "complex" melodies than developmental theory allows them, and that when they do not, they are more likely to have been constrained by environment than by innate disabilities. However, I doubt if there is any way in which the musical potential of two-year-olds can be measured accurately, because the rapid development of verbal language from eighteen months onward, *and the widespread use of verbal language as a major means of communication*, motivate the development of the verbal rather than nonverbal modes of communication.

A similar difficulty arises when assessing the influence of verbal language on music structures, and vice versa, as Anoop Chandola illustrates in his comparison of the common phenomenon of stress in patterns of musical rhythm and phrases and sentences of verbal language. The safest course is to avoid regarding either language or music as *the* primary modeling system, even though verbal language plays a leading role in the formation and transmission of cultural systems, and to treat each as *a* primary modeling system (and dance would be another) for patterns of thought and social interaction. The notion of several primary, but interdependent, modeling systems is not a contradiction in terms any more than the idea of several primary organs of the body; and it is more useful than seeking one primary modeling system such as verbal language, from which others are derived, or constructing a general model of communication and then applying it to dance, music, language, social interaction, or any other field of human behavior. The former ignores the variety of the models that different societies have chosen in creating their social, musical, and choreographic forms, and the latter runs the risk of ironing out the important qualitative differences of human experience, and hence the features that matter most when individuals choose to invoke one mode or combination of modes of communication rather than another.

A society's affective culture is enriched by the variety of primary modeling systems that people can invoke to express and educate their emotions. Richard Strauss' opera *Capriccio* portrays a situation in which a poet and a composer compete for the affection of the heroine in words and music, and much of the dialogue is devoted to a debate on the relative merits of these two modes of communication. The heroine's inability to decide who moves her more assures her of continued attention and pleasure! Although music and dance cannot be completely isolated, even for analytical purposes, from other social and artistic activities, it is their intrinsic qualities as modes of nonverbal communication and symbolic expression that elicit affective response in man and ensure that one system is not absorbed by the other; and it is the identification of these intrinsic elements that most concern the authors of the papers. Nevertheless, their field experience may have convinced them, as it does me, that one of the most valuable consequences of studying the anthropology of the performing arts is to find ways of bringing together again all the arts in performance situations in which all members of the community participate fully.

Since the practice of the performing arts can be an important factor in social change, study of the anthropology of the performing arts can, and in my opinion should, be directed toward changing, as well as understanding, the world. If any of the data or analyses in this book serve the purpose of releasing more human potential through practice of the performing arts, or make some corner of the world a better place, then its publication will be fully justified.

REFERENCES

BLACKING, JOHN
  1967   *Venda children's songs: a study in ethnomusicological analysis*. Johannesburg: University of the Witwatersrand Press.
  1976   "Dance, conceptual thought and production in the archaeological record," in *Problems in economic and social archaeology*. Edited by G. de G. Sieveking, I. H. Longworth and K. E. Wilson, 3–13. London: Duckworth.
LENNEBERG, ERIC
  1967   *Biological foundations of language*. New York: Wiley.

PART ONE

Music and Dance in Society:
General Perspectives

The Study of Man as Music-M

JOHN BLACKING

The study of music and music-making can be useful as a model for the more general anthropological study of culture, "the organized systems of significant symbols" (Geertz 1975:46) that persist in communities over time. Strictly speaking, music can only be produced by performance, and its meaning is the sense that individuals make of it; similarly, culture is invoked and reinvented by social interaction. Thus music and other cultural phenomena can be said to have no intrinsic meanings, and it ought to be possible to assign to them any meaning.

And yet the decision to invoke a system of symbols in a particular social situation, which is itself constrained by other symbol systems, can exert further constraints on behavior and action. In other words, the invocation of an organized sequence of symbols can restrict the decision-making of the very individuals who freely invented them, if only by requiring that the sequence, once begun, should be completed in a specified way.

One may ask why people should choose to invent and invoke systems of action that set limits to their freedom of choice. In the production of material goods or of sentences in a language, for example, the advantages are obvious: the constraints of a specific technical process and of syntax can generate greater freedom, through increases in the control of the environment and in the range of communication and thought. The consumption of music, however, does not have obvious social advantages, except insofar as performance may be used for purposes that are not essentially musical: for instance, focus of attention on the production of sound may bring together and consolidate the ideas and relationships of people who share nominally common political, social, or religious allegiances. As such, the constraints on free decision-making imposed by the performance of music can be justified by an expected increase in political, social, or religious commitment or activity.

. this were the only consequence of music-making, there would be ɔthing of particular anthropological or sociological interest about musical behavior and action: it could be studied as any other social activity, and its symbols could be treated in much the same way as the rules of a game. Anthropologists and sociologists would not need to concern themselves with the music so much as with the uses to which it is put and the values attached to it in the course of social interaction. Music would therefore be anthropologically and sociologically neutral, or, as Nadel suggested, an "action autonomous" (Nadel 1951:87). There need be

no link between group organization and, say, painting in oils, perspective in drawing, ornamental designs in sculpture rather than naturalistic ones, blank verse rather than rhyme, polyphony rather than homophony in music. . . . The *style* in art, then, exists in its own right, entailing and presupposing no determinate social relationships (Nadel 1951:88. Italics in original).

This is in line with the argument of Max Weber, who maintained that modern European music was rationalized within the tone system (1968), and that once this development had taken place, influenced by the scientific attitude that emerged at the time of the Renaissance, the musical system pursued an almost inevitable logic of its own.

This approach to the study of music and music-making is sociologically legitimate; but if music is to have any theoretical interest to anthropologists, it will be necessary to assume that its importance extends beyond its often arbitrary use in a variety of contexts for different social purposes, to its reciprocal influence on human behavior and action. Ultimately, the music is the most significant aspect of musical activities, not only for anyone who studies them but also for those who participate in them, and it is the special character of musical activities that is sociologically and anthropologically problematic, rather than characteristics that they have in common with other social activities. Man makes music as a patterned event in a system of social interaction, as part of a process of conscious decision-making; but there is also a sense in which music makes man, releasing creative energy, expanding consciousness and influencing subsequent decision-making and cultural invention. The anthropological study of music and music-making must therefore be concerned with the products of man as music-maker, and the processes by which feelings and ideas are expressed in patterns of sound, and patterns of sound evoke feelings and ideas. The symbolic load *assigned* to music, often arbitrarily, may be relevant in this enquiry, and performers' and listeners' views of music and musical experience are crucial data in the identification of significant musical parameters and the analysis of musical meaning. But the study of the symbolic load *of* music itself, and especially of the effectiveness of musical symbols, is its most challenging aspect, because music is a mediator between nature and culture, between feeling and form, a link between the innate, generalized automatic complexity of the body (*all* human bodies: not a few specifically "gifted" bodies), and the particular cultural arrangements of bodies that have been achieved through the medium of social interaction.

Music is therefore an ideal field for the study of relationships between patterns of social interaction and the invention of cultural forms. Nadel and others of like mind may be correct in arguing that such relationships do not and need not exist, but their case has been neither proved nor disproved. The explanation of cultural forms remains a key problem in the social sciences, and the study of music and music-making can contribute much to its solution.

This view has been well expressed by Lévi-Strauss, and especially in the Introduction to *The raw and the cooked* (1969). In comparing the special resemblance of music to myth in both freezing time and unfolding in time, Lévi-Strauss emphasizes its role in relating the inner experience of organic rhythms to the external rhythms of the music, and he claims that "music is the supreme mystery of the science of man, a mystery that all the various disciplines come up against and which holds the key to their progress" (Lévi-Strauss 1969:18). Insofar as music is a mediator between nature and culture, I can agree here with Lévi-Strauss (and with his claim (1969:18) that "musical invention depends on special gifts, which can be developed only where they are innate").

But if an understanding of music and music-making is to provide clues to further knowledge in the science of man, it must be assumed that, as in language, the power of musical invention is possessed as much by the receivers of music as by its creators and performers, and that if certain "musical" capabilities are innate, they are innate for all members of the species and not only a tiny minority. If the study of music is to reveal anything of interest to the general study of man, we must begin with the assumption (which may, of course, ultimately prove to be false) that music-making is derived from certain biologically given capabilities that are general to the human species, or at least that musical composition must have some corporate meaning to other people, beyond the separate meanings assigned by the creator and each different listener. In either case, some, if not all, of the mental processes involved in composition are also required for intelligent listening.

The composition of music has always required its *re*-composition by performers and audiences, if it is to move out of the private mind of the individual composer; and it is the *ordinary* quality of some music, its ability to transcend time, place, and social class, that makes a composer like Mozart so extraordinary. In other words, it is what Mozart has in common and can share with others that distinguishes his music, rather than what is unique about him. There is, after all, nothing extraordinary about uniqueness: all individuals, except identical twins, are biologically

unique, and all become socially unique. What makes cultural achievements possible is the ability of people to *share* feelings and thoughts, and
particularly to share with a commitment that springs from understanding
and assimilation. There is evidence, especially in the reports of ethnomusicologists, that "ordinary" people listen intelligently to music as well
as they listen and respond to language. Furthermore, composers are not
always aware of the intelligence that they employ in creating their music
(cf. Schoenberg 1951: ch. 5), because this intelligence is part of the
mechanism of the human body. Since composers value, and their critics
endorse, musical intuition, it seems hardly fair to question the intelligence
of listeners who use that same intuition to re-create the music and make
sense of its code.

Whether or not there are biological foundations of music-making, as
there are of language, music itself is not natural. Musical intervals are
social facts and not always founded on the laws of acoustics, as Alexander
John Ellis pointed out in 1885, when he measured the musical scales of
several societies and concluded:

The musical scale is not one, not "natural", nor even founded necessarily on the
laws of the constitution of musical sound so beautifully worked out by Helmholtz,
but very diverse, very artificial, and very capricious (Ellis 1885:526).

Music differs from painting in its *relationship* to nature, as Lévi-Strauss
argued, but not in its closeness to nature. Lévi-Strauss claimed that
painting is closer to nature than music because "nature offers man models
of all colors" but for music, nature produces only noises, so that "man
would be unacquainted with musical sounds if he had not invented them"
(Lévi-Strauss 1969:22). Music is in fact no less close to nature than
painting, because the model for music is man's own nature and much
music is therefore discovered rather than invented. The area of discovery
is not so much the external world of sound as the internal world of human
feelings. The creation of music can be described as a sharing of inner
feelings in a social context through extensions of body movement, in
which certain species-specific capabilities are modified and extended
through social and cultural experience. Music is a metaphor of feeling
that draws on man's own nature for many of its forms. It is because of this
that it is often "intelligible" and at the same time "untranslatable"
(Lévi-Strauss 1969:18), in the sense that any meanings can be assigned to
it as a sequence of symbols, and yet it may have only one meaning at the
time it is experienced.

Music is not intelligible unless it is "grammatical"; its code is its
message, and it is incoherent as music unless it is logically structured. (In
this respect, as in many others, music differs from verbal language, where
both ungrammatical sense and grammatical nonsense, as in Lewis Car-

roll, are possible.) And yet musical structures seem to spring from feelings as often as they evoke them. The point is that human feelings are also structured and in the transformation of feelings into patterns of sound and vice versa the innate structures of the body play a part in creation and interpretation, as well as the musical conventions of different societies and the different musical experiences of individuals.

I have argued that musical systems are not autonomous, and that the study of music and music-making therefore provides an excellent model for analyzing the invention and use of cultural forms. Relations between systems of ideas about social and musical organization can, for example, be seen in the music of the Venda of South Africa (Blacking 1967, 1970, 1973), and connections between patterns of social interaction and musical variation can be observed (e.g. Blacking 1973:71). In every performance situation social and musical decision-making is carried out in relation to the more general body of cultural knowledge, but the musical product of each situation can be "frozen" for analysis, by means of tape-recordings and films, and the details of the associated patterns of social interaction can be related to them, provided that a careful record of behavior has been made.

There are therefore two levels at which relationships between music and society can be expected: at the level of ideas and at the level of interaction in which ideas are invoked. There are also two areas of action that are involved in every performance situation: the musical and the social. Neither ideas nor musical action can be understood without reference to patterns of social interaction; for ideas and music, like everything cultural, are firstly social facts.

This does not mean, however, that all ideas and music must be epiphenomena of the social, although it is clear that they can only be expressed and shared through the medium of social interaction, and that their forms are profoundly influenced by social experience. These are elements in the formation of ideas, and especially of musical structures, that suggest they are irreducible phenomena, in the same way as language. Although verbal languages cannot be learned properly without a long period in which they are used in social situations, and their forms are affected by variations in culture and social class, language systems are not merely reflections of social phenomena; they have biological foundations (cf. Lenneberg 1967). For this reason, and in particular because it is the most extensively used channel of communication in the transmission of culture, language has been called *the* primary modeling system. Since the capacities for verbal language seem to have developed relatively late in human evolution, and the uniformity and continuity of the Acheulean stone cultures of *Homo erectus* could hardly have been achieved without sophisticated modes of communication, such as gestural "language" (cf.

Hewes 1973), there is no good reason to claim sole primacy for verbal language. Besides, language presupposes more fundamental cognitive processes, such as categorization, transformation, and particularly the symbolic transformation of experience (cf. Langer 1948:35).

The second phase of my argument is therefore that music, like verbal language, is a primary modeling system, and that what makes its study sociologically and anthropologically interesting are the features that it does *not* have in common with other social activities, and the fact that it constrains social interaction when it is invoked. It is those essentially musical features which provide the common denominator for musical and social action, both at the levels of ideas and interaction and in the areas of the musical and the social. That is to say, general relationships between music and society, and relationships between the musical and social elements in musical performance, are made possible by the extension of the primary musical modeling system into specific social contexts.

Music appears to be organized very differently from verbal language. Nicolas Ruwet, for instance, has argued (1972) that repetition and symmetry are basic features of the syntax of music: since musical meaning and communication depend on the use and perception of repetition, the essential problem in analyses of music is to identify different kinds of repetition and to assess their semantic significance. Another special feature of music is the use of mirror forms. There is a logical sequence from the observation of mirror forms in nature to the use of mirror forms in design, but not to their use in music. If, however, mirror transformations are a structure of the "mind", initially realized in musical performance, this could account for their being applied to any creative field without prior observation or experience.

What I am suggesting is that music-making may be a special way of organizing human bodies which is most commonly, but not necessarily, manifested in a variety of activities that are classed as "musical". In seeking to understand the elementary structures of human thought, music is in fact more appropriate than verbal language for revealing the purely structural requirements for a symbol *system*, as Susanne Langer has pointed out (Langer 1948:185).

But music is more than a mediator between natural and cultural forms. As a metaphor of feeling, it can both reflect and generate a special kind of social experience. Thus, the transcendental potential of musical performance provide a further answer to the question raised at the beginning of this paper. People choose to invent and invoke music, rather than other systems of action that may put fewer restrictions on their freedom of choice, because music-making offers an intensity of feeling and quality of experience that is more highly valued than some other social activities. This is not my private dogma, but a view of music that has been frequently reported from many parts of the world (e.g. Blacking 1973:50–51).

Depth of feeling and quality of experience are also critical factors in the processes of decision-making that affect the invention and use of cultural forms; and this is an important reason why the anthropological study of music could provide a model for more general studies of culture and society. People's feelings about others and about situations and institutions must be taken into account when analyzing their decisions. It is not enough to analyze structural and normative features of social systems which refer only in passing to the quality of interaction as "warm" or "close-knit", particularly when such observations are based on quantitative data, such as the number of times that certain people meet. We have to devise some way of measuring and evaluating compassion and affection, for it is ultimately these qualities which most deeply affect decision-making, and hence the use of cultural knowledge in social interaction and the distillation of social experience in cultural tradition: one particular meeting with a friend, or one musical experience, may more deeply affect a person and change the course of his/her action than a hundred meetings with the same or another friend, or a hundred other performances of the same music. This is why *processes* of interaction generally reveal more about human action than their products (cf. Blacking 1969), and why anthropological analyses of different performances of "the same" music may reveal more about man as music-maker than comparisons of many different musics *as* music — a point to which I shall return later.

The importance of feelings in social life in general and musical activities in particular, raises again the problem of meaning. How can feelings be incorporated into sociological analysis except on the basis of people's statements about them? And since in most societies feelings are very poorly labeled, how reliable can statements be, when they are inevitably expressed in metaphor and simile or by analogy — that is, in language that is not derived from or directly related to the feeling state? If music is both "intelligible" and "untranslatable", as Lévi-Strauss has described it, how can analysis of its effects on social life be measured except by reference to statements about and observations of its *non*musical attributes? Numerous musicians have insisted that "music can reveal the nature of feelings with a detail and truth that language cannot approach" (Langer 1948:191), and that if feelings could be expressed in words they would not need music (Blacking 1973:61 ff). Thus music is intelligible in terms of the feelings it evokes, but it is untranslatable *as music*. It does not represent anything but itself: it is "form in tonal motion" (Hanslick 1891). As soon as it is translated into words that describe a feeling or a scene from social life, we are no longer referring to the music but to the feeling or the event from social life; we can no longer be sure that we are discussing the effects of music and music-making on social life, since we may in reality be talking about the effects of the events to which we have said that the music refers.

The problem of analysis is similar to that faced by ethologists, who can only infer what is going on in animals' minds from what they think the animal would be meaning by its behavior if it were human. For many musicologists, the solution to this problem is to analyze and compare the structures of "sonic objects" in terms of parameters such as rhythm, melodic movement, tonality, harmony, timber, intensity and form. Similarly, the effectiveness of *music* as a symbol system, as distinct from the effectiveness of all the meanings that may be attributed to it, can only be measured in terms of the reaction of human bodies to form in tonal motion. Thus, the only reliable indicators of the effects of music are changes in pulse rate, blood pressure, alpha and beta rhythms, and so on. Even if such measurements were carried out without any distortion of a performance situation, which is probably impossible, there can be no guarantee that they indicate responses to musical phenomena, rather than to some social aspects of the performance or to associations that have come to be made with familiar patterns of sound.

Supposing it were possible to measure the effects of music with precision in the way I have described, would the results tell me anything that I do not already know? Would they tell me anything important about *music*? I know very well that some pieces of music, and some bars in certain pieces affect me more than others, and I do not think it really matters how much my blood pressure rises or my pulse quickens. I know that some performances of music that I like move me more than others. What I want to know is how I have come to discriminate certain musical parameters in the first place, and why and when some music and some performances move me more than others. I also want to know what musical features of certain pieces affect me most; how and why I choose to interpret these musical experiences in nonmusical terms; and what effects they have on my social life in general. In other words, I want to know how and why nonreferential symbols can be specifically effective in areas of social life to which they cannot possibly refer directly.

The main task of *ethno*musicology is to explain music and music-making with reference to the social, but *in terms of the musical*, factors involved in performance and appreciation. Thus music-making can usefully be regarded as a primary modeling system, a special way of organizing human bodies, whose social applications may take on a variety of forms and whose ideal aims are ritualistic and transcendental. The effectiveness of music *as music*, however, can only be described accurately in terms of musical parameters and associated physiological responses of the body. And yet common-sense knowledge proclaims that these responses are of minor significance compared to the depth of feelings and quality of experience evoked by music. How, then, are the important questions about music to be answered?

The methods of ethnomusicology, as a branch of anthropology, seem to provide the most fruitful way forward in the study of man as music-maker. Context-sensitive analyses of the deep and surface structures of music and music-making will enable us to measure with a high degree of precision processes that have hitherto belonged to the realm of the mysterious, or been attributed to the possession of "special gifts". The precision requires careful recordings of musical performances, together with descriptions of associated social interaction and both actors' and audience's analyses of the music and its effects on them. No work of art (or single performance) can do justice to the whole complexity of reality. Every work of art is a simplification based on a convention. The convention itself emphasizes "a particular aspect of nature in accordance with the interests of the particular social group or class that has created it" (Berger 1972:215). Every human response to a question about meaning is also a simplification based on a convention, and so to get closer to the reality we must try to account for the multiplicity of responses. It is a truism of modern social anthropology that the attribution of meaning tends to correlate with membership of social group or class. What we think and what we do depends very much on *who* we are socially, so that the essence of a sign or symbol rests not in the object, the product, so much as in the creative processes of making it and using it. (Listening to music, like comprehending verbal language, is as much a creative act as making it.)

Nevertheless, the aim of ethnomusicological analysis is to reveal what is peculiar to the process of making and appreciating music, as distinct from other social activities. And, as I discussed earlier, the assumption that all human beings are as capable of making music as they are of speaking a language is necessary if the results of enquiry are to be useful: the study of man as music-maker would be of very limited interest to anthropologists and sociologists if it were to be found that true musical ability was as genetically rare as some heritable disease or deformity. Thus, the analysis of who makes music and in what social contexts is only a first step towards finding out how they make it and how they describe what they make, which is the crucial part of the enquiry. Careful study of the social background of music and music-making allows the analyst to sift out action that can be described as political, economic, or religious, from that which cannot be placed in any other category than "musical". It is not that the nonmusical areas are of less importance: it is simply that the aim of analysis is to reveal modes of behavior and action that cannot be reduced to any other type of behavior.

The second phase of analysis, which is concerned with how music is made, appreciated, and described, must focus on the performance situation, and in particular on variations between one performance situation and another. Technical descriptions of the sonic parameters of the musical product and of the physiological responses of the body must be extended to incorporate multiple "ethnic" perceptions of music and music-making. Ethnomusicological research has shown that people in all societies and with greater or lesser degrees of formal musical training comprehend musical parameters very well and discriminate clearly between one performance and another, but they do not always have suitable labels with which to describe what they hear. Leon Crickmore (1968) also concluded after a carefully researched analysis of musical appreciation that music structures can be comprehended independently of personality, measured intellectual capacity, and musical intelligence as assessed by the Wing test. The task of the ethnomusicologist is to find out how different people perceive, describe, and react to different elements of musical performance, in the hope that a repertoire of essentially musical values will emerge. One example of this from the field of European classical music is the emphasis that is placed on tempo and regularity of beat when comparing different performances of the same scores.

This approach also circumvents the old arguments about what is or is not art, what is music, and what are the proper units for analysis. The "art object" by itself is neither art nor nonart; it only becomes one or the other because of the attitudes and feelings of human beings toward it. Art lives *in* men and women, to be brought out into the open by special processes of interaction. Since musical symbols have no meaning until they are shared, the processes of sharing are as crucial to musical analysis as the sonic product which provides the focus for analysis.

Similarly, even though the mullahs in an Islamic country may condemn instrumental music and insist that Koranic chant is not music, there is no problem about including it as a type of music for analysis, provided that there are people who think that it is, such as local instrumental musicians and the visiting ethnomusicologist. In fact the reasons that different people give for classifying organized sound as music or nonmusic can indicate which are the critical parameters for analysis. In two Venda children's "songs", one (*Tshidula tsha Musingadi!*) sounds like spoken verse, and the other (*Inwi haee Nyamudzunga!*) sounds like a melody (see Blacking 1973:28 and 70). But for the Venda, the former is more musical than the latter, because its monotone is further removed from the patterns of speech-tone of the spoken words.

Again, analyses of different orders of structure must begin with classifications that are socially accepted, even though these conflict with the analyst's idea of what he is supposed to be studying or seem to have little to do with the music. Thus, most Venda categories of music (Blacking 1973:38 ff and 77) refer to their social or ritual functions, and at first I was inclined to think that people made judgments about music without much attention to musical parameters. I soon found that social terminology was often used to talk about perceived musical phenomena for which there was no special vocabulary. An analysis of Venda children's songs in terms of Venda classifications and their social function revealed structural coherence that was not apparent if one viewed them in terms of parameters that might apply in Western European music (see Blacking 1967). Moreover, the Venda system focused on the performance situation as the basic unit of analysis.

The analysis of multiple perceptions of musical performance is similar to Lévi-Strauss' scheme (1963: 267 ff) for studying all different versions of a myth in order to arrive at the essential myth-making process. It is therefore curious that when Lévi-Strauss turns to the structural analysis of Ravel's *Boléro* (Lévi-Strauss 1971), he does not apply his own rules. He uses the analogy of the orchestral score in describing his method of analyzing myth, but in basing his analysis of Ravel's music on the orchestral score he is relying on only one version of the work, rather than the different perceptions of its many performers. He even dismisses the explanations of Pousseur and of Ravel himself, and so concentrates on what he implicitly defines as the "art object", rather than on the artistic process.

The surest way to understand music and discover what is unique about it is, ideally, to incorporate all "ethnic" perceptions of all available musics, and to find out on what points they agree. This should reveal the essentials of a musical process, which generates the creation and perception of products that are classified as music by some but not by others, and may consist of organized nonsound, such as Cage's silence, as much as sound. If the same performance or the same score can be understood differently, all perceptions must be treated as valid data in finding out more about the musical process. The nonmusical, or extramusical, components of the musical process must be distinguished from those that are irreducibly musical, but obviously members of one class can describe another class' music as nonmusic; their reasons for saying so should expose what, for them, are essential features of the musical process, and these same reasons may be given by the other class for calling their performance "music". The fact that one class considers certain elements to be present in the musical product, and the other considers them to be absent, is of secondary importance beside the consensus that both classes express about basic components of the musical process.

Ethnomusicological research has inevitably emphasized the need to study multiple performances and perceptions of the same music, because ethnomusicologists have rarely had a musical score available. They have had to build their "models for performance" on perscriptive transcriptions, from observation and analysis of multiple performances and the differences between them, and they have had their perception of significant musical parameters sharpened by the musicians' explanations, which often differed from the approach to which they had been accustomed.

These same methods can be applied to written music, so that the different remakings and different perceptions of a Sonata become a part of the Sonata, just as its original creation depended on pianistic tradition and a cultural environment. If we have full details of the contrasts in social circumstances, differences between performances can reveal much of importance about music as a human experience, and hence about music-making and the choice of structures with which to communicate.

A focus on musical process requires two different but complementary procedures. On the one hand, detailed analyses of single creative events may be made, on the reasonable assumption there can only be one set of explanations for each occurrence, since each decision in the process of creation involved a choice between alternatives. On the other hand, quasistatistical analyses of the *differences between* performances of a given model should reveal what features of music discourse attract people's attention in their quest for meaning, and hence are most peculiar to music. In order to reduce the number of variables, the first kind of analysis is best achieved with orally transmitted music and the second with versions of written scores. Both are based on the empirical evidence of performance, and so the primary concern is for man as music-maker rather than the music that man has made. There are also many psychological, physiological, and neurological elements that must ultimately be considered for a more complete understanding of the musical process. But until more is known about music and music-making as a special kind of intentional, meaningful human action, it will not be easy to study its behavioral aspects, since we shall not know precisely what to look for.

An ethnomusicological approach, rooted in the discipline of anthropology, therefore offers the most promising way forward in unraveling some of the mysteries of music-making. At the same time, by studying man as music-maker, and not only some men and women as musicians in particular societies, we should understand better the interaction of structure and sentiment, feeling and rationality, affect and commitment, ideas and social relations, and culture and nature in all human activities. The analysis of man as music-maker can tell us about the structures of the body and the mind, and of bodies and minds in social interaction; it can perhaps reveal the process by which feelings are crystallized in conceptual thought and cultural forms, and so provide the key to further progress in the Science of Man.

REFERENCES

BERGER, JOHN
1972 "Problems of socialist art," in *Radical perspectives in the arts*. Edited by Lee Baxandall, 209–224. Harmondsworth: Penguin.

BLACKING, JOHN
1967 *Venda children's songs: a study in ethnomusicological analysis*. Johannesburg: University of the Witwatersrand Press.
1969 *Process and product in human society*. Johannesburg: University of the Witwatersrand Press.
1970 Tonal organization in the music of two Venda initiation schools. *Ethnomusicology* 14(1):1–54.
1973 *How musical is man?* Seattle: University of Washington Press.

CRICKMORE, LEON
1968 An approach to the measurement of music appreciation. *Journal of Research in Music Education* 16(3 and 4):239–253, 291–301.

ELLIS, ALEXANDER JOHN
1885 On the musical scales of various nations. *Journal of the Society of Arts* 33:485–527.

GEERTZ, CLIFFORD
1975 *The interpretation of cultures*. London: Hutchinson.

HANSLICK, EDUARD
1891 *The beautiful in music*. [Vom Musikalisch-Schönen] Translated by Gustav Cohen. London. Originally published 1854.

HEWES, GORDON W.
1973 Primate communication and the gestural origin of language. *Current Anthropology* 14(1–2):5–24.

LANGER, SUSANNE
1948 *Philosophy in a new key*. New York: Mentor.

LENNEBERG, ERIC
1967 *Biological foundations of language*. New York: Wiley.

LÉVI-STRAUSS, CLAUDE
1963 *Structural anthropology*, New York: Basic Books.
1969 *The raw and the cooked*. Translated by John and Doreen Weightman. New York: Harper Torchbook.
1971 "Boléro" de Maurice Ravel. *L'Homme* 11(4):5–14.

NADEL, S. N.
1951 *The foundations of social anthropology*. London: Cohen and West.

RUWET, NICOLAS
1972 *Langage, musique, poésie*. Paris: Seuil.

SCHOENBERG, ARNOLD
1951 *Style and idea*. London: Williams and Norgate.

WEBER, MAX
1968 *The rational and social foundations of music*. Translated and edited by Don Martindale, Johannes Riedel and Gertrude Neuwirth. Carbondale: Southern Illinois University Press.

Toward a Cross-Cultural Conceptualization of Dance and Some Correlate Considerations

JUDITH LYNNE HANNA

There is obviously a need to "define" or, using Kaplan's phrase, to "specify the meaning of"[1] a behavior before exploring its ramifications, the complexities of its whys and hows. For the anthropologist who strives to identify, describe, and explain phenomena within a cross-cultural perspective, it is essential to use a definition that indicates the sets of features which are referents for a concept and that attempts to avoid foreclosing empirical issues. Of course, our choice of conceptual apparatus, our working distinctions, need constant refinement, and we must be alert to indications that something may be escaping us because our approach has blind spots. This paper attempts to define dance using these guidelines.

The importance of dance as a phenomenon to study derives from its near universality; its possible biological and evolutionary significance as innately derived behavior with survival value (Norbeck 1976; Blacking, this volume; Kreitler and Kreitler 1972:330); its stylistic endurance; its episodic nature, which is in some sense repeated by other actors, malleability and transformability, apparent record in antiquity, interrelation

I am once again grateful for William John Hanna's insightful suggestions. I owe much to him and to Alan P. Merriam, both of whom have given me continual support in my work in the anthropology of dance. Alexander Alland, Jr. and Conrad Arensberg, with their broad, overarching perspectives on human behavior and the arts, provided me with new ways of thinking, for which I thank them. I am most appreciative of the comments of Judy Hendin, Barbara Burnham, Jane Tyler, Pamela Squires, Joann Kealiinohomoku, Suzanne Youngerman, Gertrude P. Kurath, Adelaida Reyes-Schramm, Manjusri Chaki-Sircar, Dina Miraglia, Sharon Leigh Clark, Allegra Fuller Snyder, Gloria Strauss, Selma Jeanne Cohen, and Drid Williams on earlier versions of this paper which was originally prepared for the Pre-Congress Research Session on Art and Anthropology: Theory and Method in Comparative Aesthetics, August 28–31, 1973, Chicago.
[1] Kaplan points out that definitions are the outcome of the processes of inquiry and communication; specification of meaning is processive, hypothetical, and provisional, and it undergoes modification as inquiry proceeds (1955:527).

with other behavioral and sociocultural phenomena, and accessibility to empirical observation and film recording (Collier 1967; Sorenson 1967; Prost 1975; Sorenson and Jablonko 1975); and the relative lack of systematic study by any of the social science disciplines — see Royce (1974), Merriam (1974), Youngerman (1970), and Williams (1972) on approaches to the study of dance. Thus, dance as recurring human behavior constitutes a legitimate cultural field of inquiry.

Some people believe they have an intuitive understanding of dance. Lay people, social scientists, and even dancers, often use the term "dance" with the vague and uncritical connotations of ordinary speech. After having danced intermittently for more than two decades, I had an intuitive sense about dance without being able to articulate the necessary and sufficient criteria of its manifestation. Many definitions are accepted commonly in both the dance and social science literature — see Krause (1969), Kealiinohomoku (1970), Kurath (1960), Merriam (1974), and Langer (1953), who provide a discussion of these definitions. Kurath, Kealiinohomoku, Lomax (1968), and Williams (1978) have developed definitions which incorporate anthropological perspectives. However, I think another attempt to clarify the meaning of dance is now appropriate.[2]

A decade ago I began, as observer, participant, and field researcher, to examine dance forms ranging from classical theater ballet to popular dance, Latin American, Caribbean, African, and dance forms from other parts of the world. Over time, I began to ask myself, can we find characteristics in common about the kinds of phenomena different people call dance (or what Westerners would generally categorize as dance)? Examining dance cross-culturally in order to formulate hypotheses, to establish the range of variation of dance phenomena and their commonalities, and to demonstrate relationships among different aspects of culture or social organization, I was forced to work on an overarching analytic definition. Such a definition should, I thought, transcend participants' concepts (which undoubtedly include some criteria that other groups exclude, and debar some they encompass) and involve behavior which appears to be dance, but which for the participants concerned is not dance because they have no such concept. I have observed or read about a number of groups who seemingly have quite different ways of conceptualizing what I think of as dance. For the Ubakala of Nigeria, drum accompaniment is a necessary part of dance: the word denoting dance denoting also a drum and a play. Yet many African groups do not have drum accompaniment for dance, and some even denigrate users of drums.

---

[2]   Hopefully, the result will help the investigator to learn, in the words of Cohen and Naroll, "something useful about the theoretical problem he is investigating through the use of the category as a part of his research design" (1973:15).

Among the Tiv of Nigeria, the word for dance also encompasses activities we exclude from the performing arts: games and gambling. The Hopi Pueblo Indians of North America call dance their work (Kealiinohomoku, personal communication). Similarly among the Kuma of New Guinea, men regard dancing as a "duty" and as "work." Reay points out, however, that these terms also denote the business of the moment, that is the most pressing demand on a person's time (1959:17). Among the Australian aborigines of northeastern Arnhem Land, the term that

comes closest to a word for "dance" — the word "bongol" — has both a larger and a smaller reference than our term "dance." *Bongol* includes music as well as dancing, and at the same time it does not include the patterned steps and bodily movements performed in some of the sacred ceremonies or certain activities of the children's age group that we certainly characterize as dancing (Waterman 1962:47).

These and other examples of cross-cultural differences constituted my challenge.

For research purposes, abstract terms must eventually have (provisional) empirical indicators. The following conceptualization of dance is an etic concept, a researcher's abstraction partially generated from analyzing emic, native, definitions. This conceptualization was reached through empirical observation, a survey of literature relevant to dance, consideration of dance movement elements and the human body (the instrument of dance) in motion, and through adhering to a holistic approach (see Hanna 1965a, 1965b, 1968, 1970, 1973, 1975, 1976, 1977a, 1977b, 1977c, 1978, 1979a, 1979b). Holism does not mean an attempt to know everything, but it assumes that dance is essentially meaningful in its sociocultural context. It implies functional relations within a system but does not assume total interrelatedness nor relationships of equal importance.

Dance movement elements are those basics generally accepted by movement analysts as intrinsic to motion: space, rhythm (time), and dynamics (force, effort and quality). It is implicit that dance exists in time and space and is affected by its physical environment (light, precipitation, heat, topography, and so on) as are other motor phenomena. The instrument of dance is the human body, and its analysis is dependent on kinesiology.

Dance, in my opinion, can be most usefully defined as human behavior composed, from the dancer's perspective, of (1) purposeful, (2) intentionally rhythmical, and (3) culturally patterned sequences of (4) nonverbal body movements other than ordinary motor activities, the motion having inherent and "aesthetic" value — aesthetic referring to notions of appropriateness and competency held by the dancer's reference groups which act as a frame of reference for self-evaluation and attitude formation to guide the dancer's actions. Within this conceptualization, human behavior must meet each of these criteria in order to be classified as "dance." That is to say, each behavioral characteristic is necessary and the set of four constitutes sufficiency; the combination of *all* these factors must exist. For example, intentional rhythm as an indicator of dance is necessary. However, an activity with this property does not mean that it is therefore dance. Weight is merely added to the assumption. Some of the indicators may have more significance than others in different sociocultural contexts.

At this point, it may be useful for conceptual and historical perspective to present the definitions of dance proposed by Kurath, Kealiinohomoku, Lomax, and Williams — all of which are relevant to the anthropological study of dance — and to indicate some key points of disagreement within the conceptualization I propose. Kurath writes:

What identifies "dance," which uses the same physical equipment and follows the same laws of weight, balance, and dynamics as do walking, working, playing, emotional expression, or communication? The border line has not been precisely drawn. Out of ordinary motor activities dance selects, heightens or subdues, juggles, gestures and steps to achieve a pattern, and does this with a purpose transcending utility (1960:234–235).

It is not clear from this definition whether dance is considered only as human behavior or if it includes animal ritualization which is often referred to as "dance," a concept which I accept only metaphorically (Hanna 1977b). Dance may not always require "a purpose transcending utility." Some deities are believed to love dance, and their devotees perform for the sole purpose of appeasing them. Dances are often used in training and as motivation in work activities. In a number of cultures, dance and "aesthetics" are instrumentally motivated and used. Intentional rhythm, nonverbal body movements, and the importance of motion having inherent value are absent in Kurath's definition. Extraordinary as well as ordinary motor activities may be the material of dance. *Webster's* defines *dance* as:

rhythmic movement having as its aim the creation of visual designs by a series of poses and tracing of patterns through space in the course of measured units of time, the two components, static and kinetic, receiving varying emphasis (as in ballet, natya, and modern dance) and being executed by different parts of the body in accordance with temperament, artistic precepts, and purpose (*Webster's third new international dictionary*, s.v.).

This is the most recent definition to which Kurath adheres (personal communication, 1974). My definition differs from this one by leaving purpose open-ended (not all dance has as its *aim* the creation of visual designs), attributing cultural patterning to dance, focusing on nonverbal body movement rather than a static "series of poses" and "tracing of patterns," and emphasizing that motor activities are not ordinary and that motion has inherent value. The concept of poses may be too limiting. Twyla Tharp's dances rarely use the end-stopped poses that we are accustomed to with ballet: the dancing just keeps spiralling and shaking through every part of the dancers' bodies. Kealiinohomoku defines dance as:

a transient mode of expression performed in a given form and style by the human body moving in space. Dance occurs through purposefully selected and controlled rhythmic movements; the resulting phenomenon is recognized as dance both by the performer and the observing members of a given group (1970:28).

This definition recognizes dance as human behavior, purposeful, and intentionally rhythmical body movement. I disagree with the concepts of transience and recognition of the behavior as "dance" by members of the group. Transient means passing in and out of existence. Dance as a mode of expression may more appropriately be called ephemeral, continually becoming in the phenomenological sense. However, at another level of analysis, it may last in the memory of the performer and the memory of the observer, and sometimes in notation or film recording. Dance may affect the behavior of performer and observer beyond the dance situation. Dance in Kealiinohomoku's definition is not distinguished from nondance except by the necessity of a group having the concept of dance — see Mills (1973) and Sieber (1973) on the similar problem of cross-cultural aesthetics and whether a group has the concept of aesthetics. This condition for dance creates problems for cross-cultural studies and places undue emphasis on verbalized forms of knowing, expressing, and communicating. Her definition also omits several factors which I think are important: culturally patterned sequences of nonverbal body movements which are not ordinary, the motion having inherent and "aesthetic" value. In her definitional refinement, Kealiinohomoku states:

It is understood that dance is an affective mode of expression which requires both time and space. It employs motor behavior in redundant patterns which are closely linked to the definitive features of musicality (1972:387).

However, dance is also a cognitive mode; it can convey concepts in much the same way as verbal language, especially poetry. Redundancy does not characterize all of dance. Indeed, climaxes are often unique patterns. It is not clear how motor patterns are linked to definitive features of musicality. Some groups do not dance to music. Perhaps music is linked to the definitive features of dance!

Lomax (1968:xv) compares dance to everyday movement in order to verify the hypothesis that "danced movement is patterned reinforcement of the habitual movement patterns of each culture or culture area." Furthermore, dance is hypothesized as:

an adumbration of or derived communication about life, focused on those favored dynamic patterns which most successfully and frequently animated the everyday activity of most of the people in a culture. . . . Choreometrics tests the proposition that dance is the most repetitious, redundant, and formally organized system of body communication present in a culture (Lomax et al. 1968:223–224).

If this is a working definition, the criterion of motion with inherent, aesthetic value is omitted. Also, I submit that danced movement may not only be patterned on habitual movement patterns of a people, but may also be patterned on athletic feats and "exotic" or inverse movements requiring specific training. The proposition that dance is the most repetitious and redundant system of body communication is questionable (cf. Ekman and Friesen 1969; Ekman 1971), since dance is not "ordinary" motor activity and not everyone dances. Williams provides a relatively comprehensive definition:

dancing is essentially the termination, through action, of a certain kind of symbolic transformation of experience . . . "a dance" is a visually apprehended, kinesthetically felt, rhythmically ordered, spatially organized phenomenon which exists in three dimensions of space and at least one of time. It is articulated in terms of *dancing* on the level of the articulation of the dancers' bodies; in the body-instrument space which . . . is ninety-dimensional. It is articulated in terms of "a dance" on the level of a pattern of interacting forces; the form space of a dance . . . [is] the empirically perceivable structure which modulates in time. . . . Whatever its surface characteristics, a dance has limitations, "rules" within which it exists and which govern any of its idiomatic or stylistic expressions (1978:213–214).

This definition slights dance as socially based and culturally patterned. Furthermore, it is not necessary for dance to be visually apprehended. It may occur in the dark. For example, the Iroquois of the state of New York and of Canada have a "dark dance," a women's medicine rite which is always performed at night in complete darkness (Kurath 1964:13–14, 143–149). Dance may occur with a blind person perceiving its existence through the auditory, olfactory, or tactile senses. Furthermore, a person may dance in the absence of an observer. Kinesthetic perception appears to be an unnecessary requirement, particularly in the case of a dancer in some trance or drugged state.

From the review of previous definitions of dance, it is obvious that the proposed conceptualization is partly consensus. However, it remains close to established usage while attempting to eliminate the difficulties which have been identified. I will now elaborate the suggested necessary components of dance: purpose, intentional rhythm, culturally patterned sequences, extraordinary nonverbal movement with inherent and aesthetic value. To sustain conceptual focus, I will not employ extensive ethnographic illustrations.

PURPOSE

All dance has purpose or intent. The purpose may be primarily movement, the creation of an ephemeral, kinetic design in which concept (ideas about dance), process (what leads to performance), medium (the body instrument), and product (the dance performance) merge. In this case physical motion is the primary end, what Anderson and Moore (1960) call "autotelic" (yet Merce Cunningham, who claims the purpose of his dances is movement in itself, also breaks rules of former styles by choreographing solo dance movement which had been dueted or orchestrated with music or thematic material).

When movement is the focus, dance is viewed as a semi-autonomous system (see Table 1) separable conceptually and practically from its

Table 1.   The semi-autonomous system of dance

Process	Medium	Product	Impact–permanence
Confluence of environmental and sociocultural elements into movement choices and expression	Human body (other accoutrements possible)	Human body in motion	Dancer's and observers' memory, affect, cognition, behavior, film, notation

sociocultural context. Dance can be observed by the human eye, captured on film, or objectified by systems of graphic notation (complete autonomy of the dance is precluded by its sociocultural determinants). Meaning in dance is thus found internally in the stylistic and structural manipulation of the elements of space, rhythm and dynamics and the human body's physical control. In the embodied meaning of dance, one aspect of dance points to another rather than to what exists beyond the dance performance. Regard is more for the formal qualities and sensuous surface than for references to processes that lead to performer recruitment and dance training, movement choices, expression, and concepts that the dance may represent. Armstrong argues that a work of "art" is a thing in itself, "its own significance incarnated within its own existence and not external to itself" (1971:xvi, 31).

The purpose of dance can be understood also in terms of the larger social structure, the standardized social form through which conceptualization and action occurs. This relates to the nature of participation criteria and the dancers' relations to, and means of coping with, the broader social structure. Dance is part of networks of social stratification and other processes that organize interconnected activities of the members of a society. Maquet, among others, argues that societies strain for cultural consistency. He regards aesthetic phenomena as "parts of a system, involved in an interplay of actions and reactions with other parts of the cultural system" (1971:19).

Dance can be examined from the perspective of its sociopsychological functions (Hanna 1977b). It is within this category that the two perspectives of dance as a "self-sufficient" system and dance meshed with the sociocultural system can be conceptualized more effectively. Dance has both cognitive and affective dimensions within these functions. It communicates some kind of information — communication being used here to include the performer's intention to communicate and also the performer's transfer of information (cf. MacKay 1972). Like other cultural codes and patterned interactions, dance is a way of ordering and categorizing experience. It may even be that some statements made in dance form cannot be made in another (the manner of dance communication or style of presentation is discussed in the following sections). Nonverbal communication is used where there is lack of verbal coding, for example, in the case of shapes, emotions, and interpersonal attitudes. The dance medium has communicative efficacy as a multidimensional phenomenon codifying experience and directed toward the sensory modalities — the sight of performers moving in time and space, the sounds of physical movement, the smell of physical exertion, the feeling of kinesthetic activity or empathy, the touch of body to body or to performing area, and the proxemic sense — has the unique *potential* of going beyond many other audio-visual media of persuasion (obviously, not every individual has the full complement of sensory equipment).

Dance is a whole complex of communication symbols, a vehicle for conceptualization. It may be a paralanguage, a semiotic system, like articulate speech, made up of signifiers that refer to things other than themselves. Information necessary to maintain a society's or group's cultural patterns, to help it attain its goals, to adapt to its environment, to become integrated or to change are some of the substantive possibilities of communication. Dance may support or refute through repetition, augmentation, or illustration, linguistic, paralinguistic, or other nonverbal communication. It may anticipate, coincide with, or substitute for other communicative modes. Thus dance may communicate or provide an open communication channel that could be used if necessary.

Obviously dance may not communicate in the same way to everyone. Within a culture, differential understanding of symbols may be based on, and sometimes be exclusive to, the dancer's age, sex, association, occupation, political status groups, and so on. Someone just learning the dance may know less than the dance initiate, who may know less than the dance expert. And it may be that what is communicated is not translatable into a culture's other codes or into a different culture's concepts. The cultural outsider usually knows less than the insider. Figure 1 illustrates some kinds of variations. Some dance behavior has generally shared meaning; some is intended by the performer to transmit information; some is interactive in the sense of evoking a deliberate response from the spectator (cf. Arensberg 1972), some is aimed toward a few; some is unintended or has latent meaning. Meaning in dance is thus transcendent, going beyond or outside it (devices of symbolization are discussed in later sections).

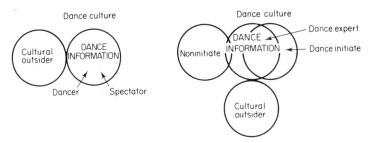

Figure 1.   Information held in common

The affective function of dance is to provide an immediate and sensuous experience. Appeal of the processual, sequentially unfolding dance form, with its arresting, seductive essence, is through all or some of the sensory modalities mentioned above. The presence of dance may evoke an emotional response or range of feelings, sometimes for pleasure or well-being, sometimes to cope with problematic aspects of social involvement. Dance as a psychological defense mechanism embodying psychologically or socially unacceptable impulses falls within this latter category; dance may gratify or deflect basic needs. What is made sensorily perceptible, such as anxiety and fear, is thereby, according to some of the psychological literature on the arts and play, accessible to purposive action by the individual, group, or society. Thus dance may be like play, rituals of rebellion, or cathartic outlets for deviance in which a segment of the psyche or world is represented in order to understand or cope with it. Symbols with established emotional associations may be employed; emotion-arousing events, people, or supernatural entities depicted; or combinations of dance elements capable of arousing emotions in themselves used, for instance rapid whirling (cf. Hanna 1975; Fernandez 1974; Firth 1973). Aesthetic motion (further discussed under nonordinary behavior) as an end in itself lies within this function.

Dance may provide affective security as a familiar experience for performer or spectator. Herein there is an emotional expectation that within a particular dance style, a dance element (for example rhythm, dynamic, or spatial pattern) will be recognized, repeated or followed by another such element at some specified point in the dance style continuum. Alternatively, dance may provide interest arousal, excitement, what Turner describes as "liminality", the suspension of usual rules (1969); what Berlyne calls the collative variables — novelty, counter-expectations (surprise and incongruity, uncertainty, absence of clear expectations), complexity, conflict, ambiguity and multiple meanings, and instability (1971:141–161); what the Kreitlers refer to as "remoteness from the habitual" (Kreitler and Kreitler 1972:163); or what Ludwig refers to as "altered states of consciousness" (1969:13). Herein, the individual dancer or observer clearly feels a qualitative shift in the pattern of mental functioning through alterations in thinking, disturbed time sense, loss of control, body image change, perceptual distortion, change in meaning, sense of the ineffable, feeling of rejuvenation, and hypersuggestibility. The pursuit of vertigo, self-loss, or giddiness through high speed is common in dance. Altered states of consciousness may be achieved through rhythmic stimulation in more than one sensory mode; aural, visual, or tactile reception can convey the impact. Kinesthetic stress, overexertion, and fatigue increase susceptibility to rhythm. Peckham (1965) argues that art forms provide "protected situations categorized by high walls of excited insulation," in which "disorientation" or "discontinuity of experience" can be savored, thus satisfying "man's rage for chaos." The drive for order, he believes, prevents man from changing his orientation when conditions within which it worked change. Art thus permits man to experience chaos symbolically without danger; it provides novelty which functions to break up old orientations.

Of course, cognitive and affective functions are considerably intertwined. Dance tends to be a testament of values, beliefs, attitudes, and emotions. Mills points out that the "cognitive and qualitative modes are banks of one stream of experience" (1971:85). Even if dance is mechanically performed and leaves the performer and observer unsatisfied or bored, these reactions are affective responses. And mechanically performed dance, usually a stimulus-response pattern, retains its essence of symbolically transformed experience; this transformation distinguishes cultural from natural movement (Williams 1972:24; Hanna 1977b).

INTENTIONAL RHYTHM

We are biologically and environmentally stimulated by rhythm, by patterned, temporally unfolding phenomena. Similar elements are repeated at regular or recognizably related intervals; there are alterations of relative quiet and activity. Such behaviors as physical work, sports, playing instruments, and sometimes fear or anxiety responses, are rhythmical Thus dance must possess more than the rhythmic pulsing flow of energy in time and space.

Although "rhythmic motion" is mentioned as a characteristic in numerous Western definitions of dance, *intended* rhythm seems to be implicit. A choreographer (who obviously need not be the dancer) may choose rhythmic variables which are then repeated; improvisation is also possible. Even in modern dancer Merce Cunningham's explorations with timing concepts free of metric pulse, and in other spontaneous, aleatoric, and improvisational choreography, one finds some intentional structuring of time. Sometimes this is based on deliberately breaking the cultural rules or parameters of dance rhythms to which the dancer has been socialized.

Dance can be viewed within several time perspectives. There is the duration of the performance itself; the duration of the interval during which the audience perceives, understands, or reacts to the dance; and the interval actually portrayed in the dance itself, which is based on the choreographer's conceptions of time — for discussions of different views of time, see Leach (1971); Douglas (1973); Doob (1971); and Schechner (1969:89–93). Rhythmic temporality in dance may be created by transformations of time itself (for instance by manipulating alterations of quiet and activity) or by content (presenting motional configurations which represent events in time). The orientation of time may be toward the past, present, or future. Durations may be successive, circular (not in a causal pattern), oscillatory (discontinuous with repeated reversals, going back and forth, or inverted), bracketed (succession and repetition are not necessary and actions not related to each other occur), or combinations of these in what Schechner (1969) calls nodes, "complicated circuitry capable of instant transformations and swift shifts of matrices", in his discussion of theatrical time.

Dance can arrest time and offer an opportunity to those with relevant predispositions and in an appropriate mood to be in a particular time frame. This means that the principles ordinarily employed in judging the duration of intervals are suspended (see Doob 1971:378–379). "Sometimes the arresting of time in art occurs because the audience is given the impression that it can master temporal intervals metaphorically and vicariously" (Doob 1971:382).

Dance may be rhythmically realized in different time frameworks. In "objective" clock time, intervals of time are discretely measured and mechanically regular through subjectively set registering devices. "Natural" time refers to ecological variables such as the fluctuation of the seasons, climatic variations, and diurnal cycle. "Biological" time centers on the human organism: heartbeat, aging, energy expenditure, fatigue factors, and so on. "Historical" time is the recapitulation of a chronological period, which may involve a compressed expression (for instance a ten-year period may be portrayed in one hour). The Ghanaian *krachi abofac*, a hunter's dance, for example, is a funeral for an animal about to die; at another time "it is both a celebration and a means for the men to purify themselves and re-enter village life . . . the dance isn't in 'ordinary time' because in it they recall what their forefathers saw in visions about how to kill animals" (Drid Williams, personal communication, 1974). In addition to a virtual condensation of time, there can be an extension. In this case, redundant expression could portray a second of time in a dance of greater length. "Future" time may also be presented in dance, and there is "psychological" or "subjective" time reflecting interest or bore- dom, high or low points. This involves recollection, anticipation, expec- tancy. Climaxes or peaks of intensification are not necessary. Another variable is "social convention" time, time reckoning as a conceptualiza- tion of aspects of social phenomena, for example market weeks or meal- times.

In addition to performance duration, audience response time, and period portrayed in the dance through time alterations or content refer- ences, and various time frameworks within which to present dance, there is dance "motor" time. *Accent* is the significant stress, the relative force or intensity with which energy is released. *Duration* is the relative length, the amount of time, of movements, phrases (groups of related movements which have their own unity, perceptible start and stop, or climax), pat- terns, and performances. *Meter* is the underlying consistent numerical grouping of beats and accents. *Tempo* is the rate or speed at which movements follow one another. Each of these elements may be simple or complex, uniform or variable within a dance, that is, dance may be heterometric, meters changing within a dance or its parts. It may also be polymetric. As ethnomusicologists note, meter can be arbitrarily demar- cated. The rhythmic patterns that characterize a group's dance tend to be culturally patterned.

CULTURALLY PATTERNED SEQUENCES

Dance is culturally patterned and meaningful. It is not universally identi- cal behavior, a proven innate, instinctive response, although the raw capacities are. At some level, dance may reflect universal body structures, experiences, and structures of the mind — what Blacking, in his article in this volume, calls the universal "collective consciousness" and "aesthetic sense" based on theories of evolution and biological development (cf. Alland 1976) — Byers (1972) discusses underlying rhythms. An indivi- dual learns dance on the bases of innate capabilities *plus* social interaction. Blacking writes that dance and music combine in a unique fashion the expression of universal structures of the body with reflections of particular realizations of those structures in different cultural environments (this volume, p. 5). Dance is a social phenomenon. As is the case with much linguistic behavior, it sometimes operates without people being aware of it (when we speak we are not conscious of the syntactic and morphological laws of our language). As individuals create verbal language and respond to it without being conscious of how they do it, so may they create and respond to dance. In this sense it lives, develops, and persists as a collective phenomenon (cf. Lévi-Strauss 1967:55–57).

Dance — as a system of ordering movement, a cumulative set of rules or range of permissible movement patterns — is one of the elements comprising culture. It reflects other cultural manifestations and is a vehicle through which culture is learned. It is certainly not equally important in all societies. Within a sociocultural system there may be classes of dance which are differentially ranked for importance. Within a class, a specific dance may be either a major or minor event. A class of dance may be part of another class or classes of events which assign rank to the dance.

Most behavior of members of a society is to some degree patterned by their culture. The distinction here must be made between cultural patterning and such symptomatic behavior as an epileptic or hysterical fit (trembling from excessive excitation of the nervous system) or a child rhythmically rocking on all fours, excitedly jumping or otherwise instinctively, spontaneously, or idiosyncratically moving. The latter is what Devereux calls "the straining of pure affect against pure (culturally structured) discipline" (1971:194) which has certain standards, criteria by which to evaluate the behavior socially, psychologically and choreologically (in terms of the intrinsic characteristics of dance movement). Motor behavior which is expressive but has undisciplined affect could be called dance only metaphorically (see Meerloo 1960) or what Langer calls a "dance motif" (1953:172), or what *Webster's third new international dictionary* includes in four of its sixteen distinctions. This means that movement styles (the particular and constant features, recurrent motifs, unique to a tradition, the way in which all the contributing elements are selected, organized, manipulated, and projected, and by which one may establish origin, place, and time) and movement structure (the appearance of the interdependent elements of space, dynamics, and rhythm as perceived through performance) of dance do not occur randomly. Even when rules are deliberately broken, this reflects cultural patterning.

Of the virtually infinite number of possible combinations of movements that can be manipulated and the dramatic variants possible, ranging from intense peaking or outstanding climaxes to the mere physiological change from repeating the same movement, only certain ones appear to be used by the dancers of a specific culture.[3] These are used within certain parameters or delimiting rules. But why is one form chosen or why does one evolve rather than another? Do functions determine form? Cultural patterning, within biological determinants or constraints (see Hanna 1977b), affects the way, if any, in which purpose and function create form; it determines the minimal and maximal sequences and configurations (or syntax) of elements.

Cultural patterning affects the sequencing of interpersonal interaction, that is, who dances and who interacts with the dancers and how, when the dance occurs, how often, how long, and why (cf. Arensberg 1972). A dance may be a solo in privacy. Sharing or "interaction" tends to occur as the performer, with or without awareness, draws upon his (or her) culture's stylistic movement inventory. The individual dances to cope with loneliness, symbolically putting himself in contact with his people; he becomes an audience to himself in beseeching himself to move as he thinks he ought to; or he perceives himself visually or kinesthetically as a detached observer — the superego may stand for society. The private solo dance is similar to what Dewey calls the inner dialogue or soliloquy seemingly locked within the self but the "product and reflection of converse with others". For "if we had not talked with others and they with us, we should never talk to and with ourselves" (1922:171). A dance may be performed for others by any number of participants. It may be performed for the dance group members themselves or for another spectator or group of spectators.

A people may take from its own inventory, borrow, or invent. Style determination may be based on psychological, historical, environmental, or idiosyncratic factors. It may be that performers' fantasies about social situations are projected onto the dance form. Some aspect of fantasy bears a relationship to a real or desired situation of a social condition. Historical relationships may be determining factors. A society's dance conventions can be viewed as elaborations of, or reactions against, earlier rules. The evolution of a style may be patterned enrichment in one direction, impoverishment in another, or additive. Alland (1976) also speaks of breaking rules. One could consider the congeniality of a dance style of a neighboring group or other factors which lead a group to adopt a style by importation and imitation, or why among a broad range of available variables, culture A becomes the model rather than culture B (cf. Hanna 1979b). Fischer (1961) points out that using known historical connections alone to explain similarities of art styles of two distinct cultures or using general features of art styles to establish historical

---

[3]   Illustrations of the infinite range of variation upon an ordinary walk, for example, from floridity to leanness, pointed toe, flexed foot, half toe, on point; small to large, high to low, forward to backward and other directions; slow to fast; light to heavy, and so on, can be found in most books on teaching modern dance at the college level.

connections is dangerous (see also Naroll 1973). A third factor in style determination may be the stimulus of forms in the natural environment. Individuals who only cultivate tend to have some different movement vocabularies than those who fish, herd, or hunt. The weaverbird's courtship patterns are the model for the Sokodae dance of Ghana's Ntwumuru (Williams and Kumah 1970). The mandrill, with its strikingly vivid facial red, blue, and black colors and bold planes, may have had an impact on the masked dancers found in West Africa, the mandrill's natural habitat. One group of Armenian dances is devoted to two types of trees, the pomegranate and apricot, both full of seeds and bloodlike red juice, embodying the female essence, and the pshat and pear embodying the male essence (Petrosian, this volume). A fourth factor may be the limitations of the human body which vary by endogamous breeding populations in terms of body-limb proportions.

It is most likely that styles evolve through the convergence of these factors plus the idiosyncratic. An individual's private nightmare or repressed desires may be expressed in a new style which is culturally congenial to what a group had heretofore found acceptable. If the new style is too unfamiliar, the behavior might still qualify as dance, bearing traces of cultural conditioning, but would not be emulated and thus perpetuated. In the United States, the development of white minstrelsy was based on the imitation of a black cripple's dance, but it blended the jig and shuffle of the extant Irish and Afro-American cultures, and so became easily accepted by the dominant culture (Emery 1972:18; Stearns and Stearns 1968:40).

Movement styles develop through psychomotor socialization patterns; they are largely dependent on observing dance, general motor activity, and dance practice. Movement styles are subject to forces of internal and external change. These occur in relation to other aspects of culture, as for example, work, economics, religion, and politics (see Theeman 1973). Dance movement style may require specialized training. Alternatively, the capability for mastering a style may develop through daily life experience. An example of the latter pattern is found among a Nigerian Igbo people in the rural areas (Hanna 1976). In the course of my fieldwork, I noticed the Ubakala dancers' ease in maintaining the common angular posture (upper torso inclined forward, pelvis tilted downward), knee flexibility, elisive hip rotations, sustained movement patterns, and stamina. This ease is developed in such activities as bending to fetch water, washing in a stream, crop cultivation, squatting to defecate, and carrying heavy loads on the head (which requires lifting high in the pelvis and subtly moving the hips). The common bending knee action gives elasticity to movement and helps to cushion irregularities in the ground surface. A dancer's projected strength is more than illusory, for at an early age young people begin to participate in such family chores as yam pounding, cultivating, wood chopping, and transporting heavy burdens. An individual's dance practice begins in the mother's womb, then on her back as she dances, and later through encouragement, even before he can walk. Youngsters regularly practice. On the other hand, those Ubakala brought up in an urban industrialized environment use Anglo-Saxon styles of motor behavior for the most part. In contrast with the diffuse kind of movement socialization to dance in rural Ubakala, dance training in the industrialized, technological American culture tends to be, as with our other activities, relatively segmented and participant specialized, with training often attempting to counter earlier movement socialization — (this is not to imply an industrial-nonindustrial dichotomy, for a number of the latter cultures have highly specialized dance training).

Dance style and structure may well be like a generative grammar. A grammar (syntax) of a dance language, a socially shared means for expressing ideas, is a set of rules specifying the manner in which movement can be meaningfully combined. There is a finite system of principles or conventions describing how the realm of semantic interpretation (referential meaning) is related to movement realization (cf. Miller 1973). Just as a key feature of human speech is that any speaker of a language is capable of producing and understanding an indefinitely large number of utterances that he never encountered, so in dance performance, new sequences of movement never previously encountered may be created by the performer with the audience able to understand these despite the lack of previous experience. Here it is necessary to distinguish between the choreographer (or improviser) and the imitator who repeats a dance conceptualized and choreographed by someone else. The choreography involves knowledge of grammar, relational rules for using a motor lexicon or corpus of movements, and semantics. Imitation merely depends on learning a motor lexicon.

NONVERBAL BODY MOVEMENTS OTHER THAN ORDINARY MOTOR ACTIVITIES, THE MOTION HAVING INHERENT AND "AESTHETIC" VALUE

What is not ordinary is obviously relative to a particular society, as are the other characteristics of dance. Identifying and analyzing these call for a general knowledge of the society involved. Awareness of human anatomy and physiology are also essential to provide a base line for the analyst to perceive the ordinary/extraordinary distinction, because the human body as the dance instrument has natural kinetic parameters and extraordinary extensions (for example through exercise or drugs). It is necessary to examine the characteristic use of the body, the postural movements that activate or are largely supported through the whole body; gestural movements that involve parts of the body that are not "supported" through the whole body (for example head, hand, or shoulder movements used in isolation); and locomotor movements that involve a change of location of the whole body from one place to another as in the postural movements of walking, running, leaping, hopping, jumping, skipping, sliding, and galloping. How the various dimensions of movement are manipulated must be observed. These are subject to measurement and recording (cf. Benesh and Benesh 1956; Hutchinson 1954; Lomax 1968; Kaeppler 1967).

One dimension, rhythm, was elaborated above; the ordinary/extraordinary distinction in space, the area used by dancers, may be found by observing the following: *amplitude* is size of movement, the relative amount of distance covered or space enclosed by the body in action; *direction* is the path along which the body moves through space; *focus* is the direction of the eyes and body; *level* varies from high with the weight on the ball of the foot or elevated as in jumping, to low with the body lowered through flexing knees, kneeling, sitting, or lying, to middle with the body in an upright position or bent at the waist; *shape* refers to the physical contour of movement design created by the body or its parts forming angles or curves; *grouping* refers to the overall spatial pattern of movement in relation to dancers' interpersonal links either in free form or in an organized pattern that involves a couple, small group, or team with or without physical links.

The ordinary/extraordinary distinction in dynamics, the effort used by the body to accomplish movement, includes the following: *force* is the relative amount of physical and emotional energy exerted, involving the indulgence of minimum or maximum spatial use through "direct" straight lines or "flexible" curves and deviations; *effort flow* is the change in expenditure of energy which qualifies movement on a continuum between degrees of uncontrolled to controlled movement, the kind of locomotion used contributing to dynamic patterns; *projectional quality* refers to the texture created by the combination of elements and relative quickness or slowness of energy released in space.

Movement perceived by dancer and spectator participants and outside observers can be extraordinary by cross-cultural agreement; extraordinary only in the performing or in the observing culture; or not extraordinary. According to the specification of dance in this paper, the movement must be extraordinary within the host culture (see Table 1).

By using the concept of extraordinary motor behavior, we may distinguish dance from many kinds of behavior. Ordinary movement tends to be diffuse, fragmentary, and unfocused on itself in comparison with dance (in athletics and wrestling, for example, the overriding concern is winning) which is more assembled, interfused, and ordered. However, some

work, sports, music making, drama, ritual, lovemaking, and play —
Norbeck (1976) includes dance within this category — actions may also
involve extraordinary body movements. These actions may have a
charismatic quality, being extraordinary contrasted with the routine,
everyday world (cf. Meyersohn 1970), departing from an ordinary state of
being to another realm of perception. These kinds of activities may also
involve special skill. As in dance, the human body may be the primary
means of expression. Even the creator (dancer) and the thing created
(dance) may be the same as in some drama and lovemaking. And,
furthermore, these activities may be separated from, a prelude to, concomitant with, a postlude to, or even merge with, dance.

The distinguishing characteristic which sets extraordinary nonverbal
body movements in dance apart from other activities is the manipulation
of ordinary motor activities within an aesthetic[4] domain with an emphasis
on the importance of movement (the fact of bodily action) and motion
(illusion and residual action resulting from the kind of movement produced). Out of ordinary motor activities, movements are transformed
into dance configurations (ordinary movements may be incorporated).

Aesthetic in its original philosophic usage (concerning what constitutes
"beauty") is derived from Western intellectual life. To use *aesthetic* in
cross-cultural studies requires that the term be broadened. In this essay,
aesthetic refers to notions of appropriateness, quality, or competency
from the dancer's perspective. Expectations are created by the dancer's
reference groups. These are significant, whatever other values or motiva-
tions are associated with dance. Groups have canons of taste arising out of
cultural conditioning. In dance, they have a recurrent minimum way of
deliberately manipulating, composing, performing, and sometimes feeling (cf. Vatsyayan 1968) the various elements for physically structuring
and meaningfully presenting a dance. These actions constitute the rules of
dance.

The aesthetic experience involves sensory elicitation of rapt attention,
contemplation of a phenomenon's immanent or transcendent meanings
at the emotional, cognitive, and behavioral levels. This experience can be

---

[4]   The subject of aesthetic discourse calls attention to the issue of dance as art *or* craft; I do
not find this to be a particularly fruitful distinction. One of the many problems with the term
"art" — Mills (1973) and Sieber (1973) discuss its ethnocentric uses — is that within a group
the criteria for and judgment of a work (product) or behavior (performance or product, as a
dance which is preserved on film) are not always established by the critics synchronically.
Avant garde phenomena may be rejected at one point in time only to be accepted at
another. Judgmental tests are not usually clear-cut. Sieber discusses the "connoisseurship or
the right of each age to its ethnocentric aesthetic," and notes "that the history of taste is a
story of constantly shifting attitudes which are not cumulative, and which are neither
inevitable nor infallible beyond the movement they are in favor" (1971:128). And
Devereux points out that art theories "hobble behind practice, painfully thinking up new
and devious ways of justifying unusual, but effective and meaningful, modes of communication" (1971:202–203).

viewed from the perspective of the performer or choreographer in whom degrees of satisfaction, closure, or purpose are felt. Aesthetic experience can also be viewed from the perspective of the audience, which differs from that of the dancer, although empathy with the creator may be intense. The spectator experience can provide a variety of feedback responses that affect future performances. These responses range from ignoring the performance to euphorically encouraging a dancer and those who contribute to the dance production during or after the presentation. Experiential variation for creator and observer depends on such factors as age, dance and life experience, innate sense of form or what we call "artistry", and mood. In some cases, the response may be less to the artistic affective aspects of a dance performance than to cognitive factors such as recognized status attributes of a dancer or the purpose of a performance (honoring a national leader, for example).

Dance has qualities which stimulate aesthetic awareness; it has non-instrumental features which go beyond what is required for work, magic, and other activities. Motion seems to have inherent value as a motivating force — the pleasure in doing or contemplating (the empathetic factor is operative here). Arnheim points out that "motion is the strongest visual appeal to attention," for it implies a change in the conditions of the environment which may require reaction, perhaps to danger or to the appearance of a friend. "And since the sense of vision has developed as an instrument of survival, it is keyed to its task" (1954:361). The impact of dance is based not only on learning and knowledge, but it also relies on "the direct and self-explanatory impact of perceptual forces upon the human mind" (Arnheim 1954:380). For a person without vision, motion has strong appeal through other sensory modes. The intrinsic merit of motion may well be related to the growth and development of the human. It is a basic means of expression after the cry — cf. Hewes (1973) on the evolution of gesture. Body language can exist without verbal language, although we interpret it in terms of existing concepts. Children delight in regular rhythmical motion, rocking, swinging, and spinning. Pleasure and power in the mastery of body movement is found in ontogenetic development.

Theatrical dance, such as the work of the Alwin Nikolais modern dance company, exemplifies aesthetic phenomena that are explicitly and primarily designed — although perhaps not always so realized — to provide an aesthetic experience in the observer and performer (Siegel 1971). Features which stimulate aesthetic awareness lie in the culturally patterned form and style of dance. It is often difficult to distinguish form from content, and therefore, content may also stimulate aesthetic awareness.

Fashioning and meaning are keys to extraordinary aesthetic motion having inherent value. Fashioning involves embellishment, distortion, deletion, rearrangement, abstraction, contrast, miniaturization, and projection of personality. Ladzekpo (1973) tells us of the Ewe of Ghana: in all their dances any movement, besides the principal motion or basic movement which a dance stands for, must have *atsia*, which literally means "style" or "display".

Meaning in this discussion is what a thing or an idea stands for. More than the relationship between a sign and its referent, a disposition to respond is involved (Morris 1955). Stone (1975) speaks of awarenesses, patterns of data in the stream of consciousness which may be attended to, behaved toward, or reported on. Meaning is communication in contexts where the participants, dancers and observers, share semantic codes.

A symbol is a vehicle for conceptualization. It helps to order behavior and is a transformation or system of transformations. Dance as symbolic behavior creates an illusion. Body locomotion and gesture, the raw material of dance, and other dance materials such as pantomime, plastic images, musical forms, play, accidental and sociocultural forms found in the environment become abstracted into what Langer describes as the "primary illusion of dance". Herein dance is a virtual realm or "play of Powers made visible" (1953:187), "not actual, physically exerted power, but appearances of influence and agency" (Langer 1953:175). The imagery and illusion of reality in dance does not, of course, negate the reality of emotion being experienced by the performer and audience. Phenix argues that dance achieves aesthetic effect through inducing a powerful illusion; the forms of the body disclosing potentialities of posture and movement that transcend normal existence and thus create a structure of heightened possibilities, the viewer being aware "that these are his own potentialities, because they are embodied in persons with bodies like his own" (1970:11).

A symbol itself is usually arbitrary. The degree of representational or abstract symbolization and the syntactic arrangement, permissive groups of movements which refer to sequences of meaning, depend on cultural patterning. Substantive content may be realistically represented as in a mimetic hunt or work activity, or distorted as in a dance satirizing or idealizing a person. Kinesthetic (muscular) imagery qualities may be employed. The instrument of dance (the body) itself may be subjected to distortion as with the body limbering demanded for the *kathakali* dance of India without which the dance cannot be performed properly.

Not only can time be altered, as discussed earlier, but scale is another form for manipulation and conveying meaning. Single concepts may be developed in dance and thus magnified. Dance costume and masks (some as large as the twelve-story house of the Dogon of Mali) are often used to enlarge movements, making them outstanding or formidable. The opposite abstraction, miniaturization, is a simplification by reduction in scale or the number of properties, decreasing formidableness (cf. Lévi-Strauss 1971:241).

There are at least six modes or devices for conveying meaning that may be utilized in dance. Each device may be conventional (customary shared legacy) or autographic (idiosyncratic or creative expression of a thing, event, or condition):

1. A *concretization* produces the outward aspect of a thing, event, or condition, for example, mimetically portraying an animal. It is an imitation or replica.

2. An *icon* represents most properties or formal characteristics of a thing, event, or condition, and is responded to as if it were what it represents, for example, dancing the role of a deity which is revered or otherwise treated as the deity. The American Hopi Indians believe the masked *kachina* dancer is supernatural and treat it with genuine awe. The icon is a human transformation found among groups which believe in possession, the supernatural manifesting itself in specific human dancing patterns.

3. A *stylization* encompasses somewhat arbitrary gestures or movements which are the result of convention, for example, pointing to the heart as a sign of love, performing specific movements as a badge of identity, or using dance to create abstract images within a conceptual structure of form, such as in many of George Balanchine's "pure" ballets.

4. A *metonym* constitutes a motional conceptualization of one thing for that of another of which it is an attribute or extension, or with which it is associated or contiguous in the same frame of experience, for example a war dance as part of a battle. It can be conceived of as a sample.

5. A *metaphor* expresses one thought, experience, or phenomenon in place of another which resembles the former to suggest an analogy between the two, for example, dancing the role of a leopard to denote the power of death — cf. Kirstein (1970) for examples in ballet.

6. An *actuality* constitutes an individual dancing in terms of one or several of his usual statuses and roles, for example Louis XIV dancing the role of king and so treated.

Meaning usually depends on context. Indeed, some scholars argue that all meanings are situational. The devices for encapsulating meaning seem to operate within one or more of seven spheres: dance as a sociocultural *event* or situation; *total human body in action*; *whole* pattern of *performance*; *discursive performance* (unfolding of a concatenation of motional configurations); *specific movements*; *intermesh* with other communication modes; and a *medium* for song, music, costume, accoutrements, or speech. Singly or in combination, the devices allow for consideration of all message material in terms of possible relations to context.

The devices are signs (indications of the existence, past, present, or future of a thing, event, or condition) that may function as *signals* when they are directly related to the action they signify, for example, a war dance to herald a battle — Hanna (1979a, 1979b) provides extended illustrations and discussion of devices and spheres of encoding meaning.

Because dance is extraordinary, it may be an attention-getting device, arresting and seductive. Thus it is useful as a medium of evocation, persuasion (Hanna 1975, 1976), and stimulation, for example, of work tasks.[5] Let us return to the distinction noted above between similar extraordinary nonverbal body movements in dance and in other behavior. It seems likely that when movement is physically utilitarian, it may be considered to be dance if other more efficient physical means to utilitarian ends were available and not opted for. Where utilitarian purpose and the aesthetic and motion emphases are involved, one finds a fusion, for example, a work dance such as that of the Nupe of Nigeria, during which women prepare a hut floor. The floor could be completed more efficiently in terms of time without the dance with its stylizations and aesthetic, affective involvement. The center of interest is the process, the movement and motion, more than the goal, although it too is certainly significant. The dance apparently motivates and sustains the task (Nadel 1942:254–255; see Kurath 1960).

COMMENT

Although this paper presents an analyst's definition of dance that attempts to have cross-cultural applicability, it does not follow that the participants' labeling of behavior, the emic system of concepts, taxonomy, and exegesis, are to be ignored. Figure 2 and Table 2 illustrate some of these considerations. Participants' perspectives provide valuable clues to combine with the analyst's observations. We learn more about the universal phenomenon of dance when we consider the categories in which it occurs within a culture. The criteria by which an individual accepts or rejects activity as being "dance" may relate to purpose, function, occasion, audience relationships, use of movement elements, accompaniment, costume, or other factors. The analyst also examines systems of human action, the dance behavior and the interaction between the participant and cocultural observer. The delineation and significance imputed by the participants (*dancer* — leader, group, instructor — and *observer* — this may include a plural category such as sex, age, education, political group) and the behavior must receive attention in order to understand dance and modify the working definition.

---

[5]   Lomax (1968) suggests dance has heightened redundancy. Since repetition is certainly an element of affective learning, it may be this quality in dance which contributes to its cardinal educational role in some societies.

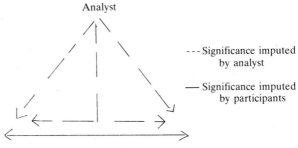

Participant dancer
  (this may be a plural
  category, for example, leader,
  chorus, instructor)

Cocultural observer (this may
  be a plural category, for example, sex,
  age, education, economic, political,
  initiated group)

Figure 2. Perspectives of dance

Table 2. Analyst's checklist

	Purpose	Intentional rhythm	Cultural pattern	Not ordinary motor behavior	Motion has inherent and aesthetic value
Participants conceptualize					
Different term					

Some related activities	Predance	During dance	Postdance
Spontaneous rhythmic movement			
Dissociation			
Mime			
Drama			
Ritual			
Work			
Song texts			
Music			

The purpose of this paper has been to present a cross-cultural conceptualization which attempts to synthesize much of what is known about dance worldwide and to distinguish dance from other behavioral phenomena. Thus dance is defined as human behavior composed — from the dancer's perspective — of purposeful, intentionally rhythmical, and culturally patterned sequences of nonverbal body movement which are not ordinary motor activities, the motion having inherent and "aesthetic" value. Obviously specifying the meaning of a phenomenon is not an end in itself. The discussion of necessary and sufficient conditions (1) indicates the set of features that are referents for a concept and provides a framework for the perception and description of reality and the rationale for associating elements of the description; and (2) identifies some important variables to be incorporated in hypotheses that lead us to understand changes within dance, and to explain and eventually predict and control the relationships of dance to other events. This would allow us to modify the outcome of a dance sequence by altering one or more related factors for educational and therapeutic purposes (Hanna 1977c, 1978). Hopefully the conceptualization presented is a step toward developing a theory of dance. The set of interrelated propositions should lead to empirical tests of function, structure, change, semiotics, psychology, and culture acquisition and patterning. It is likely that as further work is done in the study of dance, the definition will need to be refined to meet empirical and conceptual developments.

REFERENCES

ALLAND, ALEXANDER, JR.
   1976   "The roots of art," in *Ritual, play and performance*. Edited by R. Schechner and Mady Schuman, 5–17. New York: Seabury.
ANDERSON, ALAN ROSS, O. K. MOORE
   1960   Autotelic folk-models. *Sociological Quarterly* 1:203–216. Carbondale, Illinois.
ARENSBERG, CONRAD M.
   1972   "Culture as behavior: structure and emergence," in *Annual review of anthropology*, volume one. Edited by Bernard J. Siegel et al., 1–26. Palo Alto, California: Annual Reviews.
ARMSTRONG, ROBERT P.
   1971   *The affecting presence: an essay in humanistic anthropology*. Urbana: University of Illinois Press.
ARNHEIM, RUDOLF
   1954   *Art and visual perception: a psychology of the creative eye*. Berkeley: University of California Press.
BENESH, RUDOLF, JOAN BENESH
   1956   *An introduction to Benesh dance notation*. London: A. and C. Black.
BERLYNE, D. E.
   1971   *Aesthetics and psychobiology*. New York: Appleton-Century-Crofts.

BYERS, PAUL
1972 "From biological rhythm to cultural pattern: a study of minimal units." Doctoral dissertation, Columbia University, New York, Ann Arbor, Michigan: University Microfilms.

COHEN, RONALD, RAOUL NAROLL
1973 "Method in cultural anthropology," in *A handbook of method in cultural anthropology*. Edited by Raoul Naroll and Ronald Cohen, 3–24. New York: Columbia University Press.

COLLIER, JOHN, JR.
1967 *Visual anthropology: photography as a research method*. New York: Holt, Rinehart and Winston.

DEVEREUX, GEORGE
1971 "Art and mythology: a general history," in *Art and aesthetics in primitive societies*. Edited by Carol F. Jopling, 193–224. New York: E. P. Dutton.

DEWEY, JOHN
1922 *Experience and nature*. New York: W. W. Norton.

DOOB, LEONARD W.
1971 *Patterning of time*. New Haven, Connecticut: Yale University Press.

DOUGLAS, MARY
1973 *Natural symbols*. New York: Vintage.

EKMAN, PAUL
1971 "Universals and cultural differences in facial expressions of emotion," in *Nebraska symposium on motivation, 1971*. Edited by James K. Cole, 207–283. Lincoln: University of Nebraska Press.

EKMAN, PAUL, WALLACE V. FRIESEN
1969 The repertoire of nonverbal behavior: categories, origins, usage, and coding. *Semiotica* 1:50–98.

EMERY, LYNNE
1972 *Black dance in the United States from 1619 to 1970*. Palo Alto, California: National Press Books.

FERNANDEZ, JAMES W.
1974 The mission of metaphor in expressive culture. *Current Anthropology* 15(2):119–145.

FIRTH, RAYMOND
1973 *Symbols public and private*. Ithaca, New York: Cornell University Press.

FISCHER, J. L.
1961 Art styles as cultural cognitive maps. *American Anthropologist* 63:79–93.

HANNA, JUDITH LYNNE
1965a Africa's new traditional dance. *Ethnomusicology* 9(1):13–21.
1965b "African dance as education," in *Impulse 1965: dance and education now*. Edited by Marian van Juyl, 48–52. San Francisco: Impulse.
1968 Field research in African dance: opportunities and utilities. *Ethnomusicology* 12(1):101–106.
1970 "Dance and the social sciences: an escalated vision," in *Dance: an art in academe*. Edited by Martin Haberman and Toby Meisel, 32–38. New York: Teachers College Press.
1973 "The highlife: a West African urban dance," in *Dance research monograph one, 1971–1972*. Edited by Patricia A. Rowe and Ernestine Stodelle, 138–152. New York: Committee on Research in Dance.

1975   Dances of Anáhuac — for God or Man? An alternate way of thinking about prehistory. *Dance Research Journal* 7(1):13–27.

1976   "The anthropology of dance ritual: Nigeria's Ubakala Nkwa di Iche Iche." Doctoral dissertation, Columbia University, New York, Ann Arbor, Michigan: University Microfilms.

1977a "African dance and the warrior tradition," in *The warrior tradition in modern Africa*. Edited by Ali A. Mazrui. *Journal of Asian and African Studies* 12(1–2):111–133.

1977b "To dance is human: some psychobiological bases of an 'expressive' form," in *Anthropology of the body*. Edited by John Blacking, 211–232. New York: Academic Press.

1978   "African dance: some implications for dance therapy." *American Journal of Dance Therapy* 2(1):3–15.

1977c "Anthropological perspectives for the healing arts." Paper prepared for the First International Conference of Dance Therapy, Toronto.

1979a Toward semantic analysis of movement behavior: concepts and problems. *Semiotica* 25(1–2):77–110.

1979b *To dance is human: a theory of nonverbal communication*. Austin: University of Texas Press.

HEWES, GORDON W.
1973   Primate communication and the gestural origin of language. *Current Anthropology* 14(1–2):5–24.

HUTCHINSON, ANN
1954   *Labanotation*. New York: New Directions.

KAEPPLER, ADRIENNE LOIS
1967   "The structure of Tongan dance." Doctoral dissertation, University of Hawaii. Ann Arbor, Michigan: University Microfilms.

KAPLAN, ABRAHAM
1955   "Definition and specification of meaning," in *The language of social research*. Edited by Paul F. Lazarsfeld and Morris Rosenberg, 527–532. Glencoe, Illinois: Free Press.

KEALIINOHOMOKU, JOANN WHEELER
1970   "An anthropologist looks at ballet as a form of ethnic dance," in *Impulse 1969–1970: extensions of dance*. Edited by Marian van Juyl, 24–33. San Francisco: Impulse.

1972   "Folk dance," in *Folklore and folklife: an introduction*. Edited by Richard M. Dorson, 381–404. Chicago: University of Chicago Press.

KIRSTEIN, LINCOLN
1970   *Movement and metaphor: four centuries of ballet*. New York: Praeger.

KRAUSE, RICHARD
1969   *History of the dance in art and education*. Englewood Cliffs, New Jersey: Prentice-Hall.

KREITLER, HANS, SHULAMITH KREITLER
1972   *Psychology of the arts*. Durham, North Carolina: Duke University Press.

KURATH, GERTRUDE P.
1960   Panorama of dance ethnology. *Current Anthropology* 1(3):233–254.

1964   *Iroquois music and dance: ceremonial arts of two Seneca longhouses*. Bureau of American Ethnology Bulletin 187. Washington D.C.: United States Government Printing Office.

LADZEKPO, KOBLA
1973   Physician heal thyself. *Society for Ethnomusicology Newsletter* 7(4):4.

LANGER, SUZANNE K.
1953 *Feeling and form: a theory of art developed from philosophy in a new key*. New York: Charles Scribner's Sons.

LEACH, EDMUND R.
1971 *Rethinking anthropology*. New York: Humanities.

LÉVI-STRAUSS, CLAUDE
1967 *Structural anthropology*. Garden City, New York: Anchor-Double-day.
1971 "The science of the concrete," in *Art and aesthetics in primitive societies*. Edited by Carol F. Jopling, 225–249. New York: E. P. Dutton.

LOMAX, ALAN
1968 *Folk song style and culture: a staff report on cantometrics*. Washington, D.C.: American Association for the Advancement of Science.

LUDWIG, ARNOLD M.
1969 "Altered states of consciousness," in *Altered states of consciousness*. Edited by Charles T. Tart, 9–22. New York: John Wiley.

MAC KAY, D. M.
1972 "Formal analysis of communicative processes," in *Non-verbal communication*. Edited by Robert A. Hinde, 3–26. Cambridge: Cambridge University Press.

MAQUET, JACQUES J.
1971 *Introduction to aesthetic anthropology*. McCaleb Modules in Anthropology 4. Reading, Massachusetts: Addison-Wesley.

MEERLOO, JOOST A. M.
1960 *The dance: from ritual to rock and roll, ballet to ballroom*. Philadelphia: Chilton.

MERRIAM, ALAN P.
1974 "Anthropology of the dance," in *New dimensions in dance research: anthropology and dance, the American Indian*. Edited by Tamara Comstock, 9–28. New York: Committee on Research in Dance.

MEYERSOHN, ROLF
1970 The charismatic and the playful in outdoor recreation. *The Annals* 389:35–45.

MILLER, GEORGE A., *editor*
1973 *Communication, language, and meaning: psychological perspectives*. New York: Basic Books.

MILLS, GEORGE
1971 "Art: an introduction to qualitative anthropology," in *Art and aesthetics in primitive societies*. Edited by Carol F. Jopling, 73–98. New York: E. P. Dutton.
1973 "Art and the anthropological lens," in *The traditional artist in African societies*. Edited by Warren L. d'Azevedo, 379–416. Bloomington: Indiana University Press.

MORRIS, CHARLES
1955 *Signs, language and behavior*. New York: Braziller.

NADEL, S. F.
1942 *A black Byzantium: the kingdom of Nupe in Nigeria*. London: Oxford University Press.

NAROLL, RAOUL
1973 "Galton's problem," in *A handbook of method in cultural anthropology*. Edited by Raoul Naroll and Ronald Cohen, 927–961. New York: Columbia University Press.

NORBECK, EDWARD
    1976   "Religion and human play," in *The realm of the extra-human: agents and audiences*. Edited by A. Bharati, 95–104. World Anthropology. The Hague: Mouton.
PECKHAM, MORSE
    1965   *Man's rage for chaos: biology, behavior and the arts*. Philadelphia: Chilton.
PHENIX, PHILIP HENRY
    1970   "Relationships of dance to other art forms," in *Dance: an art in academe*. Edited by Martin Haberman and Toby Meisel, 9–14. New York: Teachers College Press.
PROST, J. H.
    1975   "Filming body behavior," in *Principles of visual anthropology*. Edited by Paul Hockings, 325–364. World Anthropology. The Hague: Mouton.
REAY, MARIE
    1959   *The Kuma: freedom and conformity in the New Guinea highlands*. Melbourne: Melbourne University Press.
ROYCE, ANYA PETERSON
    1974   "Choreology today: a review of the field," in *New dimensions in dance research: anthropology and dance, the American Indian*. Edited by Tamara Comstock, 285–298. New York: Committee on Research in Dance.
SCHECHNER, RICHARD
    1969   *Public domain*. New York: Avon.
SIEBER, ROY
    1971   "The aesthetics of traditional African art," in *Art and aesthetics in primitive societies*. Edited by Carol F. Jopling, 127–131. New York: E. P. Dutton.
    1973   "Approaches to non-Western art," in *The traditional artist in African societies*. Edited by Warren L. d'Azevedo, 425–434. Bloomington: Indiana University Press.
SIEGEL, ALICE B., *editor*
    1971   Nik — a documentary. *Dance Perspectives* 48.
SORENSON, E. RICHARD
    1967   A research film program in the study of changing man: research filmed material as a foundation for continued study of nonrecurring human events. *Current Anthropology* 8(5):443–469.
SORENSON, E. RICHARD, ALLISON JABLONKO
    1975   "Research filming of naturally occurring phenomena: basic strategies," in *Principles of visual anthropology*. Edited by Paul Hockings, 151–163. World Anthropology. The Hague: Mouton.
STEARNS, MARSHALL, JEAN STEARNS
    1968   *Jazz dance: the story of American vernacular dance*. New York: Macmillan.
STONE, ROSLYN E.
    1975   Human movement forms as meaning-structures: prolegomenon. *Quest* 23:10–17. Columbus, Ohio.
THEEMAN, MARGARET
    1973   "Rhythms of community: the sociology of expressive body movement." Unpublished doctoral dissertation, Harvard University, Cambridge, Massachusetts.

TURNER, VICTOR W.
  1969   *The ritual process: structure and anti-structure.* Chicago: Aldine.
VATSYAYAN, KAPILA
  1968   *Classical Indian dance in the literature and the arts.* New Delhi: Sangeet
          Natak Akademi.
WATERMAN, RICHARD A.
  1962   "Role of dance in human society," in *Focus on dance* II: *an inter-
          disciplinary search for meaning in movement.* Edited by Bettie Jane
          Wooten, 47–55. Washington, D.C.: American Association for Health,
          Physical Education and Recreation.
WILLIAMS, DRID
  1972   "Social anthropology and dance." Unpublished bachelor's dissertation,
          Oxford University.
  1978   "Deep structures of the dance," in *Yearbook of symbolic anthropology*,
          volume one. Edited by Erik Schwimmer, 211–230. London: C. Hurst.
WILLIAMS, DRID, J. E. K. KUMAH
  1970   Sokodae: come and dance. *African Arts* 3(3):36–39.
YOUNGERMAN, SUZANNE
  1970   "Anthropology and the study of dance." Unpublished bachelor's dis-
          sertation. Barnard College, New York.

Culture Change: Functional and Dysfunctional Expressions of Dance, a Form of Affective Culture

JOANN W. KEALIINOHOMOKU

This paper uses the term "affective culture" to mean those cultural manifestations that implicitly and explicitly reflect the values of a given group of people through consciously devised means that arouse emotional responses and that strongly reinforce group identity. Affective culture typically includes those behaviors, experiences, and artifacts that are perceived by the members of a society as being significant ideological referents for important facets of cultural reality. Typically, also, affective culture is recognized by persons outside the society as including those aspects of a culture that are subject to aesthetic evaluation, that command attitudes of respect, or that rivet cognitive awareness by devices that deliberately focus attention.

Affective culture is exemplified by arts and rites. For the former, this means ephemeral performances as well as tangible plastic goods. For the latter, this means political, religious, and propagandist behavior and materials. Ultimately, they all encompass one another since they reflect the essence of their culture.

Affective culture is reflective *of* a culture, and also instrumentally affecting *to* the culture. It must be a *sine qua non* of culture change theory that change and affective culture are linked. The aspect of affective culture of special interest here is dance, and the purpose of this paper is to discover what has happened to the dance forms of affective culture in two Pacific areas.

If dance reflects its culture, it must be evident that any major culture

This paper is a 1977 revised version of that presented to the IX International Congress of Anthropological and Ethnological Sciences held in 1973 at Chicago, Illinois. Thanks are expressed to my colleagues Judith Lynne Hanna and Fred Kalani Meinecke, and to my students Penne Hasson and Barbara Ryan for discussing this paper with me. Thanks also to Fred Kalani Meinecke for advising me about the placement of diacritical marks on Hawaiian words.

change will bring about change in the dance. Culture change will be reflected in the dance as either consonant or dissonant. Change can bring new forms through syncretism if the new and the old are either supplementary or complementary. Without syncretism, disparate forms may arise, and old forms may become remnants known by only a few, unless and until viable reinterpretations occur to match changing functional needs.

From observations of Balinese dance, and from its literature, it appears that it is, and has been, consistently viable and true to itself. Hawaiian dance, on the other hand, although now experiencing a new florescence, nearly became extinct. Balinese dance has always, apparently, enjoyed a good reputation among its people and the outside world, whereas since European contact Hawaiian dance often has had a poor reputation with the outside world, and it has had, at times, a poor reputation among its own people. Why was there such a contrast in the viability and prestige of these two dance cultures, and why has Hawaiian dance been able to enter a new florescence even though it was perilously close to extinction?

In order to answer these questions, I will focus on some of the forces, both internal and external, that were at work on and through Balinese and Hawaiian dance, although the major concern of this paper is Hawaiian dance.

A COMPARISON OF TRADITIONAL BALINESE AND HAWAIIAN DANCE CULTURES IN RELATIONSHIP TO THEIR SOCIAL ORGANIZATION

The Balinese and Hawaiians are particularly suitable for comparison, since both are Pacific peoples, and both achieved a cultural climax before European contact. Their emphases on complex rituals and artistic specializations have provided examples for numerous twentieth-century anthropologists. Both groups speak a Malayo-Polynesian (or Austronesian) language, although the difference in their emphasis on "word power", and their responses to outside linguistic influences will become clear later in this paper.

Traditional Balinese and Hawaiian social organizations are models of stratification. Both stress inherited ascribed status rather than competitively achieved status. Traditional Balinese society, however, has an important democratic principle in the performing arts that plunges vertically through the horizontal layers of social stratification. Hildred Geertz notes that "aesthetic expression in Bali is an activity pursued by large numbers of persons from all segments of the society" (1963:31). Balinese affective culture is a unifying device that permits participants to achieve personal recognition that is consonant with Balinese culture. Clifford Geertz describes the integrative significance:

The great collective ritual dramas, which reached spectacular levels of display, probably did as much or more toward shaping and intensifying ties between lord and subject as did politico-military adventure: in a royal or noble *karja*, literally, a "work" — the Balinese saw summed up many of the essentials of his culture . . . the lord's role as art patron linked him to village aesthetic life, in many ways the core of its existence. Some of the finest *gamelan* orchestras were owned by lords and lent to village *seka* to play. Court dancing was the model for the finest village dance, and many of the most talented young boys and girls of the countryside went to live at the court as servants in order to study with the great teachers there, some of whom were themselves but talented commoners (1970:103).

Every Balinese can, and usually does, participate in music and dance-drama — the same word applies to both dance and drama according to de Zoete and Spies (1970:266). This participation can be either ritually or theatrically oriented, and the degree to which one participates is limited only by one's talent and interest (de Zoete and Spies 1970:263). Furthermore, almost every Balinese hamlet has its own musicians, and dancers, with several occasions throughout the year during which dance is performed (Geertz 1970:87). Thus, affective culture, specifically dance, absorbs much time and attention for the entire populace. Spatially speaking, dance is culture-wide.

In contrast, in traditional Hawaii, affective culture was stratified so that the refined performing arts were relegated to a select group of specialists. Ordinary people could become those specialists, but once they became members of a hula troupe their obligations were to the chiefs. Emerson writes:

The ancient Hawaiians did not personally and informally indulge in the dance for their own amusement . . . Hawaiians of the old time left it to be done for them by a body of trained and paid performers. This was not because the art and practice of the Hula were held in disrepute — quite the reverse — but because the hula was an accomplishment requiring special education and arduous training in both song and dance, and more especially because it was a religious matter, to be guarded against profanation by the observance of tabus and the performance of priestly rites (1909:13).

In traditional Hawai'i, nonspecialists sometimes sang and danced for fun and for family rituals, but their performance "products" were qualitatively different from those that developed out of the intensive training demanded of performance specialists (cf. Handy and Pukui 1972:83–86).

Dance specialists in traditional Hawai'i were subjected to a rigorous training program where they were surrounded by restrictive taboos affecting the food they ate, where they slept, the clothing they wore, and even their conversations and behavior during nondance periods. The sacrosanct nature of the hula school was maintained by numerous rituals, and by the exclusiveness which surrounded it. The training school was out of bounds to noninitiates, and any visitor to the school had to prove his authorization by performing a special password chant (Emerson 1909:26–48).

Dance troupes were sponsored by members of the Hawaiian ruling class, and their major performances were limited spatially to areas where the general populace were not allowed (Emerson 1909:26–27). A special three-month period of the year called the *Makahiki*, associated with the presentation of the "first fruits" to the *ali'i* [chiefs], was a period when the taboos were lifted and liberties were enjoyed by all (Handy and Pukui 1972:235). The remaining nine months of the year were austere for ordinary people who could not really participate in the most significant Hawaiian affective culture.

Traditional Hawaiian performing arts had a built-in rigidity that circumscribed creative expression because of the psychic dangers implicit in every creation. One would not lightly compose songs because the words had to be checked by a language authority to be sure that the composition did not include words that were dangerous because of some hidden meaning (Jennie Wilson, personal communication).[1] Further, because of the secret *kaona* [soul] of a chant, only skilled and initiated practitioners were knowledgeable enough to participate in a meaningful way. Because of the emphasis on the deep understanding of words, young children neither participated in nor attended dance and chanting (Jennie Wilson, personal communication). As noted, the performing arts were sponsored by the aristocracy. Usually the subject matter of chants and dances concerned the patrons. Many verbal allusions could be understood only by the composer, performers, and the elite for whom the performances were dedicated. When, and if, the uninitiated were permitted to hear or view such performances, they knew from the outset that they would not be privy to full understanding of the deep meaning — for discussion of the importance of words see Handy and Pukui (1972:196–197).

Because of the supreme importance of the chants and the dangers of words, text improvisation was usually out of the question. Further, dance music always included texts; that is to say that serious music was never instrumental only, and therefore there were no opportunities for dancers to improvise with impunity.

On the other hand, in Bali, not only has every little village its own *gamelan*, it also has several "clubs" devoted to one or more performance genres. In addition, everyone is welcome to attend all rehearsals and performances, even those given for the aristocracy (Mead 1970:207). There was and is a repertoire of stories and motifs that do not require

---

[1]   Jennie Wilson was a dancer in the court of King Kalākaua, who reigned from 1874 to 1891. She was the leader of the group of Hawaiian dancers and musicians who participated in the World Columbian Exposition held in Chicago, commencing in 1893. She died in 1962 at the age of 90. I owe much of my understanding of the hula and Hawaiian culture to our long discussions.

privileged knowledge because they are in the Balinese public domain. This repertoire provides the framework for endless variations on a theme. The stories of the play hold no surprises since everyone knows them all, and audience members come and go during a performance and still know where to pick up the story (de Zoete and Spies 1970:264). For the Balinese, the fascination with a performance is for the skill used to rework and embellish the basic repertoire: "Dances come and go with some rapidity in Bali, apparently because of what the Balinese call *mud* [boredom]" (Foreign Area Studies Division 1964:181). Sometimes an entire evening's performance is consumed with the presentation of *dramatis personae*, clowning, and improvisations, so the performers never even get to the story on the first night of performance (McPhee 1970:299). In other words, Balinese show a preoccupation with art for art's sake.

Words are not so fraught with significance in Balinese dance-drama as they are in Hawai'i. Sometimes texts are spoken or sung by Balinese performers in an archaic or foreign language and the words are translated by a clown or other performer during the course of the performance (Bandem 1972:10). In fact, in Bali there are many performances that have no oral texts at all. In Hawai'i the opposite is true, and, so far as I know, every dance accompanies a song or chant; indeed the word *accompanies* is a clue to the role of dance in traditional Hawai'i.

The reader should not interpret the above paragraphs to mean that Balinese dance-drama and music performances have no ritual. On the contrary, Balinese performances are rich with ritual behavior and symbolism. For example, Balinese have dedication rites before using a mask, and have other ritual requirements before and during performances, such as placing paraphernalia in the "correct" symbolic places (McPhee 1970:191–192).

The important difference that distinguishes Balinese theatrical sanctions from those of traditional Hawai'i is that in Bali everyone can be "in" on the symbolism, but in Hawai'i this was kept as esoteric knowledge available to only a chosen few. One might suggest that the restrictive refinement of the Hawaiian system would generate a higher art form. Any evaluation of the relative merits of artistry is, of course, a moot and subjective issue. But it can be pointed out that the Hawaiian performing arts nearly specialized themselves out of existence.

ACCEPTANCE AND REJECTION OF NEW FORMS

Hawaiian esoterica did not lend itself readily to syncretism, where syncretism is to be understood as a composite or blend of two alien forms that is acceptable to the host culture. The problem here is to discover why

Balinese successfully syncretized prototypic dance forms with an introduced form whereas Hawaiians were resistant to such syncretism.

The refined Hawaiian performing arts, known to so few and so closely linked with ritual for ritual's sake, rather than art for art's sake, had no elastic yield when they came into conflict with outside forces. The traditional performing arts in Hawai'i became dysfunctional in a pragmatic sense. When Christianity, whose symbolism is public knowledge, was adopted in Hawaii by the general population, Hawaiian esotericism was threatened. This was so, of course, because Hawaiian ritual was incompatible with missionary views. Equally true is the fact that Hawaiian ritual and esoterica were known to so few that the unwillingness or inability to pass them on to succeeding generations caused much to be lost.

In Bali, where everyone had entry to the storehouse of traditions, the society at large was girded against culture loss because of its common understanding of the traditions. That body of knowledge could not be lost to future generations unless every adult member was destroyed. Indeed, the knowledge was not limited to adults, since every Balinese of walking age was permitted to watch rehearsals and performances (McPhee 1970:297).

History shows clearly that Hinduism was syncretized with ancient Balinese traditions, whereas Islam was rejected (Bandem 1972:9). Hildred Geertz calls the Balinese hold on indigenous religion "tenacious" and she states that they chose to "merge with rather than merely surrender" (1963:5). The great Hindu epics of the Mahabarata and the Ramayana were adapted by the Balinese to become the vehicles for continuing their religious and artistic performances. When the Dutch came to Bali, their influence upon Balinese dance was negligible. Apparently Balinese religion was functioning satisfactorily, and the Balinese were not so vulnerable to a Western religion as the Hawaiians were, as we shall see. In any case, outside religions were not disruptive to the ongoing integrity of the Balinese affective culture of Bali, where today, animism is still practiced as well as Hinduism. Animistic rituals are prominent in the mountainous regions, and these performances are tolerated by the more sophisticated villagers, according to the narration in the film *The miracle of Bali* (Xerox Films 1971). Neither the sophisticated nor the unsophisticated threaten each other, it appears, because each Balinese group is preoccupied with pursuing its own artistic and ritualistic activities.

In ancient Hawai'i, where a class of specialists performed for the elite, the specializations were vulnerable to outside forces because of the limited number of persons privy to specialized knowledge. In Bali, however, it was possible to develop an entire population of participants and critics. Today we can view the results of this. Bali has its music and dance-drama traditions intact and enriched. In large part this continuity was promoted by the elasticity made possible by the high value placed on dynamic innovation as well as by the large number of persons who participated. Balinese affective culture today is the legitimate offspring of its antecedents with an integrative lineage revealed by the continuity of costume, language, social organization, general behavior, and by selective adaptation of outside influences. The Balinese *modus operandi* has ensured the viability of affective culture so that even those changes brought about through innovation, culture drift, and borrowing, are consonant with the past. As Hildred Geertz says, "to be 'traditional' does not mean to be inflexible . . . the innovations of the new Indonesia are being vigorously adopted, but within traditional channels" (1963:38).

In addition to the introduction of Christianity, Hawai'i experienced two significant changes that disrupted the continuity of traditional culture: the introduction of English as the *lingua franca* for an increasingly heterogeneous population, and the forced destruction of the highly stratified social organization. The result of the first is the drastic reduction of the viability of the Hawaiian language. The fundamental basis for song creation is weakened accordingly, because English does not lend itself to Hawaiian esoteric thought. The influx of foreigners from many shores caused Hawaiians to become a minority within their own land. English is now the major language in Hawaii today, and schools using English as the mandatory language of instruction have contributed to the loss of the Hawaiian language. Today the traditional importance of words in Hawaiian affective culture is greatly undermined, and as for the former fear of dangerous words, songs are now composed with little or no regard for the significance of words. Indeed, many songs are predictably composed in English.

The second disruptive change resulted in the disintegration of the patronage system, so the performance and observance of the hula became democratized. Modern hula performers include little children, Hawaiians with limited knowledge of the Hawaiian language, and, most strikingly, even non-Hawaiians. Along with these changes a transformation has occurred in Hawaiian music and dance. The former emphasis on esoteric symbolism is nearly gone. Indeed many hula masters do not themselves know the meaning of much symbolism. They say "in ancient days certain things were important, but I never learned about them and they are lost."

Hawaiian religious rituals are usually ignored. What used to be rigid taboos are now imperfectly known, and generally viewed as curiosities. Along with this there have been drastic revisions of hula movement styles, reasons for performances, the composition of audiences, and subject matter for dances and songs. Today almost any subject can inspire the innovative hula performer who may even employ extemporaneous expression.

The recent movement to revitalize the ancient hula is developed from bits of esoterica gleaned from books or from the incomplete memories of a few descendants of classic performers. In short, the revitalization depends upon diligence of research that in the recent past became the province of dedicated scholars rather than of performers. In this sense hula has gone full cycle and the deep meanings are known to a new elite. Many of the new elite are academicians rather than dancers, and many of them are not Hawaiian. Currently, however, the actual practice of the hula is open to all.

BOUNDARY AWARENESS

I tentatively suggest that Balinese people characteristically have a realistic sense of self and their roles in their society. They have been trained to be experts in knowing themselves as Balinese and in knowing their cultural boundaries. This assumption is suggested by the extreme emphasis on space orientation and the awareness of the body-self during early socialization processes as described by Belo (1970:91–93), Mead (1970:200), and Holt and Bateson (1970:328), and reinforced by lifelong involvement with affective culture. Though Balinese fear many potential dangers, as for example, malevolent spirits, the stress is reduced because they know the rules of behavior to protect themselves. They know ways to exorcise dangers, also, if the preventative measures have not been sufficient (Holt and Bateson 1970:329). Balinese seem to have a clear awareness of their own body boundaries, of territorial boundaries, and of social boundaries. Within the confines of those boundaries they are free to participate and to participate freely in affective behavior. Balinese are aware of self and their relationships to others within their culture, and this gives a group cohesiveness that can withstand or accommodate outside pressures.

Conversely, in traditional Hawaiian culture, the majority of people were hedged in by restrictions so that the areas in which a Hawaiian could move with confidence were narrowly circumscribed. "Every person and thing had its place and function charted out for him," claims Mary Pukui (in Topolinski 1972). Bushnell writes:

The Hawaiians' code of taboos was such that . . . on one day the whole population could be shockingly, outrageously "indecent", even to sailors who were not easily shocked; and on the next day that same population could be so perversely modest as to leave those same sailors abashed and frustrated. The sailors could hardly be expected to know that the edicts of the priests, rather than an instability of the people, accounted for these extremes in their behavior (1969:14).

Because of constantly shifting boundaries, ancient Hawaiians needed continual guidance by ritual specialists. Today, those specialized tutors of appropriate behavior are gone, for all practical purposes. After 150 years of cultural infiltration by vast numbers of people representing several world views and divergent value systems, Hawaiians are left with a legacy of rigid stratified social behavior but without the knowledge to implement it. I postulate that Hawaiians literally did not know their physical, territorial, or cultural boundaries. This problem accelerated because of the fact that there are so few traditional Hawaiians. The majority of the islanders have to accommodate themselves to other heritages as well as to the Hawaiian heritage. For example, today's aesthetic, I believe, is more Western than Hawaiian. I do not mean to suggest, however, that Hawaiians have achieved a syncretism between Western and Hawaiian aesthetics. Rather, I suggest that the Hawaiian aesthetic is strongly acculturated by Western influences. That these changes have not been functionally harmonious in the past is made evident by the hand-wringing and sense of loss which Hawaiians and Hawaiian empathizers evince.

HISTORICAL OVERVIEW OF HULA

At the time of Western contact in 1778 the hula flourished for the pleasure and benefit of the aristocracy. Men and women adults danced but children did not. Women wore mid-thigh length skirts, usually of *tapa* [bark] cloth, and their breasts were bare. Men usually wore a loin cloth. *Leis* [garlands] of vines and blossoms adorned the head, neck, and ankles. Far from being happy-go-lucky "children of nature" these dancers were burdened by the *kapu* [taboo] system. The kapu system was so rigid that when it was broken, the entire Hawaiian system fell apart. Elizabeth Handy describes this.

It was not until after his [Kamehameha's] death in 1819 that disastrous disintegration of the well-wrought ancient culture set in ... in 1820 the new *Moi*, Liholiho, at the behest of the ambitious Ka'ahumanu, Kamehameha's favourite wife, had ordered priests and householders to burn all tribal, clan and family *ki'i* [symbolic "images"] in public and domestic temples and shrines. With "idol worship" went the orderly times. ... More disastrous socially was Ka'ahumanu's abolition at the same time of all *kapu* affecting eating. Thereafter, domestic life, which had hitherto followed patterns evolved through millennia requiring women and small children to eat apart from men, and isolation, of men engaged in serious labour, and of menstruating women, became helter-skelter, and neither man, woman nor child any longer knew order, status or authority in the household. The first missionaries had not yet arrived. The old order was null and void: it would be decades before a new order, based upon New England Congregationalist and French Roman Catholic *mores* was really comprehended (Handy and Pukui 1972:233).

The first missionaries arrived in 1820, soon after the cultural collapse. Christianity was an active enemy of the hula because it disapproved of anything that seemed sexual or that glorified other religious tenets.

Ka'ahumanu, one of the coregents who inherited the monarchy from Kamehameha the Great, was converted to Christianity. A powerful and forceful woman, she had instigated the destruction of the taboo system and the restrictions that kept women in bondage. In her push for emancipation, Ka'ahumanu was an ancestral spirit of the women's "lib" movement of today. As a self-styled visionary of a new day for the Hawaiian people, sans taboos and enriched by Christianity, she "discouraged the hula" (Pukui 1936:1). Because of the traditional veneration in which the *ali'i* [chiefs] were held, Ka'ahumanu's edict did much to eliminate outward signs of the hula, and to force the remaining practitioners underground. What Ka'ahumanu could not foresee was that the entire social organization of which she was a part was becoming dysfunctional.

From Ka'ahumanu's time until the reign of King Kalākaua (1874–1891), the hula was generally in ill repute and sometimes it was legally banned. Apparently, however, hula practitioners continued dancing *sub rosa*, since there were sufficient numbers of hula masters to respond to Kalākaua's summons when he wanted to restore the prestige of the hula (Pollenz 1950:229). Hula masters and their students appeared from all the inhabited Hawaiian islands to perform at Iolani Palace in Honolulu. This period of Kalākaua's reign is generally regarded as a golden era for hula. Kalākaua is called "the merrie monarch" and clearly he was a true patron of the performing arts. He had a special interest because he was himself a composer of some note.

During that era, two basic outfits were worn for dancing. The first included a cotton skirt, gathered at the waist, of knee length or above. Hanging from the waist and over the cotton skirt was a Gilbertese-inspired coconut-strand skirt (Jennie Wilson, personal communication). A cotton blouse with puffed sleeves was worn with the skirts. The dancer wore flower leis around head, neck, and ankles. The latter enhanced the thick-legged look that had been so admired from early times. Sometimes the anklets were made of woolen yarn because they would last longer than flowers. The second basic outfit, worn for newly composed "modern" songs, incorporated European clothing of the day that was fully demure and completely covered the body. The skirt was long, and sometimes had a bustle. The blouse was prim with a high neck and leg-of-mutton sleeves. The outfit was completed by a stylish coif and high-heeled shoes (Emerson 1909:photograph facing p. 250). There were no ankle leis with this outfit. Leis around the neck and head were of vines or made of flowers such as carnations and plumeria (frangipani), recently introduced to the islands. These costumes were for women, of course. Apparently few men danced the hula by this time, although they continued to participate as chanters and musicians.

After Kalākaua died the hula again fell into disrepute. According to Jennie Wilson, when she and a group of hula dancers and musicians performed at the Chicago World Columbian Exposition of 1893, the first time the hula was performed in the mainland of the United States, she and her group inadvertently contributed to the bad reputation of the hula with the "come-on" song they were required to sing to urge audiences to see the "naughty hula". By the turn of the century, Jennie was to reap the bitter results of this reputation. She told me that island people would spit at her because she was a hula dancer.

By the end of the twenties and for at least three decades, the hula existed primarily as a tourist attraction. Only barely on the side of respectability, hula was equated with "hootchy-kootchy" entertainment. Many readers will recall that they have associated the word "hula" with performers wearing cellophane skirts. Few considered the hula as a form of serious or religious art, despite the efforts of Emerson who, a generation before, published a book through the Bureau of American Ethnology, entitled *Unwritten literature of Hawaii*. He sentimentally pleaded for understanding of the hula as part of "the genius of the Hawaiian" (1909:13).

By the thirties many of the traditional hulas had disappeared. Hawaiian authority Mary Kawena Pukui (1936:2) informed a group of knowledgeable islanders from Kaua'i in 1936 that there once was a hula self-accompaniment called *'ili'ili* [stone castanets]. In 1950, however, Pollenz reported that hulas with 'ili'ili were being performed (1950:233). During the past thirty years the use of 'ili'ili has become common, and it would surprise many dancers to realize that these had been almost forgotten.

During the thirties, forties, and fifties, hula was performed for tourists in nightclubs, for photographers, and to welcome ships. One seldom saw a man perform the hula, and even the musicians were most often women — of course, the hula continued to be performed alfresco for a *lu'au* [feast] by island people for island people. Hula studios were legion in the islands and also on the mainland. Almost every town on the mainland claimed at least one "hula-hula girl" — usually someone who had taken six lessons on a passenger ship or else had learned from a self-teaching phonograph record. Many hula "teachers" combined minimal formal hula training with maximal feeling for "showbiz". Characteristically, dances were concerned with novelty topics. One of the most popular hula songs, "Keep your eyes on the hands", carried the message that although the hula was tantalizing, it was considered "naughty" and was not acceptable to a puritanical morality. Paradoxically, it became the fad to have little girls learn the hula. It seemed to be a "cute" joke to have naive children perform what their elders were ashamed to enjoy.

During these years the costumes included three basic styles: a bright green *tī* leaf skirt, that looked both exotic and enticing when bare thighs played peek-a-boo through the leaves, worn with a strapless, sleeveless cotton blouse; a sarong, probably popularized by Dorothy Lamour in her south sea islands films; or a fitted *mu'umu'u* (*holomu'u*) that reflected the Western aesthetic for the svelte figure. Gone was the puffy, concealed look of the late nineteenth century. Gone was the admiration for thick ankles. By the thirties and forties it was usual for a dancer to wear flowers on one ankle only. By the sixties ankle leis were omitted as a rule. The battle cry during these years was "give the tourist what he wants." It is questionable whether anyone, including the tourists, really knew what they wanted. Apparently they were looking for something titillating and exotic, and were willing to have their tastes directed by what was shown to them.

Still, there were a few practitioners of the hula who took the dance very seriously — some as an art form, some for its mystical relationship with Hawaiian esoterica, and some because they were fearful that all ancient Hawaiiana would be lost. By the end of the fifties, those serious attitudes accelerated. Scholars began to notice the hula as a form worthy of their attention, and began to scour for any bit of information concerning it. This new interest was reflected in the establishment of the University of Hawaii Committee for the Study and Preservation of Hawaiian Language, Art and Culture. Noteworthy is the fact that the whole syndrome of researching, archiving, categorizing, and analyzing was not a Hawaiian tradition but was Western in concept — cf. the discussion of Hawaiians' traditional negative attitude toward curiosity in Keene (1970:56–57).

Along with this surge of interest in preserving the old, Americans in general became more sophisticated in their tastes and increasingly cynical toward tourist ploys. Tourists became wary from having heard too many snide comments about being victimized by commercial, "phony" performances, and they wanted to seek out the "authentic". The principle of supply and demand doubtless contributed to the renewed interest in the ancient hula.

PROBLEMS OF REVITALIZATION OF THE HULA

A reactionary movement in the United States has encouraged various minority groups to find or reaffirm their ancestral cultural identity. Concurrent with this is a movement by many white Americans who feel that their own cultural heritage has become so amorphous that they want to attach themselves to a new identity that has become theirs through discovery rather than through inheritance. They hope to find new meanings in their lives via an exotic culture. For the former groups, the drive is one of cultural survival or revival; for the latter, a kind of self-indulgence promoted by feelings of alienation. For both, this powerful drive for meaningful identification has influenced their contemporary world view.

Everywhere in America the stage has been set for a resurgence of affective culture, and Hawai'i is no exception. People in Hawai'i are strongly motivated to revitalize the more traditional hula, but of course what is being produced has to be anomalous traditional hula. There has been too much discontinuity of the ancient functions for Hawaiian dance to have an actual reconstruction. The Hawaiian context is irretrievably altered. The taboos cannot be enforced or observed as acts of faith.

Few are capable of creating the psychically powerful chants that were the *raison d'être* of the ancient traditional hulas because few have more than a casual command of the Hawaiian language. Name songs (*mela inoa*) for the ali'i are seldom composed. A name song was composed in 1972 on the occasion of a visit to the Hawaiian Islands by the queen of Tonga, as is consistent with the feeling that "name songs" should be composed for *Polynesian* royalty. The loss of the monarchy at the end of the last century wiped out one of the major catalysts for holding the Hawaiian people together. To be sure, those descended from the chiefs are still venerated but these descendants have little influence today on the populace as a whole. The composition of name songs has not been transferred to honoring new rulers because an elected official can be a common person by birth. Further, as Americans, Hawaiians are distrustful of politicians. Name dedicatory songs and hulas performed today are commemorative: for example, when hula dancers dedidate a performance to Kawika (David Kalākaua) they must do it to his memory. Where are the hulas for the surrogate ali'i? To the governor? To the president? The very thought is amusing because the new-style chiefs are cognitively dissonant within traditional Hawaiian cultural contexts.

Legends are depicted in song and dance, but they are more often tales of history than about the ancient Hawaiian gods because most hula teachers and dancers are Christians. Mormons, for example, are not likely to emphasize dances about non-Christian gods. Seventh Day Adventists restrict their hula dancers to performing, in modest costumes with necklines that dip no lower than the clavicle, only those songs that are sentimental and morally acceptable to them. But, I am not aware of any hulas composed for the Judeo-Christian god, or for Jesus Christ.

Hawaiians become disenfranchised from their traditional culture, but there is, however, a new day coming for them, but not one that could have been envisioned by their ancestors. Their old emphasis on ascribed status and inflexible roles crumbled under the onslaught of people who value competitive achievement, progressive change, and personal fulfillment. Traditional hulas were functional only in traditional social organization and religion. The hula became dysfunctional in the face of the changes which affected it. As noted previously, traditional Hawaiian culture was becoming dysfunctional even before the arrival of Christian missionaries.

FUNCTIONAL REINTERPRETATION OF THE HULA

The hula is becoming viable again having undergone a reinterpretation that reflects the social organization of contemporary society at large, as viable affective culture always does. Popular hula is no longer geared solely to the tourist trade, and serious hula is no longer an antiquarian relic.

Hawaiians are in the process of closing the gap of their cultural lag in terms of discovering self, community, and territorial boundaries within the greater society of which they are a part today. Thus, the correlation of "selfhood" and affective culture is becoming consonant, incorporating "Hawaiianness" with a new social organization, a new world view, and a new aesthetic. This emergence is a product of sufficient time combined fortuitously with the new moods of the day, and is built on the Western concept of scholarship.

Audiences have become more knowledgeable and appreciative. Non-Hawaiians have a new cross-cultural awareness resulting from their search for something "authentic". Western *mores* have changed sufficiently to allow that sexually overt behavior can be aesthetic also. Increasingly, audiences are able to view, for example, the pelvic rotations of the hula without having to pigeonhole that behavior as savage or vulgar.

On the other hand, contemporary island people, who include every genetic combination of Polynesian, Oriental, and European ancestry, are becoming more comfortable with the hula. They are less "shamed" by doing it in public. Young women who are shy and circumspect in everyday life are not reticent to perform hula movements that are very sexual. Even staid matrons unblinkingly watch their daughters, some of whom are very young, perform these overtly sexual movements.

Despite the emphasis upon learning ancient hulas, the transmission of these hulas is untraditional. The hula complex, through this renewed interest, has become big business and a universal institution in the islands. Here is a partial list of those individuals and organizations that benefit economically from the resurgence of interest in the hula:

hula teachers;
students of hula who will earn wages from performances;
students of hula who are preparing to become teachers of the hula;
music stores that carry accompanying "implements" and recordings;
general stores that also carry "implements" and recordings;
musicians, both men and women;
garment sellers;
fabric sellers;
seamstresses;
florists;
gardeners who grow flowers suitable for leis;

lei makers;
tour guides;
hotels; and
nightclubs

Hula has become the *pièce de résistance* for every program in the islands. It is taught as part of the physical education curriculum in the public schools, and is included in music courses taught in the university and colleges. This widespread use of hula is not altogether new, having begun in the thirties, but the prestige that is associated with it and the acceleration of numbers of participants are new developments.

Within the past decade other striking changes have occurred. More adults are studying the hula seriously. More boys and men are performing the hula. The huge variety of costumes includes simulated tapa cloth to resemble pre-Christian days (although women's breasts are not bared), through every style used for dancing for the past 200 years. Hula practitioners insist on historical appropriateness for costuming and behavior according to the style of the hula being performed. Instruments that became nearly obsolete are being used again. More and more dance studios are rewarding excellence, experience, and completeness of repertoire with graduation exercises that are frankly modelled after the ancient graduation (*uniki*). Particularly remarkable is the great variety in choreography, the richness of repertoire, and the high standards that hula masters expect of one another.

Pageants and competitions are increasing, as are the number of people involved. Competition encourages dedication and excellence. Young women taking part in contests at the annual Merrie Monarch Festival are judged for appropriateness and creativity — the inclusion of the idea of creativity is especially noteworthy, the traditional emphasis having been on accuracy rather than on creativity — cf. Keene's discussion of Hawaiian avoidance of creatively conceptual activities (1970:56–67). The requirements specified that the entrants be unmarried and between the ages of eighteen and twenty-five; they did not specify that a contestant had to be genetically Hawaiian, or that she had to worship at the hula shrine.

An important feature of the Merrie Monarch Festival is the enactment of the court of King Kalākaua in which ordinary persons dress and behave as the personnel of the court. For the three-day duration of the festival they are to all intents and purposes, the members of that court. All hula dancers, both group and individual performers, face the court rather than the audience during their dancing. They enter with a bow to the court, and exit by walking backwards to avoid turning away until they are out of sight. I was struck by the idea that King Kalākaua has become a mythic reason for performance similar to the Hindu king of the Ramayana cycle in Bali.

Just as the Balinese promote creativity, and focus their dance-drama on a legendary hero rather than a current politician, today's Hawaiians have let an historical hero serve a similar function. Just as the Balinese, by knowing all the "stories", can concentrate on form and style instead of content, so too can modern-day hula practitioners and audiences concentrate on form and style. If the "givens" are common knowledge, the understanding of the "word" will become increasingly dispensable. Also, as in Balinese affective culture, everyone in Hawai'i may participate, limited only by talent and interest. These new adjustments in the hula are consonant with competitive Western culture, with its stress upon individual achievement. Spatially, hula is now culture-wide, and it can be performed at any time of the year. Indeed numerous occasions are contrived especially for the performance of the hula.

CONCLUSIONS

If a society experiences radical changes such as Hawaiian society did, in its living patterns, in its religious and belief systems, and especially in its social organization, there is little left of the original *unless* its affective culture can maintain its viability. The paradox here is that although affective culture influences the rest of the culture, it also reflects it. Therefore, it appears that affective culture must change in order to parallel any major changes in the rest of the culture.

This predictably brings ambivalence to the people who are part of such a culture. Referring specifically to the Hawaiian people, Hawaiians value a need to maintain a sense of cultural identity and they are striving desperately toward that end. At the same time, most Hawaiians could not, or would not if they could, go back to the significant features of precontact Hawaii. For example, Christians would be unwilling to renounce their religion, the Western-educated would be unfit to rely solely on the Hawaiian language and Hawaiian knowledge, women would be unwilling to put themselves under restrictive taboos regarding food habits, bodily hygiene and modes of dress, and people generally would chafe under the old class structure and taboo system. In short, any attempt to return to the old Hawaiian ways would soon be rejected, even if it were possible, and regardless of the sentimental but unrealistic longing for such a return.

The demands of a new religion, the dependence upon new technology, the advantages of a democratic government, and the spirit of self-fulfillment have been accepted, and the Hawaiian people would not be willing to give up these things. Still, they yearn to hold fast to some measure of "Hawaiianness" and that measure seems to center on Hawaiian affective culture. Yet because of their symbiotic relationship with the rest of the culture, the arts will be maintained only in truncated or spurious forms unless they can be reinterpreted satisfactorily.

Such a satisfactory reinterpretation of affective culture is being achieved by those who identify with Hawaiian culture (and as we have seen, many of those persons may not be genetically Hawaiian at all). This reinterpretation seems to be consonant with the new value system. It is not a developmental syncretism, but an acculturated reinterpretation. Its manifestation is largely confined to the Hawaiian Islands, and this specific location has helped to identify it as Hawaiian. Because so few people are really Hawaiian and so few of the old cultural attributes are still viable, the restriction in space is extremely important to that identification.

Ultimately, the Western culture that almost killed an already ailing patient became instrumental in saving its life. The Western values of an economic, competitive, achievement-oriented ethos, plus the propensity for analyzing, categorizing, studying, and archiving finally became interiorized into a new life-style for a group of non-Western people. Instead of killing the patient, Western culture became homeopathic medicine, and restored the patient.

Hawaiian affective culture is not viable through syncretism as Balinese affective culture is. Hawaiian affective culture lives because it has been metamorphosed. Why do I call it reinterpretation rather than syncretism? Because traditional Hawaiian culture was neither supplementary nor complementary to the new life-style. The metamorphosis occurred after a long period of time, characterized by dysfunctional culture lag, and that gap was closed only after a deliberate attempt was made to let the hula serve new needs and fill new functions.

REFERENCES

BANDEM, I. MADE
    1972   Dramatic dances of Bali. *Viltis* 31 (2):9–12.
BELO, JANE
    1970   "The Balinese temper," in *Traditional Balinese culture*. Edited by Jane Belo, 85–110. New York: Columbia University Press.
BUSHNELL, O. A.
    1969   "Hygiene and sanitation among the ancient Hawaiians," in *Hawaiian Historical Review*. Edited by Richard A. Greer. Honolulu: Hawaiian Historical Society.
DE ZOETE, BERYL, WALTER SPIES
    1970   "Dance and drama in Bali," in *Traditional Balinese culture*. Edited by Jane Belo, 260–289. New York: Columbia University Press.
EMERSON, NATHANIEL B.
    1909   *Unwritten literature of Hawaii*. Bureau of American Ethnology Bulletin 38. Washington, D.C.: United States Government Printing Office.

FOREIGN AREA STUDIES DIVISION
1964   *U.S. Army area handbook for Indonesia*. Department of the Army
Pamphlet 550–39, September. Washington, D.C.: The American University.

GEERTZ, CLIFFORD
1970   *Peddlers and princes*. Chicago: University of Chicago Press.

GEERTZ, HILDRED
1963   *Indonesian cultures and communities: study guide*. New Haven, Connecticut: HRAF Press.

HANDY, E. S. CRAIGHILL, MARY KAWENA PUKUI
1972   *The Polynesian family system in Ka'u, Hawai'i*, second edition. Rutland, Vermont: Charles E. Tuttle. (Originally published 1958. Wellington, New Zealand: Polynesian Society.)

HOLT, CLAIRE, GREGORY BATESON
1970   "Form and function of the dance in Bali," in *Traditional Balinese culture*. Edited by Jane Belo, 322–330. New York: Columbia University Press.

KEENE, DENNIS T. P.
1970   "Ethics and environment: the kapu system," in *Molokai studies: preliminary research in human ecology*. Edited by Henry T. Lewis, 52–64. Honolulu: Department of Anthropology, University of Hawaii.

MC PHEE, COLIN
1970   "Dance in Bali," in *Traditional Balinese culture*. Edited by Jane Belo, 290–321. New York: Columbia University Press.

MEAD, MARGARET
1970   "Children and ritual in Bali," in *Traditional Balinese culture*. Edited by Jane Belo, 198–211. New York: Columbia University Press.

POLLENZ, PHILIPPA
1950   Changes in the form and function of Hawaiian hulas. *American Anthropologist* 52:225–234.

PUKUI, MARY KAWENA
1936   "Ancient hulas of Kaua'i." Edited by Ethel A. Damon. Unpublished manuscript, Kaua'i, Hawai'i.

TOPOLINSKI, JOHN
1972   "The hula of ancient Hawai'i." Unpublished manuscript, Honolulu.

XEROX FILMS
1971   *The miracle of Bali, a film in three parts*. Stamford, Connecticut: Xerox Films.

PART TWO

Case Studies in Dance

Totemic Dances of Armenia

E. KH. PETROSIAN

Totemic dancing is a traditional form of religious culture with pronounced ethnic features. For this reason, it has always been of interest to ethnographers. Every new detail about it is important, for it may help in making generalizations while reviewing a substantial amount of analogous collected material.

Totemic dancing during the early stages of social development has been well covered in the literature. The Armenians are one of the oldest nations in Asia Minor. They developed a high level of civilization and state organization in antiquity and adopted Christianity in the third century. It is clear that totemic dancing, which survived different social and religious formations, has been subject to changes in the course of time. Hence, studies of it are important in making a comparative historical analysis. Armenian totemic dancing is marked by archaic forms which are in a state of transformation under the new socialist conditions.

Studies in folk dancing have been under way in Armenia for a number of years and are being carried out by a special group of ethnographers. The group's task is the description, study, and publication of folk dances and traditional theatrical shows in different ethnographic regions. The work is of a comprehensive nature, texts, music, and movements all being recorded on paper (the latter by Lisitsian's system).

The field research has accumulated a substantial amount of material on totemic dancing, which is divided into four groups:
1. Dances devoted to tree totems;
2. Dances devoted to bird totems;
3. Dances devoted to fish and reptile totems;
4. Pantomimic dances devoted to animals.

The Armenians have preserved numerous patterns and dances related to invocation ceremonies that were part of the fertility cult. These have been preserved to this day under different names. One group of such dances is typologically uniform; each dance within this group is named after a tree to which it is devoted. These are the *khiki tsar* [incense tree]; *nyrni tsar* [pomegranate tree]; *tandzi tsar* [pear tree]; *fesida lokh* [pshat tree]; and *tsirani tsar* [apricot tree].

These dances are accompanied by singing. The text is usually a love story and is made up of couplets separated by a refrain. The pear tree song contains a repetition of this phrase: "What am I to do? The pear tree is dead"; that devoted to the pshat tree repeats the line: "The pshat tree is in blossom"; the one devoted to the incense tree repeats the line: "There is an incense tree in front of our house and there is one in front of your house," and so on.

The refrains of folk songs are highly archaic and, to a certain extent, indicative of the original content of a dance-song.

The melody consists of two movements, adagio and moderato, having different themes. This is typical of Armenian folk dance music. Songs which go with dancing are performed in unison.

All these dances are performed solo by women and all show a uniform pattern. During the first movement, the adagio, the dancer finds herself in the middle of the dance floor, with her arms outstretched at shoulder level or a little higher; in time with the melody, the arms make little fluttering movements and slowly go up and down, right and left. At times the movements of the arms are not symmetrical, but parallel. Simultaneously, the performer either does a kind of soft tap dancing or slowly turns about several times.

During the moderato the dancer moves in circles with little *pas-chassés*. The arms move more rapidly, imitating waving branches of a tree, while the feet and the torso sway as if they were a tree trunk.

No Armenian wedding is without solo dancing. It is tremendously popular, although people no longer remember what lies behind the dancer's movements, nor see any connection between these movements and the name of the dance. People usually ascribe realistic and secular content to these dances. Looking at them from a theological point of view, however, allows us to draw certain conclusions, since the Armenians used to have some dances devoted to the mother tree (the pomegranate or the apricot) and some to the father tree (the pshat or the pear). These trees were ascribed an important role in the fertility cult. The apricot and pomegranate, full of seeds and juice as red as blood, embody the female essence, while the pshat and the pear embody the male essence. The incense tree fruit was used to make aromatic oil for torches and also was burned at pagan ceremonies. Even today, Armenians of the Christian faith burn incense in churches and holy places and at cemeteries.

It is probable that at one time dances devoted to father trees were performed by men. The moderate tempo and subsequent secularization of these dances account for the fact that they are performed by female dancers.

In the early twentieth century the foregoing dances were performed in holiday national costumes. Medieval manuscripts, however, contain miniatures that throw further light on specific features of these dances. One such miniature dates back to the thirteenth century, and depicts two naked female dancers with long hair and in leaf-shaped caps. Both hold imitation trees, one apparently being a pomegranate and the other a pshat, that is, a father and a mother tree. The first tree has three diverging branches with symmetrical leaves and with a fruit at the end of each branch.

The women's long hair and leaf-shaped caps allow us to surmise that the miniature is a reflection of the oldest totemic dances pertaining to the fertility cult.

Another miniature is contained in a handwritten medieval gospel which was illustrated in Cilicia in the thirteenth century. It portrays a half-naked woman dressed in red, with long hair and with a cornucopia in her mouth, and a male dancer in a network of branches on top of which sits a bird, presumably an ancestor. This is a fragment of an ancient mystery play related to the cult of fertility.

According to historians and writers of the early Middle Ages, the cult of trees featured prominently in the Armenians' pagan beliefs. Well known are sanctuaries surrounded with groves and forests with sacred trees; priests used to tell fortunes by the rustling of their leaves. Even today, trees growing by Christian churches are believed to protect people from disease, the evil eye, and all kinds of misfortune, and to fulfil their wishes. To ingratiate oneself with such a tree it is necessary to attach to it a scrap of one's clothing. It is possible to cite many examples of elements of the cult of trees and totem dancing that have been preserved to this day.

Featuring prominently in Armenian traditional art are dances related to the worship of birds. Birds nest in trees, and therefore these dances played an important role in the cult of trees. Testifying to the great significance of dances related to bird totems is the fact that in the Middle Ages there were two words for "dance", *par* and *kakav*, the latter also meaning "partridge". An essential element of the kakav was jumping; it originated from totemic dances which involved dancers disguising themselves as partridges. Today the word *kakavich* is a general term for a dancer, but originally it denoted a cult dancer performing the totemic dance devoted to the partridge.

The kakav dance as such has not survived, but we still come across a number of elements imitating birds in many dances. The dancing tradition has retained steps that imitate the swaying gait of a bird. Such dances are generally known by the name *shoror* [swaying]. These dances are only performed by men, either alone or in group.

The usual step in the group dances involves shifting one's weight from one foot to the other with both regular and irregular rhythms. Performers stand side by side in line, their arms bent at the elbows, holding each other's little fingers. The arms make smooth round movements and the bodies sway right and left.

The solo shoror consists of two movements, the adagio and the moderato. During the first movement the dancer is in the middle of the floor with arms wide open and with a red kerchief in each hand. The dancer starts with small fluctuating movements of the body; his arms sway like the wings of a soaring bird and only the head remains motionless. The second movement, the moderato, is an imitation of a bird jumping to and fro.

The pantomimic dance, *araghil* [stork], was also performed by a man. The dance involved some disguise, the performer, squatting and taking a shepherd's crook, was then covered with a sheepskin coat turned inside out. The dancer put his hand and arm with the staff in one of the sleeves. The end of the staff that jutted out was wrapped in rags so that it looked like a stork's head. The dancer jumped to the music, swaying the staff. In this way he imitated the gait of a stork and the movements of its head.

A number of other totemic dances are named after birds: *kryngaven* [crane]; *khaz-khaz* [goose]; *karapdal* [swan]; and *khavku par* [hen]. The kryngaven deals with some habits of cranes. The leader of the dance is referred to as "mother". The men who line up behind are "younglings".

The dance consists of a multiple repetition of two of its parts. During the first, the dancers follow in circles after the mother, their arms wide open and swaying a little like a bird's wings in flight. In the second, they imitate a crane's cry. On the mother's signal, the younglings gather in the center of the floor. In the course of subsequent repetitions of this movement, they imitate cranes drinking water, pecking seeds and gravel, collecting twigs, making nests, and so on.

The khaz-khaz is an imitation of geese, with the lead dancer, or mother, gradually stripping off his clothes and the younglings following suit. Gradually, the dancers strip off all their clothes. This apparently signifies a multiplied image of the ancestor totem. The khavku par and karapdal are also based on the mother and younglings pattern. During Shrovetide unmarried young men walked on stilts, with long trousers hiding them, this game being called "the storks' game".

Today, all the dances devoted to bird totems are performed without appropriate costumes. We know, however, how it used to be done in the Middle Ages. The title pages of some manuscripts dating back to the thirteenth century contain several pictures of dancers in bird masks and with branches of a sacred tree in their hands. They wear light tunics without a hint of plumage imitation. The bird ancestors cult and the idea of their protection and ties of blood with them feature prominently in the Armenians' beliefs. The cult found expression in all types of traditional art, especially in folklore, fine arts, and, as has been shown above, in dancing.

The bulk of totemic dances are pantomimes in which dancers are disguised as animals: a billy-goat, bull, bear, camel or monkey. These dances are performed solo and only by married men. The dancing is done on Shrovetide and at wedding parties. Dancers are disguised to imitate their ancestral totems. A "goat" would dance making jumps and all sorts of comic movements, making *pas-chassés* in circles and walking on all fours. If it was a religious procession at the end of the nineteenth century, a "goat" and those who accompanied the dancer went dancing from house to house asking for gifts. Being given a gift of some food, the dancer blessed the family. In all parts of Armenia, a "goat" would wear a sheepskin with two sickles attached at the neck so that their blades looked like horns. The face and head of the dancer were covered with a goatskin with openings for the eyes and mouth. A bell was tied to his neck with a string; when pulled by the string, the bell rang.

Group dancing, when dancers imitate jumping goats, is known as *kochari*. Dancers stand abreast, holding each other's hands. The tempo of the dance ranges from moderate to fast. Squatting and butting an imagined opponent are followed by high jumps.

In the Middle Ages, pantomimes in which dancers were disguised as goats and bulls were very popular. The clergy turned a blind eye on them, which probably accounts for the fact that some gospels contain miniatures depicting dances of the tribal period.

The totemic dance known as "the bear" was performed both solo and by a group. A solo dancer would waddle comically, go down on his hands and knees, hug female spectators, and mockingly make to frighten children. The high point of the show was the bear's "death", when the audience loudly expressed its grief and gave gifts to the bear's master. When the latter had been given enough he would make an inconspicuous sign and the bear would rise from the dead. He would dance again gaily and then run away. For this dance, a performer used to be covered with a bearskin or a sheepskin.

Group dances imitating bears were only performed by men. Each held a partner's hand by putting his arm under his raised left knee. The dancers would jump to the right on one foot, while the audience would shout rhythmically "A bear's dance, a bear's dance!" The pattern of the dance and the absence of the music, whose role is played by the audience's shouts, are indicative of the primitive and apparently archaic nature of the dance.

Miniatures dating from the fourteenth to the seventeenth centuries testify to the fact that pantomime dancing was widespread. It is difficult to find out, of course, what its purpose was at the time. Yet we can picture the way it used to be done: dancers were clad in bearskins, accompanied themselves on musical instruments, sang and danced with fruit in their hands.

We have accumulated substantial material on pantomimes with performers disguised as monkeys. These were solo dances, in which the dancers would use a candle, some fruit, or a stick, their dress consisting of sheepskins, sheepskin mittens, and a conch-shaped thick felt cap or a dried and specially processed cow's stomach that was normally used for keeping cheese. A dancer's face would be daubed with flour or soot, and bells would jingle at his chest and neck. The "monkey" danced with a lit candle, juggled with fruit, and played a tambourine, his bells jingling all the time. He would try to make passes at an old woman as if he were in love with her, mimic the affected ways of women, the way they tidy their homes, and so on. The dance ended with the monkey's "death". The audience would express their sorrow and collect gifts. All of a sudden, the monkey would jump to its feet, dance again, then snatch the gifts and run away.

Judging from the contents of the dance, the death and rising from the dead; a love affair; juggling with fruit (which is supposedly a magic ritual pertaining to the cult of fertility); and its accessories (candles, fruit, and fire, which are all sacred symbols), one may surmise that dancing of this type originally was totemic and then followed the course of the evolution of religion, ceasing to exist early in the twentieth century.

The pantomime known as "the camel" is similar to that described above. A camel would also walk around on all fours, "attack" the spectators, die, and rise from the dead, making the spectators grieve and rejoice.

A comparison of these survivals of totemic dancing, with their images of trees, birds, and animals to some monuments of fine art of the Middle Ages, allows us to fill in some gaps in the process of the development of this complex phenomenon. Imitative dancing of ancient times gradually gave way to totemic dancing, which began to play a major role in the totem multiplication ceremony; then it became a part of the Christian ritual of the god who dies to rise again; and eventually it ceased to exist during the early twentieth century. Yet, despite all the changes in the patterns and contents of dances, they have preserved their original roots. Hence, even today's studies of these dances allow one to penetrate the essence of such a complicated phenomenon as totemism.

Kolo na Kolu: *The Round upon Round in Yugoslavia*

OLIVERA MLADENOVIĆ

There are many kinds of dances in Yugoslavia, but it is rare to find one as interesting as the *kolo na kolu* [round upon round]. Unusual, attractive, and conditioned by the dancer's strength and skill, its greatest appeal lies in its visual effect, and not surprisingly, it is sometimes considered to be concerned more with physical exercise than with traditional, popular creation. However, this dance belongs to a very old tradition, and one not confined solely to Yugoslavia. We can classify it with some well-known ritual dances of magical import, although it has long since changed its original social function, becoming in turn chivalrous, and later simply entertaining, and even humorous.

Kolo na kolu presents itself as a vertical extension of a dance formation. The most straightforward consists of a closely formed circle of men, turning slowly while singing, and carrying an equal number of dancers on their shoulders (sometimes the upper layer of dancers may be reduced by half). The ultimate development is found in the formation of two-storied, even three-storied circles, which may be combined with an additional outward circle, generally of women.

An estimation of the extension of kolo na kolu throughout Yugoslavia, may be gained by reference to existing literature. It was danced until recent times in Herzegovina, Montenegro, and Sandžak, a locality near Travnik, and may also be found as an isolated phenomenon, among peoples of different religions, Orthodox, Catholic, and Muslim, in Bosnia, Serbia, Croatia, Slovenia, and Macedonia.

The oldest description of kolo na kolu dates from 1799. Near Zurich, during the Napoleonic Wars, the Serbs and Croats fighting in the Austrian army took advantage of any respite from battle to vie with each other in dancing skills as well as in feats of strength. And so the Croats, numbering about sixty, constructed the dance in the following way:

twenty men stood on the ground, while a further twenty men went up on their shoulders, encircling one another with their arms, and the remaining twenty men repeated the procedure, so that there were three circles of men, one above the other. Then holding these positions they sang and slowly turned (Šumarski 1846). Information from the Russian scientist Rovinskii (1897) suggests a somewhat different kind of this round dance being performed in Montenegro. The upper circle was half the size of the lower one (numbering twenty men) and the third one was made up of three to five dancers. In Herzegovina, kolo na kolu was known as "carrying the tent" and was danced by the Orthodox and the Muslims. In the north-western regions of Bosnia, the Serbs performed the same dance. The young people underneath sang "This is the way we dance the round, dance the round" while those above replied "No not like that, but like this, dear cousin!" In northern Bosnia, the kolo na kolu named the *Hopa* was danced by immigrants from western Serbia, and any young girls present joined in the singing.

In Serbia, this round was danced in two far-distant and ethnically different areas. The Wallachians of eastern Serbia performed "the two-storied house", where the dancers aloft took special care not to lose their balance and tumble down, as this would be met by howls of laughter and ridicule. The second example comes from Sredska, near Prizren, in southern Serbia. Thirty years ago, the day after Easter, people gathered together near the church of St. Nicholas, the women singing and dancing rounds, the men performing feats of strength and building a "citadel", which consisted of a small circle of men bearing three others on their shoulders, who in turn supported one dancer carrying a glass of wine in his hand. While those underneath turned slowly, the dancer pronounced his "benediction": "This year has not been bad, let next year be better. Long live God's people. God give us mutual understanding and peace." And then: "The person who casts a spell on someone will make it stick like a burr to an egg. The person who casts a spell on the children will never hear a male child crying in his house. He who casts a spell on sheep will bleat like a sheep. He who casts a spell on the cattle will bellow like an ox." Finally he drinks up, throws his glass in the air, and shouts "So many drops in the glass, so many enemies!" (Vlahović 1931). In Sirinić a forecast is made, depending on which way the glass falls — "heads or tails" — as to whether the forthcoming year will be fertile or not.

In the Balkan peninsula, with the exception of Yugoslavia, the kolo na kolu still exists in Bulgaria. One of these forms is of particular interest. Young girls dance around a tree, while those above hold on lightly to its branches (Katzarova-Kukudova 1971). Kolo na Kolu is not known to the Albanians or the Greeks.

There are dances found outside the Balkan peninsula that are similar at least in some aspects to the Yugoslavian kolo na kolu. The Georgians call it *orsartula* or *zemkrelo*; the Svans *marmikela* and *marmuldikela*; the Tushins *korbegela*, which is still danced in the more complex manner, the men dancing in an outward circle, enclosing the women within, and the *zemkrelo* standing in the middle. The Ossetians performed the *naerton simd*, using more than two hundred men, aged between thirty and forty-five, and giving particular preference to the strongest and most skillful. The men below stood in close formation, holding on to one another by the waist, and turning slowly, first to the right and then left. Those above held one another less tightly. Each dancer stood directly on the shoulders of the dancer beneath, rather than being spread between two, as in most of the Yugoslavian versions. At the end of the song, those above called out to their partners below "Bow down before us", the latter replying: "So that you can fall down!" (Tuganov 1957:8–9).

Bardavelidze (1957) has given a detailed description of the Tushin korbegela. She writes:

The Tushins forecast the future in accordance with the way the procession in two tiers is performed with accompanying songs. If they sing out of tune, get their legs tangled up, or one of the dancers loses his balance, or if the harmony of song and dance is broken, then according to Tushin belief, this heralds a bad crop, foot-and-mouth disease, illness among men, while the correct performance ensures fertility, increase of the cattle, and the happiness and well-being of the people (1957:55–56).

Parallels may also be drawn in regions geographically much closer than those in the Caucasus but not as regards the choreography. At Easter, in the Ukrainian village of Tiškovce, young people build a "church", in the shape of a stationary kolo na kolu (Moszyński 1934:2). In the Rumanian *kalusari* there is a similar form to the Slovene *turn*. Traces of warlike dances remain throughout Central Europe, where a dancer bearing a flag is raised up by the crossed swords of the other dancers (Wolfram 1951).

Curt Sachs discovered an affinity between the kolo na kolu, and the initiations in which "a person can *be* danced (1938:54), this and active dancing being of the same value. For example, in the Juaneño tribe in California, those dancers taking part in ritual dance acts relating to their rites of passage, from puberty to manhood, form a round on the shoulders of the older dancers when they are tired (according to other examples, one takes the young man in one's arms or on one's back), the intention being not to stop the dance as this would break up the rite. Curt Sachs' beliefs have been accepted by Yugoslavia's ethnochoreologists, the Yanković sisters, and reiterated through their examples from Herzegovina, Montenegro, and Slavonia.

On the other hand, according to popular belief, the Montenegrin kolo na kolu is a relatively recent choreographic innovation, appearing at the time of the battle with the Turks, and portraying important elements of chivalry and love of liberty, an explanation approved by some Yugoslavian scientists.

However, as may be gathered from all the types of round dance already mentioned in Yugoslavia and in reference to other countries, especially those forms found in the Caucasus, it is possible to draw different conclusions, stressing rather the ritual-magical content of the dances to ensure continued fertility and health. The most authentic confirmation for this view is provided by the dancer standing at the top of the "citadel" in Sredska who carries a glass of wine in his hand and presses with his stick on the dancer below him. The words of the benediction, here as well as in Georgia, refer to cattle breeding, also of particular importance as regards the livelihood of the majority of its inhabitants. Another aspect to be found in Georgia, but not appearing in Yugoslavia, is the fulfillment of everyone's wishes, meaning the prosperity of the rural area, which depends on the harmony of song and dance produced by the participants in the Tushin korbegela.

This recalls a detail noted among the Wallachians of eastern Serbia, where the young people accompany the tottering pyramid with their derisive laughter and cries until it finally succumbs and tumbles down (this corresponds to the final dialogue between the lowest circle and the highest amongst the Ossetians on the Caucasus and the Bosnians in Yugoslavia). Furthermore, concerning the kolo na kolu, we can appreciate without differentiation, the skill and strength of the dancers, as well as their endurance.

The absence of magico-ritual elements in the kolo na kolu among the people of the Dinaric area in Yugoslavia, docs not mean they did not exist. Chivalrous elements have easily predominated when the struggle for freedom has identified itself with the struggle for existence itself. Thus in free Montenegro the kolo na kolu retained its social function by developing chivalrous characteristics, whereas under different socio-historical conditions in Sredska, for example, the kolo na kolu retained for a longer period, the religio-magical aspects of the dance as related to fertility. The presence of other ritual elements, expressing the cult of the dead, or initiation procedures, merely confirm that the kolo na kolu belongs to a very old tradition.

Moreover, this underlines the striking and unquestionable conformity existing between the Yugoslavian and Caucasian round dances as well as the similarity between the Lezgi couples dancing *lekuri*, and the Montenegrin *skoke*. However, the question still remains, if the kolo na kolu is a truly Yugoslavian choreclogical phenomenon originating in the South-Slav and Balkan peninsular area, or whether we shall find traces in Albania and Greece, which would argue the case for an ancient Balkan tradition, implying closer ties with the Caucasus, as already noted by scientists (Kulišić 1963).

REFERENCES

BARDAVELIDZE, VERA V.
1957 *Drevneishie religioznye verovaniya i obryadovoe graficheskoe iskusstvo gruzinskih plemen* [Early religious conceptions and ritual graphic art of the Georgian peoples]. Tiflis: Akademiia Nauk Gruzinskoi SSR.

KATZAROVA-KUKUDOVA, RAINA
1971 Hadži Dambo kula gradi [Hadži Dambo is building a tower]. *Bulgarska Muzika* 5:39–45.

KULIŠIĆ, ŠPIRO
1963 *Tragovi arhaične rodovske organizacije i pitanje balkansko-slovenske simbioze* [Traces of archaic kinship organization and the question of Balkan-Slavic symbiosis]. Belgrade: Izdanja Etnološkog društva Jugoslavije.

MOSZYŃSKI, KAZIMIERZ
1934 *Kultura ludowa słowian* [Folk culture of the Slavs], volume two: *Kultura duchowa* [Spiritual culture]. Krakow: Polska Akademia Umiejętności.

ROVINSKII, P. A.
1897 *Chernogoriia* [Montenegro], volume two. Leningrad (St. Petersburg).

SACHS, CURT
1938 *World history of the dance.* Translated by Bessie Schönberg. London: George Allen and Unwin.

ŠUMARSKI, STANISLAV
1846 Gradja za povestnicu serbsku [Materials for Serbian history]. *Serbskii Letopis'* 73:54–57. Budapest (Buda).

TUGANOV, M. S.
1957 *Osetinskie narodnye tantsy* [Ossetian folk dances]. Tskhinvali: Gosizdat Iugo-Osetii.

VLAHOVIĆ, MITAR
1931 Sredačka župa. *Zbornik za etnografiju i folklor Južne Srbije i Susednih Oblasti* 1.

WOLFRAM, RICHARD
1951 *Die Volkstänze in Österreich und verwandte Tänze in Europa.* Salzburg.

The Study of Folk Dancing in the Soviet Union: Its State and Tasks

M. IA. ZHORNITSKAIA

The study of folk art — music, dancing, dramatic art, and so on — is one of the principal concerns of Soviet ethnography. However, until recently dances were not recorded systematically, and the absence of such recording prevented ethnographers from describing the development of the dance. Before the revolution, folk dancing was not the subject of any special study, a fact partly due to the difficulty of recording dance as an artistic creation and a kind of syncretic folk art in which poetry, choreography and music were organically blended. In order to record it a person had to possess a knowledge of philology, choreography and musical folklore. In addition, there was no unified international system of recording folk dances. Although attempts were made in many countries, including Russia, to create various systems of recording dances, they all were far from being perfect,[1] so ethnographers and folklorists, as a rule, recorded texts of songs and dance tunes without describing choreography. The earliest choreographic publications in Russia were of the round dances by Chubinskii (1872–1878); Lysenko (1875); and Gnatiuk (1909), with a general description of the choreography involved. The first attempts at transferring the best folk dances on to the stage (Belorussian dances, for instance) were also made before the revolution.[2]

Studies of folk dancing in Soviet times were facilitated by their close connection with the practical tasks advanced by the victory of the revolution and the need to record the richest multinational art of folk dancing

[1] Back in 1892, in Paris, a book on this subject by an actor in the Russian emperor's theaters was published in French (Stépanow 1892). Later it was translated into Russian, and A. Gorsky, a teacher at the Saint Petersburg theatrical art college, compiled a table of signs on the basis of this system.
[2] This was being done by the founder of Belorussian theater, I. Buinitskii, in 1910 (Smol'skii 1963:65; Churko 1964).

and bring it within the reach of the masses. Soviet scholars' first scientific observations of the development of folk dancing date back to the twenties and thirties. The Ukrainian composer and choreographer, V. Ver-khovinets (1919) created a simple and generally accepted method of recording folk dances, in a work published in several editions (Ver-khovinets 1920, 1925). Undoubtedly his system was influenced by the fact that round dances had already begun to be recorded in the Ukraine before the revolution. Apart from that, Verkhovinets generalized the principles of recording and the schemes of Shukhevich (1902) and Iush-chinin (1910). In doing this he also used and perfected the experience of Zoder's method of recording (1911), which was quite rational for his time, including graphic designation of male and female dancers, descriptive characteristics of movements, graphic positioning, as well as all the information on the history and present state of the dance.

Verkhovinets not only described the technique of performing many *pas* of the Ukrainian dance, but also drew attention to their component parts (morphology of movement). Already at that time Soviet ethnographers and folklorists devoted much attention to perfecting the system of recording dances. In 1926 N. Ivanov evolved a sign system for positioning the performers on the stage, and K. Sotonin worked out in 1928 a notation system for recording human body movements.

The recording methods used by choreographers, which were elaborated by Verkhovinets, were further perfected by the Soviets Margolis (1950); Tkachenko (1954, 1967); and Humeniuk (1964). These methods are used for describing folk dances of almost all the peoples of the Soviet Union: Russian, Ukrainian, Belorussian, Armenian, Tartar, Latvian, Lithuanian, Georgian, Yakut, Moldavian, and so on. The essence of the descriptive method lies in singling out the melodic pattern and dividing movements (pas) into measures, with a verbal description of the elements of movements. Illustrations are also used: graphic schemes of the spatial composition of the dance and photographs or sketches of specific movements and poses, but they just complement the record. This system was approved in 1950 and recommended to choreographers at their conference in the Krupskaya All-Union Folk Art Club.

Other systems of recording movements and staging have been evolved in the Soviet Union, too. The most detailed system of this kind was worked out by Lisitsian (1940), whose "kinetographic" system makes it possible to record any movements of the human body. This is a very detailed method, although complex in its application, and she used it to record 1,100 Armenian and 50 Kurdish dances and many theatrical performances.

More recently, a comparatively new system for recording dance movements was offered by the Latvian scholar, Suna (1965). Soviet scholars center attention around the problem of choreographic recording, which has repeatedly been discussed in world literature, and put forward questions of creating a unified international system of recording folk dances. This is important since music experts have already begun using the latest achievements of cybernetics for their purposes. These achievements enable them to identify and systematize various aspects of a wide range of melodies (Goshovskii 1964, 1968, 1971; Lomax et al. 1969).

The basic principles of studying folk dancing in the Soviet Union are determined by a concept of ethnography as a science dealing with the stable ethnic features of peoples' life in connection with their ethnogenesis and ethnic history up to the present time, a concept currently prevalent in this country. Such a concept, which takes into account, in a most comprehensive manner, a consistent historical approach stemming from the methods of historic materialism, presupposes an examination of folk dancing historically, in its formation and development. Specific features of ethnographic investigation are: the use of all historical sciences (including archaeology, which allows study of the earliest sculptures and paintings) and other branches of the social sciences (music and folklore studies, linguistics, paleography, and so on); a wide application of a method of direct observations of modern forms of traditional dancing; and the execution of special fieldwork investigations for the purpose.

The study of Russian round dances began during the first postrevolutionary years. The first attempt to review what had been done was made by Vsevolodskii-Gerngros (1933). From 1923 to 1933 he organized the ethnographic theater attached to the ethnographic department of the Russian Museum in Leningrad, where old Russian folk dances were performed (Lutskaia 1968:40). Back in the twenties the first expeditions to study folk dances in various regions of Georgia were organized. In 1923 a group headed by Kote Maryanishvili and including the choreographers, G. Barkhudarov and S. Sergeev, went to Khulo, in Georgia, to study local folk dances there. In the thirties an expedition was sent to lower and upper Svanetia with the choreographer, D. Dzhavrishvili, who filmed eleven Svan folk dances and their nine versions (Gvaramadze 1966).

Beginning in 1930, systematic studies began in Armenia, with Lisitsian at first conducting work in Yerevan and then organizing expeditions throughout the republic's entire territory (Lisitsian 1958). Gerasimchuk did a great deal of work studying folk dances in some regions of the Carpathian Ukraine and published a book in Polish (Gerasimchuk 1939). M. M. Vladykina-Bachinskaia, on the initiative of K. V. Kvitka, head of the folk music department at the Moscow Conservatory, began to study slow round dances in 1940, the results being summed up in Vladykina-Bachinskaia (1951).

A broad program of studying and collecting folk dances of the peoples of the Soviet Union was launched after the Second World War. Expeditions were sent to many regions of the Russian Federation with predominantly Russian populations (*Russkie narodnye tantsy* 1949; Ustinova 1955, 1957, Kniazeva 1962); the Baltic republics (Toomi 1953; Lingis et al. 1955; Lasmane 1962; Suna 1964); the Central Asian republics and Kazakhstan (Azimova 1957; Abirov and Ismailov 1961); and Moldavia (Oshurko 1957). Investigations were still going on in the Ukraine (Gerasimchuk 1956; Humeniuk 1963),[3] and in the Transcaucasus (Gvaramadze 1947, 1956; Dzhavrishvili 1958; Lisitsian 1956). A long-term project was launched to study folk dances of the people of northern Siberia (Zhornitskaia 1964; Timasheva 1959a, 1959b). Folk art clubs organized in 1936 were turned into scientific and methodological centers conducting a great deal of work and accumulating various materials on modern choreographic folklore. On the basis of this material a series, "Tantsy narodov CCCP" [Dances of the peoples of the USSR], began to be published in Moscow, containing recordings of various folk dances and their costumes and contexts. For the first time in our country, materials on the folk dances of a majority of the Soviet people were published. These collections covered a vast amount of material, exceeding that contained in the international ethnographic and folklore literature. What is important is that the material on folk dances of some of the people of the Soviet Union became a component part of their general ethnographic description (*Khoreohrafichnvi fol'klor* 1960; *Ukrainskie narodnye tantsy* 1964).

Modern technical means make it possible to tape and videotape dances. With a view to interpreting folk dances and theatrical folklore correctly, scholars have recorded all the details of their performance. Many folk dances and theatrical performances no longer exist or have been forgotten, so scholars had to recreate them on the spot on the basis of what they were shown by old folk who remembered them. For this purpose questionnaires were prepared to help fix more exactly the setting, place of action, and so forth. In 1959 a bibliographical reference list of literature on the Soviet peoples' folk dances was published (Zosimovskii 1959). Petermann (1967) includes some of the literature published in subsequent years.

By the sixties, comprehensive analyses of folk dancing had already been compiled in a number of union and autonomous republics. The results of these historical and ethnographical studies were summed up at the VII International Congress of Anthropological and Ethnological Sciences in Moscow in August 1964. There was a special section on folk theater and choreography at the congress (see Gurvich 1964). The Soviet

---

[3]   Data on Ukrainian folk dances are published from time to time in the Kiev ethnographical magazine *Narodna Tverchist' ta Etnohrafiia*.

scholars' papers characterized certain specific features of the dances of various Soviet peoples: round dances of the Russian population near Moscow, specific features of Ukrainian folk dances, dances of the people in the Carpathian Mountains, folk dances of the Armenian and Georgian peoples, specific features of Latvian folk dances, and traditional dances of the peoples of Yakutia.

Since that time new monographs on folk dancing have appeared in the Soviet Union. Special mention should be made of Goleizovskii's work (1964), which is the first and only comprehensive work on Russian folk dancing. Goleizovskii makes an original analysis of the sources of folk dances in close connection with the life, customs and cultural development of the people. He does not confine himself to analyzing folk dances and games, giving much information about peoples' rites, customs, and beliefs, and recreating many pictures of their life, work and leisure. As far as the Ukraine is concerned Humeniuk (1968) completed a large work on its folk dancing, and Vasilenko (1965, 1971) devoted his work to the vocabulary of the Ukrainian folk scenic dance. He justly remarks that the principle of classifying choreographic vocabulary is of great importance not only for the development of lexicology but also for folk dancing as a whole. Suna (1967) continued studying folk dances in Latvia. Gravitskas (1967) defended a candidate's dissertation on folk dances in Lithuania. The materials on Belorussian folk dancing were synthesized in a candidate's dissertation by Churko (1964). Koroleva (1970), on the choreographic art of Moldavia, traces the development of folk dancing from its sources to the formation of the professional art of dancing. Avdeeva's work (1965) is the first attempt to analyze the history of Uzbek dancing. The dances of Georgia were analyzed in a doctoral dissertation by Gvaramadze (1966). It should also be noted that a number of books containing recordings of folk dances in some republics were also published. They examine the basic movement of folk dances: many books have prefaces giving historical outlines of dancing and its development (Sokolova 1964; Adamkova and Starikov 1963, 1964; Chudak 1966; Petrova-Bytova 1964).

Soviet scholars — ethnographers and choreographers — display an ever-growing interest in research into folk dancing. One of the greatest achievements of this research is the elaboration of a historical and ethnic typology of this aspect of culture. Although in a number of cases questions of classification of folk dancing are examined in a different manner, the most widely accepted principle is that based on genre and theme. According to it, genres are considered as a historical category generalizing the origin and development of folk dancing of a definite historical period. Due account was taken of the social function of dancing in the people's cultural life, the forms of its existence, the specific stylistic features of the text of choreography and music, as well as the particular manner of performing the dances. In this connection, questions regarding the origin of dancing in human labour occupy an important place.

On the basis of these criteria Humeniuk (1963) defined Ukrainian folk dances as round dances, genre dances and topical dances. These genres have themes and stylistic peculiarities of their own which became established in folk dancing during a specific period of social development. In their artistic aspect, they differ from one another qualitatively. The same principle of classification is used by Aslanishvili (1957), who divided Georgian folk dances into the same categories, and by Lingis et al. (1955) for Lithuanian dances, to mention but a few.

Such an approach to folk dancing is based on examining the genres in their artistic, historical, and ethnographic aspects (Chistov 1968). Studying the whole complex of cultural phenomena, Lisitsian emphasizes the synthesis of folk dancing and theatrical performances, which stimulate the creation of poetry, music, theater and dancing as an art. She studies all these forms of folklore as parts of a single whole. The author combines an analysis of historical and artistic aspects (which is good, in principle) with a linguistic analysis of a great number of terms related not only to dances, games or theater but to movement in general. Such an analysis not only helps us to understand the principles of Armenian folk dancing, but also contributes to understanding the social and cultural basis of each dance form, and thereby makes it possible to tie a dance to a certain social structure and even to date it approximately within the limits of a given structure. Due to the application of her ingenious "kinetographic" system Lisitsian succeeded in recording material with a great degree of scientific accuracy. Systematic descriptions of song, dance and other melodies, and of instrumental accompaniment and specific features of folk instrumental music (its key, rhythm, and form) are essential features of the monographs on folk dancing in the Soviet Union. The genesis of recorded dance patterns, melodies, and texts can be traced only with the help of a thorough analysis of their choreography. Studies of different dances made it possible to differentiate local regions of the territory under observation: in the Ukraine, for example, where there are five local regions, the basic ones are its central and eastern parts, as well as its western regions. The remaining local regions have different kinds of dances, supplementing, to a certain extent, these two main parts of the republic. A study of folk dances in ethnographic regions of Armenia has been conducted on a broad scale (Petrosian and Khachatrian 1965; Khachatrian 1968, 1971).

The structure of the various versions of Yakut round dances, which we singled out for consideration, is explained by the specific geographical and historical conditions in which they exist (Zhornitskaia 1966, 1972). Some groups of the population led an isolated life and were influenced only by their Evenki, Even and Russian neighbors. According to our data and the names of the principal round dances, not counting the Yakut *osuokhai*, the following comparatively large areas can be defined among the Altaic peoples of Yakutia and contiguous regions (excluding the Amur basin):

1. Southwestern with variations of the names *yekhorye*, *dya'urya*, and *yekhor*, including Evenkis, Buryats (at least in the west) and the southeastern groups of Evens;
2. Northeastern area of the Even: *'edye*;
3. Southeastern area of the east Evenkis: *deryode*;
4. Northwestern area of the Dolganis: *'eiro* (Taimyr and contiguous regions of Yakutia).

Thus we have been able to define large areas where round dances existed (among Yakuts, Buryats, Evenkis, Evens, Yukagiris, and Itelmens) and where there were individual imitative dances (among Chukchis, Koryaks, and Eskimos).

These data deserve the attention of researchers in order to establish the most important choreographic complexes throughout the entire country (zones, regions, dialects). The material accumulated enables scholars to begin comparative studies of the dances of the Soviet people. This important problem could obviously be dealt with in a special atlas of folk dances in the Soviet Union, although the list of subjects recommended for national atlases by the International Commission on Atlases and for the proposed ethnographic atlas of Europe and adjacent countries does not mention dance (Bruk and Tokarev 1968), even though this same paper mentions maps of dances in the first Swiss ethnographic atlas.

However, the available data show that Russian, Belorussian, and Ukrainian folk dances have a common origin, and folk dances in the Transcaucasus have common stable specific elements. The same is true of folk dances in the extreme northeast of Siberia, and so on.

These aspects of folk dancing can be revealing if due account is taken of the history of production techniques used by the people in question, their living conditions, socioeconomic and cultural relations with neighboring peoples, and concomitant geographical factors. All this makes it possible to establish well-founded concepts about the historical type, level, origin, and peculiar structure of a genre repertory of the dances studied, and its ethnic ties, and to use the material on folk dancing for elaborating problems of ethnogenesis and ethnic and cultural history. In this way the material on folk dancing reveals its ethnic and cultural content and it will be possible to relate to the areas of distribution of definite complexes of material culture and rites, and to ethnolinguistic and ethnoanthropological areas. The wide range of diverse material used for studying folk dancing raises the question of working out a proper classification of these sources (Sadokov 1970:38–39).

The proximity of dancing devices and the peculiar features of the dances of various peoples can serve, along with other data, as an important additional argument in reviewing the historical and ethnographic nearness or remoteness of the cultures compared, as well as past contacts and ethnic interconnections between peoples.

The dance, a theatrical heritage of the Soviet people, contains many beautiful examples of culture. A timely revealing and recording of this heritage will enable us to preserve the folk dancing and theatrical art of these peoples and ascertain the contribution of each people to world culture, as well as ensuring the further development of folk dancing. The study of the existing dance as well as the theatrical heritage of the Soviet peoples, as an original historical source helping to trace specific features of the life and customs of these peoples, is a most important task. The need for a thorough study of folk dancing calls for greater attention to methodological questions, for the continuing absence of uniform methods of recording and uniform terminology seriously hampers the exchange of experience in this field.

REFERENCES

ABIROV, D., A. ISMAILOV
  1961   *Kazakhskie narodnye tantsy* [Kazakh folk dances]. Alma-Ata.
ADAMKOVA, A. A., S. E. STARIKOV
  1963   *Udmurtskie tantsy* [Udmurt dances]. Izhevsk.
  1964   *Chuvashkie tantsy* [Chuvash dances]. Cheboksary.
ASLANISHVILI, SH.
  1957   "Narodnaia tantseval'naia musyka" [Folk dance music], in *Gruzinskaia Muzykal'naia Kul'tura* [Georgian musical culture], 63ff.
AVDEEVA, A. A.
  1965   "Traditsii i novatorstvo v uzbekskoi khoreografii" [Traditions and innovations in Uzbek choreography]. Candidate's dissertation, Tashkent.
AZIMOVA, A.
  1957   *Tantseval'noe iskusstvo Tadzhikistana* [Dance art of Tadzhikistan]. Dushanbe (Stalinabad).
BRUK, S. I., S. A. TOKAREV
  1968   Mezhdunarodnaia konferentsiia po etnograficheskomu atlasu Evropy i sopredel'nykh stran [International conference on the ethnographic atlas of Europe and its bordering countries]. *Sovetskaia Etnografiia* 5:152 ff.
CHISTOV, K. V.
  1968   Fol'klor i etnografiia [Folklore and ethnography]. *Sovetskaia Etnografiia* 5: 10ff.
CHUBINSKII, P. P.
  1872–1878   *Trudy etnografichesko-statisticheskoi ekspeditsii v zapadno-russkii krai* [Transactions of the ethnographico-statistical expedition to western Russian territory], seven volumes. Leningrad (St. Petersburg).
CHUDAK, G. S.
  1966   *Kalmytskie tantsy* [Kalmyk dances]. Elista.

CHURKO, IU. M.
1964 "Natsional'nyi balet na belorusskoi stsene" [National ballet on the Belorussian stage]. Candidate's dissertation, Minsk.

DZHAVRISHVILI, D.
1958 *Gruzinskie narodnye tantsy* [Georgian folk dances]. Tiflis.

GERASIMCHUK (HARASYMCHUK), R.
1939 *Tance Huculskie* [Hutsulian dance]. Lvov.
1956 "Razvitie narodnogo khoreograficheskogo iskusstva Prikarpat'ia" [Development of folk choreographic art of the Carpathians], part one: "Issledovanie gutsul'skikh tantsev" [Research on Gutsul dances]. Candidate's dissertation, Kiev.

GNATIUK, V. M.
1909 Materialy do ukrains'koi etnolohii [Materials on Ukrainian ethnology]. *Vydae Ietnohrafichna Komisiia Naukovoho Tovarystva im Shevchenka u L'vovi* 12. Lvov.

GOLEIZOVSKII, K. Y.
1964 *Obrazy russkoi narodnoi khoreografii* [Images of Russian folk choreography]. Moscow.

GOSHOVSKII, V. L.
1964 Fol'klor i kibernetita [Folklore and cybernetics]. *Sovetskaia Musyka* 2:74–82.
1968 *Ukrainskie pesni Zakarpat'ia* [Ukrainian songs of Transcarpathia]. Moscow.
1971 "U istokov narodnoi muzyki slavian" [At the sources of Slavic folk music], in *Ocherki po muzykal'nomu slavianovedeniiu* [Studies of Slavic music]. Moscow.

GRAVITSKAS, V.
1967 "Iskusstvo tantsa" [The art of dancing]. Candidate's dissertation.

GURVICH, I. S.
1964 O rabote sekstii VII Mezhdunarodnogo Kongressa Antroplogicheskikh; Etnograficheskikh Nauk [On the work of a section in the VII International Congress of Anthropological and Ethnological Sciences]. *Sovetskaia Etnografiia* 6:161 ff.

GVARAMADZE, E. L.
1947 *K voprosu o proiskhozhdenii i morfologii gruzinskogo tantsa* [On the question of the origin and morphology of Georgian dance]. Tiflis.
1956 "Osnovnye voprosy gruzinskoi narodnoi khoreografii" [Basic questions of Georgian folk choreography]. Candidate's dissertation, Tiflis.
1966 "Gruzinskii tantseval'nyi fol'klor" [Georgian dance folklore]. Doctoral dissertation, Tiflis.

HUMENIUK, A. I.
1963 *Narodne khoreohrafychne mystetstvo Ukrainy* [Folk choreographic art of the Ukraine]. Kiev: Akademia Nauk.
1964 Zapys pryntsypy klasyfikatsii narodnykh tantsiv [Notes on the principle of classifying folk dances]. *Narodna Tvorchist' ta Etnohrafiia* 4.
1968 "Narodnoe khoreograficheskoe iskusstvo Ukrainy" [Folk choreographic art of the Ukraine]. Doctoral dissertation, Kiev.

IUSHCHININ, I.
1910 *Hahilky dlia shkoly: desiat' narodnykh zabav zi spivamy v 2–3 holosy* [Easter songs and dances for school: ten folk amusements with singing for two and three voices]. Lvov.

KHACHATRIAN, ZH. N.
1968   *Pliaski Dzhavakhka i ikh osobennosti* [Dances called Dzhavathka and their characteristics]. Seriia Obshchestvennykh Nauk 3.
1971   "Armianskie norodnye pliaski Dzhavakhka (Dzhavakheti)" [Armenian folk dances called Dzhavakhka (Dzhavakheti)]. Doctoral dissertation.

Khoreohrafichnyi fol'klor
1960   *Khoreohrafichnyi fol'klor* [Choreographic folklore], volume one: *Ukraintsi* [The Ukrainians]. Kiev.

KNIAZEVA, O. N.
1962   *Tantsy Urala* [Dances of the Urals]. Sverdlovsk.

KOROLEVA, E.
1970   *Khoreograficheskoe iskusstvo Moldavii* [Choreographic art of Moldavia]. Kishinev.

LASMANE, M.
1962   *Latyshskie narodnye tantsy* [Latvian folk dances]. Riga.

LINGIS, IU., Z. SLAVIUNAS, V. IAKELAITAS
1955   *Litovskie narodnye tantsy* [Lithuanian folk dances], volume two. Vilnius.

LISITSIAN, S.
1940   *Zapisi dvizheniia (kinetografiia)* [Recording of movements ("kinetography")]. Moscow and Leningrad.
1956   "Starinnye pliaski i teatral'nye predstavleniia armianskogo naroda" [Old dances and theatrical performances of the Armenian people]. Doctoral dissertation, Yerevan.
1958   *Starinnye pliaski i teatral'nye predstavleniia armianskogo naroda* [Old dances and theatrical performances of the Armenian people]. Yerevan.

LOMAX, ALAN, IRMGARD BARTENIEFF, FORRESTINE PAULAY
1969   Choreometrics: a method for the study of cross-cultural patterns in dance. *Research Film* 6(6):505–517. Institut für den Wissenschaftlichen Film.

LUTSKAIA, E.
1968   *Zhizn' v tantse* [Life in the dance]. Moscow.

LYSENKO, M.
1875   *Molodoshchi: zbirnyk tantsiv ta vesnianok (hry, spivy, vesnian, dytiach, divoch, zhinoch i mishani* [Youth: a collection of dances and spring songs (games and spring songs of children, maidens, women, and mixed groups)]. Kiev.

MARGOLIS, E. M.
1950   *O zapisi tantsa* [On the recording of the dance]. Moscow.

OSHURKO, L. V.
1957   *Narodnye tantsy Moldavii* [Folk dances of Moldavia]. Kishinev.

PETERMANN, KURT
1967   *Tanzbibliographie: Verzeichnis der in deutsche Sprache veröffentlichten Schriften und Aufsätze zum Buhnen-, Gesellschafts-, Kinder-, Volks- und Turniertanz zowie zur Tanzwissenschaft, Tanzmusik und zum Jazz.* Leipzig: Bibliographisches Institut.

PETROSIAN, E. KH., ZH. N. KHACHATRIAN
1965   Sobranie proizvedenii armianskogo tantseval'nogo i teatral'nogo fol'klora [Collection of works of Armenian dance and theater folklore]. *Sovetskaia Etnografiia* 1:155–158.

PETROVA-BYTOVA
   1964   *Chetyre kamchatskikh tantsa* [Four Kamchatka dances]. Petropavlovsk-Kamchatski.
Russkie narodnye tantsy
   1949   *Russkie narodnye tantsy* [Russian folk dance]. Moscow.
SADOKOV, R. L.
   1970   *Muzykal'naia kul'tura Khorezma* [Music culture of Khiva]. Moscow.
SHUKHEVICH, V.
   1902   *Hutsul'shchyna* [Hutsul country], part three. Lvov.
SMOL'SKII, B. S.
   1963   *Belorusskii musykal'nyi teatr* [Belorussian music theater].
SOKOLOVA, L. A.
   1964   *Mariiskie tantsy* [Mari dances]. Ioshkar Ola.
STÉPANOW, W. J.
   1892   *Alphabet des mouvements du corps humain: essai d'enregistrement des mouvements du corps humain au moyen des signes musicaux.* Paris: P. Vigot.
SUNA, H.
   1964   *Sistematizatsiia khoreograficheskogo materiala: metodicheskaia zapiska po arkhivnomu khraneniiu i sistematizatsii fol'klornykh materialov* [Systemization of choreographic material: methodological note on archival holdings and the systemization of folklore materials]. Vilnius.
   1965   Novaia sistema kinetografii — zapis' khoreograficheskikh dvizhenii [The new system of "kinetography" — the recordings of choreographic movements]. *Izvestiia Akademii Nauk Latviiskoi SSR* 5:214ff.
   1967   *Latviešu rotaļas un rotaļdejas* [Latvian round songs and round dances]. Riga.
TIMASHEVA, L.
   1959a   *Tantsy narodov severa* [Dances of the peoples of the north]. Magadan.
   1959b   *Tantsy narodov Krasnoiarskogo kraia* [Dances of the peoples of the Krasnoytarsk territory]. Krasnoyarsk.
TKACHENKO, T. S.
   1954   *Narodnyi tanets* [The folk dance]. Moscow.
   1967   *Narodnyi tanets* [The folk dance]. Moscow.
TOOMI, U.
   1953   *Estonskie narodnye tantsy* [Estonian folk dances]. Tallinn.
Urainskie narodnye tantsy
   1964   *Ukrainskie narodnye tantsy* [Ukrainian folk dances]. Narody Evropeiskoi Chasti SSSR 1. Moscow.
USTINOVA, T. A.
   1955   *Russkie tantsy* [Russian dances]. Moscow.
   1957   *Berech' krasotu russkogo tantsa* [To preserve the beauty of the Russian dance]. Moscow.
VASILENKO, K.
   1965   "Voprosy razvitiia sovremennogo ukrainskogo narodno-stsenicheskogo tantsa" [Questions of the development of the contemporary Ukrainian folk-stage dance]. Candidate's dissertation, Kiev.
   1971   *Leksyka ukrainskoho narodno-stsenichnoho tantsiu* [Lecture on the Ukrainian folk-stage dance]. Kiev.
VERKHOVINETS, V.
   1919   *Ukrainc'ka khoreohrafiia: teoriia ukrains'koho narodnoho tantsa* [Ukrainian choreography: theory of the Ukrainian folk dance]. Kiev.

1920   *Teoriia ukrains'koho narodnoho tantsa* [Theory of the Ukrainian folk dance]. Poltava.

1925   *Vesnianochka* [Spring songs]. Kiev.

VLADYKINA-BACHINSKAIA, M. M.

1951   *Russkie khorovody i narodnye pesni* [Russian dances and folk songs]. Moscow.

VSEVOLODSKII-GERNGROS, V. N.

1933   *Igry narodov SSSR* [Dances of Soviet peoples]. Moscow and Leningrad.

ZHORNITSKAIA, M. IA.

1964   Narodnye tantsy evenov i evenkov Yakutskoi ASSR [Folk dances of the Evens and Evenkis of the Yakut ASSR]. *Sovetskaia Etnografiia 2.*

1966   *Narodnye tantsy Iakutii* [Folk dances of Yakutia]. Moscow.

1972   "Izuchenie tantseval'noi kul'tury amguemskikh chukchei" [Study of dance culture of Amguen Chukchis], in *Itogl polevykh rabot Instituta etnografii ANSSSR za 1917 god* [Summary of the work of the ethnographic institute of the Academy of Sciences of the USSR since 1917], 157–163. Moscow.

ZODER, R.

1911   Wie zeichnet man Volkstanzen auf. *Zeitschrift des Vereins für Volkskunde* 1.

ZOSIMOVSKII, V.

1959   *Bibliograficheskii spravochnik po khoreografii* [Bibliographic reference guide on choreography]. Moscow.

PART THREE

Cross-Cultural Studies of the Performing Arts

Continuity and Discontinuity in Song Styles: An Ordinal Cross-Cultural Classification

S. LEE SEATON and KAREN ANN WATSON

SUMMARY

An investigation into the relationship of contemporary song styles and the American counterculture (Seaton and Watson 1972) involved the nonmetric replication of the cross-cultural factor and grouping analyses of Alan Lomax's cantometrics project (Lomax 1968).[1] Ordinal multidimensional scaling (Young 1968) produced a circumplex configuration for the thirty-one cantometric variables. Hierarchical clustering (Johnson 1967) of the variables indicates that the circumplex which had not been noted by Lomax does conform, however, to originally hypothesized models for song styles. Following normal interpretation of circumplex configurations (Guttman 1954), it is possible to extend beyond the discrete model stage and identify a specifically musicological continuity following the work of Levelt et al. (1966). In this paper a taxonomic world song style map is presented for ninety sample cultures, and interpreted in accordance with the underlying circumplex structure.

The cantometrics project involved a cross-cultural study of the folk songs of 233 societies.[2] The basic datum is the percentage of songs characterized by the presence of a descriptor feature within each culture's song sample (Lomax 1968:34–74). In all, songs were measured in terms of thirty-one variables. These may be conceptually grouped into four general categories: (1) vocal stance, (2) group relationship (singer to accompaniment), (3) musical elaboration (textual and melodic), and (4) rhythm. Table 1 displays the full set of variables along with the

---

This is a revised and expanded version of a paper read by Seaton at the Third Annual Meeting of the Classification Society (North American branch), April 25, 1972, Chicago.
[1] Replicative aspects are reported in Watson and Seaton (1971), and in Seaton and Watson (1972).
[2] Raoul Naroll (1970) published the raw matrix as an appendix to his survey of cross-cultural studies. Reviews of the cantometrics enterprise were generally cautiously supportive (Driver 1970; Downey 1970).

Table 1.   Cantometric variables and rotated configuration

Point identity	Label	1	2
A	Solo and explicit	0.318	−0.381
B	Solo, explicit, and moderate	0.347	−0.318
C	Interlocking vocal group	−0.357	0.246
D	Overlapping vocal group	0.043	0.463
E	Simple alternation	0.371	−0.076
F	Exclusive dominant	0.321	−0.348
G	Polyphony	−0.109	0.553
H	Polyphony for females	−0.070	0.556
I	Tonal cohesiveness	0.045	0.586
J	Rhythmic cohesiveness	0.128	0.521
K	Wordiness of text	0.375	−0.254
L	Repetition of text	−0.744	0.033
M	Nonexplicit text	−0.643	0.242
N	Free vocal rhythm	0.159	−0.414
O	Vocal counterpoint	−0.250	0.307
P	One-beat orchestra rhythm	−0.703	−0.215
Q	Unison orchestra rhythm	−0.731	−0.199
R	Accompanying orchestra rhythm	0.465	−0.098
S	Orchestra counterpoint	0.142	−0.279
T	Orchestra polyrhythm	0.180	0.458
U	Wide melodic interval	−0.701	0.104
V	Narrow melodic interval	0.226	−0.457
W	Embellishment	0.234	−0.425
X	Elaborateness	0.246	−0.427
Y	Moderate delivery	0.427	0.100
Z	Narrow voices	0.122	−0.480
1	Wide voices	−0.026	0.617
2	Mean number of instruments	0.436	−0.037
3	Precise enunciation	0.386	−0.338
4	Slurred enunciation	−0.418	0.482
5	Nasality	−0.218	−0.524

configuration derived from the multidimensional scaling.[3] The corresponding configuration is presented in Figure 1.

The configuration is based on the ordinal scaling of missing-data correlation coefficients. The two-dimensional solution had a Kruskal's stress of 0.134 ("fair to good") with Torgerson's index at 0.996. The two-dimensional solution had a Kruskal's coefficient of stress of 0.134, indicating a fair-to-good fit for the data. The moderate lack of fit therefore is to be attributed to violations of the triangular inequality (7.23 percent) in the correlation matrix, due to missing-data ill-conditioning.

Inspection of the configuration suggests that two distinct sets encompass all the variables. In fact, the configuration is striking in a number of respects. First, the variables appear relatively tightly knit within their

---

[3]   A subsample of 147 cultures was drawn from the original 233 on the basis of identification of a compatible unit in the *Ethnographic atlas* (Murdock 1967). This helped to minimize missing data.

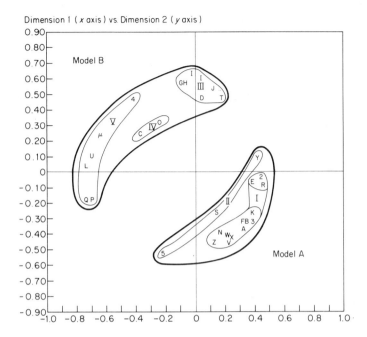

Figure 1. Cantometric variables: ordinal scaling and clustering

groupings. Second, the overall pattern of the variables is arclike. Third the arcs, if continued, would meet and form a remarkably symmetrical ellipse. These features suggest that the interpretation of the plot must proceed both at the level of the clusters of variables and at the level of the overall structure of the configuration.

Lomax (1968:16) set out two "contrastive models" for song performance: "the highly individualized and group-dominating" Model A, and "the highly cohesive, group-involving" Model B. The characteristics anticipated to be associated with each model are listed in Table 2. Although the dimensional representation clearly suggests a two-model

Table 2. Lomax's hypothesized cantometric models for song styles

Model A	Model B
Solo	Choral, multileveled, cohesive
Textually complex	Repetitious text
Metrically complex	Metrically simple
Melodically complex	Melodically simple
Ornamented	No ornamentation
Usually noisy voice	Usually clear voice
Precise enunciation	Slurred enunciation

interpretation, numerical clustering methods permit a more explicit stepwise procedure for testing the hypothesized models.

Figure 2 displays the dendrogram derived from diameter-method hierarchical clustering of the correlation matrix. As the "clustering value" is the maximum diameter, that is, the smallest correlation, of the clusters at that level, a parsimonious grouping of variables may be achieved by taking as a cutoff point the shift from positive to negative-valued diameters. At level 27 (clustering value = 0.002), five distinct clusters are formed. The boundaries are traced in Figure 1 by the narrow lines and labeled with Roman numerals. In the next clustering step, V and IV are merged. The clustering continues with the formation of superclusters (levels 29 and 30) prior to the final union of all points into a single grouping.

Identification of the membership of the first cluster (I) indicates that there is a common factor of precision running throughout and that virtually all conceptual categories are represented. Ornamentation in style and constraint in expression, that is, individualization in performance, are the core features. Cluster I is joined by Cluster II, a small grouping of nasality, moderate delivery, and orchestra counterpoint (specialized constraint items), to form the hypothesized Model A.

Cluster III is a tight grouping of cohesiveness features, with the additional feature of wide voicing. The cohesive group-orientedness of this cluster is accented by the presence of the two polyphony variables.

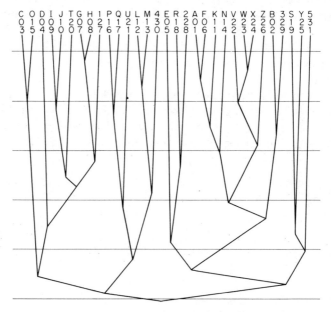

Figure 2.   Cantometric variables: hierachical clustering dendrogram

Cluster IV is a two-member group of vocal coordination features. Nonornamental and open, Cluster V, which joins with IV at the next clustering step, neatly contrasts with the characteristics of Cluster I. The supercluster of IV and V merges with the Cluster III cohesiveness items to form Model B.

Models A and B are joined at level 31 (clustering value $= -0.742$), thereby completing the aggregation process. No variables are isolated from the major arcs. This indicates a conceptual unity to the cantometric selection of variables.

There can be no doubt that the nonmetric configuration and clustering clearly confirm Lomax's originally hypothesized models for folk song styles. The clustering of the models into distinct classes further confirms the empirical findings of intracultural homogeneity of musical styles (Lomax 1962:431). This point is particularly significant for the interpretation of the overall pattern.

THE CIRCUMPLEX

Unfortunately Lomax has not provided a musicological rationale for his models. Rather than being "concerned about the way that musical symbolism works", Lomax designed the cantometric variables to "locate sets of musical phenomena cross-culturally" (1962:42). The description of musical behavior is set apart from the theory of musical performance (cf. Downey 1970). Models A and B, as descriptors, do provide contrast sets in the cross-cultural context, however, the musicological groundwork for a theory of performance remains. One research strategy would be the intensive investigation of specific variables and their performance significances. Another — and the one pursued here — is to adopt a reductive approach, namely, analyzing the structure in the data, and thereby developing a context for separate items. Item selection is thus subordinated to explanation of the configuration *in toto*.

The fact that the variables formed cluster arcs indicates that the underlying structure of the data is a circular ordering, or a circumplex (Guttman 1954:324–325). As a circumplex, all of the variables are of the same level of complexity — figuratively lying equidistant from the origin on the circumference of a circle. The implication, then, of the circular configuration for the cantometric data is that there is only *one* underlying dimension operative in the song-style space. The two models represent a *continuity* of musical styles.

The interpretation of the circumplex as *unidimensional* is that the distances within clusters represent the relative "musical utility" of a style characteristic with respect to other intracluster variables. Psychomusicological evidence for such a "musical utility" function is given in an article by Levelt et al. (1966), who, using multidimensional scaling of reported perceptual similarity, derived a three-dimensional configuration from judgments of musical intervals. Their identification of the configuration was in terms of "extremity" or "infrequency of occurrence" (1966:174). However as their sample was monocultural, "musical disutility" might easily be judged "extreme".

There is further supportive evidence which may be extracted from a reinterpretation of their findings. First, the authors accept the three-dimensional solution with an averaged (for simple and complex tone intervals) stress of 0.113 rather than the two-dimensional configuration with an averaged stress of 0.179. They do this in spite of findings that the third dimensions are uncorrelated when the configurations are matched (Levert et al. 1966:170).[4] This suggests that the two-dimensional solution is to be preferred for further analysis. The authors in fact do abandon the third dimension and proceed to the interpretation of the common dimensions. Here again, they seem to run counter to their findings. In fitting a curve to the matched configuration the authors selected a parabola: "although an ellipse was found to give a better mathematical fit, the parabola was preferred because we could not think of a meaningful interpretation of a closed scale" (1966:173). Set in the context of a cross-cultural study, the mathematically superior ellipse is also the ethnomusicologically better solution. As cultures tend to manifest homogeneity in styles, an operative "imperative of selection" in the decisions underlying musical performances is not surprising. The open parabola, then, *is characteristic within* a musical tradition (that is, Model A or Model B). Considered cross-culturally, however, the two models' parabolas are opposed on their principal axes. Their intersection produces the ellipsoidal circumplex of Figure 1.[5] The discontinuity between models A and B is simply the result of the infrequency of occurrence of mixed modalities of style due to the intracultural judgments of extremity.

The ordinal circumplex in the cantometrics data provides a strong theoretical perspective — a theory of musical utilities — from which the original list of thirty-one variables may be refined and extended. The fact that this theory deals in continua of styles rather than simple binary oppositions may sober some contemporary structuralists. Methodologically the field of analytic procedure between nominal measures and metric measures of style has only been scratched by the ordinal tech-

[4]   Levelt et al. do offer interpretations of the specific dimensions (1966:174–178). However their analyses seem strained and reflect an ethnocentric bias toward evaluation.
[5]   Fitting two polynomials to models A and B yielded an averaged coefficient of determination of 74 percent (A = 66.5 percent and B = 81.5 percent) whereas a quadratic solution accounted for only 45.2 percent of the variance in the configuration. The pattern of coefficients for the two polynomials is quite similar: $Ya = -0.538 + 0.205Xa + 1.82X^2a$ and $Yb = 0.530 - 0.015Xb - 1.07X^2b$. The differences in the signs of the coefficients reflect the mirroring of the parabolas across the origin.

niques used here. In addition to multidimensional scaling of similarities, rank-ordered *preferences* may be conditionally scaled without any inter-subjective comparison of utilities (cf. Green and Carmone 1970:ch. 4). In this procedure, individual stylists or cultural traditions may be scaled idiosyncratically solely on the basis of their own choices. In the present analyses, comparisons are made as if all cultures share the same utility function. Although this assumption of shared functionality *is* supported by the identification of the circumplex, the potentiality of field data on cantometric preferences is great for both replication and refinement.

THE WORLD SONG STYLE MAP

The circumplex configuration may be used to interpret a taxonomic world song style map constructed by applying the dimensional and clustering procedures already discussed to the transposed (variable by culture) data matrix. The original cantometric sample was again reduced from 147 to 90 units in the interests of computing costs and limitations. The two-dimensional stress was 0.185 ("moderate to poor").[6] The rotated config-uration is listed in Table 3, and plotted in Figure 3.

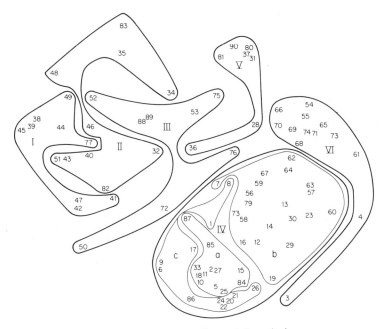

Figure 3.   World song style map (ordinal scaling and clustering)

[6]   Guttman-Lingoes SSA1 was used to calculate an initial configuration which was then rotated to varimax simple structure.

Table 3.   Cantometric ethnic units and rotated configuration

Point identity	Name	Coordinate 1	Coordinate 2
	American Indian (North and South)		
1	Aymara	−0.0368	−0.6116
2	Bora-Witoto	−0.0125	−0.8667
3	Jivaro	0.4173	−1.0506
4	Campa	0.8454	−0.5914
5	Camayura	0.0123	−0.9680
6	Huichol	−0.3218	−0.8619
7	Pima	0.0388	−0.3921
8	Yaqui	0.0979	−0.3856
9	Totonac	−0.3176	−0.8197
10	West Apache	−0.0987	−0.9249
11	Navaho	−0.0605	−0.8977
12	Zuni	0.2492	−0.7176
13	Hopi	0.4067	−0.5473
14	Creek	0.3058	−0.6331
15	Iroquois	0.1126	−0.8723
16	Yuchi	0.1734	−0.7146
17	Kiowa	−0.1396	−0.7533
18	Blood	−0.1016	−0.8875
19	Washo	0.3324	−0.9244
20	Poma (northern)	0.0725	−1.0378
21	Poma (eastern)	0.0738	−1.0372
22	Haida	0.0465	−1.0867
23	Puyallup	0.5379	−0.5905
24	Nootka	0.0474	−1.0646
25	Caribou Eskimo	0.0531	−1.0069
26	Carrier	0.2348	−0.9677
27	Slave	0.0077	−0.8614
	New Guinea		
28	Motu	0.2326	−0.0720
29	Kakoli	0.4244	−0.7379
30	Abelam	0.4298	−0.5849
	Oceania		
31	Palau	0.2443	0.3406
32	Ulithi	−0.3367	−0.2062
33	Yap	−0.1074	−0.8575
34	Manus	−0.3377	0.1192
35	Hawaii	−0.5291	0.3424
36	Mangareva	−0.1251	−0.1922
37	Samoa	0.2005	0.3604
	Old high culture		
38	Turkmen	−1.0221	−0.0057
39	Japanese village	−1.0784	−0.0667
40	Sherpa	−0.7252	−0.2185
41	Temiar Semang	−0.5858	−0.4744
42	Pwo Karen	−0.7974	−0.5109
43	Burma	−0.8516	−0.2530
44	Thailand	−0.8877	−0.0630
45	Malay	−1.1023	−0.0876
46	Iban	−0.7044	−0.0617
47	Tagbanua	−0.7783	−0.4775

Table 3.—*(continued)*

Point identity	Name	Coordinate 1	2
	Old high culture		
48	Java-Sunia	−0.9367	0.2400
49	Egyptians	−0.8346	0.1030
50	Shluh	−0.7626	−0.7497
51	Kurds	−0.8899	−0.2610
52	Kerala	−0.6944	0.1088
	Africa		
53	Malinke	−0.1250	0.0398
54	Diola-Fogny	0.5472	0.0645
55	Mamou	0.5271	−0.0423
56	Shilluk	0.2097	−0.4461
57	Nandi	0.5454	−0.4576
58	Dinka	0.1663	−0.5836
59	Nuer	0.2430	−0.3977
60	Bushmen	0.6695	−0.5591
61	Mbuti	0.8344	−0.2248
62	Xhosa	0.4592	−0.2529
63	Sotho	0.5586	−0.4284
64	Zulu	0.4245	−0.3135
65	Bemba	0.3725	0.0237
66	Luvale	0.6170	0.0595
67	Chagga	0.2928	−0.3481
68	Sakalava (Madagascar)	0.4876	−0.1834
69	Tanala (Madagascar)	0.4526	−0.0868
70	Luba	0.3685	0.0669
71	Fut	0.5855	−0.1990
72	Fon	−0.2865	−0.5171
73	Toma	0.6983	−0.1156
74	Mende	0.5333	−0.1023
75	Wolof	0.0095	0.1183
76	Hausa (Zazza)	0.1145	−0.2315
77	Amhara	−0.7252	−0.1619
78	Galla (Gibe)	0.1099	−0.5516
79	Afar	0.1869	−0.4952
	Europe		
80	Basques	0.1979	0.3817
81	Dutch	0.0542	0.3099
82	French Canada	−0.6378	−0.4141
83	Naples	−0.5127	0.5072
	Arctic Asia		
84	Ainu	0.1581	−0.9216
85	Yukaghir	−0.0228	−0.7302
86	Chukches	−0.1415	−0.0156
	Tribal India		
87	Abor	−0.1757	−0.5633
88	Gond (Mugon)	−0.4111	−0.0326
89	Gond (Magon)	−0.4088	−0.0292
	United States		
90	Popular circa 1950	0.1270	0.3978

Lomax used a revised version of the *Ethnographic atlas* (Murdock 1967) scheme for the regional grouping of individual cultures (Lomax 1968:29–33). The regional boundaries noted in Table 3 are derived from that listing. While the distribution of cultures in the configuration does support, in general, the culture-area typology, numerical clustering again sharpens the classification. Using the zero-correlation cutoff point, the dendrogram (Figure 4) reveals a six-cluster pattern which transcends purely regional boundaries. The six-cluster top of the dendrogram is reproduced in Figure 5 in condensed form. The sociocultural labels applied to each cluster are impressionistic and should be taken as heuristic.[7] However, the stepwise pattern of aggregation is significant in its own right. First, there is a basic dichotomous split which would be anticipated in view of the discontinuity of the generative circumplex configuration in the cantometric variables. Second, the next order of decomposition is balanced as both branches of the dendrogram serially bifurcate into tripartite divisions. Cluster I, "High cultures", is formed of the classicisms of Ethiopia and Egypt as well as several advanced Asian cultures. Cluster II, "States", is composed of both Western folk traditions and independent Asian and Oceanic styles. Together Clusters I and II form the core of a supercluster of elaborated musical styles. Cluster III, "Old kingdoms", which is made up of a mixture of Indian and African groups, joins the first two to complete a "Civilizations" supercluster of elaborated musical styles. The corresponding divisions of the remaining groups show a large isolate of American Indian and African "tribal" cultures, Cluster IV. The subclusters of IV are identified in Figure 5 as "Warriors", "Pastoralists", and "Hunters". Cluster V is a "High folk" group of Western and Oceanic traditions. Cluster VI's "Villagers" is a broad collection of agriculturalists with a curiously large number of sheep herders (six out of thirteen). Clusters V and VI are joined with IV in creating a supercluster which, for lack of a better term to contrast with "Civilizations" must be called "Primitives". Again it should be emphasized that at this stage in research such labels are largely mnemonic.

The musicological continuities underlying the cluster configuration may be identified by intensive examination of the patterns of scores of the cantometric variables within each cluster. A profile analysis of each cluster consists of finding the variables which are most characteristic of the cultures in the cluster. In the present case, eighteen variables (eight from Model A and ten from B) received at least three scores of eighty percent or more and had at least half of all grouped scores of fifty percent or more for the six clusters. The pattern of responses to these eighteen are displayed in Table 4. Once again the basic A/B discontinuity is present. However, there is overlapping between models and clusters, which is

[7]   Hypotheses relating social structure to musical style are examined in Lomax (1962).

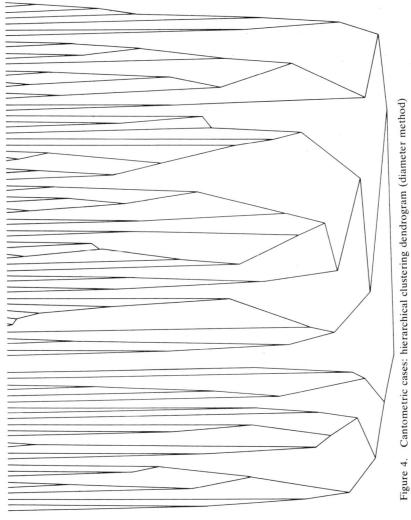

Figure 4. Cantometric cases: hierarchical clustering dendrogram (diameter method)

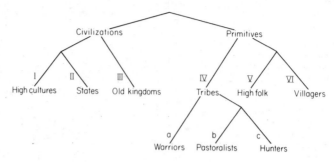

Figure 5.　Condensed dendrogram for cantometric clusters

indicative of the circumplex structure. Explicating the precise pattern of scoring will greatly assist in understanding the dynamics of cross-cultural classification in music.

Clusters I, II and III are united on Model A by common scores on two core variables. Narrow voices (26) and nasality (31) form a shared element of constrained vocal stance which underlies the "civilized" supercluster. The set of core variables for Model B and clusters IV, V, and VI includes rhythmic cohesiveness (10) and wide voices (27). The open style of the "primitive" supercluster members is further underlined by strong showings for the polyphony variables (7, 8) and another cohesiveness factor (9). Similarly, the controlled style of "Civilizations" is indicated by partially shared elements of precise enunciation (29) and textual elaboration (11).

The contrast dimension for models A and B is vocal stance. The features on this basic diagnostic are "narrow" versus "wide" voice. There is no overlap between superclusters on this dimension, and as such it is a perfect predictor of cluster-model scoring. Each individual cluster may be singled out by additional consideration of within-bloc contrasts and idiosyncratic variables. Clusters I and VI may be identified by their antipathy for B and A variables, respectively. They are archetypes of the two great musical styles. The remaining clusters cross model-theoretic boundaries and present heterogeneous scores. Orchestra rhythm differentiates clusters II and V. The features are "accompanying" and "unison", with the scoring running opposite to the general model pattern. Therefore Clusters II and IV are accounted for (predicted) but not defined by the intersection of the dimensions of vocal stance and orchestra rhythm. The additional and idiosyncratic variable of "solo and explicit" (1) is needed to complete the definition of Cluster II. Clusters II and IV are identified by a commonality which bridges the discontinuity. They share noncontrast core variables: nasality and rhythmic cohesiveness. They are accounted for, then, by the intersection of the principal dimensions of contrast and commonality, continuity and discontinuity.

Table 4.   Cantometric scores by cluster region

Model A		I	II	III	IV	V	VI
1	Solo and explicit		×				
5	Simple alternation	×					
6	Exclusive dominant		×				
11	Wordiness of text	×	×			×	
18	Accompanying orchestra rhythm	×				×	
26	Narrow voices	×	×	×			
29	Precise enunciation	×	×			×	
31	Nasality	×	×	×	×		
Model B							
7	Polyphony					×	×
8	Polyphony for females					×	×
9	Tonal cohesiveness					×	×
10	Rhythmic cohesiveness		×	×	×	×	×
12	Repetition of text				×		
16	One-beat orchestra rhythm				×		
17	Unison orchestra rhythm		×		×		
21	Wide melodic interval				×		
27	Wide voices				×	×	×
30	Slurred enunciation				×		

Note: × indicates at least three scores 80 percent or more and at least half of all grouped scores 50 percent or more.

CONCLUSION

Song styles have been found to reflect a basic data structure of continuity and discontinuity. That such a structure may still yield a unifying theory for cross-cultural research was indicated by the identification of a config-uration with known analytical properties. Specifically, the ellipse formed by the opposition of two parabolas along their principal axes suggested the development of a theory of musical utilities. The evidence necessary for testing the theory remains to be collected. However, conditional scaling of individual cultural judgments of style preferences appears to be a promising research strategy.

In light of the evident circular ordering in the ellipsoid, an assumption of a universal utility function was made. The resultant interpretation of the configuration was that of a unidimensional circumplex. The circumplex with its pattern of within-model continuity and between-model discon-tinuity dictated the adoption of the comparative perspective in ethno-musicological interpretation. Further research into the nature of musical symbolism must be consciously comparative if it is to avoid latent biases induced by mixing different models for utilizing the parameters of musi-cal style.

The world song style map produced a taxonomic ordering of the 90 sample cultures. The overall display generally corresponded to the well-known culture regions of Murdock's *Ethnographic atlas* (1967), the basic split being between "Civilizations" and "Primitives", understood as heuristic labels. The musicological split was between Lomax's "individualized" Model A and "group-oriented" Model B. Detailed profile analysis of the scores of separate clusters across the significant variables substantiated the circumplex pattern of continuity and discontinuity. The findings of that analysis may be neatly summarized paradigmatically (see Table 5). The contrasts between model-theoretic features of voice and orchestra form a sixfold classification of song style clusters. The parsimony of this classification suggests that these dimensions may be the major distinctive features in defining musical utilities. Future research probably would benefit by concentrating on these variables for assessing judgements of musical preferences.

Table 5.   Cluster/model summary

| | Vocal stance | |
Orchestra rhythm	Narrow	Wide
Accompanying	I	V
Not marked	III	IV
Unison	II	VI

REFERENCES

DOWNEY, JAMES C.
   1970   Review of *Folk song style and culture: a staff report on cantometrics*, by Alan Lomax. *Ethnomusicology* 14(1):63–67.
DRIVER, HAROLD E.
   1970   Review of *Folk song style and culture: a staff report on cantometrics*, by Alan Lomax. *Ethnomusicology* 14(1):57–62.
GREEN, PAUL E., FRANK J. CARMONE
   1970   *Multidimensional scaling and related techniques in marketing analysis.* Boston, Massachusetts: Allyn and Bacon.
GUTTMAN, LOUIS
   1954   "A new approach to factor analysis: the Radex," in *Mathematical thinking in the social sciences.* Edited by Paul F. Lazarsfeld. Glencoe, Illinois: Free Press.
JOHNSON, STEPHEN C.
   1967   Hierarchical clustering schemes. *Psychometrika* 32:241–254.
LEVELT, W. J. M., J. P. VAN DE GEER, R. PLOMP
   1966   Triadic comparison of musical intervals. *British Journal of Mathematical and Statistical Psychology* 19:163–179.
LOMAX, ALAN
   1962   Song structure and social structure. *Ethnology* 1:425–451.
   1968   *Folk song style and culture: a staff report on cantometrics.* Washington D.C.: American Association for the Advancement of Science.

MURDOCK, GEORGE
1967 *Ethnographic atlas*. Pittsburgh: University of Pittsburgh Press.

NAROLL, RAOUL
1970 What have we learned from cross-cultural surveys? *American Anthropologist* 72:1227–1288.

SEATON, S. LEE, KAREN ANN WATSON
1972 Counter-culture and rock: a cantometric analysis of retribalization. *Youth and Society* 4(1):3–19.

WATSON, KAREN ANN, S. LEE SEATON
1971 "McLuhan, Lomax, cantometrics and rock: a multivariate test of the retribalization hypothesis." Paper presented at the seventieth annual meeting of the American Anthropological Association, New York City, November 19.

YOUNG, FORREST W.
1968 "A FORTRAN IV program for nonmetric multidimensional scaling." L. L. Thurstone Psychometric Laboratory Report 56, Chapel Hill, North Carolina.

Rice-Planting Music of Chindo (Korea) and the Chūgoku Region (Japan)

RURIKO UCHIDA

Chindo (Chin Island) is located in the Yellow Sea, just off the southwest of the Korean peninsula. The island is 420 square kilometers in area and has a population of 110,000. The history of the island goes back to the *Kudara* period in the sixth century, and since ancient times has been known as the "island of granary" and also the "island of song". Eighty percent of the inhabitants are farmers. The island is also famous for its dogs. Usually the people marry a fellow-islander. In funeral rites men carrying the coffin sing funeral songs accompanied by drums and gongs, and the bone-washing burial custom has been kept up. There are three kinds of religion: Buddhism, Confucianism, and Shamanism. The natives give *kj* [mutual aid] for rice planting, weeding, harvesting, money saving, and on such occasions as weddings and funerals.

At the time of rice planting a leader hangs the *book* [drum] in front of his body and beats it to the rhythm of work. The leader (sometimes a singer stands beside the leader) and many rice-planting women, sing folk songs alternately, accompanied by an ensemble of *chango*, a special Korean drum, *book*, *chin*, a gong and *kengari*, a small gong (see Plate 1). There is a very similar rice-planting performance in the Chūgoku region on the mainland of Japan (see Plate 2). Comparing the rice-planting music of both districts, the problem of musical, poetic and ethnological similarities and differences between them will be discussed.

SIMILARITIES

Ethnographic

1. The structure of the performance of rice planting (gathering the seedling and transplanting it) is very similar.

Plate 1.   Rice planting in Chindo, Korea

Plate 2.   Rice planting in the Chūgoku region of Japan

2. Rice planting is carried out by the cooperative work group, called *ture-kj* in Korea, or *yui* in Japan.

3. After rice planting, *suresim*, a banquet is held in Chindo. In the Chūgoku region a similar custom exists.

4. For the purpose of praying for a good harvest a number of ceremonies are held in Chindo, such as *Ryutosai* (June 15), *Hyakchù* (July 15), *Chusoku* (August 15) and New Year (January 15). Chusoku and New Year are the most important ceremonies, when rice cakes, made of newly harvested rice, are offered to ancestors, and a dance, *kankanswore*, is performed. At New Year the forecasting of the next year's rice harvest is carried out in many ways, such as "welcoming the moon", tug-of-war, and so on. They also dance *nonak*, a Korean farmers' dance, visit and congratulate every household. In the Chūgoku region there are also harvest ceremonies in autumn and at New Year. In autumn ears of newly harvested rice are offered to the ancestors and at New Year forecasting ceremonies are held and young men visit and congratulate each household.

5. After the harvest the old rice contained in the holy pot in Korea, or fine straw bales in Japan, is replaced with newly harvested rice. The idea of the "grain spirit", believed to be the "ancestor's spirit", is evident in the ceremony.

6. The time schedules for cultivating rice, and the techniques of agriculture, are similar in the two places.

Musical

1. The music consists of vocal solo, vocal unison and instrumental ensemble.

2. The tonal system of rice-planting songs is based on the fundamental tetrachord.

3. The function of music in rice planting is to pray for an abundant harvest and to increase the efficiency of the work.

4. Rice-planting women plant to the rhythm of the music. The tempo is always set by the leader drummer and so he controls the efficiency and speed of the work. Sometimes the tempo becomes faster and faster.

5. The ensemble music of Chindo is a type of the *nonak* farmers' music, a primitive style which was cultivated and became the artistic *nonak* dance. The musical performance of rice planting in Chūgoku region is called *dengaku*, a primitive style similarly cultivated to become the artistic dengaku dance. But after the composition both styles are changed greatly.

DIFFERENCES

Ethnographic

1. In Chindo the performance of rice planting consists of two elements, work and music, but in the Chūgoku region a third element, religion, is added. In Japan the planting of rice is associated with belief in the god of the ricefield, called *tano-kami*, and rice planting itself is a form of ritual.

2. In Chindo the cooperation of a group continues from the gathering of the seedling to the harvest, but in the Chūgoku region the group cooperates only in the gathering of the seedling and in its transplanting.

3. The most important ceremony in rice cultivation in Chindo is the *kirkonegi*. Men and women weed the ricefield to the rhythm of a musical ensemble three times during the summer, and after the last weeding *kirkonegi* is held. The tenant leader who has the richest annual yield, riding on a decorated cow, parades with the other workers. On the way home, the nonak is danced, and a banquet is held. In the Chūgoku region no such custom exists, the important ceremony being the rice planting itself.

4. In Chindo, at the time of rice planting, a farmer tills a ricefield using one or two decorated cows, selecting a single furrow, while in the Chūgoku region farmers till using a procession of many (sometimes thirty to fifty) decorated cows along many furrows.

5. In Chindo, rice-planting women wore the traditional white clothes, *chima* and *chokori*, later replacing the chima by trousers as it is inconvenient for working. In the Chūgoku region, women now dress in a traditional farming garment, the kimono, and tie their sleeves with a red sash, *tasuki*.

Poetical

1. The topics of the songs sung in Chindo are love, personal history, the transience of human life, the promotion of loyalty, the encouragement of agriculture, and so on. There is a strong influence of Confucianism in the poems, which are often improvised by farmers as they are sung. The subjects of songs sung in the Chūgoku region are the sun, flowers, fruit, wine, love, and so on. Besides these songs there are ceremonial songs for the god of the ricefield. They are divided into the morning song, the day song, and the evening song. Most of these songs are described in the poetic textbook, *Taue-zōshi*, of the fifteenth century.

2. The syllabic structure of the rice-planting song in Chindo is very free, whereas in the Chūgoku region 5-5-6-4-7-7-4 or 5-7-5-7-5 are characteristic.

Musical

STRUCTURE. A characteristic musical structure of a Chindo rice-planting song, composed of two melodies, A being quite fast and B being variable, would be: A(solo)–A(unison)–B(solo)–A(unison)–B'(solo)–A(unison)–B(solo)–A'(unison)–B(solo)–A(unison), whereas that of the Chūgoku region might be: A(solo)–B(unison)–A'(solo)–B(unison)–C(solo)–D(unison)–C'(solo)–D(unison). In both places solos are sung by a leader and unison parts are sung by the rice-planting women.

SCALE.

Chindo

Here A, D, and E are important tones, the A–D combination comprising a fundamental tetrachord, its disjunctive motion being a characteristic feature of the south Korean folk song. E and B are flexible tones, accompanied by a kind of descending appoggiatura. F is also flexible and B appears rarely.

Chūgoku region

Here the A–D and E–A combinations comprise the fundamental tetrachord.

RHYTHM AND TEMPO. The rhythmic pattern in Korean music is called *chantan*. There are three kinds of chantan in rice-planting songs in Chindo, *chunmori* [andante], *chunjunmori* [allegretto], and *chajin-chunjunmori* [allegro]. The basic rhythm is twelve time, that is, four times triple time. This form of song is influenced by the Korean monoopera, *pansori*, a widespread art in the southern part of Korea. Thus a drummer plays the chantan of book, the leading instrument of Pansoli, as follows:

In the Chūgoku region there are many rhythmic patterns of the drum, but they are all in duple time. An example is:

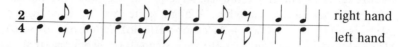

The work movements of Chindo are based on triple time and those of the Chūgoku region on duple time, depending upon the basic rhythmic feeling of the Korean and Japanese people.

VOCAL TECHNIQUE. The vocal technique in Chindo is characterized by strong glottal activity, while in the case of the Japanese farmers of the Chūgoku region this is slight.

INSTRUMENTS. The musical ensemble in Chindo consists of kengari, chin, chango and book. The musical ensemble in the Chūgoku region consists of *tazutsumi* or *ō-daiko*, a large drum; *kodaiko*, a small drum; *chappa*, a small cymbal; *kane*, a small gong; and sometimes a *shinobue*, a kind of flute, is added.

CONCLUSION

Rice planting in which the leader and the rice-planting women sing folk songs alternately to the rhythm of labor, accompanied by the musical ensemble, as in Chindo and the Chūgoku region, has been widespread through eastern and southeastern Asia ever since transplanting ceremonies have been held. The function of the music, which is to pray for a good harvest and to increase the efficiency of labor, is the same in all places, but the musical features, such as rhythm, tonal systems, heterophony, vocal techniques, interpretation, and instruments are very different.

APPENDIX 1. RICE SONGS

Rice-Planting Song

Noted. R. Uchida
Chūgoku region, Japan

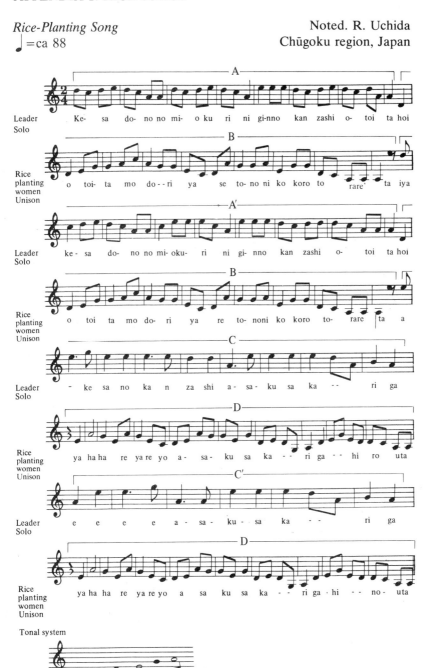

"Mossori" *Rice-Planting Song*
"Chunmori"

Andante ♪ =ca 88

Noted. R. Uchida

"Chindo" Island, Korea

↳ =A kind of special descending appoggiatura.

Leader Solo: o gi yo ho hoi yo ho ho - la sang --- sa lo - se

Rice planting women Unison: o gi yo ho hoi yo ho ho - la sang --- sa lo - se

Leader Solo: jo gi to nof ko tzu gi to nof ko du re pang op si man simkjotzuke

Rice planting women Unison: o gi yo ho hoi yo ho ho - la sang -- sa lo - se

Leader Solo: sang sa soli nun - e di lul kattaga te lul tza tza a ta sie nun te

Rice planting women Unison: O gi yo ho hoi yo ho ho - la sang -- sa lo - se

Leader Solo: u li in seng un hang pon ka mjon ta si o chi lul mo ha ta ni

Rice planting women Unison: O gi yo ho hoi yogi ho - yo ho la sang -- sa lo - se

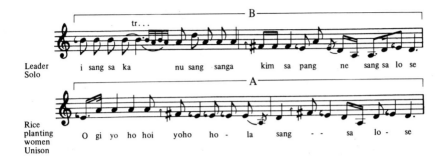

The Status of Women in the
Performing Arts of India and Iberia:
Cross-Cultural Perspectives from
Historical Accounts and Field Reports

BONNIE C. WADE and ANN M. PESCATELLO

We believe that the arts of a culture reflect the values of that culture, not only by their contexts, but also by who creates them. Yet the arts are usually neglected by analysts of *en vogue* issues in world societies. Through an examination of the status of women in the performing arts of India and Iberia, we hope to offer a fresh dimension for evaluating the general status of women in those societies and, perhaps, the potentiality for involvement of female performing artists in their nations' "Women's movements". This paper represents only an exploratory foray into the subject, serving as the basis for a larger study.

The focus in this paper is on music, dance, and theater-film forms in both their historical and contemporary perspectives. Taking into consideration regional variations in practices, and sometimes in personnel, we concentrate on the position of female performers in relationship to the overall position of performers and the place of the performing arts in Indian and Iberian cultures.

The task is at once easy and impossible, partly because of the interdependent nature of the arts, music being performed independently of the other arts, but dance rarely being independent of music. In Asia, "there is . . . no exception to the rule that all classical and semi-classical drama must be accompanied by music, and a majority of modern plays . . . embrace this aesthetic principle" (Bowers 1960:25). The same is true of Indian theater and dance, which "have been indispensable adjuncts of one another" (Bowers 1960:38). In Iberia, "music . . . inseparably allied to its natural partner the dance, has always been the life breath of the . . . people" (Chase 1959:17). Theater, too, from premedieval Christian

This paper, presented in 1973, represented work from written accounts and participant-observer work in India and Iberia.

festival dramas to twentieth-century cinema, has been allied with music and dance as an indispensable part of Iberia's artistic tradition.

Ideally it would be helpful to supply the reader with relatively thorough information on the perceptions, roles, and status of Indian and Iberian women throughout the long history of those cultures, but our comments on this important subject must be brief. Literary and legal evidence indicate that from the end of the Vedic period (500 B.C.) the life-style of Indian women was increasingly circumscribed by class and family relationships. Especially after the impact of Islamic influence (from the early thirteenth century), particularly in northern India, the seclusive principle of *parda* worked to deprive women from the cradle to the grave, of all contacts with males other than their husbands and other members of their immediate families. Since independence in 1947, a spate of legislation has guaranteed equal rights and opportunities to women. These are, however, theoretical legal measures passed by an urban-based government; their implementation is almost wholly dependent upon a largely illiterate, rural, and tradition-bound populace.

In many ways Indian and Iberian societies exhibit similarities, although they have arrived at and justify those similarities according to their own particular rules. Codes of law have not been kind to the Iberian woman: those of Castile, the peninsula's most powerful region, have classified her with children, invalids, and delinquents in terms of rights. But in practice, women fell on hard times as a result of the increasingly uncertain and turbulent conditions in medieval Iberia, that necessitated new systems of social relationships under which women became increasingly "protected", that is, excluded from serious involvement in everyday activities, and increasingly submissive to their menfolk. Legally, contemporary Iberian women are still disadvantaged in such areas as suffrage, divorce, and inheritance. A woman's major occupation is "being a housewife", and, consequently, unlike present-day Indian women, are rarely to be found in business, politics, or even the professions. In marital relationships Iberian women conform externally to the role of the virtuous and submissive wife, but it has been suggested that she accepts the perception of her role as a second-class citizen in exchange for *de facto* power within her home and family (Kenny 1966).

Having presented, all too briefly, the legal and traditional status of women in India and Iberia, we shall turn to the main discussion on the performing arts and the status of female artists. Music, dance, and drama have been integral to the cultures of the Indian subcontinent and the Iberian peninsula. From ancient times, music, dance, and mime all have been intertwined with drama: principles of aesthetics; details of theatrical production; concepts of melody, rhythm, and musical structure; and the rich vocabulary of movements of classical dance styles, have remained to present times. What are now the performing arts of India were in ancient times the ritual arts, and their association with worship has never been lost. Another important perspective here has been a clear separation of the arts, documentable as early as the fifth century A.D. in northern India, into two spheres: those of the elite and those of the masses. It is also clear that people at all social levels have participated in and enjoyed music, dance, and theater, from performances in inner sanctums of temples to village courtyards, to royal courts.

To the traditional performing arts have been added the productions of the world's second largest film-making nation. Films have continued the centuries-old reliance of Indian theater on music and dance, but they now compete with folk drama, and, as more and more villages receive electricity, even threaten its existence.

In the live performing arts the pace of change has been slow, and overall a sense of tradition and continuity prevails. Today tents and open-ended outdoor theaters are still preferred to the enclosed proscenium stages introduced by the British to an audience that enjoys meandering in and out of night-long presentations. Musicians, dancers, and actors, performing within a tradition in which improvisation is a crucial determinant, and time is *not* of the essence, continue to respond in ways they find familiar and comfortable.

Until about the fifteenth or sixteenth centuries, the basic aesthetic theory and structure of the performing arts in Spain and Portugal were similar. Differences there were, but they were between secular and sacred, between urban and rural, between folk and classical, and between various regions of the peninsula, particularly between those of either Moorish or Christian traditions. The areas of Iberia, particularly southern Spain, that remained under Muslim influence witnessed changes in genres of performing arts and in types of performances. Instrumental music occupied an important place in those areas of Iberia where Muslims penetrated and particularly where they remained. On the other hand, in the northern areas of Iberia, and especially among the rural populace, the medieval troubadour tradition was a powerful one.

Music, dance, and theater appear to have been enjoyed by various groups among the common people. Throughout all of Iberia they have been integral to sacred ceremonies (religious pilgrimages, feast days, and the like), as well as indispensable to official activities, festivals, and secular events of many kinds. Folk music has been closely allied to dance, and together they have constituted a rich repertoire for entertainment, particularly in the countryside. In general, folk music and dance have enjoyed greater popularity than folk theater, at least in terms of endurance.

Regional styles of music, dance, and theater are numerous throughout

Spain and Portugal — the *flamenco* of Andalusia, in southern Spain, is perhaps the best known to foreigners. Urban counterparts to regional rural genres include the Negro patter songs and mulatto dances born of the fifteenth-century urban theater repertoire and the seafaring-based *fado* songs, which found their greatest audiences in the poorer sections of Portugal's cities. The urban theatrical milieus have dominated the urban folk traditions and the development of Iberia's classical performing arts. These too, have reflected both sacred and secular features and have enjoyed preeminence in the entertainment environment of both elite and commoner. From sacred observances and from secular festivals the theatrical tradition developed into one of the most popular forms of entertainment, and that has now been joined by cinema.

The status of performers in any culture is determined by several factors, among them: who performs (that is, who can do what); the function of the performance, and the value attached to it. The status of performers in India has undergone considerable change as each of these factors has been altered by circumstances and by time.

In Indian mythology, males in particular are associated with music and dance. An aspect of Lord Shiva especially popular in Tamil country (southern India), where religious dancing was part of the earliest known tradition, is that of Lord of the Dance (Nataraj).[1] The Gandharvas, heavenly musicians, were all males; their female counterparts were the Apsarases, beautiful and libidinous, mistresses of gods and men (Basham 1954:317).

In ancient times, well-born Indian men and women were encouraged not only to patronize the graphic and performing arts, but also to become somewhat proficient in them. Accordingly, the study of music and dance was quite widespread. At the same time, the temples that were rich in monies and land employed musicians and dancing girls for ritual services (Brown 1947) and professional theater troupes for festival performances. The arts themselves were highly respected because of their association with worship, and consequently performers were accorded respect for their talents. This respect extended to the host of trained professional musicians, dancers, and actors who provided the bulk of such entertainment even though their position in society was not high.

In ancient times in India there seems to have been no social proscription on women dancing or performing music, whether they were courtesans or respectable women. A Tamil poem[2] describes this scene:

---

[1]   The most famous sculptures of Nataraj are from the *Cōḷa* period, eleventh century A.D.; they are cast in bronze and now housed in the Victoria and Albert Museum, Bombay.
[2]   *Pattuppaṭṭu Maduraikkāñji* [The garland of Madurai], written in the third or fourth century in honor of the second-century Paṇḍyan king Nedunjeliyan.

In the evening the city prostitutes entertain their patrons with dancing and singing to the sound of the lute (*yāl*), so that the streets are filled with music. . . . Respectable women make evening visits to the temples with their children and friends, carrying lighted lamps as offerings. They dance in the temple courts, which are clamorous with their singing and chatter (Basham 1954:204).

Thus, there were two kinds of performers and three kinds of status. There were highborn and lowborn performers with their respective social statuses; there was the high status of the arts themselves because of their religious-entertainment function; and there was the (exceptional) status accorded to the skilled and well-trained among the lowborn. These last are, however, to be distinguished from the casual performers traveling in circus-type troupes, the musicians, bards, acrobats, jugglers, dancers, and others who graced the carnival circuit and were outcasts of proper society. The status of performers in Iberia has not undergone the changes that have occurred in India. There has been a stratum in the lower ranks of society specifically reserved for performers, whether musicians, dancers, or actors. Iberia, unlike India, has little documentable material concerning the performing arts until well into the "Christian" era. There are a number of pre-Christian vases depicting dancers, but the earliest beginnings of consistent documentation concerns the dances and songs of church festivals in the sixth century A.D. An edict from the Third Council of Toledo (A.D. 589) condemned the introduction of unholy songs and dances into religious festivals and also prohibited the singing of funeral songs by the people, possibly because they were associated with a non-Christian cult to the deity of death (Chase 1959:19). Communal singing and dancing also appear in other records of this time because the Church discovered early that the people's fondness for these art forms might be used to lure them from paganism to Christianity. Liturgical drama and its conjunctive associates, dance and chant, flourished throughout the peninsula from the early seventh to early eighth centuries onward.

The *juglar* [jongleur] was the major performer of secular music in medieval Iberia. Some juglares were part of traveling troupes; others were patronized by nobles or wealthy families. Although they were male, the term came to be applied to all who earned their living through public performance. As this rubric eventually came to include the dregs of society who performed for their suppers in one-night stands, as well as the most superb and famous artists, a classification system was developed. Juglares were instrumentalists; *remedadores* were pantomimists and mimics; troubadours who wondered from court to court were *segrieres*; those who had little or no skill or manners and were strictly street performers, whether in music, acrobatics, magic, or the like, were *cazurros* (Chase 1959:34–35). In Portugal, the juglares (*jograis*) were further subdivided into three types: string players, wind players, and percussion players.

Also included in this rather elaborate classification system were singers of the beautiful lyrical-poetic *cantigas*, composed in Portuguese Galician, the chief language of the peninsula in the twelfth century. Because Galicia (in northwestern Iberia) was the home of Iberia's most famous shrine, Santiago de Compostela, we have records of both professional and lay singers of pilgrim songs. Another category of performers consisted of the *juglares de cantares de gesta*, or specialists in reciting or singing the epic poems that were so crucial for maintaining the morale of a Christian people constantly at war. It was said that:

> kings and princes . . . commanded the *menestrilles* and *juglares* to appear with their lutes and viols and other instruments so that they might play and sing the ballads that were composed about the famous deeds of knights (Menéndez Pidal 1924:376, translated).

Most or all of these performers were men or young boys.

For Iberia, as for India, a distinction must be drawn between women who performed publicly during religious festivals and those in the professional performing arena. Since early times, women in Spain and Portugal have been performers in public festivals and religious *autos* [morality plays], even dancing in both. But it is conjectured that, in terms of professional appearances, women's participation was circumscribed. For example, female characters in plays were impersonated by boys in Spain as elsewhere in Europe, although actresses were permitted on stage in public squares, at *corrales* [a Spanish theatrical form], and in traveling troupes earlier in Spain than elsewhere in Europe.[3]

By the beginning of the "Middle Ages" in India (about the fourth century A.D.), highborn women were no longer being educated in the arts or in other subjects, as they had been previously. In fact, the only educated women were courtesans, who continued to become skilled musicians and dancers. In southern India the dancing-girl tradition remained associated with the temples, but the social status of its practitioners was low. Particularly in northern India it appears that reverence for the arts was no longer sufficiently strong to discount lower social status.

During the Middle Ages (about A.D. 325 to 1565) the image of the *apsaras* had become the image of any female who could perform in public: her public performance could not be separated from her sexuality. When this applied to village as well as town or court, to theater troupes, and to individuals, performance of music and dance seemed to have become the purview of low-caste females and prostitutes.

---

[3]   The English theater was unaccustomed to the appearance of actresses on stage in the mid-seventeenth century and hissed them or pelted them with rotten apples whenever they appeared with French troupes (see Malone 1800:130–131). In Germany, apparently as late as 1717 no actresses were allowed on stage (*Shakespeare Jahrbuch* 1885:236).

But there were many levels of prostitutes, and at one level, rather more a companion-courtesan than a for-hire "hooker", she was likely to be a beautiful, often wealthy, and culturally accomplished woman, comparable to the *hetaera* of ancient Athens or the *geisha* of Japan. Particularly during the golden Guptan days (A.D. 320 to 540), these trained courtesans were accomplished musicians, dancers, actresses, and singers, as well as the chief purveyors of manners, wit, and wisdom. They were, in essence, the cultured companions to highborn and wealthy Indians, their presence demanded by changes in Indian society (at a time and for reasons that we cannot document) that were producing the social seclusion and intellectual isolation of highborn Indian women. Later in the Middle Ages the position of such companion-courtesans lost its luster and became demeaned.

In Iberia the generally low esteem in which entertainers were held is documented in some thirteenth-century laws which, in preventing clergy from partaking in dramas, suggested that only people of certain classes could perform. Singers, instrumentalists, dancers, and actors who made their living in public squares were declared "infamous" by King Alfonso X and without civil rights by the Church (Rennert 1909:254). At least until the turn of the twentieth century, any actor or actress of theater or film in Spain "who dies in his profession cannot be buried in soil consecrated by the Church" (Rennert 1909:255).

The opprobrium toward performers in Iberia probably resulted from the growing involvement of the Church in later medieval times, an involvement encouraged by the proselytizing fervor of the reconquest crusades. The popularity of religious festivals, celebrations, and public festivities increased, but "pagan" and secular ideas, "immoral" in nature, crept in to the extent that plays and public music and dance performances were considered clownish and lewd. Clergy, who had been a major source for actors in comedies, dramas, and particularly in farces, were no longer allowed to perform. Despite the watchful eye of the Church, dramatic and musical activities continued to flourish, and we know that clergy continued to perform because the Council of Aranda, in 1473, enacted a decree condemning abuses of performers in religious feasts and "forbidding other festivals in which theatrical plays, masks, monsters, shows, . . . derisive speeches . . . [and] recitation of lewd verses" were a part (Rennert 1909:253–254).

Most musicians and dancers, then, performed in conjunction with theatrical performances, both secular and sacred. Dancers more than musicians enjoyed great reputations, carrying on a tradition famous since the days of Juvenal and Martial, the Roman writers who had noted the renown and importance of dancers and dancing in Iberia. Even as late as the nineteenth century it was ascertained not only that dancing was the most popular of the performing arts in Iberia, but that everyone, from the king and royalty to the general populace, was a performer of dance (Monreal 1878).

In the Muslim Middle Eastern tradition introduced into India, the arts were not connected with religious worship. There is still argument as to whether or not Mohammed himself condoned singing and dancing, for they were associated in his culture with sex, alcohol, and entertainment, all reprehensible in his puritanical milieu. Professional musicians were, for the most part, on the level of servants, however well trained and skilled they might be. In Muslim courts of India, then, the performing artists encountered cultural attitudes that threatened their very existence.

What emerged was a compromise in the form of an internal hierarchy. Musicians who entered in formal court sessions (*darbār*) were among the most highly respected in Hindustan (northern India), but even the "superstars" among them were just employees of the court. Among darbār musicians, vocalists had the highest rank, with accompanists on stringed instruments next, and percussionists below them. Entertaining in the harem was another set of musicians and dancers, clearly of lesser status than darbār musicians.

In Mogul courts, women were not allowed to perform in any capacity at darbār, and dancing girls entertained only in the harems. Outside the courts in northern India, courtesan dancers continued to perform and eventually gained a reputation as *nautch* girls. They maintained a reputation for such unrestrained eroticism in their skillful dancing that Muslims eventually relegated nautch performances to brothels and insisted that if their dances were performed publicly, they had to be done by young boys (Bowers 1960:48). *Kathak*, the primary classical dance style of northern India today, is a synthesis of the court dancing tradition and a respectable form of the nautch. It is unusual in that it is danced by men as well as by women.

In southern India musicians were not under such pressure to convert to Islam, nor was the Hindu reverence for the arts challenged. Musicians continued to regard music as a type of *yoga*, a path to salvation, and were commonly referred to as saint-singers. Many highborn individuals studied the arts, and consequently the status of performers and performances remained high relative to their northern counterparts. Under British rule the situation in southern India remained fairly stable, while in the north the status of professional performers and performances reached a nadir.

With the temple dancing girl (*devadasi*) of southern India resided the dance tradition that was recorded in the *Nātya Śāstra* and in temple sculpture. Also associated with sex, the devadasi tradition was allowed to continue only because of its direct connection with the temple. Finally, in the 1920's that particular caste (*jati*)[4] was abolished by provincial law and the surviving tradition was forced underground. Today that dance tradition, *bharata natyam*, in its untainted form, is a classical one, moved to the concert stage. It is still primarily the purview of women, but nowadays whoever wishes to learn it may do so.

The medieval juggler/troubadour performance tradition remained strong in Iberia and was enhanced by the development of the secular drama, which first appeared in the pastoral playlets of the late fifteenth to early sixteenth centuries. Balladry had enjoyed an enormous following among all classes of rural and urban peoples in Iberia, and the balladeer was joined, from the end of the sixteenth century, by guitarists, who were major performers for the secular dramatic forms. The popular theater which had developed fully by the end of the sixteenth century, through the efforts of one Lope de Rueda, provided for the continuation of musicians as accompanists to dramatic presentations.

Apparently it was the general situation throughout most of Europe that women began to appear on stage in place of young boys in female roles in the later Middle Ages. Then, just as mysteriously, they began to disappear from arenas of public theatrical performance in the sixteenth century, *except in Spain*, and did not appear again in public performances in the admission-fee theaters until about the middle of the seventeenth century. The freedom for women to act in Spain in the sixteenth century is documented in several sources, including one that mentioned that a married actress, no matter how famous, could not make a binding legal contract without her husband (Pérez Pastor 1901:15; 1906:153). Why women could act on the public stage in Spain during the sixteenth century when they were banned from similar appearances elsewhere in Europe we have not yet been able to determine.

In the seventeenth century a semipopular, semiclassical form of opera, the zarzuela, created by Calderón de la Barca, enhanced the place of dramatic and musical performers. The zarzuela, a musical drama, included both singing and dancing and thus required either that the actors be proficient as singers or dancers, or that specialists of song or dance be able to perform the dramatic roles in the play. The zarzuela quickly achieved popularity and became, in different forms, the purview of both classical and folk theater. In the folk theater tradition of zarzuela, players of guitars, mandolins, tambourines, and castanets became extremely important; for the most part they were males.

Other sixteenth-century changes had relieved, somewhat, the particularly low status of musicians within theatrical troupes. Music accompanying plays performed in the public squares had been provided "by one or

---

[4] *Jati* is India's generic term for caste in the class-caste or *varṇa-jati* system of social stratification.

two persons 'who sang an old ballad without the accompaniment of a guitar' [Cervantes] behind a woolen blanket, which served as a curtain, and which separated the dressing room from the stage" (Rennert 1909:62). One Pedro Navarro brought the musicians onto the public stage, and thereafter, from that new position, they continued to provide music before and after the performance of a farce, or between acts of a *comedia* (Rennert 1909:62–63). After 1640, the number of musicians in a theatrical troupe greatly increased, probably as a result of the popularity of autos-da-fé, the religious morality plays (Pérez Pastor 1901:37, 220; Sanchez-Arjona 1898:126, 203–204).

In addition to this increment in personnel, in the seventeenth century it was noted that women were gradually being introduced on the stage in the place of boys, although the performances of boys of good appearance and rouged, attired as women, were held by some to be even a greater objection (Rennert 1909:137). This was obviously in reference to a short period of time in the late sixteenth century when females were banned from the stage, as their counterparts elsewhere in Europe had been for a much longer time. The growing popularity of theatrical presentations and the consequent increase in the number of theaters and players throughout Spain and Portugal in the time of Lope de Vega found "the dances, songs, expensive costumes, and the acting, not only of women, but of women disguised as men" (Rennert 1909:143).

An index of all Spanish actors and actresses from 1560 to 1680 shows a substantial percentage of women in the profession. Women worked in two types of dramatic companies: both those in which players worked for a salary and those in which they worked for shares. Readings of the contracts indicate not only a profusion of women in the companies, but an equality of salary and treatment. In addition, women served as managers of companies, were in charge of finances, and kept custody of the chests in which were deposited the earnings of the company (Pérez Pastor 1901:145–148).

In actuality, by the seventeenth century there were at least eight kinds of acting companies, and women performed in five of them. Three types, the least important in the performing classification system for theater, were itinerant and usually consisted of performers from the lowest classes of society. The *bululu*, a single performer, was almost invariably a male; the *naque* consisted of two men who acted and played the drum; and the *gangarilla* comprised three or four males, one of whom played the fool, while the youngest, usually a boy, played women's roles.

There were five types of larger troupes. The *cambaleo* usually consisted of five men and a woman, whose role was to sing and to be in charge of distributing the food. In general, she seems to have enjoyed preferred treatment, because one of the men carried her on his back and a bed was always hired for her while the men slept in the straw (Rojas Villandrando

1603:132–140). The *agarnacha* consisted of five or six men and a woman, who played the leading lady roles, while a young boy played any secondary female characters. This troupe gave private performances and was hired for festivals, as was the *boxiganga*, comprising two women, a boy, and six or seven men. The *farándula* had three women and eight to ten men, while the largest type of troupe, known as *compania*, was the one company that contained a mixed-class group including trained actors and actresses and "even very respectable women" (Rojas Villandrando 1603).

The seventeenth century produced, for the first time in Iberia, stars of the classical theater. In Spain the most famous actress was Maria de Riquelme, considered not only to have been talented and beautiful, but also to have led an exemplary life. Another star was Maria Calderón, who, after her days of glory on the stage and as a favorite of Philip IV and mother of his son, Don Juan of Austria, became an abbess of a convent in Guadalajara (Hume 1907:208). Most of the actresses, however, were from the lower classes and evidently espoused and lived very turbulent lives, keeping alive reputations of entertainers as immoral and deservedly outside the pale of proper society.[5]

The position of women in Indian theater can be traced with some degree of accuracy. At least into Guptan times (about the fifth century A.D.) both men and women were part of professional theater troupes. But theater was also affected by the increasing isolation of women in society in general. About the tenth century A.D. in southern India a movement of fervent religious devotion (*bhakti*) began, which was to have a sweeping impact on much of the subcontinent. Proselytizing saints, realizing the power of theater for their own purposes, organized troupes that excluded women, because to them their presence was a threat to the creation of the pure, ascetic life which all were urged to live. Troupes such as the Nattuva Mela of Andhra Pradesh, which had included women, were reorganized in the fifteenth century as strictly male organizations in order "to preserve the purity of the form" (Raghavan 1969:33). With very few exceptions, women were effectively banned from the theater stage, whether rural or urban, folk or classical. A striking instance of the extensiveness of this ban is seen in *kathakali*, an all-male form of dance-drama. Kathakali was developed in Kerala, on the southwestern edges of the subcontinent, in a region that is traditionally matriarchal and in which women have been influential in public affairs and have a reputation for considerable degrees of freedom in society in general. Yet even in this area, so deeply had the ban on women penetrated that kathakali had been, and remains, an all-male form.

---

[5] An example of this is cited in competitive performances between a Jacinta Herbias and an Antonia Infante, as noted in Sanchez-Arjona (1908:304).

The banning of all respectable women from any performing arena meant a very low status for any woman who did perform publicly, but such public performance is to be distinguished from village communal dancing and singing at festivals or on other ritual-holiday occasions. Even in villages, however, public dancing of women had been condoned only on special occasions — and those have usually been religiously oriented in some way.

Among classical dance styles, the dance-drama kathakali is an exception, for classical dance — including the fourth major style, from northeastern India, *manipuri* — is a female-associated art, that is to say, the *performing* of classical dance is done largely by females; the *teaching* traditionally has been done by males. This is an important factor in determining the status of women even in an art form dominated by their sex: in Indian culture it has been the *teachers* who have been respected most, and they have been *male*!

Temple sculptures in southern India (where most of the pre-Muslim Hindu architecture and sculpture is still intact) depict women playing drums and cymbals; the goddess of music, Saraswati, is most often sculpted playing a *vīna* [a stringed instrument]. In folk music today, women still play percussion instruments, but as a general rule, melody-producing and percussive instruments are the purview of men. In the sphere of classical music it has not been acceptable for women to study drumming, and for the most part they leave performing on percussive and melodic instruments to men.

The professional dancing women in Mogul courts in Hindustan were accompanied by male *sāraṅgī* and tabla players whose rank was below that of darbār musicians. Rajput miniatures (the famous style of court paintings of the seventeenth and eighteenth centuries in northern India) and other paintings show women playing instruments, but the context is obviously the harem, and this instance of female instrumentalists seems to have been a rare one. Bharata natyam, kathakali, manipuri, and kathak all are accompanied primarily by male musicians, as are all forms of folk theater.

When court patronage declined in northern India and musicians were on their own professionally, the male–female role assignment continued for some time. Sons of musician families became musicians, while daughters married sons of other musician families. Women who had been dancing girls in the courts and their daughters were practically the only female performers, and they were either dancers or singers, as had been the custom at court.

With the independence movement and the cultural renaissance, beginning in the mid-nineteenth century and continuing until the present, came numerous changes. Musicologists, for the most part Hindus, began soliciting audiences for concerts and students for music classes in an effort to reacquaint the populace with its musical tradition — and with the historical tradition that stated that the study of the arts was the mark of any cultured individual (see Wade 1971). The result has been that women now are numerous on the concert stages of both northern and southern India, and they generally continue to espouse singing as the suitable medium for their performance. The leading vocalist of southern India today is a woman, and in northern India there are several famous and highly respected female vocalists. A small but growing number of women now play melodic instruments; among them, Sharan Rani, the sarodist, being the most prominent. Two traditional patterns remain, however: women still do not drum, and, for the most part, men remain the teachers in the performing arts.

With the influence of court patronage, particularly after the turn of the eighteenth century, changes also came to the performing arena in Spain and Portugal. These nations began subscribing eagerly to western European standards in the classical performing arts. The important performing arena was shifted from royal chapels to royal courts; kings and princes sent their singers and dancers to Italy for training and recruited Italians to Portugal and Spain to train native performers. Increasingly, classical performers grew in reputation and came to occupy an enviable position in certain social circles. While the court elites patronized classical performers, in the public theaters burlesque and ballet retained a great appeal for the masses, and the performers of these art forms enjoyed a great public following. There was no segregation of performers according to sex, and equal numbers of females and males became famous as singers, dancers, and actors in the performing arena. But as in India, the purview of instrumental music remained male, although there were female as well as male teachers of song, dance, and acting.

It should be remembered that although female performers in Iberia did not undergo the long banishments and oblivion of their Indian sisters, they did succumb to occasional periods of disfavor, as during the brief period in the sixteenth century. It has been shown that the female enjoyed an active and prominent place in the musical life of medieval Iberia. As a *juglaresca* or *juglara* she "sang, played, and danced for the entertainment of kings and nobles", while at other levels of society she was a featured performer at events enjoyed by the general populace (Chase 1959:33). These women, carrying their involvement into the post-Renaissance period, retained a fame for singing; indeed, this was their major activity as the centuries passed. And, as in both the Indian tradition and in other aspects of the Iberian performing music tradition, they frequently accompanied themselves on castanets and tambourines (Chase 1959:34) — percussive, not melodic instruments.

By the eighteenth century, female performers in Iberia had expanded the scope of their public performances. With the writings of Ramon de la

Cruz, whose life spanned the latter two thirds of the eighteenth century, there was a resurgence of popularity for the "lyric theater" and its female stars. The first great actress-singer star of this performing art form was María Antonio Fernández. She and another female star, María del Rosario Fernández (La Tirana), were the dominant performers and stars of the dramatic and musical stage.

Although there was a lull in theater and music in general during the nineteenth century, in today's Iberia female performers have eased into star positions and joined musical and dramatic troupes in substantial numbers, especially in Spain. One of the best and most prestigious theater companies today is operated by the multitalented Ana Mariscal, who writes, directs, produces, and stars in her repertory productions. And one of the very finest music and dance troupes in Spain is the *Teatro Zarzuela*, an organization begun by two Spanish ballet stars, Maria del Sol and Mario La Vega, for the purpose of presenting anthologies of regional Spanish music and dance. Female singers, dancers, and actresses seem to be in abundance and seem to suffer no more stigma and no less fame than their profession allows for male performers. The Mariscal and Teatro Zarzuela experiences do not seem to be isolated events in Iberia, at least in Spain.

The Second World War and the ensuing external and internal political rearrangements and realliances created considerable change in both India and Iberia. Since independence and the artistic renaissance, high-born Hindus are again studying the performing arts, either to become professionals or for their own enjoyment. Many Muslim musicians and professional performers consider their art forms a type of worship, and through that reintroduction route both the arts and the status of performers are being raised to the level of respect due them in traditional thought. For Indian and Iberian women especially, three media have become noticeable avenues to social mobility and also provide professions in which women enjoy economic and social parity with men: film in India, flamenco in Spain, and fado in Portugal.

Although today in India there are three primary theatrical forms — folk, urban professional, and film — the position of women in the cinema industry provides an example of social change and the influence that a successful "new" cultural form can exert on more traditional ones. When India's first great film maker, Dadasaheb Phalke, was looking for female performers, he was thwarted because "no decent Indian woman would think of acting in a film" and "he could not ask a decent woman to do so" (Barnouw and Krishnaswamy 1963:13). Several prostitutes whom he asked to perform refused also, so Phalke had to turn to what was customary — handsome and slim young males to play heroines. He was eventually able to persuade a Maharashtrian woman to play the lead female role in his second film. In 1919 he had his own daughter play Krishna (a male role!), and in the 1920's he had several women in his film company, although the social stigma still remained (Barnouw and Krishnaswamy 1963:20).

In the 1920's respectable women and prostitutes both agreed to perform for the cameras, and some even became stars. In particular, Anglo-Indian girls, who tended to fill professions considered borderline or nonrespectable by high-class Hindu and Muslim Indians, began an involvement in films that gave them an honored position in society, while helping to give "respectability" to the role of female performers. In the early 1930's, however, a beautiful daughter of a respected Bengali family, Devika Rani, who had been educated most of her life in Europe, and her actor-director husband returned to India with their own films. Devika Rani became a star and with another Brahmin star, Durga Khote, made more respectable the role of women in Indian films. The increasing respectability of music and dance performers and the pressure from India's Cinematograph Committee from the 1920's onward further helped to enhance the reputation of film actresses.

Music and dance have been extremely important elements of Indian films. An analysis in 1959 showed that there were 7.7 songs per film; 70 percent were sung by the hero, 23 percent by a heroine who did not dance. In 70 percent of the films the heroine sang and danced (Bose 1959).

Once it had become acceptable for girls to act in films, categories were devised to supply them: "ordinary" girls, who might appear in crowd scenes, and "decent" and "superdecent" girls, accepted for high-society roles and court scenes. These girls were paid wages depending on their categories; those who could also dance were paid more (Barnouw and Krishnaswamy 1963:163).

Many women are now stars in films in regional languages, and a few have become "superstars" by virtue of their fame in Hindi-language films. Until recently, in fact, the shift to "superstar" fame by a regional-to-Hindi film route was more common for females than for males. Many of these stars are excellent singers and dancers: a good example is the beautiful artist Padmini, who excels in both acting and dancing (Barnouw and Krishnaswamy 1963:262).

The successes and relative respectability of women in films has affected a few folk theater forms. In *nautanki* of northern India, for example, women's roles have traditionally been played by young boys. After the 1959 Suppression of the Immoral Traffic Act, numerous prostitutes and nautch dancers followed the example of film actresses and joined nautanki troupes. In Kanpur there was even a company solely of female performers (Gargi 1962:84). However, in folk theater most female roles are still played by men and young boys.

Professional urban theater troupes, which are a relatively unimportant dramatic form in India today, have also felt some influence from film and have permitted women to appear on stage. They have been mostly courtesans and singing-dancing girls, however, and few have risen to stardom (Gargi 1962:153, 161).

In Iberia to this day opera singers, ballet dancers, and theater actors are patronized by the elite upper and middle classes, while the common people flock to folk festivals, rural and urban. As in India, exceptional status is accorded those who manage to become "superstars", and although it is still difficult for performers to enter the ranks of *la crème de la crème* of society, these performing media are avenues for upward social movement.

As film has been an extremely important medium for social advancement for Indian female performing artists, so flamenco and fado have been for their Iberian counterparts. The famous actress "La Caramba", an Andalusian, appears to have been one of the earliest stars of the singing style we know as flamenco, which was a major vehicle for female singers long before it achieved international fame in the eighteenth century. Both flamenco and bullfighting "stem basically from the common people" and "are the two most probable ways that the commoner can break out of his social and economic level" (Pohren 1972:30).

Flamenco is an art form that is also a philosophy; in its audible and visible sense it consists of song, dance, acting, and the music of the guitar. *Cante* [song] is deemed by Spanish aficionados the most important element, "the preferred mode of expression" — as opposed to the dance and the guitar (Pohren 1972:48). Although most flamenco singers are male, regardless of the style of cante or its region of origin, there does not seem to be a stigma against female singers. The criteria for performing appear to be artistic rather than social.

Guitar is played only by men: "With a few notable exceptions, the guitarist is the least paid, and the least acclaimed of flamenco interpreters" (Pohren 1972:71). He must be intimately familiar with cante and dance, as well as with his own art.

The subtle art of flamenco dance is espoused by many female performers. Dancing is the aspect of flamenco best known to the non-Spanish public, the aspect most dramatic and seemingly easy to appreciate. Nearly all *tablao del flamenco* [commercial flamenco clubs] feature dancers, but unfortunately the quality of dancing is said to be greatly influenced by the tastes of nonaficionados. Both men and women dance flamenco, with traditional differences defining their respective styles: male dancers emphasize footwork, which symbolizes strength and virility, while female dancers emphasize movements of the shoulders, arms, hands, and fingers. The female dancer's motions express femininity and passion, and sex appeal is supposed to be a motivating force, though she must never display it in an obvious come-hither manner.

Fado, the urban song style of Portugal best known to non-Portuguese, is commonly associated with female entertainers, accompanied by male instrumentalists on *viola*, a plucked stringed instrument with metal strings, and guitar, for that is the form in which it is presented in many nightclubs in Lisbon. In fact, however, dramatic Lisbon-style fado is sung by both men and women, while the more lyrical Coimbra-style fado is rendered most often by men.

Fado developed in the port sections of Portugal's cities, sung in bars by women who have been depicted wearing full, multicolored skirts and white blouses with colorful shawls draped gracefully over the shoulders. That they were not the most ladylike and highborn of women is suggested by the stances in which they are pictured (for example, standing with one leg propped up on a chair). Traditional Lisbon *fadistas* today drape themselves in black — black shoes, black dresses, black shawls — and their intense dramatic airs leave the expression of sensuality more to the texts of their songs than to their physical appearances. Contrasted with this are their nightclub counterparts, wearing slinky, low-cut dresses of any color, with the barest suggestion of a black shawl (a long fringe) worn so as to conceal nothing.

Male performers of Lisbon fado appear to perform in casual dress, but Coimbra *fadistos* wear traditional long black capes, as do their accompanists, who stand, rather than sit, to play. In both styles of fado, the song is central, the text of the song the reason for the form.

SUMMARY

Women in the performing arts of any culture are certainly one of the most visible groups of females. At this point in our study, we must conclude that in Iberia and India their status is linked first to the status of women in general in those cultures, and second to the status of the particular art in which they perform. For example, when Indian women were secluded to the point that only prostitutes were leading public lives, then the only women who performed in public were prostitutes — or were considered so even if they were not. Centuries later, when the movement for independence enlisted the active support of women, drawing them into the public arena again, the effect was felt in the performing arts.

Once a woman does participate "on stage", her status in society becomes involved with the position of the art she is performing. In Iberia, for example, she would have a higher status as a ballet dancer or opera singer than she would have as a member of an itinerant drama troupe catering for small towns. In other words, the status of the art in her particular society would accrue, in part, to the artiste. In India, this is more difficult to define not only because of the complexity of definitions of social status but also the status of genres and performers within the classical traditions.

Within the sphere of a particular art, the roles of women appear to be traditionally defined. In flamenco, for instance, both women and men are acknowledged to be fine singers and dancers. But in both Iberia and India it has not been customary for women to specialize in solo or even accompanying melody instruments. This difference in roles may or may not be linked to a difference in status.

As to the possible involvement of female performers in women's movements in India and Iberia, at this point in our research we can draw only tentative conclusions. Women entertainers are part of a particular socioeconomic status group. Many performers in Iberia and India are of low status, and low-status groups in general have little power to effect changes in the status quo in such traditionalist, elite-oriented societies. Furthermore, although the women on stage in India and Iberia might be more visible and more audible than are other women of their status, they tend to be apolitical, more devoted to their art than to sociopolitical movements. In this they do not seem unlike their male colleagues. Another factor to be considered is the artist's fear of loss of audience should she become involved in "causes". It would seem that there is more likelihood of involvement among the lesser-known performers and the novices. In Spain, for instance, women are beginning to join the ranks of bullfighters, and many have the express purpose of changing the laws regarding women in bullfighting and in society in general. Whether or not this activism will extend to female entertainers, and especially to "super-stars", remains to be seen.

REFERENCES

BARNOUW, ERIK, SUBRAHMANYAM KRISHNASWAMY
  1963   *Indian film*. New York: Columbia University Press.
BASHAM, A. L.
  1954   *The wonder that was India*. New York: Grove.
BOSE, ASIT BARAN
  1959   Analysis of all films reviewd in *New Statesmen*, 1959. *New Statesmen*, India.
BOWERS, FAUBION
  1960   *Theatre in the East: a survey of Asian dance and drama*. New York: Grove.
BROWN, PERCY
  1947   *Indian architecture: Buddhist and Hindu periods*, second edition. Bombay: D. V. Taraporevala and Sons.
CHASE, GILBERT
  1959   *The music of Spain*, second edition. New York: Dover. (Originally published 1941.)
GARGI, BALWANT
  1962   *Theatre in India*. New York: Theatre Art Books.

HUME, MARTIN A. S.
　1907　*The court of Philip IV: Spain in decadence*. London: Eveleigh Nash.
KENNY, MICHAEL
　1966　*A Spanish tapestry: town and country in Castile*. New York: Harper and
　　　　Row.
MALONE, EDMOND
　1800　*Historical account of the English stage*. London: Basil.
MENÉNDEZ PIDAL, RAMÓN
　1924　*Poesía juglaresca y juglares*. Madrid.
MONREAL, JULIO
　1878　"Los bailes de antaño," in *Cuadros viejos*. Collected by Julio Monreal.
　　　　Madrid.
PÉREZ PASTOR, CRISTÓBAL
　1901　*Nuevos datos acerca del histrionismo español en los siglos XVI y XVII*.
　　　　Madrid.
　1906　*Bulletin hispanique*. Paris.
POHREN, D. E.
　1972　*The art of flamenco*, third edition. Seville: Society of Spanish Studies.
RAGHAVAN, V.
　1969　The classical and folk in Indian music. *Music Academy Journal* 39.
　　　　Madras.
RENNERT, HUGO ALBERT
　1909　*The Spanish stage in the time of Lope de Vega*. New York: Hispanic
　　　　Society of America.
ROJAS VILLANDRANDO, AGUSTÍN DE
　1603　*El viage entretenido*. Madrid: Francisco de Robles. (Reproduced 1901
　　　　as *Viaje entretenido*. Coleccion de Libros Picarescos, Madrid.)
SANCHEZ-ARJONA, JOSÉ
　1898　Noticias referentes á los anales del treato en Sevilla desde Lope de
　　　　Rueda hasta fines del siglo XVII. Seville.
Shakespeare Jahrbuch
　1885　*Shakespeare Jahrbuch* volume 21. Weimar.
WADE, BONNIE C.
　1971　"Music, an Indian synthesizer: an artistic response to the search for
　　　　identity." *Papers presented at the Twenty-Eighth International Congress
　　　　of Orientalists*. Canberra, Australia.

PART FOUR

Case Studies in Music and Folklore from Asia and Eastern Europe

The Functions of Folk Songs in Vietnam

CONG-HUYEN-TON-NU NHA-TRANG

Music and poetry are close to the hearts of the Vietnamese, of whose lives they are an intimate part, for through them these basically sentimental people find the most comfortingly appropriate outlets for their emotions. The use of music has traditionally been, and still is, an unquestionably necessary part of a ceremony, a celebration, or a festival. The Vietnamese love to compose or copy favorite poems to give or to recite to one another as presents on special occasions. Proverbs and proverbial sayings exhibiting most of the stylistic devices of poetry are widely quoted, and even the cursing that low-class people exchange among themselves when enraged is poetry in prose, full of rhymes and rhythm.

There exists an intimate relationship between these two forms of art. Vietnamese is a singing language of five tones. Poetry, composed of monosyllabic words arranged in different tonal and rhythmic patterns, reads both melodiously and rhythmically, thereby possessing two of the basic elements of music. A tendency of poems to be sung follows naturally, particularly among the Vietnamese common people, who, unlike the elite, cannot transmit their poetry through writing and printing — nor do they have the leisure or education for studious composition and recitation. Lines of verse spontaneously composed, or having orally circulated for generations, are transmitted through song by the common people. Almost always they are used as song texts which they sing to the various existing folk melodies. Folk songs, the result of this customary and natural combining of poetry without writing and music without instrument, were and are cherished most by the Vietnamese populace in their oral tradition. With these two properties, folk songs are primarily designed for entertainment. Most Vietnamese struggle continuously for subsistence against intense heat, storm, flood, and drought. The singing of folk songs, the only form of entertainment that seems to match the majority's pattern of income and leisure, helps to ease the pain of work and to release them from the pressure of everyday activities: a function apparently universal and by no means peculiar to Vietnamese folk songs. The discussion in this paper is more concerned with the functions of folk songs which are significant in the context of the culture and society of the Vietnamese populace, among whom they transmit information of all kinds, and promote the consciousness of group identity and group unity. A brief introductory note on melody and text, the two components of folk songs, will help to clarify the points to be discussed.

To date, more than three dozen melodies of Vietnamese folk songs have been recorded. Thousands of song texts, in verse, have also been collected. The same melody can be attached to various folk songs, and the same song text is not always sung to the same melody. However, the geographical and occupational distribution of the folk melodies is more limited than that of the texts. Generally a melody matches the rhythm of some special physical activity. It follows that the melody of sampan girls' songs is different from those of rice pounders. Moreover, due to differences in temperament and in the pitch ranges of the dialects, folk melodies of the same occupational group differ from north to south. One may be reasonably sure of the birthplace of a folk song by its melody. On the other hand, most song texts are distributed widely throughout the country: some transmitted unchanged, others with some slight variations. This is particularly the case with lyrical texts devoted to expressing a mood or a feeling, like those of love songs, which make up the largest portion of Vietnamese folk songs. The transmitted texts are adapted to different melodies in different parts of the country, resulting in numerous traditional variants. The greater mobility of song texts seems due to the fact that both their form and content are highly acceptable to every Vietnamese, no matter what part of the country he comes from, what dialect he speaks, or what occupation he has. The lyrics are in the language he understands, in the rhyming patterns with which he is well acquainted, and are easily adaptable to the melodies of his community. What the texts contain facilitates further their transmission and acceptance. A common Vietnamese can associate the familiar features of landscape mentioned in folk songs — from a winding river to a tiny path, from a rice field to a bamboo grove — with those of his beloved village. Moreover, he can also recognize typical Vietnamese sentiments shaped by the particular sociocultural traditions that he shares and appreciates.

Keeping in mind the ease with which the texts are transmitted and maintained through constant use, we will now return to the functions of folk songs. Throughout generations of feudal rule and foreign domination, only a tiny minority of the population has had the privilege of obtaining an education. The vast majority of the people, composed mainly of peasants, have remained illiterate (Thuan-Phong, n.d., 71–72).

For education, or the sharing of knowledge and experiences, they have had to depend on word of mouth, for which folk songs can best serve the purpose, for information stated in rhyme and put to music is easy to memorize and transmit.

In Vietnam, where agriculture is the economic base, information on agricultural technology and related animal husbandry is most vital. Folk songs play the role of an agricultural almanac, transmitting important information through generations of Vietnamese peasants who cannot read and write. A few examples will suffice. We find a folk song that spells out the preparation for a winter crop which is reaped in the tenth month of the lunar year:

Tháng giêng là tháng ăn chơi,
Tháng hai trồng đậu, trồng khoai, trồng cà.
Tháng ba thì đậu đã già
Ta đi ta hái về nhà phơi khô.
Tháng tủ đi tậu trâu bò
Để ta sắp sủa làm mùa tháng năm.
Sớm ngày đem lúa ra ngâm,
Bao giờ mọc mầm ta sẽ vớt ra.
Gánh đi ta ném ruộng ta,
Đến khi lên mạ thì ta nhổ về.
Lấy tiền mười ke cấy thuê,
Cấy xong rồi mới trở về nghỉ' ngỏi.
Cỏ lúa dọn đã sạch rồi,
Nước ruộng với muồi còn độ một hai.
Ruộng thấp đóng một gàu dai,
Ruộng cao thì phải đóng hai gàu sòng.
Chờ cho lúa có đòng đòng
Bấy giờ ta sẽ trả công cho nguồi.
Bao giờ cho đến tháng mười,
Ta đem liềm hái ra ngoài ruộng ta.
Lúa gặt ta đem về nhà,
Phơi khô quạt sạch ấy là xong công.

The first month is for festivals,
We grow beans, sweet potatoes, eggplants in the second month.
Beans are ripe in the third month
We gather and dry them in our yards.
In the fourth month we purchase buffaloes and oxen
To get ready for the cultivation of the winter crop in the fifth month.
Rice grains are then soaked in water,
To become rice seeds when sprouts appear.
In our rice fields, we sow rice seeds
Which are pulled up when grown into seedlings.
We hire people to transplant them.
Time for rest comes at the completion of rice transplanting.
When grass is removed and seedlings are in order
The water level in the fields goes down a great deal.
We use a bucket with long ropes to supply water to a rice field on low ground,

And two buckets with long handles are needed to bail water into a rice field on
   high ground.
With the appearance of young rice grains
We can pay the hired hands.
When the tenth month finally comes,
With sickles we reap the harvest in our rice fields.
The rice we gather is brought home
Dried and winnowed, and the work is done.

Only a general outline of the work is presented here. There are many folk
songs that specify in detail the methods of plowing, harrowing, sowing,
and rice transplanting. On plowing and harrowing, the peasants
remember:

Răng bừa tám cái còn thủa
Lười cày tám tấc đã vừa luống to.
Muốn cho lúa nẩy bông to
Cày sâu, bừa kỹ, phân cho thật nhiều.

While a harrow with eight teeth is still large-toothed
A plowshare of eight decimeters in length is just right for big furrows.
For the rice plants to bear ample grains
We must plow deeply, harrow carefully and use sufficient fertilizer.

The experience with weather tells them when seedlings are ready to be
transplanted:

Mạ chiêm ba tháng không già
Mạ mùa tháng rười ắt là không non.

While seedlings for the summer crop are not old when they are three months of
   age,
Seedlings for the winter crop are certainly not young when they are one and a half
   months old.

Seeds for a summer crop are sowed in the cold season. In cold weather,
seedlings grow slowly and therefore are only ready after three months. In
the meantime, seeds for a winter crop sowed in summer grow quicker into
seedlings, and therefore are ready to be transplanted after forty-five days.
It is important to know the timing, for premature seedlings or overgrown
seedlings cannot promise a good crop. Advice for rice transplanting is
also offered in folk songs:

Lúa mùa thì cấy cho sâu
Lúa chiêm cấy cạn nhảy mau mà về.

Seedlings for winter crops must be planted deeply into the soil;
But, as we can transplant seedlings for summer crops shallower, we can finish our
   work faster.

Fertilizer for rice plants is also recommended:

Việc cấy lúa phải cần bón đất,
Các chất màu tốt nhất là phân.

In rice planting, it is necessary to fertilize the soil,
And manure is the best fertilizer.

Folk songs also provide hints to judge the future harvest. Rain is the most significant indication. Of summer crops, an experience is thus related:

Lúa chiêm đủng nấp đầu bờ,
Hễ nghe tiếng sấm mở' cỏ mà lên.

Rice plants in summer that stand hiding at the edges of ricefields
Happily shoot up at the sounds of thunder.

It is believed that rice seedlings transplanted in the cold season to grow in the following warm season need rain with thunder and lightning to be at their best. Similarly, a bad winter crop is bound to result from rain not coming at the prescribed time:

Mồng chín tháng chín không mùa,
Mẹ con bán cả cày bừa mà ăn.

If it does not rain on the ninth day of the ninth month
Mother and children can be sure that they have to sell their plow and harrow for
    subsistence.

When the peasants have to part with these essential tools, it can only mean that the crop is a complete failure.

Animal husbandry is an important part of the rural economy. The Vietnamese peasants need buffaloes and oxen to till their fields. Though buffaloes are stronger than oxen, in dry regions where water is not sufficient for buffaloes, oxen are used in plowing and harrowing. Thus, these animals are most essential in rice cultivation. When choosing them they can turn to folk songs for guidance:

Trâu năm sáu tuổi còn nhanh,
Bò năm sáu tuổi đã tranh cõi già.

Buffaloes of five or six years of age are still fast
While five- or six-year-old oxen are about to reach old age.

The appearance of a buffalo is also suggested as a determining factor:

Xa sừng mắt lại nhỏ con,
Vụng đàn, chậm chạp, ai còn nuôi chi.

Buffalo with horns far apart and eyes very small
Are too clumsy and slow to be worth keeping.

Raising chickens is an additional source of income, if care is taken to choose the right kind of chicken:

Nuôi gà phải chọn giống gà
Gà ri bé giống nhủng mà đẻ mau.
Nhất to là giống gà nâu
Lông to thịt béo về sau đẻ nhiều.

One should choose chickens of good breed to raise.
Spotted chickens, though small, lay eggs easily and often.
Chickens of brown color are biggest
Thick-breasted and fleshy, they are prone to be productive.

The circulation of folk songs on agriculture and animal husbandry has been limited to the rural communities of Vietnam, which as late as 1945 still embraced more than ninety percent of the total population of the country (Nguyen Khac Kham 1967:79). In the period of postwar reconstruction, while industrial employment will undoubtedly be developed, agriculture will remain an important part of the Vietnamese economy, undertaken by a large sector of the population. Much physical destruction brought about by the war will have to be repaired before any mental handicap like illiteracy of the majority can obtain serious attention. And until illiteracy is eradicated, it seems quite conceivable that folk songs will remain an effective way of communicating and recording information. But, even with a future high literacy rate, the folk song may continue to play a role in communication, for information is more interesting and easier to memorize when put in the form of the traditional folk song so familiar to the Vietnamese peasant, regardless of whether it is transmitted through singing in the open rice fields or through modern media like radio or television.

Also related to the lack of literacy is the function of the folk song in courting. Unable to write love letters or love poems, young peasants, both men and women, use folk songs to inform each other of their feelings. This they do while carrying on their daily activities, or during some annual festivals when they are presented with an opportunity to lay bare their hearts through singing. Witness a young man's subtle approach through one of the most popular love songs:

Hôm qua tát nước đầu đình
Để' quên chiếc áo trên cành hoa sen.
Em được thì cho anh xin
Hay là em để' làm tin trong nhà.
Áo anh sứt chỉ đường tà,
Vợ anh chủa có, mẹ già chủa khâu.
Áo anh sứt chỉ' đã lâu
Mai mượn cô ấy vào khâu cho cùng.
Khâu rồi anh sẽ trả công

Ít nủã lấy chồng anh sẽ giúp cho.
Giúp em một thúng xôi vò,
Một con lộn béo, một vò rượu tăm.
Giúp em đôi chiếu em năm
Đôi chăn em đắp, đôi tằm em đeo.
Giúp em quan tám tiền cheo
Quan năm tiền cưới lại đèo buồng cau.

Yesterday while bailing out water near the village temple
I hung my tunic on a lotus branch then later forgot to pick it up.
If you have found it, dear young girl, please give it back to me
Or, you may want to keep it as a token.
The stitches are loosened on the seam of my tunic
I have no wife to fix it, and my old mother has not been able to.
The stitches have been broken for a long time
I ask you the favor of sewing it for me some time.
I will repay you for your sewing
By helping you when you get married.
I will help you with a basket of steamed glutinous rice,
A fat pig, a jar of condensed rice wine.
I will help you with a pair of sleeping mats to sleep on
A pair of blankets to cover yourself and a pair of earrings to wear.
I will help you with one coin eighty for the engagement fee paid to the village
One coin fifty for the marriage fee and a bunch of areca nuts.

Whether or not his tunic is actually missing is not important. What matters is that it serves as a very delicate opening for his proposal to the girl he loves. The first intimation of special affection on his part is indicated by the way he addresses her. He calls her *em* and himself *anh*. Literally, *em* is translated as younger sister and *anh* as elder brother. However, in the context of a man–woman relationship, this is a pair of endearing terms used by two people in love. The nature of his interest in the young girl is spelled out when he suggests that she keeps the tunic as a token of his affection. His declaration of love is followed by a statement of his marital status, which informs the girl of his availability. The last part of his approach is presented in terms of a fair give-and-take arrangement, very suggestive of that between an intimate couple: the woman takes care of the man, and he provides her with material comfort. The proposal cannot be more beautifully and more subtly stated, because all the things he lists as repayment for her sewing his tunic are exactly the traditional items that a bridegroom is expected to provide for the wedding.

The transmission of practical information essential to agricultural livelihood and performance of courtship among the illiterate are two important roles of communication played by folk songs in Vietnamese society. A third role is the transmission of geographical and cultural attributes of Vietnam and the Vietnamese. Through folk songs, the people are informed of other parts of their country, of a hero in another village or town who fought for their independence, of the same customs or ethic prevailing from north to south. But more than just being informed, the people are imbued with a sense of pride. This leads to the second major function of folk songs which we will now explore: their role in inculcating a consciousness of national identity and national unity in the minds of the Vietnamese populace.

The Vietnamese have an intense love for their country. Their country is the land that nourishes them, that is marked with the graves of their ancestors and inhabited by people who speak the same language and share the same history, customs and traditions with them. It is a country they have frequently protected against invasion by outsiders. In fact, it has been an inviolable law that the land of Vietnam belongs to the Vietnamese. This concept is cherished in folk songs:

Nủớc non là nủớc non trời
Ai chia đủợc nủớc, ai dời đủợc non.

Our waters and mountains are heaven's waters and mountains;
No one can divide water, no one can remove mountains.

The term *nủớc non* (water mountain) in the first line, which names the two most distinguishing physical features making up the Vietnamese landscape, is used to refer to "country". Heaven is omnipotent. By saying that the Vietnamese land is heaven's property, the folk song accords to it an inviolable nature. The second line presents this nature in a more concrete light. As much as one cannot cut up water and transfer a mountain to another place, one cannot divide or alter the shape of the country they stand for. This line, with the tone of a challenge, laden with self-confidence, to outside interference, seems to reassure the Vietnamese that the land which they inhabit is theirs to keep. This land to which they are attached serves as a foundation for their group identity. Vietnamese ethnicity reckoned in terms of this specific territory is time and again reconfirmed and strengthened by folk songs:

Nồi đồng lại úp vung đồng:
Con gái xủ Bắc lấy chồng Đồng-nai.

Just as a bronze pot is fittingly covered by a bronze lid,
A girl from the northern part of the country is married to a man from Dong-nai region.

Dong-nai, that is, Saigon, formerly referred to the southern part of Vietnam. The folk song precisely states that people from all parts of the country have the same ethnic identity, just as a bronze pot and a bronze lid are of the same kind.

The desire to see the land retain its identity in the terms in which their own identity is asserted makes the Vietnamese hostile to anything that threatens to violate the land's unique nature. In this connection, a most often cited folk song goes:

Ta về ta tắm ao ta
Dù trong dù đục ao nhà vẫn hỏn.

Let us return to bathe in our own pond;
Whether its water is limpid or troubled, the pond at home is still better.

A Vietnamese peasant's pond is better than any other in the sense that he can feel free and comfortable in it, because it is his own. The folk song thus advocates an adherence to everything considered uniquely Vietnamese that sets off Vietnam from other countries, and a rejection of anything unfamiliar, inconsistent with the Vietnamese way of life. In order to shield the beloved country from outside violation, it is necessary to have unity among the people. National unity is sung of repeatedly in folk songs:

Bầu ơi thương lấy bí cùng
Tuy rằng khác giống nhưng chung một giàn.

Dear gourd, please love this winter melon;
Though of different breeds, we share the same trellis.

Of different classes and lineages, the Vietnamese depend on the same land for survival, just as creeping branches of gourd and winter melon depend on a trellis for support. Sharing the same destiny, they should have compassion for one another. The word *thương* arbitrarily translated as "love" here refers to the feeling of closeness and mutual assistance among people who find themselves on the same boat. Another folk song is more specific:

Nhiễu điều phủ lấy giá gương,
Người trong một nước phải thương nhau cùng.

In the manner that a piece of red cloth covers a glass stand,
People of the same country must love one another.

The word *thương* [love] is more clearly specified here. It refers to affection, help, protection, as suggested by the cloth's shielding of the glass stand against dust. The folk song advocates this sentiment of love, whose several nuances point to group unity, to solidarity. In both songs, the land is indicated as the basis for this sentiment.

It is probably this ethnic consciousness related to territoriality, as propagandized most effectively through folk songs, that has played a considerable role in providing Vietnamese with a formidable unity and resilience, as evidenced by their successful struggles against the far greater forces of the Chinese, the French and the Americans. However, love for the country is solidified not only through a limited number of folk songs which promote ethnic consciousness and territoriality. The whole corpus of Vietnamese folk song in another way can evoke patriotic feelings in the Vietnamese. Emotional responses to music are chiefly learned reactions shaped by usage and association. The singing of folk songs is a daily activity in Vietnam. Folk songs are heard everywhere and any time of the day or night, by a sampan girl crossing a river, a peasant thrashing his rice in the moonlight, a mother putting her baby to sleep, a buffalo boy sitting on his animal's back, a fisherman stretching his net to dry. Through intensive repetition, folk songs are ingrained in the mind of the Vietnamese people and become associated with their community — the land that nourishes them and the people with whom they have interacted since birth. Due to this internalized association, the singing of a folk song, with a familiar melody or a familiar text, always triggers in a Vietnamese memories of his community and rekindles his warm feelings of attachment toward it. In this connection, lullabies are the most significant form of folk song. While, for example, occupational folk songs are heard mainly where and when related occupations are performed, lullabies are sung wherever there are babies, three or four times a day whenever a baby needs to sleep. The widespread and frequent use of lullabies is associated with the typical and moving image of the Vietnamese mother holding her infant child and singing in a rhythm that harmonizes with the sound of the swinging hammock. Hence, the singing of a familiar lullaby brings back the memories of that gentle image and turns one's heart to its related environments. And all Vietnamese lullabies can, to a certain degree, affect Vietnamese emotions this way, for they all sound familiar to him in virtue of their being easily recognizable. The melodies of lullabies are smoothly rhythmical, peaceful. The refrains are limited in number and also similar to one another. They range from "Ạ hời ời, hạ hời hoi" in the north, to "À ờ . . . ờ" in the center, to "Ầu ờ . . . ờ" in the south. The content centers mainly upon advocating good conduct and solidifying Vietnamese values, the most important being the country. It is true that a baby to whom these lullabies are sung is still too young to comprehend what is said to him. However, with time, he cannot help internalizing the familiar melody, and as he grows older, the words begin to register in his mind when he hears them sung to his siblings or neighbors. In this light, every common Vietnamese grows up with lullabies and is bound to have a very strong emotional response to this form of folk song, which is closely associated with his homeland.

The functions of folk songs as a medium of communication in economic and emotional life, and as a means of propaganda in the political life of the Vietnamese, have been shown briefly here. The future roles of Vietnamese folk songs, when the country is industrialized and the educational level much higher, cannot, however, be foretold. Until then, while much pain and energy is required to rebuild the country, Vietnamese folk songs will probably continue to assume the significant role they have been playing to date.

REFERENCES

NGUYEN KHAC KHAM
    1967   *An introduction to Vietnamese culture.* Tokyo: Center for East Asian Cultural Studies.
THUAN PHONG
    n.d.   *Ca-dao giang-luan* [A discussion on folk songs], second edition. Saigon: A Chau.

The Aboriginal Music of Taiwan

MIDORI D. HIMENO

Much excellent research has been done recently on the Taiwan aborigines in both the fields of ethnology and cultural anthropology, but unfortunately nothing has been written about their music. Their present civilization, partly urbanized and permeated with Christianity, has made their music, which was closely connected with their daily life, meaningless. As a result, the Taiwan aborigines' traditional music is in a critical condition and likely to disappear. In fact, this music contained almost all of essential significance in their culture. So now it is urgently necessary to investigate and record it. Since at the time of writing this investigation is still continuing, this paper constitutes an interim report and no *definite* conclusions are drawn, but it is not anticipated that those conclusions which are present are likely to change in the future.

THE TAIWAN ABORIGINES AND THEIR CULTURE

There are ten tribes among the Taiwan aborigines — Atayal, Saiseat, Bunun, Tsou, Shao, Paiwan, Puyuma, Rukai, Ami and Yami (see Map 1). With the exception of the Yami tribe, which has been proved to have close connections with the Philippine Islands, we do not know exactly where they lived before they came to Taiwan. The cultural elements of these tribes are very similar in most respects. For instance, all except the Yami had a religious tradition of headhunting. But some tribes, such as the Atayal and the Paiwan, had the custom of tattooing, while others, such as the Ami and the Bunun, did not. The intertribal differences are greater in music than in other cultural elements, though when their music is subdivided into smaller elements, many factors universal among the tribes can be found. Even so, there are fairly distinct differences, so that

Map 1.   Taiwan distribution of aboriginal tribes.

upon hearing one of their melodies it is usually possible to tell which tribe produced the music.

This report deals particularly with the music of two tribes who live on the east coast of Taiwan — the Ami and the Puyuma. These two are discussed because they are among the earlier settlers who built villages, and they engage in agriculture and fishing, so their way of life is more stable. Their music is more closely related to their daily lives than in other tribes, and they show a special talent for it. They use music in all situations. Finally, these tribes live in a flat district which is convenient for research!

THE RESEARCH

Both the Ami and the Puyuma tribes originally had a few musical instruments — musical Jews' harps and bows — but now those instruments have been lost and their music consists only of songs or chants, accompanied by a few kinds of bells. Though there are some solo songs, most are sung in groups of several persons, so it was very important for this research to gather enough performers in a village or community who could sing well. Most of the singers were over forty, though there were a few villages in which the youths sang traditional songs well. The research was carried out in the comparatively important villages, collecting ethnological material in the daytime from the older people who no longer worked, and at night recording their music. It was a very difficult job transcribing and analyzing all the songs collected (over five hundred).

Music of the Ami Tribe

The Ami tribe has a natural talent for music, and their songs are the best among the Taiwan aborigines. The thirty villages researched cover all five subdivisions of the district — Nan-shi Ami, Hsiu-ku-luan Ami, coast Ami, Pei nan Ami and Hêng ch'un Ami. Though we divided the Ami tribe into five subdivisions by their cultural characteristics, we can also divide them into two main groups, the north Ami and the south Ami. We can find some differences between these groups. Their language differs a little, for example, the north people call their own age groups *sular* and the south, *kaput*. Their way of dressing differs also. Finally we can also find differences in their music. The chief characteristics of the Ami tribe's music are:

1. The scale is pentatonic, based on the tetrachord, but using several modes.

2. They count in dual time, although sometimes we find songs which are counted in six-eight time. There is no triple time.

3. The melodic form is usually descending.

4. The song style is usually call and response, though sometimes we find solo songs or simple choruses. Almost all have a solo part and a chorus part.

5. The chorus part is usually sung in a kind of polyphonic style with two to five voices, though some are sung in unison.

6. Their vocal technique requires a skilled singer who sings in melismatic style. The tension in the voice is produced by a narrowed mouth and vibrated from the forehead. They are fond of rather high-pitched voices and anyone who can produce a high-pitched voice and remember the text well is considered to be a good singer. Sometimes they use falsetto.

7. The text of the old songs frequently has a meaningless part or is sung in a dead language. Sometimes they add improvised words.

8. The Ami people like to "make" songs.

Among the various aspects of their music the call-and-response style is the most important and interesting. It can be divided into several patterns:

1. Solo and solo, question and answer style;

2. Solo and chorus, question and answer style, with the chorus part sung in unison;

3. Solo and chorus, question and answer style, with the chorus part sung in polyphony;

4. Solo and chorus, with the solo part taking the initiative and the chorus acting as a kind of accompaniment;

5. Solo and chorus, with the soloist singing an introduction and the chorus following in polyphonic style; and

6. Chorus and chorus — this variety is rare.

In the second, third, fourth, and fifth examples, the solo singer is the leader of the group. A unison style is popular with the north Ami, while the south Ami like to sing in a polyphonic style.

In the Ami tribe each age group sings particular kinds of music. They also sing particular kinds of songs for the various parts of the year's cycle and their life cycles. An attempt at classifying these songs is as follows:

1. Religious songs: from festivals (moon-viewing), headhunting, magic, from magical physicians, and so on;

2. Work songs: weeding songs, logging songs, building songs, and so on;

3. Songs for assembly, sociability and amusement, which may be, for example, for a drinking feast, for greeting or farewell, or for a singing match with another village.

These songs can also be divided into two categories: simple songs and songs accompanied by a dance, the dancing being usually performed in a group. There is also a kind of shaman or magical physician, for whom these songs are quite important.

Music of the Puyuma Tribe

Originally, the Puyuma people were divided into eight groups, which correspond to today's eight villages, all of which were visited. The Puyuma tribe also has age group classifications, but differing from those of the Ami tribe, and some groups are forbidden to sing. The chief characteristics of their music are:

1. Their scale is pentatonic but one mode is dominant. This mode differs from the Ami tribe's modes, but they also use another mode which was "imported" from the Ami tribe.

2. All music is composed in dual time. There are no examples of triple time.

3. The melodic form is usually descending.

4. The song style contains solos, chorus and antiphon. There is also a kind of chanting, for example, a chant for headhunting. The chorus is sometimes sung in unison, and sometimes in a polyphonic style which is much simpler than that of the Ami tribe.

5. The classifications are almost the same as the Ami's, but among the Puyuma tribe nursery songs and children's play songs, which are not common among the Ami, can be heard.

They have borrowed some of the Ami tribe's music, which can be easily distinguished. They dance, especially at festivals, and their dancing is performed in a group. They also have shamans or magical physicians. The music in the eight villages is nearly the same except that the music of T'ai P'ing village differs slightly from the rest, a fact supporting a tradition that long ago the people of T'ai P'ing village were brought as slaves from the western part of Taiwan.

SUMMARY

Considering the Taiwan aborigines as a whole, we can find almost all "primitive" forms in their traditional music. As mentioned above, there are as many musical differences between the tribes as there are other cultural differences. The Ami have the greatest variety of musical types, the most important of which are the use of antiphonal call-and-response forms, polyphony with two to five voices, transposition, falsetto, chromatics, and harmony (which is probably the result of polyphonic singing). The Atayal, Saiseat and Yami tribes are different from the Ami in that they have much simpler music. The Bunun, Tsou and Rukai tribes are also different, while the Puyuma and part of the Paiwan tribe show similarities in their construction of the musical scale, but are all different from one another.

Today the younger people of the Taiwan aborigines are interested only in popular music, despite their excellent traditional music. As a result, one fears that their traditional music will gradually be forgotten and disappear. This disappearance will be a great loss to all of us, so the research will be continued and the traditional music recorded to preserve it. It is hoped also to find some clues to the question of the origin of the Taiwan aborigines.

Finally, one thing should be noted. There is a theory that the Taiwan aborigines' music was once greatly influenced by the Chinese because their music also has a pentatonic scale. But the aboriginal pentatonic scale consists of a tetrachord, while in the Chinese scale, one fifth is dominant, so this is very unlikely.

Contemporary Music of the Maclay Coast

B. N. PUTILOV

The Soviet expedition on board the *Dmitri Mendeleev* in 1971 included a team of ethnographers who, apart from strictly ethnological and anthropological research, were to collect material on the music and folk songs of Oceania.

From July to September the expedition visited New Guinea, the New Hebrides, New Caledonia, Fiji, Western Samoa, the Gilbert and Ellice Islands, and the island of Nauru. In almost all these places the Soviet team carried out field research, made tape recordings of folk songs and traditional music, studied musical instruments, and collected material on contemporary music and the basic trends of present-day folklore.

In places where we could not visit villages and meet singers in person we contacted local radio stations and obtained from them high-quality recordings of folk music. The result of this collecting was a wealth of diverse material which gives one an idea of the contemporary folklore of some regions of Oceania and also makes it possible to draw some general conclusions of a comparative nature.

The Maclay Coast of New Guinea was of special interest to the expedition from the point of view of ethnography and folklore. Soviet ethnographers were landing here one hundred years after the ethnographer Miklukho-Maklai, from whom the region takes its name, to carry out research into changes that have occurred in those years in the life, social organization, and culture of the inhabitants, to collect material on their present-day conditions, and to add new data to Miklukho-Maklai's work. The ethnographic research also included folklore studies.

Some of the problems pertaining to local folklore were suggested by Miklukho-Maklai's diaries and ethnographic articles. Folklore and studies in folk songs and music featured prominently in his program of research in New Guinea. He made detailed descriptions of local musical instruments, some of which he brought back and are on display in the Museum of Anthropology and Ethnography of the Academy of Sciences in Leningrad. Miklukho-Maklai described some traditional festivities of the Papuans and analyzed their folk songs. He wrote down the texts of some songs and collected data on their theater, dancing, and games. All these materials, most valuable for studies in the folklore tradition of one hundred years ago, can also be used as a reference point by modern scholars.

Of course, Miklukho-Maklai did not make an exhaustive analysis of the local folklore, because he worked on strictly ethnographic problems. The Soviet expedition was to add new details to his observations and make a fresh investigation of a number of problems such as the genre composition of Bongu folk songs, their functional relations and, of course, their musical characteristics. It must be remembered that there was no recording equipment in Miklukho-Maklai's day, so one of our major tasks was to record folk songs and thus fill in the gap in our knowledge of the musical culture.

In the organization of fieldwork and in the methods of collecting folklore material, we followed principles evolved by several generations of Soviet folklore specialists. We strove to explain to the people the essence and basic purpose of our work to ensure understanding on their part. Our recording sessions were meant to cover all the age and sex groups in a village, so as not to leave out any essential aspect of the local folklore. Our basic aim was to discover, on a comprehensive basis, types and functional systems of village folklore, primarily of folklore pertaining to everyday life. In other words, we looked not for rarities or relics, but for everyday features of local music which determine the standards and nature of contemporary musical culture of the village.

Following in the footsteps of Miklukho-Maklai, we tried to study all the available musical instruments, describe them, establish their functions, and record their sound. We found that almost all the instruments described a century ago have been preserved, with the exception of the *orlanai*, a type of nutshell threaded on a set of strings tied to a handle, and the *dyubonu*, a coco leaf with a lengthwise slit. Both instruments were known to the villagers, but neither was available. On the other hand we found some instruments that Miklukho-Maklai had not mentioned and we also made some corrections regarding the terminology and descriptions of known instruments.

One of the most widespread musical instruments in the village of Bongu is the *bembu*, a hollow bamboo pipe some sixty centimeters long, open at one end and of varying diameter. The bembu is used to accompany singing, both solo and choral, being struck on the ground in time with the singing. Not a single song is performed without such accompaniment. Although Miklukho-Maklai did not mention this instrument, it is doubtless traditional. It is probable, however, that he meant the bembu when he wrote: "Another musical instrument is a bamboo stick which is struck on thick tree trunks" (Miklukho-Maklai 1951:109).

Another instrument not mentioned by Miklukho-Maklai is the *congon*, a bamboo pipe approximately as long as the bembu, closed at both ends and with a slit along its entire length. Part of an adjoining section of the same bamboo trunk is used as a handle. Struck with a stick, the congon produces a high, harsh sound.

The *lob-lob-ai* is a painted wooden blade tied with a string to a long bamboo stick. With fast rotation of the stick, the wooden blade cuts the air with a wailing noise. This instrument is said to be used during initiation rituals and to have a magical function. No description of the lob-lob-ai occurs in Miklukho-Maklai's writings but a number of such wooden blades are to be found in his collection of instruments.

Miklukho-Maklai referred to the *ai-kabrai* as a common musical instrument, describing it thus

It is a bamboo pipe some two meters long or even longer, and some fifty millimeters in diameter; the partitions at the joints are removed, so that it is one hollow pipe. One end of it is put in the mouth, no matter how wide the opening; into it the Papuans blow, holler, howl, bellow, etc (1951:106).

When we asked for an ai-kabrai we were shown a bamboo pipe some thirty centimeters long, into which a performer shouted loudly. When we asked for a long pipe we found that it was called an *ai-damangu*; the performer blew it with all his might, producing a deep sound.

All the other instruments we saw in Bongu correspond to Miklukho-Maklai's descriptions. We noted only some minor differences in their names.

The *mongi-ai* (Miklukho-Maklai refers to it as the *monki-ai* or *munki-ai*) is a peeled and dried coconut with openings at the upper end and on one side. Blowing into one of these openings produces a shrill, piercing sound.

The *ilol-ai* is a kind of trumpet made of a hollowed-out, cherry-colored fruit that resembles an elongated pumpkin widening toward one end. With reference to the same name, Miklukho-Maklai drew a trumpet made of a hollowed out tree root (1951:107). He referred to the one made of a hollowed-out pumpkin as the *khol-ai* (1951:106). Like the ai-damangu the ilol-ai is designed to amplify and distort the human voice.

The *shyumbin*, which Miklukho-Maklai called the *tyumbin*, is a bamboo flute with two openings on opposite sides. In a drawing by Miklukho-Maklai the player holds it sideways, like a European flautist. Today it is held lengthwise.

The *tora* is a huge signal shell (resembling a triton shell) with an opening at its narrow end. When blown it makes a low, deep wailing sound.

The percussion instruments include, in addition to the bembu, the *okam*, a drum made of a hollowed-out tree trunk; one end is open, while the other is covered with monitor skin. The outer surface of the okam is decorated with intricate woodcarving, the richest ornamentation being in the middle, the narrowest part of the drum. Carved handles are also provided. This is a favorite instrument, as it was in Miklukho-Maklai's day. Although also being used to accompany singing, its chief purpose is to accompany dancing. Each dancer uses his own okam to accompany his dancing and the singing that goes with it.

As in the old days, the villagers widely use an enormous signal drum, the *barum*, made of a hollowed-out tree trunk. An ordinary barum is two and a half to three meters long and up to eighty centimeters in diameter. The back of it is cut off at a right angle while the front is moulded into a head of a fish or the bow of a boat. On the upper side, covering almost the entire length of the drum, there is a slit which is quite narrow for such a huge trunk. The player strikes the drum with a special wooden stick, the *toba*. The barum's sound is powerful and clear and can be heard for miles around. A system of well-known signals has been evolved and are used in various situations. The barum is also used to accompany singing.

Thus, musical instruments in the village of Bongu have not changed much over the past hundred years. This stability is especially striking in contrast with other parts of Oceania where the traditional system of musical instruments has disappeared almost completely. The Bonguans have managed to retain the traditional system, and, moreover, have not adopted a single modern instrument of those that are currently tremendously popular all over Oceania, including New Guinea and in regions quite near Bongu.

Yet it can be said that the traditional system is on the way out. The only instruments still commonly used are the bembu, okam, and barum: percussion instruments meant to accompany singing and dancing and to communicate signals. Wind instruments become rare and gradually fall out of use.

Miklukho-Maklai wrote of the bamboo flute: "It is a favorite instrument with the Papuan youth. ... Music lovers never part with their tyumbins and never stop playing them either in solitude or in small groups" (1951:109). I spent much time trying to find out about the shyumbin and only on the third day of intense search did villagers bring me two flutes. It turned out, however, that not a soul could now play them the way it used to be done a hundred years ago. It is notable that other wind instruments aroused a lively interest among the villagers; it was clear that the Bonguans did not hear them very often.

The functions of the local instruments have also changed in some ways.

Miklukho-Maklai wrote that a number of instruments were under a strict taboo. With the exception of the okam and a few other instruments, all, and especially the ai-kabrai (apparently both this and the ai-damangu), the ilol-ai, and the mong-ai, "were forbidden to be used or even be looked at by women and children. One sound of any such instrument was enough to chase all the women and children from the village" (Miklukho-Maklai 1951:109–110). These musical instruments were kept in men's houses and adult males played them in secrecy outside the village.

To my regret, I could not find out to what extent the tradition of special use of some musical instruments by adult and young males has been preserved. Judging from what has been stated above, it is improbable that it is still firmly rooted. We can say with certainty, though, that women and children are no longer forbidden to look at or listen to these instruments. The villagers brought the ai-kabrai, ai-damangu, mongi-ai, ilol-ai, and lob-lob-ai, to the village square and played them for us in the presence of a great number of people.

The relative stability of the local system of musical instruments is, doubtless, related to the general state of the folk song and folklore tradition in the village of Bongu.

We made a series of recordings of songs performed by groups of men, women, young men, girls, and children. The musical style and the poetic and functional aspects of the folklore of all these groups was marked by a high degree of uniformity and could not always be precisely differentiated by age and sex. Its systematization is largely based on the principle of the genre function, the latter being most strongly manifest in folk songs of the village of Bongu. Thus far, there are very few songs that are not related to some aspect of everyday life. Apparently, the process of the evolution of nonfunctional lyric songs is only beginning. This is one of the manifestations of the archaic nature of the local folklore.

We recorded a number of work songs, a form with which both men and women would start their series of songs, a fact indicative of their popularity.

Functionally, local work songs may be divided into three types, the first, sung by fishermen while pulling out their nets, becomes part of the work process, the rhythm of the song and a repeated melodic phrase being distinctly associated with rhythmical movements of hands pulling out fishing nets. The second type is a women's song, sung by women while men are clearing land for vegetables. Because the people are cultivators this type of song is heard quite often, and although there is little rhythmic relation between the song and the work in this case, it is clear that the workers need the song. Finally, the third type is sung by men before planting taro, while starting work on a new vegetable garden. It is possible that this type of song is supposed to have magical power to secure fertility.

We were especially interested in songs whose function and content were related to wars and clashes among different tribes in the past. We heard one song which used to be sung before setting out for war. It seems that old military folklore has been largely forgotten. We could not obtain any data on epic songs.

Another prominent group of songs is related to all kinds of rituals. Of course, we were unable to find songs pertaining to the entire set of local rituals, but we did record songs of the two principal cycles: songs related to the initiation ritual, and funeral songs, or lamentations (*aran*).

The ritual of initiation continues to play an important role in Bongu's social life and still remains compulsory for youth here. We recorded such songs performed by old and young men who had been subject to that ritual. Special songs are usually sung when young men are on their way to the village from the woods after performing the ritual. According to the singers, these songs are meant "to bring back the young men to the village and instruct them as to how they should act and what they should say to their wives." Here is how young men explained another song: "When we go to the woods to cut off our skin, and when we are about to leave the woods, when we come back to the village, then we sing this type of song, and when the morning comes, we come back home." We also found that songs accompany the circumcision and the incision of marks on the young men's bodies. One such song was sung for us, in strict confidence, by an old man who performs those operations.

Funeral songs, or laments, described by Miklukho-Maklai, are still a tradition in Bongu. In addition to being an accompaniment to funeral rites, they are also an expression of grief. Old men told us their parents' story about seeing Miklukho-Maklai off: as he was leaving, the whole village joined in an aran.

As far as we were able to find out, laments are performed in the house of a deceased person by his relatives. They may be sung in chorus, men and women together, and they do not differ as regards the sex, age, or family status of the deceased. This means, in particular, that the laments do not contain any specific differentiating features and are clearly a general expression of sorrow. The Bonguans do not seem to have the tradition of a funeral repast.

At first, the recording of laments caused some difficulties. The villagers seemed loath to sing an aran "just for nothing". I patiently asked them to perform an aran, emphasizing at the same time that I wished all the villagers good health and long life. Eventually they led me to a remote corner of the village and there, out on the veranda of a hut, sang a series of them. On the following day it was much easier to make some young men sing arans; they did so right in the village square.

Other songs have a functional content pertaining to some typical situation of local life. One such song is performed when an "uncle" from one village is going to give something, some pigs for instance, to an "uncle" from another village. When they are preparing for a festival they ask inhabitants of another village to come and take part, they sing a song so that the guests come with food — taro, pigs, nuts, breadfruit, and other things. One song is used to accompany a specific type of dancing (dancing and singing are done only by girls and young men, with no married men or women taking part). Some songs are performed by men and serve as an accompaniment for dancing at ceremonies and festivals. A number of such dance-pantomimes were performed for us in the village square, the dances being accompanied by the beating of okams.

The musical and poetic structure of all the local song types seems to be basically the same. Only a special musicological analysis can provide detailed and accurate answers regarding the nature and extent of that similarity and the specific features of the song types. I believe that such an analysis will disclose a typological similarity of the music and a predominance in it of a single musical type.

These observations also apply to the poetic structure of local songs. The first thing to be noted in this respect is that we did not hear any improvised songs, such as Miklukho-Maklai described. The texts we heard, with all their simplicity, are quite traditional, that is, they have been learned by heart and are not the results of improvisation.

As in Miklukho-Maklai's day the songs are very simple in content. Normally they are a repetition or a slight variation of a phrase, one or two words, or even one word. The words of a song are not directly associated with a situation, or with the song's function, the imagery being of an associative nature, and typical of most local songs. For example, one fisherman's song contains a repetition of the word *kanajo* [seagull]; one aran repeats the word *sandanu* [cock]; a lyrical girls' song repeats the word *popoja* [wind].

Elements of modern musical culture (youth songs to a ukulele accompaniment, or modern hits) are all around Bongu, and can already be heard in neighboring villages. Yet the folklore of Bongu still retains, in striking integrity, its traditional and partially archaic nature.

REFERENCE

MIKLUKHO-MAKLAI, N. N.
   1951   *Sobranie sochinenii* [Collected works], volume three, part one. Moscow and Leningrad.

Rituals and Songs of Weather in Georgian Poetic Folklore

KSENIA SIKHARULIDZE

Weather ritual, and verse songs and legends connected with it, is known throughout the world. It began in the distant past, being as old as the most ancient forms of agriculture, and is thus important not only to the future of agrarian poetry but also to the study of the development of a word-and-music art form.

Man in captivity to nature depended entirely on the weather, a fact demonstrated in the Georgian saying "Weather was working and laborers were boasting." Struggling for existence, whether in hunting, agriculture, or woodsmanship, man felt in earliest times the usefulness of suitable weather, and so it was that primitive man thought it important to perform various kinds of rituals in order to bring it. With these rituals came creativity in words and music. In spite of regional variations in flora and fauna, songs and poetry related to weather rituals in different parts of the world are found to possess certain similarities. This is true although the weather-connected rituals and poetry and music of each people have their national characteristics.

It is well known that many pagan rituals were blended with those of Christianity to become part of the original form of divine service. The character and the theme of weather ritual and weather poetry were essentially determined by the weather at the time, that is, by drought, rain, or hail. These rituals and verse songs were dedicated to gods who were considered to be the rulers of weather. In the complex heathen pantheon the god of the sky (clouds or weather at an earlier time) was the highest — and one might posit a connection between this and the worship of celestial bodies, depicting well the close connection between the weather and the seasons and the effect of celestial bodies. The residence of the gods, of course, was the sky, and for this reason weather rituals were usually performed on high ground. In this respect Georgian customs, and particularly the Svan, Khevsureti, and Tushin ones, are of interest.

In Svanetia, until recent times there was preserved a celebration called *Khatarashoba*, dedicated to weather. Khatarashoba was a big celebration which took place in February on a mountain near the church. There, "magic plowing" was performed, and the villagers would take the icon out of the church and carry it to the village.

In the village of Khevsureti Pirimze [Sunface], St. George, or Queen Thamar, were considered to be the rulers of the sky. It was believed that Pirimze kept a giant as a slave, so that when people offended her she would go to the god and fill baskets with hail, load the giant with them, and have him cover the area with it. Khizanishvili (1940:70–71) writes: "Sunface is held in high respect; days are singled out for the prevention of hail in Khevsureti: Friday, Saturday and Monday." The rituals for removing hail are performed from the beginning of June. In the lately discovered Khevsureti documents, weather ritual performed on a high mountain was called Satsvero [of the apex]. Countryfolk used to go to the castle there to slaughter cattle and drink beer.

The ritual was performed until the corn matured, and then a three-day holiday was celebrated during which, in the place where people prayed, a kid was killed, boiled, and eaten, and the remains left at the top of the castle. Guts and other organs were minced and thrown away on the other side of the mountain. The Khevsureti weather ritual, performed in both good and bad weather is considered to be the oldest.

Among people in other parts of the world, the heathen gods considered to be the sources of life had other names. Ilya the prophet was one, as were the Slavic god Perun, the Scandinavian Piorgen, and others, all equivalents of the Georgian sun god. In western Georgia the ritual of weather bore the name *Kokhindjroba*, in the east, in Kartli, Kakheti, and Imereti, they were called *Lazaroba* and *Gondjaoba*; we meet the names Lazarus and Gondja in many Georgian verse songs.

In Kakheti one also finds the use of a stone figure in the performance of weather rituals. Patriotic and class elements are also noteworthy here. In the Kvareli district Gondjaoba is connected with an historical legend analogous to the myth about Daphne and Apollo. According to legend when Kakheti was invaded by an enemy the inhabitants fled to the forest, among them being a woman named Gogolashvili who went with her baby in its cradle. She became very tired, and, when approached by the enemy, bent down and pleaded to god: "I don't want to fall into the hands of Tatars, turn me to stone." The god listened to her and turned her to stone. The inhabitants of this village can to this day show you a stone which they call a woman-stone. During bad weather a group of women used to go to the stone. One of the women, also named Gogolashvili, would touch the stone and say "Come on, my aunt." The women then turned the stone and threw it into the water, saying "God, award us with rain," or "God, award us with the eye of the sun." Then they went barefoot back to the village, took a toy Gondja, and splashed people who were approaching with water.

The rite of Lazaroba took the form of a women's carnival. The text of the song contains a prayer to the god of weather. The contents of the prayer was determined by the weather at the time. In times of drought, the participants in the carnival sang:

Oh, Lazarus, Lazarus,
Bring clouds on the sky!
God, give us dew,
We don't need any more the eye of the sun!
God give us mud!
We don't need any more drought!

During rainy periods the song took this form:

Oh, Lazarus, Lazarus,
Take away clouds!
We don't need any more dew,
God, give us the eye of the sun!
We don't need any more mud,
God give us drought!

These texts, which were written down in Kartli, had their own melody (Chikhikvadze 1960:184). The whole cycle of texts of weather prayer has reached us. One version of the transcribed text of Lazaroba reads like this:

Lazarus comes to the door,
He rolls his eyes,
He goes up and down,
Looks like the moon.
Oh, Ilya, Ilya,
Why! I did not offend you,
I presented you
One goat and a kid,
We do not need any more drought,
God, give us mud!

According to the second version given by one of the women who took part in Lazaroba, the women who performed the song went barefoot, handing out candles and toys and asking for provisions. Then they put some women to the plow. They carried the plow to the water and with the collected provisions they made sacrifice (Sikharulidze 1956:49–50). The magic plowing of water during bad weather was well known among other people (Snegirev 1837:vol. 3, p. 156). According to the narrator they threw the toy Gondja into the yard of anyone who did not reward the carnival participants in order to destroy his family life (Sikharulidze 1958:366). Asking for provisions on behalf of Gondja is a custom also met in a text written down in Svanetia in the 1870's (Umikashvili 1937:378). For comparison it is also worthwhile looking at another text transcribed in the past century (Takaishvili 1918:vol. 1, p. 21).

I splashed on Gondja
Vardo — Mananasa!
God, bring rain,
Vardo — Mananasa!

The magic splash of water over Gondja recalls the Polish and Silesian Maruana, the Icelandic Mara, the English nightmare, the Czech Morus, and so on, Maruana, which is represented by a straw dummy of a woman, is the same as the Georgian Gondja. They drowned it in water on the seventh of March, singing: "Death climbs up fences, looking for profit" (Snegirev 1837:vol. 3, pp. 8–12).

The Georgian texts of worship, among those of other nations, assert that Ilya the prophet replaced the highest god, Perun. According to the oldest Georgian belief, the traveling of Ilya the prophet through the sky by carriage caused thunder and lightning. The mythology of horse and sea must be studied in the context of subjects connected with the gods of weather and fertility. The belief in a connection between horses and the sea is common throughout the world. This belief is described in the myth of Amiran. Ivane Dzhavakhishvili (1928:141–143) was right when he considered the father, Kamar-Ketus, wearing a fiery helmet, to be the lord of clouds. According to some versions of the myth, the father, Kamar-Ketus, and his army create weather — rain or storm (Chikovani 1947:279). In the belief of Pahava, rain is the tears of the mother of Kamar.

Among the Georgians, as among many people of the world, different functions of the heathen pantheon are combined, such as those of weather, fertility, agriculture, and animal husbandry. From this point of view, there is a close contact between songs and poetry about the seasons. In this instance we can notice one peculiarity of folklore: the genetic relationship among poetic genres. Dramatization of the struggle between spring and winter, meeting with the first rain of spring, celebrating the first of May, and so on, took place in Georgia too. According to the different rituals and rites in the texts of some songs is the very interesting Easter round dance song: "Christ is risen, make merry, thank the herald." Easter rituals represent the desire for the transformation into spring of the characteristic influence of winter. The dramatization of the struggle between winter and spring is represented in these lines of another Easter round dance:

Yesterday the son of a bitch
Crossed the door of the sky;
He was dressed in a Circassian coat;
His hat, covered with roses,
Touched the breeze.

The boy with the hat of roses caressed by the breeze is a symbol of summer. This is contrasted with bad winter weather:

The breeze is in love with the sun,
And the storm with bad weather.

The participants in the Easter round dance are against bad weather:

We should like good weather
Better than rainy weather.

The dance ends with a eulogy to fertility:

We prefer the full jug
To the empty pitcher   (Takaishvili 1918:vol. 1, p. 163)

In this complex text, heathen in origin but later Christianized, the rites related to spring, weather, and fertility are performed simultaneously. No doubt there is a relationship between the concepts of weather and of dying gods and gods raised from the dead. Men's thoughts were directed to suitable weather on the calendar of celebrations. This shows in the poetry of everyday life. An interesting example of this appears in the text of a children's song:

Rain, rain, come,
Come down in a pot,
There are many pots
Full of seeds   (Sikharulidze 1938:49)

It is probable that people greeted the first rain of spring singing this song, and in addition to asking for good weather, asked for fertility. So the seed is mentioned here not for fun. This opinion is strengthened by the evidence of a Russian spring song in which they asked the first rain of spring for a heavy harvest:

Rain, rain!
Go on the old woman's rye,
Go on the old man's wheat,
Go on the girl's flax,
Pour out of the bucket   (Snegirev 1837:vol. 3, p. 15)

The kindness of rain is depicted in a Georgian verse song. It is possible that earlier it was a song of glory:

Glory to the Holy Father!
He decided to build up a country,
He gave clouds to the sky,
And there is rain   (Takaishvili 1918:vol. 1, p. 378)

The song was sung while using the threshing floor, and contains requests for good weather:

Come, wind
And mix corn,
I'll bake bread
And make children happy   (Takaishvili 1918:vol. 1, p. 329)

It is noteworthy that in Khevsureti, up to the end, they had a celebration of wind. It took place in the middle of March. People thought that if anybody did not obey the celebration rites, wind would throw down haystacks. People used to say: "There is rain (or snow) for a happy man and wind is blowing for an unhappy one."

In most songs we can see hatred and fear of winter. The Georgian saying: "May you have the kind of winter you deserve" is seen as a curse. It is from this point of view that we must note the cycle of verses about months. These verses are not ritual in origin, but are of everyday life and represent weather suitable for the seasons of the year. Describing the climatic features of the months, they underline the special difficulties of the winter months, December and January. Examples of this are:

At the beginning of December
Storms started,
Mills were frozen,
Nobody could make them move   (Kotetishvili 1934:188)

January is coming
As a snake of September   (Takaishvili 1918: vol 1, p. 327)

The designation of months showing a mood of spring depends upon the climate of a region. In southern Georgia this appears in poems dedicated to February, but in the mountainous areas, where in February it is very cold, people show their fear of the severity of this month.

It is interesting that in many parts of the world April is considered to be the time for meeting the spring. People show this in various ways, but it is noteworthy, however, that even people with different beliefs have the same custom of deception on the first of April (Snegirev 1837:vol. 1, p. 43). The Georgians say: "Today is the first of April, it is very easy to deceive." This was not simply a custom. It had the same meaning in spring rites as in a wedding ceremony. During the wedding procession people used to see the bride and bridegroom off while telling lies and shooting into the air. It is possible that the habit of playing tricks on the first of April was intended to ward off evil forces that might interfere with the rebirth of nature, the spring, the deity raised from death. Attempting to frighten off evil forces was a habit among Georgian farmers. In Khevsureti, when it was hailing, people used to shoot into the air.

With the ritual and poetry of weather is connected the celebration of May. Among Slavs this celebration signified the transition from spring to summer (Snegirev 1837:vol. 1, p. 48).

Celebrations of the first and seventh of May have been observed to the present day in Georgia. On the first of May women sang and danced in a ring. People also believed that the rain of May helped hair to grow. The song of the seventh of May said:

There is rain of the seventh of May,
Hair is down to the feet.

In connection with the rituals of weather and legend songs, the poetic folklore of the celestial cycle must be noted. Being a captive of nature, man noticed from the beginning the meaning of this cycle for agriculture. This was the basis for worship of the celestial cycle, which was reflected in different branches of art. Many people believed that the sun was a totem. According to the Ossetian legend, Queen Thamar conceived her son from a sunbeam which shone through the window (Miller n.d). In Georgian poetic folklore the image of Queen Thamar is connected with the heathen deity of weather, Pirimze. According to the legend nobody knew winter in Georgia until Queen Thamar imprisoned the Star, or the Lord of Weather; it was eternally spring (Sikharulidze 1961:81–82, 254–261). Benevolent weather created the totem of the sun and the cult of the stars. The sun was the source of life, an idea preserved in Georgian folk tales as a charming fable.

According to one of the folk tales the mother of the sun instructs the mother of a boy who is dead in the daytime but alive at night:

Take the water with which the sun washes his face and it will cure your son. Go down the same way you came up. Stay there until morning. At dawn collect the early dew — this is the water. Take it and sprinkle with it the face of your son and he will be as alive in the daytime as he is at night.

The mother did so and her son came to life (Takaishvili 1918:vol. 2, pp. 4–8).

In Georgia, the sun and the moon were considered not only to be royal totems but also the source of life. This is well illustrated in a Megrelian song:

The sun is my mother,
The moon is my father,
Small stars are
My sisters and brothers   (Dzhavakhishvili 1928:54)

The rituals or dramatizations of the struggle between winter and spring showed how a man depending on weather looked at the sun with hope. That is why people thought that at Easter the sun rose playing and dancing. So believed people in Russia and in Iceland (Snegirev 1837:vol. 1, p. 18), as well as in Georgia. Celebration of Easter is a transformation of heathen spring celebrations. Traces of sacrificing of goats, kids, and sheep to the sun during the rituals of asking the heathen god for good weather are preserved up to the present day in poems of the sun's cycle:

Rise, sun,
Come into our yard,
Shine on the cattle yard,
I'll kill for you a sheep   (Sikharulidze 1970:37–38)

Verses analogous to this can be found in Russian folk song, when children sing to the sun:

Sun, fine weather,
Look out of the window   (Snegirev 1837:vol. 1, p. 18)

There were many poems in Georgia which were part of the worship of the sun and now take their place in the children's repertoire. A good example of this is a poem which a Georgian child learns as he starts to speak:

Sun, rise, rise,
Don't hide in the mountains,
The man is killed by cold,
Poor man is wallowing here.

The texts of Georgian work poetry reveal the connection of agriculture with songs dedicated to the sun. Some of the songs were performed during group work. The children's poems probably had the same function we have spoken about above. According to texts recently discovered, at the beginning and at the end of work a group of workers sang to the sun:

Sun, come, come,
Light up over the world,
Long live your creator!
You are a candle for the world   (Sikharulidze 1970:37–38)

During the process of work they sang for good weather:

Oh, morning, morning,
How charming you are
My morning,
The sun lit up
And woke up all beings   (Sikharulidze 1960:249)

In the process of work dew is spoken of affectionately:

I woke up early in this morning
And touched dew
At first we have to thank God
And then his strength.

Dew, as we have seen from this folk tale, was considered to be water with which the sun washed his face. In this poem heathen and Christian gods, the sun and the creator, are joined.

Laborers at the end of the day's work used to say farewell to the sun, singing his glory. For example, one song can serve which keeps a trace of mythos:

Sun is going down,
Taking his seat in the nest
Where he put the golden egg,
A chicken of pearl   (Sikharulidze 1960:294)

From the point of view of the ritual of weather and poetic creation there must be noted a poem, "The sun and the moon," in dialogue form. In this verse a realistic picture of the meaning of celestial bodies for man and agriculture is given. The superiority of the sun over other bodies is underlined there. At the same time the poem retains traces of a great celebration of the awakening of nature. This poem and others from the cycle of celestial poetry raise many interesting questions. In answering them, we shall solve many complex problems of mythology. Investigation of rituals of weather and the poetry connected with them has a great meaning for research into the hopes, expectations, and consolations of people over the centuries.

REFERENCES

CHIKOVANI, J.
  1947 *Amiran chained.* (In Russian.)
CHIKHIKVADZE, G.
  1960 *Georgian folk song.* (In Russian and Georgian.)
DZHAVAKHISHVILI, I.
  1928 *The history of the Georgian people*, volume one. (In Georgian.)

KHIZANISHVILI, N.
1940   *Ethnographic notes.* Tiflis. (In Georgian.)
KOTETISHVILI, V.
1934   *Folk poetry.* (In Georgian.)
MILLER, U.
n.d.   *Ossetian studies*, volume three. (In Russian.)
SIKHARULIDZE, K.
1938   *Children's folklore.* (In Georgian.)
1956   *Georgian folklore reader*, volume one. (In Georgian.)
1958   *Essays*, volume one. (In Georgian.)
1960   *Poetry of folk rites, Georgian folk poetry*, volume one. (In Georgian.)
1961   *Georgian historical folklore*, volume one. (In Georgian.)
1970   *Georgian folklore reader*, volume two. (In Georgian.)
SNEGIREV, I.
1837   *Russian folk celebrations and superstitious rites*, volumes one and three. Moscow. (In Russian.)
TAKAISHVILI, E., *editor*
1918   *Folklore,* two volumes. (In Russian.)
UMIKASHVILI, P.
1937   *Folklore*, volume one. (In Georgian.)

On the Hungarian Variants of South Slavic Folk Songs and Tales

MADELEINE V. ANDJELIĆ

South Slavic ethnic groups dispersed in various regions of Hungary even today continue the customs and folklore (folk poetry, epic songs, folktales, and so on) which they brought with them when they migrated to the new country several centuries ago. However, under the influence of new environmental conditions and new circumstances of life, and despite the desire to preserve tradition untouched, it has changed little by little, and at the same time folk poetry, epic songs, and prose have also undergone modifications and transformations. These transformations are also influenced by the accelerated rhythm of modern life which spares neither the village customs, nor the traditional milieu in which folk songs are best cultivated and conserved.

For the most part the songs of contemporary singers are those heard on radio and television, or those which are culled from written compilations.

The researcher Vlajko Palavestra, who spent the end of 1962 and the beginning of 1963 in Hungary gathering folklore material, succeeded in hearing the folk songs of Szőreg (Sirig), a village six kilometers from the city of Szeged. It was in the household of Bogdan Jovanov, a seventy-year-old man, that his daughters-in-law, two Serbians and one Hungarian, sang the songs which they had learned while listening to the radio from Novi Sad.

They sang the widely known song *Andjelija vodu lila* [Andjelija poured water], then another, also well circulated, of the *dodola* type-songs associated with the custom of praying during a drought:

Our doda begs God, hola dodo, hola dodole
That it may rain a little, hola dodo, hola dodole.

They also knew some facetious songs (*šalajke*), for example:

Hola Sirig, you are scattered on the hillside,
You are a beautiful nest of vagabonds.

The singers then narrated in detail the old customs of Christmas and other festivals which have been preserved and are still celebrated in the same fashion as in the past.

It is possible to appreciate to what extent the small South Slavic ethnic groups dispersed in Hungary maintain and retain tradition by reading *Narodni kalendar*, a people's almanac which appears each year in Budapest and which is intended, for the most part, for villagers of South Slavic origin. In response to the wishes of the subscribers, of those who read it, the almanac contains folk songs and tales, but there is also some interest shown for articles concerning customs. The epic songs published in the almanac are often only well-known songs taken from the collections of Vuk Stefanović Karadžić. Those from these collections which have appeared in the almanac since its first appearance two decades ago are: "Marko drinks Ramazan wine" (1959), "Predrag and Nenad" (1960), "The wife of Hassan-aga," "Marko recognizes the sword of his father" (1962), "Prince Marko and Bey Kostadin," "Czar Lazar and czarina Militza" (1963), "The first climb made by Prince Marko," "Marko hunts with the Turks," "Old man Voujadin," "Prince Marko and the eagle," "Prince Marko and Bey Kostadin" (1964), "The battle of Micher," "The Marriage of Janko Sibinjanin" (1966), "Prince Marko and Moussa Kessedžija" (1967), "Tomorrow will be the fair day of Vid" (1968), and "Old man Novak and Prince Bogosav" (1969). Included also are songs taken from other collections: "The redeemed girl (the marriage of Ive de Senj)" (1959), "Empty Daničić" (1963), "Prince Marko and his cousin Ognjan" (1967), and "Prince Marko and the fairy of Pechter" (1969). Exceptionally popular songs have even appeared twice: "Marko recognizes the sword of his father" reappeared in 1966 and "Prince Marko and Bey Kostadin" in 1965.

In addition to the songs mentioned, in which heroism is glorified and the great deeds of the favorite characters of South Slavic epic tradition, especially those of Prince Marko, are praised, we find lyrical songs, some from the Karadžić collections "The girl complains to the rose," "The stag and the fairy," but for the most part collected in more recent years. Stjepan Velin published the lyrical songs of the Bunivetch (*Bunjevci*) and the Shocatz (*Šokci*) which he observed in Baja and its surroundings (1969); some old songs of the Bunivetch of Vantzaga (1966); the ballad "The immurement of the breakfast maid," the variation of the well-known ballad of the immured mother (1969); and songs which describe the customs of the Bunivetch which are sung in Santovo, Bereg, and Monochtor (1971). Here is an example from the last group:

I love the brunette in the evening twilight
When the ducats jingle around her neck.

Popular songs of Gradiste, Koljnive, Narde, of the village of Petrovo Selo, and of Chitz of the Croatians (1961, 1964, 1967) have also been published, including the well-known "I am a rose until I have no husband" (1961), "Where do you come from little girl?" (1963), "All the tiny birds of the forests," noted by Marthe Tangl (1967); and street songs (*bećarac*) such as "The window is high, and I am a little girl" (1967). One also reads with pleasure the treatises on the history of the ethnic groups, the Bunivetch and the Shocatz (1968); the descriptions of the customs of Pomaz, of Lower Martinzi (Donji Martinci), and of the forest of Legrad; of the customs of Ivan Krijes at Felsőszentmarton (Gornji Martinci) noted and published by Marie Fekete (1969); and the Christmas customs among the Shocatz in Baranja, noted and published by Čizmić (1969).

All the ethnic groups are similar in that songs about fairies are popular, but songs which praise and glorify the great deeds of Prince Marko are preferred even more. Let us analyze some of these songs and tales noted by researchers over the years. Prince Marko is equally popular among all people of South Slavic origin: Serbs, Croats, Bunivetch, Shocatz, Slovenes, and others, especially those who live a rural life. In village gatherings (*divân*) the favorite subject of recitations or of stories is the personality of Prince Marko. The narrators are mostly old men; women tell stories and recite only rarely. Besides the stories culled directly from the Karadžić collections there are variations, made up by the singers and narrators, which may be longer or shorter and with more or less original supplementary parts. The contents of the tales about Prince Marko correspond to known songs: sometimes these tales embody the legendary themes of widespread European folktales; other times the subjects of South Slavic folktales are incorporated. In 1971, in the area of the Drave river, Djuro Šarošac collected, along with other songs, one song about Prince Marko. One of the singers who served as a source for this valuable and interesting material was eighty-four-year-old Simon Kokorić of the village of Drávasztára (Starina), near the Yugoslavian border. While collecting ethnographic and folkloric data in the regions of Baranja area Ernö Eperjessy (1968) encountered, by chance, this old man who had a rich imagination and who sang while playing bagpipes. A cobbler by trade, he was a "friend" of the fairies who, according to him, taught him various crafts such as the making of clocks and bagpipes, weaving, basketry, and other trades. He insisted he had magical capabilities inherited from his mother. To prove that the fairies punished him because at one time he did not want to sing to them and play the pipes he showed a burn on his left hand (Dőmőtőr 1968, 1972).

Eperjessy and Dőmőtőr verify that he is really and truly a poor man but that he is esteemed by his fellow citizens and jokes are not made about him. He is often invited to weddings and other feasts to sing and play the pipes. Despite the small number of songs in his repertoire, Eperjessy thinks that it would be useful to pay more attention to him and to try to rescue from oblivion at least part of the treasure he possesses.

Up to now, only three of his songs have been collected: one about fairies, another about Prince Marko, and one about the Hounadis. The song about the fairies, which has no title, and the other "Miloš i vila" [Miloch and the fairy] are only faint memories of Serbo-Croatian folk songs taken from the Karadžić collections: their elements and facts are wholly mixed together and confused. The song of the fairies could be considered as a synthesis of what information can be about them in the songs of these collections. The fairy Ravijoila and the mountain fairies, including the evil Zagorkinje are found in the song. These "sister" fairies can be either noble and generous or treacherous, they recount their adventures and deeds to one another when they meet. Kokorić imputed to the fairy Ravijoila that, after dinner in the king's palace, she

Slit her young son's throat
So this evil race might perish.

(Dőmőtőr 1968:342)

Such a deed is not known in South Slavic folk poetry, but it is found in a modified version in the tales of European peoples.

The song about the hero Prince Marko ("Miloš i vila") is only an impoverished variation of the one from the Karadžić collection. Kokorić remembered only the principal elements of this song: Prince Marko and his chosen brother Duke Miloch, identified by Kokorić and Miloš Obilić, which bears witness to the fact that he knew Serbo-Croatian folk poetry in detail, were traveling on horseback across Mount Mirotch (in the Kokorić song the mountain's name is not mentioned, which means either that he forgot its name or that he had never known it at all). Marko asks his chosen brother to sing to him, but Miloch hesitates since he is afraid of the fairy (again Kokorić does not know that the fairy is jealous of the beautiful voice of Miloch, who has, according to the popular South Slavic folk song "an imperial throat . . . more beautiful than that of the fairy"). However he finally begins to sing; the fairy shoots an arrow to kill him, but Prince Marko catches the fairy and, according to the South Slav song:

He hits the fairy in the chest
While throwing her rudely to the ground,
And beating her with his club,
He knocked her about from right to left,
While beating her with his golden club.

Kokorić's variation says only: "He seized the fairy and threw her to the ground." The fairy in his song, as in the Karadžić one, gathers medicines to heal Miloch. Kokorić does not mention the geographic names which are found abundantly in Karadžić's song: Mount Mirotch, the Poretch region (Porečka krajina), the Vidin region (Vidinska krajina), the Timok waters (voda Timokova), the village of Breg (selo Breg). Kokorić recites the song in decasyllabic verse, but his decasyllables are not always the pure and rhythmic decasyllable of South Slavic epic poetry. In his recitation he also has verses of six, seven, and twelve syllables:

Sing, my brother, without fear of the beautiful fairy;
The fairy does not want to touch any Serb.
. . . .
He speaks softly some words to his Charatz:
"My good Charatz, my dear friend,
Catch the fairy for me!"
. . . .
Charatz threw three spears toward the sky.

(*Narodni kalendar* 1972)

The question arises: where did Kokorić learn these songs? He was illiterate; he could not read for himself the Karadžić collections. He probably heard the songs from his predecessors, as singers and narrators normally learn them, but he simply maintains that he learned them from the fairies who according to his own words, still kept in touch with him even at that time.

During his work as a researcher, Eperjessy encountered another narrator who is also worthy of attention. He was the fisherman Andrija Hideg, from the village of Felsőszentmarton (Gornji Martinci), who died a few years ago at the age of ninety. As he grew old, he went blind, but he kept the gift of narrating in an appealing manner. His father was a Hungarian shepherd; his mother Croatian. He heard the tales he knew from the Croatians while fishing along the banks of the Drave. His repertoire of tales was rich. Almost everything he narrated referred to the personality of Prince Marko. His tales were prose versions of South Slavic folk songs, in which one could recognize the songs' decasyllabic structure. Here are some of their titles: "Prince Marko and the black Arab," in two versions; "The three-headed Arab," "The wedding of Prince Marko," also in two versions; and "Prince Marko and Janko Sibinjanin." These tales are in manuscript form, still unpublished, but the tale "Miloch and the Fairy" was published with the Kokorić song (*Narodni kalendar* 1972). All of Hideg's tales are from the Karadžić song collections, faithfully rendered in prose.

By comparing Kokorić's song and Hideg's tale "Miloš i vila" on the one hand, and the South Slavic epic song "Prince Marko and the fairy" on the other, we can conclude the following: Kokorić's song is an abridged, shortened, verse variation, in contrast to Hideg's tale which is a sweeping narrative interspersed with elements from the imagination of the narrator. Hideg introduced some altogether personal elements, including the seven mountain fairies who lived on Mount Jamina. The youngest of these, one of the actors of the tale, is only seventeen years old. In Hideg's version Marko encourages Miloch, who was healed by the young fairy, to marry her, and Miloch obeys, but in two months he lets her return to her sisters the fairies. Hideg did not follow the epic narrative. He interspersed his narrative with dialogues which resembled conversations of people of his own social environment: "'Don't do it like this,' said Marko. 'Take her as your bride. You will be a better man.'" Or: "She spent two months at his home as his wife, she slept beside him in his bed. After two months passed, she told him: 'Mijo, you have completely neglected me.' 'But, why?'" Marko has wine and some brandy. He commands the fairy to bring the liquor and a glass. She obeys, pours the drink and they drink.

That Hideg learned this tale, and all the others too, in the form of the epic song, is proved by the decasyllabic lines intermingled with the fabric of the narrative: "*'Don't do that, my friend Prince Marko, allow me to go into the green mountain'*", "when they were going from Mount Jamina to another mountain *Prince Marko quickly seized his mace* and threw it toward her", "*So if I do not then heal his eyes*, he will have me burned by fire" (*Narodni kalendar* 1972:66; emphasis added). Moreover, he uses elements characteristic of South Slavic epic poetry: the mace, the golden club, the green mountain, and so on, but Hideg did not remember the names mentioned in the South Slavic epic: Miloch of Pocerje is, according to him, Miloch of Poselje; Mount Jamina is also his own invention.

Kokorić and Hideg prefer not to use the traits of brutality and impulsiveness which are attributed to Prince Marko in the South Slavic epics: they disregard them or tone them down.

The fact that Prince Marko and his chosen brother are the favorite traditional characters among the ethnic groups where folklore materials have been gathered up to the present time is again witnessed by an unpublished song which Vlajko Palavestra heard from Milena Bogdanov, who was born Milena Božić in Deska. This song, which she learned from her father, merits attention, and it is published here in full:

Hola, the falcon looks for a quiet place,
He doesn't want it to be up above on the fir tree,
But in the valley where the tent becomes white,
But in the valley where the tent becomes white.

Hola, in the tent is the heroine,
She drinks the wine and does not worry,
Singing, happy, in her charming voice,
And her song animates the grey falcon;
And her song animates the grey falcon.

Hola, I have served two Serbian heroes,
I have served Miloch and Prince Marko,
Marko taught me to drink wine,
Miloch, to sing beautiful songs;
Miloch, to sing beautiful songs.[1]
                    (Vlajko Palavestra, personal communication, October 29, 1972)

We see that the characteristic features of the two heroes, Marko and Miloch, are pointed out here: Prince Marko is known for his predilection for wine; Miloch for his famous voice.

Traditions and folk songs have been extremely well preserved by the South Slavic ethnic groups in Hungary. A historical factor has contributed to this fact: from the early fifteenth century there were families of great Serbian lords who owned vast feudal estates in these regions. They were formerly the subjects of epic songs. One of these wealthy families, the Jakšićs, whose seat was in Nagylak, was known for legal proceedings between two brothers, Stevan and Dimitrije, over the division of the estate. There even exists a monograph which deals with this subject (Szentkláray 1898). The argument between the two brothers was transformed into song. Because of its beauty, this song is among the best of the South Slavic epics:

"Confide in me my friend the grey falcon,
How do you bear life without wings?"
The falcon answers with a piercing cry:
"Without my wings, life is similar
To the life of the brother who no longer has a brother."[2]
                                                    (Karadžić 1932:575)

---

[1]   Hej, soko bira di će naći mira
      Neće gore na visokoj jeli,
      Već u doli, di se šator beli,
      Već u doli di se šator beli.

      Hej, pod šatorom delija devojka,
      Vino pije, ni briga joj nije,
      Pesumu peva i od glasa mila
      Cisto rastu na sokolu krila,
      Cisto rastu na sokolu krila:

      Hej, služila sam dva srpska junaka,
      Služila sam Miloša i Marka,
      Od Marka sam piti naučila,
      Od Miloša pesme prisvojila,
      Od Miloša pesme prisvojila.

[2]   "Kako ti je, moj sivi sokole,
      Kako ti je bez krila tvojega?"
      Soko njemu piskom odgovara:
      "Meni jeste bez krila mojega,
      Kao bratu jednom bez drugoga."

In his tale "Miloch and the fairy" Hideg remarks: "Listen, Charo, my good horse, as you feel without your limbs, so I feel without my brother."

Current research and collecting expeditions, as well as those to come in the future, will be able not only to give us the answer to the question of how Hideg arrived at this sentence, but also to unmask many important and interesting problems in the domain of the folklore sciences. They will help us to discover how tradition is kept, how it is transmitted from one generation to another, and how it passes from one area to another. We hope that the answers to the numerous questions asked will not be long in coming and that research work will give us some important results.

REFERENCES

DŐMŐTŐR, TEKLA
1968 A vilák ajándéka [The world gift]. *Filológiai Kőzlőny* [*Philological Review*] 14(3–4):339–346.
1972 "Zwie Zauberer aus Südungarn," in *Volkskunde: Festgabe für Leopold Schmidt*. Edited by Klaus Beitl, 381–390. Vienna: Verein für Volkskunde.

EPERJESSY, ERNŐ
1968 Borbála napi hiedelmek, szokások és a nyelvcsere kérdése [St. Barbara's day beliefs and customs and the language question]. *Ethnographia* 79(4):560–587.

KARADŽIĆ, VUK STEFANOVIĆ
1932 *Srpske narodne pjesme* [Serbian folk songs], volume two, Belgrade: Državna Štamparija.

Narodni kalendar
1959–1972 *Narodni kalendar*. Budapest: Demokratskog Saveza Južnih Slovena.

SZENTKLÁRAY, JENŐ
1898 *A Csanád-egyházmegyei plébániák tőrténete* [The Csanád district parish history]. Timisoara (Temesvár), Rumania.

The Rumanian Folklore Calendar and Its Age Categories

EMILIA COMIŞEL

The great variety, originality, and social and artistic merit of the Rumanian folklore calendar gives it an important place in the national culture. It has arisen out of economic and social conditions no longer prevailing, and has retained echoes of a specific view of life and the cosmos, of ancestral spirituality and technical experience, and of literary and musical documents belonging to the successive cultures, pre-Indo-European and Indo-European, at a time prior to the splitting of these into distinct peoples, and finally from some of the direct ancestors of the Rumanians, the Geto-Dacians and the Latins. The assimilation of this cultural treasure by each specific people, according to the psychic factors they possess, and within the framework of local magico-religious systems and specific living conditions, gave birth everywhere to original types of manifestation and development, thus confirming the spiritual originality and creative force of different races. The universality and quasi-universality of certain seasonal ceremonies, founded upon myths, beliefs, and superstitions, and developed from ancient religious practices, is the consequence of a common material and spiritual genetic inheritance. Their permanent function in daily life and their ability to reinforce bonds of solidarity of structure and way of life within the framework of specific societies helps provide a better existence for all, giving assurance of stability in time and space, although in the dialectic process of permanent adaptation to life's demands, mutations in function, form, and content have been experienced. As they are passed down by word of mouth from one generation to the next, these complex manifestations include a certain number of

This work is based on personal research, carried out over more than three decades, generally made in situ, and on the large quantity of material available in the archives of the Ethnological and Folklore Institute at Bucharest, and finally data from known sources (see References).

factors with differing elements, of an economic, magical, religious, judicial, or artistic order, breathing life and vitality into these structures, and giving them precise roles and definite meaning both to community life and to the individual. In the course of the long and complex process of social evolution, the ancient feasts, myths, and symbols consecrated to the pre-Indo-European and Geto-Dacian pantheon gods, changed into rituals of a more utilitarian nature, then into opportunities for collective entertainment, as new elements, of an artistic nature, were introduced. Within the framework of these intrusions at various moments in the evolution of the cycle, that is, these interpellations, dislocations, superimpositions, and accumulations of features, a process comes into being whereby each man does his best to subordinate them to his vital needs and to his cultural-artistic horizon, determined by new conceptions of the world and society. Annually recurring customs become impressive dramatic spectacles enlarged by artistic additions of a more entertaining nature — literary, musical, and choreographic, and though wholly integrated with the life of modern man, relating in different ways to the actual conditions of life and work.

The folklore calendar is founded on the sidereal year, important in terms of agriculture and pastoral production and labor, making it easier for the Rumanian peasant to acquire an organic understanding of this life: a fundamental unity of organic life developing at two cosmic levels, "the vegetal level, considered to be the spring of life, and the human level" (Eliade 1968:258), corresponding to the analogy "woman/field, giving birth/sowing," and "mental synthesis" which has been "essential for the evolution of humanity" and was not "possible until the discovery of agriculture" (Eliade 1968:304).

Formally linked to the ecclesiastical calendar and partially influenced by it, the rural, ethnographic, calendar rests upon dates and periods representing the beginnings and ends of seasons: essential times in the different stages of agricultural and pastoral labor.

In correspondence with changing social conditions, the customs and festivals, and their ceremonies, rituals, and practices, represent complex syncretic actions with differing functions, practiced and respected by both sexes and all ages. The feasts, customs, and rituals refer to several themes: death and the annual renewal in nature; agricultural labor; and daily life, including relationships between young people and within the family. In the past it was normal for the fertility of the soil, and the fecundity of women and animals, indeed the very social equilibrium, to be assured and maintained by the performance of such ceremonies.

Within the framework of these seasonal ceremonies, we can discover several ritual categories: those which are *linked to agricultural and pastoral labor*, such as seed preparation, plowing the fields, sowing and harvesting crops, sheepherding, and transhumance; or those *linked to fixed annual holidays and to the domestic cycle*. By analyzing each rite within the context of the ceremony to which it belongs, several general features emerge: certain ceremonies are universal; others are regional, known only in a limited geographical area or ethnic locality; some have developed artistic aspects having their own peculiar characteristics, with a great variety of theme, style, and composition, from the simple recitation of verbal formulas or the outline of a few dance steps, to the highly artistic, structured choreography, intonation, and rhythm. The same rite may have a different, even a directly opposite, meaning, if performed in different ceremonies — an example being the sprinkling of water in agricultural, wedding, and funeral ceremonies. Also the same rite may be performed in different ways, by one or more age groups. For example, ritual *firelighting*, for purification, fertility, or commemoration purposes, may take place on beaches, in fields or yards, at gravesides or in the middle of the village, in various forms — a pyramid; a wheel covered with flaming straw; special torches called *hodaitze*, made from branches broken from trees in a certain way, or gathered in the village, or even procured in secret — on certain fixed dates or during certain times of the year. Some ceremonies practised in the past exclusively by one age category have since been adopted by others — for example, the *colindat* and the *Udatu* [ritual sprinkling of water on young girls]. The time and place are important conditions in the practising of rites, but some may happen without any fixed date or place established for their performance; others may be celebrated at different times of the year and at different times of the day or night. Some ceremonies may be repeated during the course of the year — for example Udatu at Epiphany, Shrove Tuesday, St. Theodore's Day (the first Saturday of Lent), on Easter Monday or Tuesday, on May 1, and so on.

By analyzing these various syncretic manifestations, it is obvious that the full value and meaning cannot be understood, and moreover cannot be studied adequately, *without* relation to the age categories, each of which had a particular function and position in the framework of the ancient village, and whose organization of social and cultural life was strongly regulated by tradition. Taking into account these typological categories observed by the Rumanian ethnomusicologist Constantin Brăiloiu (1932), and by applying them to the seasonal ceremonies, we are able to delineate the following age categories: *children* (sometimes their sex is designated in a particular ritual); *young people* (girls and boys); *couples married for one year*; *mature couples*; and *women* (adult and the aged).

However, it was the young bachelors who featured in the greatest number of functions: the "initiation" of adolescent girls (the principal of these being the *hora*, a round dance); organization of relationships between young girls and boys and between family members; organization of feasts and community entertainments during the year; respecting the traditional norms of morality and the perpetuation of the species; and ensuring the fertility of the soil by virtue of their cultural affinity with the forces of nature. Their judicial function was no less important, ranging from moral sanctions to corporal punishment; the *bricelatu* and the *alegerea craiului* [electing the prince]; the *strigarea peste sat* [outcry over the village]. Although they will soon disappear, the young men's "associations" still retain significant elements and attributes which are probably traces of brotherhood initiations (Eliade 1968, ch. 4), often concerning strict regulations, by which one could not enter the respective brotherhood without fulfilling certain *age qualifications* (from 16 years to engagement), tests of *valor and virility* (ability to use arms, horsemanship), of *moral behavior*, of the *learning of customs*, and of the candidate's *artistic repertory*. Then again they were submitted to various strict obligations and taboos: money payments, meetings on certain days and at precise times, exile from home for a limited period, a solemn oath, abstinence from dancing, speaking, and so on. Certain of these initiation rites remain: a candidate may be tossed in a blanket three times or may even be thrashed, a *juni* [youth] custom, and so on.[1] Each association or brotherhood[2] is brought to order at St. Nicholas, on Easter Sunday or between Easter and Whitsun. They each have their leaders, their particular jargon and their well-defined characteristics, their insignia (banners, firearms, a club, a sword or sceptre, jewelry, special ceremonial costumes, and so on).

In Table 1 there is a detailed presentation of the various customs and of the age categories which as a rule practise them. Note that the great majority of participants are young people; that the customs are grouped around particular dates and periods of the year. Note the times when these customs are practised, the extremely diverse terminology for the same custom, and the repetition of some customs during the cycle.

Some feasts are respected or honored by means of certain taboos, such as on eating particular foods, performing certain tasks, dancing, enjoying oneself; others are commemorated by lighting fires in different places, and doing charitable acts (*pomeni*) in remembrance of the dead, the *moşi* [ancestors]; or bestowing blessing on the countryside, animals, men, freeing them from disease, protecting them from wild beasts, evil spirits. Other feasts include a complete artistic repertoire.

Certain ceremonies linked to the calendar year will now be described, revealing their internal structure, their significance, and the various ways,

---

[1]   These are two regulations of the *juni* of Brasov (of 1881 and 1894) known to this day. See Muşlea (1930); Chelcea (1942); Dimitrie Cantemir (1872–1901); and Buhociu (1971).
[2]   *Ceata junilor* [group of youths]. They have various names like *bute* [farriers]. Their leader is called *primar* [first], *jude* [judge], or *birău* [mayor], and his aids *chizăş, pirgar, cămăraş, vătaf mic*, and so on.

Table 1.   The Rumanian folklore calendar in 1972

Date	Occasion	Participants	Time
The winter solstice and the winter cycle (December 23 to January 6)			
Dec. 23–24	*pizari, prichi, kiţu-miţu*, and star songs (with or without stars)	children	day
Dec. 24–26	*colinde* (with or without masks)	young people	night
	profane theater	young people	day, evening
	religious theater	children	day
Dec. 31–Jan. 1	*colinde*	young people	night
Jan. 1	*Plugul* (with or without a masked procession), with *buhaiu*	young people	night
	sorcova, plugușorul, Vasilca	children or adults	day or evening
	ghicitul (*vergel* or *leruit* [predictions])	young women	night
	traditional fires	children, men	day, night
Jan. 6	*Boboteaza* [Epiphany]: horse racing	young men	day
	ghicit [divining]	girls	night
	udatu [sprinkling of young girls], continues between Epiphany and Shrove Tuesday	young people	morning
Jan. 8	*ziua babelor* [old women's day]	women	evening, night
Cîslegile, from Epiphany to Shrove Tuesday, a period rich in weddings			
Jan. 16–17	*Sf. Petru de iarnă* [St. Peter of Winter]		
Jan. 16–18	*Circovii de iarnă*		
Jan. 25–Feb. 2	*Filipii*		
Feb. 1	*Trifon* [Tryphon]		
Feb. 2	*stretenia, Ziua ursului* [bear's day], *Gurban* or *Arizan*	adults	day
Feb. 1–3	*Filipii*		
Feb. 10	*Aralampie* [St. Charalanbos]		
Feb. 11	*Sf. Vasile* [St. Basil]		
Feb. 12	*Sîmbăta morţilor* [Remembrance Saturday] *focuri* [fires], *pomeni* [alms]	women	day
Feb. 24	*Dragobetele: infrăţitul tinerilor* [young people's fraternity]	children, young people, girls	day
Mar. 1	*mărţişorul*	children, young girls	day

Table 1. (*continued*)

Date	Occasion	Participants	Time
Lent (*March 8 to April 22*)			
Mar. 8	*Lăsata secului: strigarea peste sat* [outcry over the village], *priveghi* [vigil] or *moroleucă*, also on March 14, April 17, 19, 20 *cucii* [cuckoos], with masks; *focuri* [fires]	young people young people young people	day, evening day, evening day, evening
Mar. 8–15	*Săptămîna nebunilor* [Fools' week]: *ziua cornilor, maimusi*, etc.	young people	evening
Mar. 9	horse racing, alms	young people	day
Mar. 9	*muceninii*, [market] alms, *Dați, copii, cu maiele*: beginning of plowing	women, children	day
Mar. 14	*Toaderii* [St. Theodore] *Homanu* *Bîlciu lu Sîn Toader* *haide-n tîrg*, (Sîmti)	young people young women those married during the year children, young people	day morning, evening morning, evening day
Mar. 17	*Sf. Alexie* [St. Alexander]		
Spring equinox (*March 21*)			
Mar. 25	*Bunavestire* [Annunciation]		
Mar. 26	*Blagoveştenie*: fires	women	day
Apr. 14	*Lăzărelul*	women	day
Apr. 15	*Floriile, moşii de florii* [Saturday before Palm Sunday]	women	day
Apr. 18	fires	women	day
Apr. 19	*Toconele*, fires	children	day
Apr. 22	*Paştile* [Easter Saturday]: *plugaru* [plowman] alegerea craiului [choosing the prince] *bricelatu* (*vergelatu*) *milioara* (*lioara* or *jocu felegii*)	young people young people young people young people or children	evening, day evening, day evening, day evening, day
Apr. 22–23	*udatu* [sprinkling] *însurăţitu* (*Mătcălău*), fires; also on April 29	young people, girls everyone	day, morning evening, day morning
Apr. 22–29	*junii* [young people]	young people	night
Apr. 23	*Sîngeorz* [St. George's Day] *Arieţu* (*sîmbra oilor, alesu* or *roscolu*) Govia horse racing *udatu* *rouratu* *infrăţitu* (*mătcălău*) *ghicitu* [prediction] *focu vie* [roaring fire]	young people adults (men and women) young people, girls young people young people, girls girls everyone young people, girls shepherds	day three days day, evening day day morning day evening, night day

Table 1. (continued)

Date	Occasion	Participants	Time
Spring equinox (March 21)			
Apr. 25	*Marcu boilor* [St. Mark the Apostle]	adults	evening, day
Apr. 26	*Paştele blajinilor* [Easter for the good-natured]		
Apr. 30	*udatu*	young people, girls	day
	fires	everyone	morning, evening
May 1	*armindenu* [May-day]	everyone	morning, evening
after May 15	*udatu*	those married during the year	morning
May 25	*Sf. Ioan* [St. Joan], date not fixed:		
	Caloïan (Scaloïan, Ene, Mumuliţă de ploiţă, etc.);	children	day
	paparuda (păpălugă, dodoloaie, etc.)	young girls, children	day
	sulu	children	evening, day
Jun. 1	*Rusalii: căluşu*	young people	evening, day
	bou înstruţat [decorated ox]	young people	evening, day
	infrăţit	young people, girls	evening, day
	rusitori		
Jun. 9	*Aliseiu*		
Jun. 19	*Ispas*		
Summer solstice (June 22–23)			
Jun. 24	*Drăgaica*	young girls	day, evening
	fires	everyone	evening
Jun. 29	*Sf. Petru* [St. Peter]: *Cununa (buzduganu)*	young people, adults	day, evening
Jul. 20	*St Ilie (Sîntilia)* [St. Elias the Prophet]	young people, adults	day, evening
	fires	young people, girls	day, evening
Jul. 27	St. Panteleimon: horse racing	young people, girls	day, evening
Autumn equinox (September 22–23)			
Sep. 8	*Sf. Maria* [Nativity of Our Lady]		
Sep. 24	*Sf. Tecla* [St. Thecla the Martyr]		
Sep. 26–28	*Berbecarii*		
Oct. 18	*Sf. Luca* [St. Luke the Apostle]		
Oct. 26	*Sîmedru* [St. Demetrius]: *Drumitriţele* fires	everyone	day, evening
Nov. 8	*Moşii de toamnă (Sf. Mihail and Gavril* [St. Michael and St. Gabriel the Archangel])		
Nov. 9–14	*Filipii de toamnă*		
Nov. 30	*Sf. Andrei* [St. Andrew the Protoklite]: *ghicitu* [prediction]	young people	night

historically and geographically speaking, in which they are known, plus the themes and structure of the artistic repertory.

WINTER CEREMONIES

In the past, winter cycle customs were probably practised exclusively by young bachelors. They were centered on the pagan feast of the resurrection of the sun, and on beliefs referring to the significance of New Year's Day (up to the sixteenth and seventeenth centuries the beginning of the year was celebrated on March 1), and of the first day of the agricultural year. According to ancestral belief, all changes (of season, age, social state) needed to be accompanied by well-defined rites, symbolic acts which purify by means of their influence and repetition — according to the recurrent ritual drama of death and resurrection during the winter and spring cycles, when zoomorphic and phytomorphic masks are used.

During this time, men tried to predict the future by observing the phenomena happening around them, and by trying to influence the future with all kinds of active and passive rites: predictions (*ghicitul* [fortune-telling]);[3] the *colindatul* [active rituals] of children and young people, sometimes with masks; and *urarea* [wishes], which augur well for a happy and prosperous new year. Such wishes might be effected by means of a plow, real or symbolic, by a *bouhai*, a membranophonic instrument, a friction drum, comprising a taut skin stretched over a hollow wooden vessel, a cask, with a string across it, which when drawn recalls the lowing of oxen at the plow; by *sorcova*,[4] or *vasilica*;[5] in the *staging of wedding productions*; by impressive *masked processions*;[6] by *mime and drama productions*, for example the masque parodying death and resurrection; in the lavish *communal banquets*; by *songs and dances*; in the *exchange of gifts*; by the *sprinkling of young girls*; by the *lighting of fires* in various places, and the *ritual of encircling the fire* and *jumping over it*; and by *horse racing* (*incuratul cailor*).

As to the colindat, young people are the main participants, going in groups, from house to house, singing and reciting verses with special or satirical themes, accompanied by wind instruments, such as bagpipes, flutes, or more modern instruments; membranophones, such as the

---

[3] Also called *vergel* or *leruit*, often accompanied by special sung verses.
[4] Young tree shoots or twigs decorated with flowers.
[5] A doll or pig's head, decorated with ribbons and flowers, and carried by gypsies singing special verses.
[6] Typical disguises are those of a goat, a stag, a bird's head with a long beak, and other zoomorphic masks: camel, horse, ram, billy-goat, and ox. Others are disguised as grotesque characters, as old men, old women, as a man and his wife, as a shepherd, a herdsman, a gypsy, a priest, a choirboy, a doctor, or a devil. Some are covered in straw; some carry bells, large and small, or silent flutes or drums. A pig's bladder may be worn on the head.

bouhai or the *dobă*, a small drum decorated with leaves, and noise-making objects: large and small bells, whips, chains, and so on. In fertility rites the flute–drum association is common all over the world (Collaer 1963:38). The colindat, in common with many other ceremonies, has a well-defined structure; it develops in stages, in various places, with certain regional differences as follows: (1) the preparations, rehearsals to learn the procedure, may be made by young girls in the evenings — a laborious way of spending a winter evening; or they may take place at a particular house, with a family, a *gazdă* [host], chosen as the focal point for the rituals; (2) the choice of the leader and his adjutants; (3) the collection, in the host house, for the final festive meal of all the food and drink received as presents by members of the group; (4) the engagement of the instrumentalist who accompanies the *colindători* [*colinde* singers] — the word *colindat* itself meaning the execution of the repertoire, which varies according to the age, sex, occupation, and position of those for whom the good wishes are intended, as well as being influenced by the place where the colindat happens (at the roadside, beneath windows, indoors, and so on); (5) the dance to which members of the receiving family are also invited; (6) the giving and receiving of gifts and thanks for them, sometimes in the form of humorous verse; and (7) *the last of the banquets and holidays*.

The children's colinde is in fact a request for a particular present such as money or confectionery, but it includes a wish for prosperity and happiness. Various little rituals, such as searching the ashes in the hearth, or touching the walls of the house or the stables with special twigs, may also be incorporated.

The young people's colinde is different, however, referring to wide-ranging story themes, often of a legendary nature, with agrarian, hunting, pastoral, nuptial, or cosmogonic themes referring to abundance and fertility. Religious themes, with apocryphal subjects or subjects owing something to folklore, were added later by the church and adopted by the children, sometimes carrying a star made of colored paper, hence *star songs*.

The tunes belong to various styles enveloping different stages of musical development. The music is for the most part of early composition, the tunes being simple, syllabic, based on one or two formulas either identically repeated or changing in rhythm, which may be giusto-syllabic or *aksak* (Brăiloiu 1932). The architectonic form is enlarged by one or two refrains. The sound material is organized according to archaic principles: bi- tri- tetra- and pentatones, with hexatonic or heptatonic systems occurring more rarely.

The rite determines the poetic and musical structure of the artistic repertoire, which may include asymmetric forms, premodal structures, complex rhythms originating from several systems, and the grouping of pieces in a suite. The colinde, with its profane and optimistic contents in wishing everyone a happy and prosperous new year, has helped greatly to maintain confidence in a better future.

SPRING CEREMONIES

Another conspicuous day in the calendar is *lăsata secului* [Shrove Tuesday], the eve of the day when fasting for Lent begins. Some of the ceremonies from the winter cycle are carried over into this period, with others whose celebration can continue for up to a week. These include *strigarea peste sat,*[7] *cucii* [cuckoos], *săptămina nebunilor* [fools' week],[8] *Toaderii* [St. Theodore's Day], *înfîrtăţitu* or *însurăţitu,*[9] *homanu,*[10] *tîrgu mireselor* [a fair for people married during the year].

Strigarea peste sat is a complex ceremony, having several functions, religious, purifying, and restoring the forces of nature.[11] Young boys, standing opposite each other, near enormous fires, shout across the village, in satirical or humorous verse, the names of couples in love, unmarried girls, and those who have transgressed the traditional moral code, or who would like to impose a new set of morals in opposition to the taste and sensibility of the community, or finally they cry out the particular moral failings of members of the community. The custom has a deeply moral and educational meaning. Near the fires, which pairs of young people and children sometimes jump over, huge wheels covered in straw and flowers revolve,[12] torches are carried, or rings of fire are drawn by means of circular movements of the arm, holding burning embers in the fingertips; they also use sticks covered in burning rags and having an old

[7]   Also called *hodaiţe, citirite,* or *priveghi* [vigil], from *per vigilium,* a vigil for the ancestors, a term which shows affinity with the cult of the dead. It has no fixed date.

[8]   This has other names implying trickery: *fărşang, ziua cornilor, maimozi, măimusi,* and so on.

[9]   An old form of social relations between villagers, the custom of "being intimate like brothers" (*însurăţitul* for girls and *înfîrtăţitul* for boys) is highly developed in some areas. It is accompanied by several ceremonial acts, such as making crowns and bouquets of flowers; and eating the *colac* [bread in the shape of a circle], in certain areas called *brăduleţ.* In some villages it is cut with a silver coin. The crowns of flowers are used for kissing through; and the participants dance around a fruit tree or in a circle one after the other; the communal meal has a special menu. The ceremony is described with verses in which one calls upon health and friendship. The recitative melody is based on a two-note chord having a structure of a fourth. Sometimes it is developed further.

[10]   A *homan* song is an incantation against going bald. The song is preceded by picking the *homan* or *iarba mare* plant, which is rewarded by bread and salt (left at its root); by fires, feasts, and dances. The songs are varied and belong to several stages of evolution of music. A song may be slow, of good quality, and based on the prepentatonic minor, or it may be recitative, in a prepentatonic major. They may share a single phrase, possibly with differing cadence.

[11]   See Varagnac (1948); Marian (1898–1901); Manolescu (1967); and Comişel (1967).

[12]   A rite found among the solstice ceremonies of numerous European peoples (Mircea Eliade, personal communication).

shoe at the end. Eventually the stick and shoe is thrown away over the graveyard, having first made all sorts of shapes. In certain areas, the rite is associated with the sound of the horn or the trumpet, the ringing of bells, with the sprinkling of water on young girls, and the bathing of young boys (at one time it was believed that these baths protected the boys from disease throughout the year). Elsewhere, masks are worn, during fool's week, cucii, and St. Theodore's, men dress as women, make up their faces, cover their heads with large leather masks, and with colored paper decorated with feathers and reeds.[13] And these carnival revelers come and go throughout the village, going into houses, disturbing the young women and girls' evenings, jumping, dancing, singing, reciting satirical poems and making the women and girls dance. The "cuckoos", dressed as hunters, ladies, kings and queens, drummers, janissaries, married couples, barbers, or warders, carry sticks with torn shoes or a piece of rubber hanging at the end, with which they touch passers-by to protect them against evil. They are then harnessed to the plow to make three furrows round the village. They receive gifts, and in the evening there is a festival comprising dancing and a large meal. Happy times and cheerful dances close the festivities.

Other spring ceremonies must be kept going and followed by the young people, in which they celebrate the renewal of plant life, and the defeat of winter and the forces of darkness. Some of them will retain memories of ancient feasts consecrated to the gods of vegetation and fertility (Lazăr, Caloianu, and so on), very old beliefs concerning rites to hurry along the arrival of the new season (children and men turn the soil with their feet and with sticks, adults "threaten" the winter, and so on), to stimulate and regenerate the forces of nature, to assure "manna" to the cultivated fields and to the animals, by means of "energy centers" (woman, purity, trees, lavish meals, rejoicings). The regenerative power of these "centers" is based upon the idea of solidarity which the ancestors linked with agriculture and women (Eliade 1968:ch. 9).[14] Even to this day fires are lit on particular days; houses and other buildings are decorated with boughs and leaves (young men put them at their sweetheart's doors); boys and girls cover themselves in green leaves (*síngeorz*, *paparuda*) reciting or singing verses of invocation and good wishes, performing games (*lilioara*) and going through the village in two-wheeled carts covered with grass (*govia*). In addition to ceremonies common to other times of the year, they celebrate those relating to agricultural work: *plugaru* [plowman], *alegerea craiului*, *bricelatu*, *junii*. They consist of a certain number of

---

[13]   The masks have specific names: "emperor", "demon" and so on. The maskers go through the village making jokes and grotesque gestures. The *Toaderi* are mythological beings and have nothing in common with the St. Theodore of the ecclesiastical calendar.
[14]   Up to the beginning of the century, only women had the right to sow the corn and to reap. Even today, certain plants are sown only by women, and thus accompanied by a complex ritual (Eliade 1968:29).

ceremonies having regional differences and lasting for several days, for example, for the "plowman" ceremony, the young man who was the first to plow his field is chosen, with a few helpers, who send the invitations. Often a child's blouse is thrown from the top of the church bell-tower; and if nobody catches it a new choice is made. The plowman is decorated with leaves and has straw attached to his feet, belt, and hat, which also bears giblets and a reddened egg. He is then carried on his friends' shoulders, at the end of a harrow, up to the nearest river and thrown in. Then those present are sprinkled with water before returning to the hero's home for the beginning of the festivities. Sometimes the action is complicated by a trial in which the guilty's punishment consists of blows with a rod or small board (*bricela*) on the soles of the feet. The trial is conducted in front of the church, while the culprit, held by his feet and hands, face downward, is carried round the church. Also a standard (*steag*) is flown from the roof of the *plugar*'s house to send out good wishes. There is dancing and a meal consisting of food brought by the girls, who give their partners red and white eggs for each dance — an opportunity to get to know one another with marriage in view. After the feast, the young people are entertained at the homes of those couples newly married during the year.

Fools' week, one of the prettiest, most complex and original spring customs of the *junii* still exists in a small area in a disjointed form. Made up of several ceremonies and rites, the custom lasts a week and happens in a variety of places traditionally consecrated to its practice (on high ground, in front of the church, in the road, or in the center of the village). The meaning of certain rites has not yet been discovered, but others are surely reminders of the sun cult, known to the Geto-Dacians, in which feasts and processions took place on high ground. Certain ritual youth functions (relations with the forces of nature and with girls) or matrimonial rites, and certain initiation and marriage practices, during a period when excesses of all kinds, festivals, banquets, and so on, are deemed necessary for the regeneration of nature, are also reminiscent of this cult. In *ingroparea vătafului* [burial of the group leader], branches are placed in front of the leader's house, and commemorative rites to put evil to flight are performed — gunshots and bell ringing: shots fired from special weapons called *tresturi*, special bells rung only by young men and women.

The *ceata junilor*, consisting of fifteen to fifty people, elects its leader and his helpers: *vătaf mare* [great leader], *vameş mare* [great officer], *vames mic* [petty officer], the only ones who are allowed to carry the *buzdugan* [club], a kind of mace in bronze, lead, or wood, and to organize entertainments for the week (in the past, for the whole year). Each of these three in turn is required to offer a meal to the whole group, every evening. The *juni* wear costumes with garlands of flowers over them, and ribbons on their hats; they take up arms, small or even large bells, and masks. Two of them are disguised as patriarch and precentor. Preparation begins a fortnight before Easter when they go to high ground and form a circle (*horă*), each person throwing the club into the air three times, and being required to catch it before it falls to the ground. Those who do not manage this are held up to ridicule and have to pay a fine. Beginners are welcome (at one time with special rites) to practise wielding the baton, to dance, and so on. The ceremonies of throwing the baton, of leaving the *vătaf*, and the lavish meals with special dishes, which the young people and the audience share, take place every day. In addition, on the Monday, the young men leave in three groups, with the *lautars* [fiddlers], in leaf-covered wagons, to get the eggs they receive, presented in a certain way, from the girls, who give them food and drink after sprinkling them with water (and later perfume). On the Wednesday the young people go riding, adorned, both riders and horses, with garlands of flowers, carrying fir trees which they plant at their leaders' or sweethearts' doors. Masked people arrive, moving grotesquely and playing the fool; there is a dance with the girls who had not until then been permitted to do so. On the Thursday each young man from one of the leaders' houses is thrown three times over a blanket, a practice repeated the following day with those absent the previous evening, but this time in public. The "burial" of the leader includes the whole funeral ritual, songs and lamentations; the leader is tied to a ladder and carried to the top of the hill, where he is released to slide down it; a special dance, which is also known at weddings, called *cățeaua* [bitch], is performed, but this is practised more or less in secret. In it young men strip to the waist, those who are slow being beaten with straps. Under the influence of the church, custom has experienced some modification: the addition of a large number of riders grouped in various categories; the performing of religious formulas, the laying down of green branches at crucifixes beside the road; and fixing crucifixes to the fir trees which are carried.

Certain evolutionary aspects of the *arminden* customs are very interesting. A tree is left at someone's door on March 1, often at a girl's by a boyfriend. This custom has gradually acquired additional significance, becoming a symbol of beneficent power, of love, fertility, and of family prosperity. Children go around gently tapping houses, stables, cow stalls, and animals with green willow branches, which are then burnt to safeguard the men and animals from evil, and to keep away hail, thunderstorms, and so on. This also became a distinctive sign of the leader's house in certain customs, and later a symbol for international workers' freedom.

SUMMER CEREMONIES

During the cycle of summer feasts which reflect man's unbounded happiness, and also his care not to exhaust the soil, besides the events which are constantly repeated (*înfârtâţit*, *udatu* [sprinkling], and horse racing) we find ceremonies and rites invoking rain: *caloïan* [dolls], *paparuda*, or relating to the beginning and end of harvest: *Drăgaïca*, *cununa* [crown], and *căluşu*, a symbolic dance. Apart from the Drăgaïca and *căluş*, the rites have no fixed date nowadays.

Lazărul and Drăgaïca are two customs having certain elements in common: the *mireasa* [bride] and the *mirele* [bridegroom], bearing small crowns of flowers and leaves on their heads; the *steagul* [banner]; gifts received in kind; and an expanded repertoire (a unique kind of suite composed of one or several vocal melodies, with a poetic text, followed by some dances, and either the Lazărul, performed by six- to twelve-year-old girls, or the Drăgaïca, danced only by virgin girls who are good dancers). Lazărul is a survival from the ancient cult of the god of plant life, whereas Drăgaïca is a complex rite concerning fertility at the beginning of the harvest. For Drăgaïca a bridegroom is always chosen, though in fact it is a girl in disguise, with an axe on her shoulder, whereas the other girls, adorned with wild flowers and carrying "swords" (sticks), are dressed in white, a symbol of purity. Also wearing necklaces and bracelets, and infants' clothes tied to their hands and waists, they go from house to house, singing and dancing. One of the Lazărul themes concerns the mourning for the loss of a child who died in a forest. A Drăgaïca poem describes the custom concerning the coming of harvest. The taboo against leaving the group for three (or seven) years, and on entering the church, is similar in the *căluş* custom.

During the period of ripening, prehistoric man tried to influence the forces of nature, knowing essentially that rain, if it came at the required time, constituted the main element for a prosperous year, so the paparuda custom had a precise date in the past, and was also performed every time there was a drought. Nowadays the performance is truncated: in place of poetry there are merely verbal formulas to invoke rain and wishes for a good crop. A little girl or boy is covered in foliage arranged in a special way, goes along the village streets, enters houses, singing and dancing, and is sprinkled with water. Little girls aged between five and seven years accompany the child, sing, and receive gifts. Little by little the custom has been modified, firstly through its adoption by small children, then by gypsy children, nowadays it has nearly disappeared.

Caloïan (or *scaloïan*, *ene*, *mumuliţă de ploiţă*, and so on) retains mythological and festive elements from the god of plant life who dies and is reborn every year. Children make one or several dolls, usually of clay, and having special names; they are placed on a piece of wood and covered with flowers, red eggshell, and lighted candles. The children simulate a funeral ceremony, with lamentations and the service sung by a child dressed as a priest; the doll is then buried in cultivated fields or near a well, to be disinterred three days later and taken to the edge of a stream where the children throw it into the water along with the lighted candles and flowers, at the same time throwing water over each other. Then respect for the dead (*pomana*) is shown by the funeral meal, food being brought by the parents. The young people in the village also take part in the final rejoicing. If there is not enough food, the young women wrap up a rolling pin to resemble a baby and go from house to house asking for more.

The harvest rites and ceremonies are enriched by artistic elements. For example cununa, a ritual concerning the last sheaf of corn, which is known to many Europeans and non-Europeans alike, comprises several ceremonies, including the departure of a number of girls and boys (field workers) in a procession, accompanied by *lautars* [fiddlers]. They go to the fields which require reaping, and when they have finished their work, make one or even several crowns using the nicest ears of corn, and place the crown on the head of a "pure" young girl (or boy), and return to the house chosen for a meal, that is, to the person who owns the field. On the way they sing together, in heterophony, songs with stories derived from literature, some belonging to the wedding ceremony; they sprinkle water on the one wearing the crown; and on arrival at the welcoming house, recite an "oration" made up of comical verses, with fanciful elements describing all the stages of work in the field, from plowing to baking the bread, which resembles the *pluguşor* of the New Year; they express wishes for prosperity, health and happiness; they attempt to carry off the crown, as in the marriage ritual; to run three times round the table laden with food; and they eat their meal together accompanied by songs and dances. In particular regions, the last sheaf is tied with red string as an offering to the spirit, to the soil, to the wheat, and is kept indoors; the thread may be plaited in a special way. The poetry and songs are more varied than those in other customs. Besides the mythological theme glorifying the forces of nature, by way of a dispute between the sisters Sun and Wind, there are themes concerning former work relationships between farmers and shepherds, descriptions of the customs, and so on. The melodies have a serious character and a high artistic standard.

AUTUMN CEREMONIES

The cycle of autumn feasts is not so rich in its manifestation of folk arts.

For St. Demetrius (*Sînmedru*), when the agricultural year is over, fires are lit, children, and in the past young people too, dance around and shout: *"Hai la focu lu Sînmedru"* ["Come and see St. Demetrius' fire"],[15] and the burning wheels are spun again. The adults perform all kinds of rites, to protect themselves from the coming bad weather in winter and

[15]   The French have the same custom (Varagnac 1948).

the animals from all evil forces, involving various work and eating taboos, fires, and acts of charity (*pomeni*) in remembrance of their ancestors (*moşi*). The present names of these special days are significant: *mărcinii* [thistles], *Filipii de toamnă*, *berbecarii* [goats], *martinii* [bears].

The analysis of the folklore calendar helps us to discover more about the ancient culture of the Rumanian people which keeps its essential heritage as its base but is further enriched by traits that are essentially new. Some of the calendric customs are widely diffuse, common to many peoples in Europe and Asia. All these elements from the folkloric calendar reveal an archaic origin, where it is possible to discover traces of old cults of the sun, of plant life, of the dead, of the waters, and of animals (the ox, the bear, and so on). The great diversity, originality and antiquity of the folklore calendar proves the continuity of the Rumanians' presence in this region, as the heirs to an ancient culture which they have adopted and assimilated creatively. Moreover, it also proves a unity of form and content in the calendrical customs, out of which interesting regional differences have arisen. After two thousand years these particularly complex customs, having originated in prehistoric times, have lost at least some of their old meanings through conditions created by technical, economic, and social revolution, but remain as folk manifestations of great artistic value providing an entertaining social quality.

REFERENCES

BRĂILOIU, CONSTANTIN
   1932   *Esquisse d'une méthode de folklore musical*. Paris: Fischbacher.
BUHOCIU, OCTAVIAN
   1971   Über den Rumänischen Burschenbund. *Kurier der Rumänischstudenten* 11:21–23.
CHELCEA, ION
   1942   Organizarea tradiţională a tineretului în viaţa satelor noastre [Traditional youth organizations in our village life]. *Revista Fundaţiilor Regale* 9(5):340–362. Bucharest.
COLLAER, PAUL
   1963   Carnaval et rites printaniers. *Bulletin de la Société Royale Belge d'Anthropologie et de Préhistoire* 73:29–43.
COMIŞEL, EMILIA
   1967   *Folclor muzical* [Musical folklore]. Bucharest: Editura Didactică şi Pedagogică.
DIMITRIE CANTEMIR, VOIVODE OF MOLDAVIA
   1872–1901   *Operele principelui Demetriu Cantemiru* [Principal works of Dimitrie Cantemir], volume one: *Descriptio Moldaviae* [Description of Moldavia]. Edited by A. Papiu Ilarianu. Bucharest: Societatea Academica Româna. (Originally published 1715.)
ELIADE, MIRCEA
   1968   *Traité d'histoire des religions*. Paris: Payot. (Originally published 1953.)

MANOLESCU, GABRIEL
  1967 Despre originile, semnificaţiale şi tipologia unui obicei străvechi: strigarea peste sat [On the origins, significance, and typology of an ancient custom: the outcry over the village]. *Folclor Literar* 1. Timisoara.

MARIAN, SIMION FLORIAN
  1898–1901 *Sěrbătorile la Români* [Holidays of the Rumanians], three volumes. Bucharest: Editiunea Academieĭ Romăne.

MUŞLEA, ION
  1930 *Obiceiul junilor braşoveni* [Customs of the youth of Brasov]. Cluj: Institut de Arte Grafice "Ardealul".

VARAGNAC, ANDRÉ
  1948 *Civilisation traditionelle et genres de vie*. Sciences d'Aujourd'hui. Paris: Albin-Michel.

PART FIVE

Aspects of the Musical Process

The Role of Songs for Children in the Formation of Musical Perception

GHIZELA SULIŢEANU

Study of the psychological aspects of the "children's" folk song repertory highlights two important problems that have hitherto been neglected in ethnomusicology: firstly, little is known about the category of folk songs usually called lullabies, and secondly, methodical study has rarely been attempted, possibly because of past failures. However, current developments in ethnomusicology would suggest that psychology should receive as much attention as acoustics, physiology, aesthetics, or sociology, in explaining all aspects of musical folklore.

Because a musical event is a conscious human activity, we must investigate thoroughly its means of expression, so that we may reach ground that is common to many sciences concerned with the psychophysiological nature during the first phylo- and ontogenetical stages of evolution. The psychology of the child should, in the last analysis, provide the decisive arguments.

By the category of folklore designated "for children" we understand in fact two subcategories of songs performed by those who take care of the child. The function of these songs is either to lull a child to sleep, in which case they are lullabies, or to amuse the child when he is awake by lifting him up in the arms, playing with his fingers and palms, tickling him, moving his hands and feet, teaching basic body movements, responses to the natural environment, and so on. I have called these *amusement songs* (Suliţeanu 1969a). These two subcategories are not sung to children of exactly the same age group, but more consecutively, since lullabies may be sung to a child of two months up to about two-and-a-half years, whereas the amusement songs usually being at seven to nine months and continue up to about four to five years, by which time the child has his own repertoire.

This folklore repertoire appears to be essential to the development of children's musical perception, and at the same time it may provide information about the very sources of music in human experience.[1] Thus the folklore repertoire for children becomes an important element in the development of musical perception. It is the means by which a gradual transition is made from the auditive perception of the first year of life to the formation of basic musical nuclei. These nuclei will form the base of the future musical language which the child will begin to appropriate from the third year of life, the period in which music appears to us to be perceived and consciously performed. Up to this stage the child remains totally submissive to the sounds heard in his environment.

The music of the songs is performed by adults, who intuitively use melodies and rhythms that may more easily be understood by children. This musical language is made up of primary elements, and appears in children's songs as a manifestation of instinctive creation,[2] handed down as part of the body of education, knowledge, and culture that has accumulated during the millennia in which human thought has evolved.[3]

In these songs, communication between adult and child involves two different operations. On the one hand there is the performance of the adult in a language accessible to children; and on the other hand, there is the process by which the child develops his musical perception and then performs consciously — a process that does not depend on the adult performance for its social value.

Characteristic features of children's songs are the musical nuclei of the intervals of minor second, perfect fourth, major third and minor third as well as a series of short musical motifs obtained by combining them.

I   II

---

[1] There are attempts by ethnomusicologists to discover the sources of music by tracing the evolution of musical expression by comparative studies of the music of tribal cultures. A more suitable approach to this problem would be to study the formation of musical language in the ontogenetic evolution of the child.

[2] The results of the experiment designed to find out the origins, genesis and structure of the melodies of lullabies, confirms their psychophysiological nature. With the aid of a heterodyne tone-producing apparatus a transcription was made of the parlando performance on the words *hani-nani* and *lule-lule*, executed during the rocking. By noting, in hertz, the rhythmical parlando of the sounds reproduced by the apparatus, as well as their musical transpositions, one can detect a correspondence which provides evidence that the simple intonation generated by the "rocking" function of these words releases musical nuclei that are specific to lullabies (Suliţeanu 1969b, 1970).

[3] Even when some evolved melodies appear in the subcategory of lullabies, having originated from other categories (songs or dances), they are subjected to rhythmical modifications and the addition of onomatopoeic phrases and musical fragments necessary to the function of lulling children to sleep.

All these nuclei are also characteristic of the children's musical repertory, but there is the important difference that while the adults who perform the songs are used to a more developed musical language, the children who sing the same patterns are just beginning their musical experience.

The perception of musical sound involves a series of psychophysiological operations in which reception and performance acquire a new auditory dimension, so that musical sounds are differentiated from all other sounds. Musical perception includes two principal and interdependent forms: the perception of rhythm and the perception of melody. An earlier phase depends on the process of psychophysiological transformations effected during the passage from a premusical stage to the musical one. Before this there exists only the general auditory perception of sounds in which musical sound has not yet been specifically identified.

Following the normal process of the appearance and development of musical perception in the environment in which a child develops, we can differentiate four principal phases corresponding, albeit approximately, to different age groups: (1) from two to nine months; (2) from nine months to two years; (3) from two to three years; and (4) from three to four or five years of age.

The first phase is characterized by baby talk, or babble, signifying the child's reaction to moments of well-being and of interaction with other people. Toward the middle of this phase appear the claiming cries, the interrogative exclamations and the pleasure babble, and toward the end the imitative babble in response to other people's incitement. There is also the tendency to imitate different sounds, and a reaction of pleasure on hearing music. It is during this period that the child begins to discern the songs addressed to him, and especially the musical language of lullabies.

In the second phase babbling is replaced by different onomatopoeic syllables that have semantic value for children. This phase also belongs to the earlier repertoire of oral competence from which both language and music will be formed. At the end of this stage appear the first premusical inflexions. They are distinguished from the earlier sounds by a more musical intonation of the different phonemes.[4] At the same time the child's reaction to music grows more acute, and toward the end of this stage he tries to live through different rhythmical movements. He also develops his tendency to imitate and to repeat syllables in a musical fashion. In spite of this, the child's attempts at musical performance belong mostly to the incipient premusical stage.

In the third phase the child distinguishes musical sounds from other

---

[4]   The first and second phases are being investigated in an attempt to transcribe all these kinds of musical expression in children from the second month of life up to three years of age.

sounds. He tries either to accompany the songs that are sung to him or to engage in prose dialogues, but at first he can manage only short fragments. Song 6 in the appendix is a transcription of such a game from Turkey, and in it the two-year-old child tries to participate in a dialogue with his grandmother. In song 5, which is a Rumanian poem sung while the child is lifted in the arms, we can observe the same musical transformation of the words springing from the emotional impact of the movement. In both cases the women add a touch of melody to the words, and in song 6 the child's performance shows how his participation already depends on what the game means for him. Toward the conclusion of each phrase, imitation and repetition continue with increasing intensity. Although there is enough evidence to assume that a process of conscious musical creation has begun, on the basis of the different nuclei and musical motifs which he can perform, the clumsiness of actual performance suggests that we are in fact confronted by a premusical stage. The child shows an ability to assimilate melodies that are based on the musical range of the children's repertoire. His natural development helps him to appropriate them, and we can observe how, little by little, intervals that are at first poorly consolidated begin to emerge as the musical nuclei characteristic of his future musical repertoire. At the end of this stage children can retain a limited musical repertoire, though they cannot guarantee performance to order. We are at the beginning of the process of conscious music making. Songs performed by parents or grandparents together with the child or children whom they held in their arms were recorded several times, and, for the sake of experimentation, separate recordings were made with only the children performing. The transcriptions of these in songs 7 and 8 prompt some speculation about the children's musical interpretations at this phase of development:

1. The child's tendency to follow the musical outline is subject to an instability that is specific to this age.
2. There is an abundance of sounds situated at the frontier of verbal language, that is, there is musicalized speech.
3. Words are not used freely.
4. Appoggiaturas are used to help the melody along.
5. Semitones are common as a result of intonation that is close to speech.
6. The tempo is adapted as far as possible to a speed that the child can manage.
7. The rhythmical structure of the melody is emphasized.

In the fourth phase, assuming that the child has mastered the previous phase, he very soon develops his musical skills and consolidates them by repetition, in a way that is specific to the children's repertoire. The child becomes more and more involved in games accompanied by songs, and in general does not perform any song without moving his hands and feet. In this period ditties addressed to animals and birds in the child's environment are common. They are sung with musical intonation, but are not regarded as songs: for the child the words and the bodily movement of the ditty are his chief concern, but because of his innate musical impulse he sings using a limited repertory of between two and four musical nuclei in all performances. Each time one or two of the following nuclei are selected and repeated throughout the ditty:

These nuclei represent spontaneous musical expression issuing from the innate psychophysiological potentialities of the child.

All the other melodies subsequently learned are based on these primary nuclei. Song 13 is from the game *Dorul Marioarelor* [Yearning of Mary-es] performed, in a context which the child categorizes as musical, together with the actions of the game. These early steps in musical performance mark the stage in which innate capacities are superseded by a deeper comprehension of music and more and more integration into the musical language of the society.

There is a qualitative difference between musical nuclei that recur in the songs "for children" and those in the repertoire performed *by* children. In order of appearance the interval of a perfect fourth comes last in the children's repertoire, whereas in the adults' repertoire for children it is almost as common as the major second. Also, in the children's repertoire, three small motifs observed in the adults' repertoire of songs for children do not appear because they seem to belong to a more advanced stage of musical development.

Besides noting the phases of ontogenetical evolution in comparison with the formation of musical perception during the first five years of life, we may also consider the evolution of the children's musical repertoire up to the age of puberty. The operations of coding and decoding musical perception begin with lullabies and with lightly "melodized" words during the first six months of the child's life. As the child develops his power of perception, his musical perception also will be more and more crystallized according to the demands of the cultural environment. In the urban milieu the category of "songs for children" may be absent. It can be reduced to simple caressing and humming or even other kinds of song, which offer the child rudiments of rhythmical verbal and musical structures.

Frequently the mother or others who try to teach the child some songs from the children's repertoire sing together with the child, whose voice is in this way directed toward learning by imitation and forming on this basis new temporary associations. In this situation the learning process is assisted by movement, words, and the prevailing affective mood. The musical performance of a child appears rather as a conditioned reflex than as a conscious approach to music. It is enough for an adult to give a signal which the child recognizes as the song or to make a movement from the associated game, and the child will begin to hum and so express the desire to revive and joy in reviving moments of pleasure.

In the category of songs for children we can often notice verbal language in the form of parlando and melodic parlando such as spoken interruptions in prose and verse in the subcategories of lullabies and amusement songs. In such cases we have seen how the verbal language influences musical inflexions, especially when reflecting the affective mood of the performer toward the child.

Of special importance is the evidence of a close connection between affective speech and music. We can postulate the hypothesis that between the age of two months and three years the child had the same musical capacities that he manifests in a preverbal and premusical ontogenetic. phase. Subsequently he forms of it his musical performances which remain for a long time closely related to the verbal language. Although premusical performance appears before the formation of verbal language, verbal language appears first in the child's consciousness, whereas conscious musical perception appears relatively much later. A one-year-old child can begin to speak but a song can be consciously and correctly intoned only from the end of the third phase, that is, possibly at three years of age.

In the formation of musical perception, rhythm plays an important role. It appears as a support and impulse to the child's musical memory, being consolidated long before consciousness of melody. In spite of the fact that the child responds to rhythm accurately with his body, he does not become conscious of rhythm per se until he has developed his consciousness of melody. The child cannot distinguish the rhythm from the accompanying movements. This is possible only at a subsequent stage between six and seven years of age and this seems to depend not on the development of musical perception, but on the evolution of his thought.

There exists a similarity not only between the melodies of the folklore category *for* children and that *of* children, but also between their rhythms. Because the common factor in each case is the response of the child, this phenomenon is natural in spite of the possible differences that may appear in the adults' interpretation.

The ethnomusicologist Constantin Brăiloiu (1956) affirmed the universality of children's rhythms without being able to give a reason. An answer to this problem has been suggested by evidence of a primary rhythmical time that generates rhythms psychophysiologically and is manifested through kinesthesia (Suliţeanu 1958). Conventionally centered on the value of a quarter note, this "primary rhythmical time" also appears consistently in the folklore category "for children". Here it appears through clapping, through the sequences of lifting up the child in the arms, or passing the fingers over the child's body, and in all movements with which the grown-up accompanies his vocal performance.

We notice that although the child's movements have hitherto been disordered, they begin to acquire equilibrium and constancy. The "primary rhythmical time" of the movements is reinforced during the performance with the adult, so that the child relates it to all subsequent vocal-poetic and musical manifestations. Thus is developed a rhythmic framework on which may be based any kind of rhythmic structure.

Finally, we approach the problem of the child's internalization of musical language as a stage in the process of musical perception. There has been no special research into this, but it can be assumed, on the basis of some results obtained in research into adult musical perception, that the temporary musical association of the child allows inner performance to accompany the perception of the adults' execution. We can observe it from his humming or even his singing in concert with adults. But we do not know if the child can at this age, four to five years, conceive of the music without exteriorizing it in performance.

In conclusion, we may say that the data offered by studying the repertoire is of great importance not only for ethnomusicology but also for other sciences such as musicology, linguistics, psychology, physiology, sociology, and indeed any other science interested in the ontogenetic development of the child as compared with the influence of the environment. As for ethnomusicology, the study of the development of musical perception allows us to observe, on the morphological basis of first musical manifestations, how the whole musical tradition, with its rich and complex ramifications, comes into being and develops.

The study of children's expressions and behavior in relation to their earliest musical repertoire is one of the essential chapters of ethnomusicology.

APPENDIX 1.

Mg. 4144 n (II)   Gropeni, jud. Brăila
                                          Inf. Manda *Prodan*, 44 ani
1. Rep. pentru copii   Culeg. G. Sulițeanu, 18. IV. 1972
Cîntec de leagăn (pentru Cristinel)   Trans. G. Sulițeanu, VII. 1972

[♩ = 152]

Aᵢ = deą   na = ni   pu = iu   ma = mi

Mg. 4033 d (II)

Biica – Suceava
Inf. Domnica *Irimescu*, 38 ani
Culeg. G. Suliţeanu, 5. X. 1971
Trans. G. Suliţeanu, I. 1972

2. Cîntec de leagăn

Mg. 4083 i II (var.h)

3. Rep. pentru copii
Cîntec de leagăn

(♪ = 192)

Kobişniţa – Negotin – R. S. T. Yugoslavia
Inf. Nada lu *Raţa*, 49 ani
Culeg. G. Suliţeanu, XII. 1970
Trans. G. Suliţeanu, II 1972

Mg. 2827 f A

4. Cînteg de leagăn

(♪ = 264)

Orig. Dodeşti – Fólciu – Bîrlad
Inf. Catrina G. *Stoica*, 66 ani
Culeg. G. Suliţeanu, VI. 1965
Trans. G. Suliţeanu

Mg. 1048 l
5. Folclor romànesc
Centec divertisment

Orig. Berlovenii Vechi – Banat
Inf. Floarea *Imbrescu*, 49 ani
Rech. G. Suliţeanu

(♪ = 264)

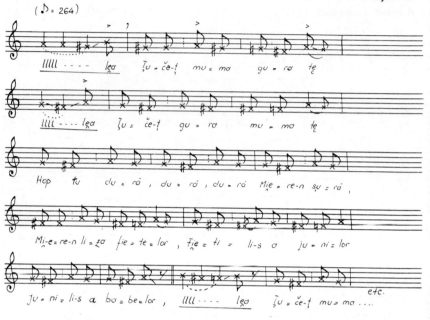

Mg. 3125f

Inf.

6. Folclor turcesc

Orig. Ada-Kaleh – jud. Mehedinţi
Nazire *Geambolat*, 56 ani
Bairam *Geambolat* 2 ani
Rech. G. Suliţeanu, 1966

(♪ = 132)

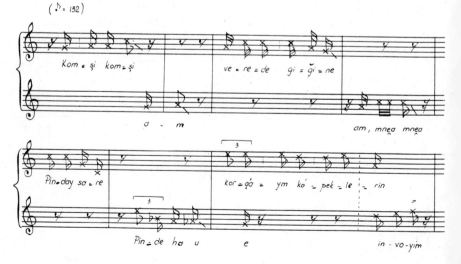

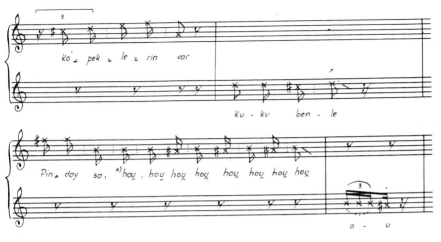

x) *Imitation d'aboiement*

Mg. 3416

7. Folclor sàsesc

Folk Song for Children

Orig. Blājel – Medias – Sibiu
Maria *Klein*; Katerina *Klein*, 60a
Inf. Herta *Klein*; 27a; Adelheit *Klein*, 2,8a.
Horst D. *Klein*, 3,10a
Rech. g. Sulieanu, II. 1968

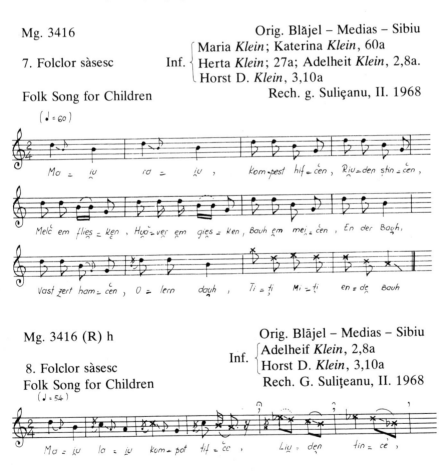

Mg. 3416 (R) h

8. Folclor sàsesc
Folk Song for Children

Orig. Blājel – Medias – Sibiu
Inf. Adelheif *Klein*, 2,8a
Horst D. *Klein*, 3,10a
Rech. G. Sulieanu, II. 1968

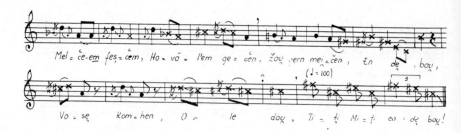

Mel = ce-em feș = cem, Ho = vă = l'em ge = cen, žaŭ ŗern mei = cen, En de bou,

(♩ = 100)

Vo = șe Kom = hen, O = le dou, Ti = ți Mi = ți en = de bou!

Mg. 3840 II aa

Totoi (Dumitra) jud. Alba
Inf. Carolina *Nichimis*, 38 ani
Culeg. G. Suliţeanu, 6. VIII. 1970
Trans. G. Suliţeanu, XI. 1971

9. Rep. pentru copii
joc cu degetele copilului

(♩ = 160)

Ă = sta me = re cu pur = če = i Ă = sta me = re cu gi = ță = i

Ă = sta ži = če hoi a = ca = să C-o fa = cut ma = mo plă = čin = te

Și le-o pus pe cup = tor S = o pus mi = ța pă = ži = tor

Și mi = ța s-o mi = ni = at Și pe tă = ti le-o min = cat

Mg. 4033 f II

Bilca – Suceava
Inf. Domnica *irimescu*, 38 ani
Culeg. G. Suliţeanu, 5. X. 1971
Trans. G. Suliţeanu I. 1972

10. Rep. pentru copii :
Divertisment – săltare în braţe

(♪ = 200)

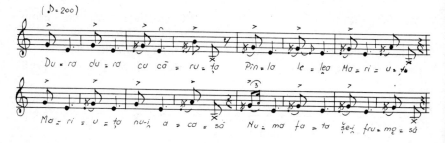

Du = ra du = ra cu că = ru = ța Pîn = la le = lea Ma = ri = u = ța

Ma = ri = u = ța nu-i a = ca = să Nu = ma fa = ta șe-i fru = mo = să

Cu šer = šei di gi = vo = šei   Cu sol = bŏ di no = vŏ lei

Orig. Bacău – Moldova
Inf. Haia *Wertenştein*, 70 ani
Rech. G. Suliţeanu

11. Folclor evreiesc
Folk Song for Children

Ai, oi, he = me = rl , Kim te mir en ké = me = rl , ih

Vil dir e = pes va - ţn, Şi - sa - leh ţen ə - ţn

Bir en de kri - gia leh' Kin - der en de vi - gia - leh

Kimt Moi - se Flah - ţer , En moh a grois ge - lah - ţer ha!ha!

Mg. 4083 d (v)

12. Rep. pentra copii
Divertisment, săltare pe genunki

Kobişniţa (Negotin) – limoc
R. S. F. Yugoslavia
Inf. Natalia *Popovici*, 67 ani
Culeg. G. Suliţeanu, XII. 1970
Trans. G. Suliţeanu, II. 1972

Dur dur du = ru = ion , Du = pŏ ca = sa lui Sto = ion ,

Te = ti = li cu ţur = či = li , Da , Dă = na = či cu mă = čiu = či = li ,

Să le spar = gă nu = či = li , Să le um = ple bu = či = li

i hu hu! ——

13. Folclor grecesc
Folk Song for Children

Ellenika Dimotica Tragoydio
Tom. III, Atena, 1963
p. 392, nr. 1

14. Folclor lipovean
Folk Song for Children

Orig. Bucuresti
Inf. Elena *Popov*, 27a
Rech. G. Sulițeanu, 1966

Mg. 3836 d (v)
15. Rep. copii : "Dorul Marioarelor"
Children's Game:

Orig. Dumitra, jud. Alba
Inf. Eug. *Gofa*, 13 ani și
grup de copii

REFERENCES

BRĂILOIU, CONSTANTIN
  1956 *La rythmique enfantine*. Paris: Elsevier.

SULIȚEANU, GHIZELA
  1958 Kinestezia și ritmica folclorului copiilor: contribuția psihologiei la studiul comparat al folclorului muzical [Kinesthesia and rhythm of children's folklore: a psychological contribution in the comparative study of musical folklore]. *Revista de Etnografie și Folclor* 3:211–227.

  1969a "Le rôle des chansons pour enfants dans le processus de formation de la perception musicale." Paper presented to the Congress Savez Udrujenia Folklorista Yugoslavia, Herceg Novi. September.

  1969b The experimental method in ethnomusicology. *Revista de Etnografie și Folclor* 5:369–382.

  1970 "Cîntecele de leagăn ale poporului român" [Lullabies of the Rumanian people]. Paper commissioned by the Rumanian union of composers.

Pattern Perception and Recognition in African Music

GERHARD KUBIK

The present work can be nothing more than an introduction to this field of research, since the study of the musical ethnology of Africa is still only in its infancy. We shall determine in what manner auditory complexes in Black Africa can be perceived, recognized, interpreted, and understood by musicians and participants of the most varied ethnic, linguistic, and cultural heritages. First of all we shall be treating the relevant processes exclusively in their musical context. Extramusical implications or associations with sound complexes are dealt with in another work (Kubik 1974). All phenomena which have a direct or indirect relationship with pattern perception and pattern recognition in the field of music and dance of Black African cultures fall within this field of investigation. They must be carefully recorded with adequate samples.

How do African musicians grasp auditory complexes as patterns? Are there specific criteria for pattern perception and interpretation, which hold good for the whole of Black Africa or for certain areas of musical style? In what way can music and dance patterns be defined from an intraethnic standpoint, from the standpoint of the musical culture of the performers and participants? How is musical terminology in the various African languages related to the perception and recognition of patterns? What breadths of variation exist in the perception and interpretation of patterns within given African musical cultures, subcultures or between musical personalities? To what extent can a pattern appear in a variant form and still be recognized and interpreted as the same pattern by the members of a given musical culture? These questions, which are but a few among many which will arise as this investigation proceeds, call for some sort of methodological orientation. Mental processes which are auditively relevant cannot be understood directly by the means available to musical ethnology. They have to be determined by indirect means, from the *behavior* of the participants and the statements they make, and a terminology has to be established by implication.

To show how important *behavior* is, I will mention an example from the musical ethnology of eastern and central Africa. In Busoga (southern Uganda) and neighboring areas the players of wooden xylophones take them apart after a performance. The xylophone slats and banana trunks are stored in a shady place, such as a house, so as to prevent their drying out in the blazing sun. Before being played, the instrument has to be reassembled. With the Basoga there are fifteen or more slats, so in order to make it possible for them to be laid quickly on the banana trunks in the form of a scale, they are numbered by the musicians. Otherwise it would be necessary to strike each slat and listen to its note before laying it in position.

In one case which I myself documented in this region, at Bumanya (Kubik 1964a) as well as in another case among the Azande in Zemio, in the Central African Republic (Kubik 1964b) the numbering always began with the highest slat and followed the pitch step by step downwards.

From this behavior of the musicians it is possible to draw conclusions regarding their conception of scale. The numbering carried out for a purely practical purpose shows features which cannot be regarded as merely fortuitous. It makes it obvious that Basoga and Azande musicians (1) regard their note material as constituting a progressive series according to pitch, and (2) regard this scale, contrary to what happens in the Western countries, as *starting from the highest frequency*.

Such a conclusion also agrees with Wachsmann's observations in regard to the procedure employed by the neighboring Baganda for tuning harps and xylophones (Wachsmann 1950, 1957).

Statements made by specialist members (musicians) or nonspecialist members of the society concerned are also of the greatest importance and make it easier to track down the formative processes of pattern perception and interpretation in music. However, it is not always easy to interrogate the informants directly. Wherever they are only used to one possibility, that of their own culture, as a rule they possess no designations and often not even descriptive identification.

A terminology specific to a given culture only becomes possible where phenomena have to be *distinguished* from an intracultural standpoint. An ethnic unit which only knows a single dance will have no name for it, but only a generic name for "dance". However, where a number of dances are customary there will soon be a need for distinctive designations so as to make it possible to refer clearly to them. In this way a terminology is gradually built up. A guitarist who uses nine different modes of tuning for his instrument (cf. Kubik 1972b:48; 1973) will in all probability possess a terminology for this, but not a guitarist who only has one method.

A musical ethnologist cannot expect an ethnic group whose entire music approaches an equiheptatonic system of notes to have a name for this pattern, or that the people belonging to the musical culture concerned will be able to define it themselves. Relevant questions are therefore superfluous.

Rhythmic patterns in some types of African music are also often identified terminologically by "describing" them by means of verbal or purely syllabic formulas. These also serve as a mnemonic aid and play an important part in situations of teaching and learning. If a rhythmic pattern is to be played, it is possible to utter the relevant syllables to the musician in order to make it clear to him which pattern he is supposed to play. In African music mnemonic syllables or verbal formulas also perform the function of a nomenclature for identifying the associated rhythm forms.

Patterns play an important part in African music (Nketia 1962, 1963). From the point of view of perception psychology Corcoran wrote "The word 'pattern' usually does refer to stimuli which differ on many dimensions" (Corcoran 1971:20). Auditive stimuli, for example sequences of notes, can vary both in frequency and in amplitude. Nevertheless, what a pattern actually *is* has up to now defied definition. Koetting (1970:121), in an important work which shows a new reflective attitude on the part of "Westerners" when they encounter other cultures, writes: "in the absence of further information I always define as a pattern the longest consecutively repeating sequence."

A central problem of pattern perception is to be found in the question: How is it possible for a complex stimulus, such as that of beats in a given arrangement in time, a series of notes having a definite relationship as regards frequency or a sound spectrum, to be perceived as something which forms a unit, as a whole, as an entity which is distinctly separate from other stimuli occurring at the same time? What is responsible for the fact that in our "nervous system", in our perceptive capacity, a whole is "built up" from fragmentary mental impressions?

In our narrow field of research in African music it is obvious that wherever a pattern is perceived the elements which constitute this pattern are somehow *ordered* in relation to one another. This inner order produces a force of cohesion which in the end gives rise in our perceptive capacity to the effect which causes these fragments to come to life as a whole. Koffka (1935:98) wrote: "Things look as they do because of the field organization, to which the proximal stimulus distribution gives rise. ... It means that we have to study the laws of organization."

One can say: patterns are always structured — on the relationship between whole and structure in the wider framework of the cultural sciences, cf. Stiglmayr (1970). But what is implied by this proposition that patterns are structured? It implies that patterns can be broken down into subsections, into subpatterns. These in turn can once again be structured. The proposition also implies that a number of patterns together can form a superior whole, a superpattern.

Patterns fluctuate into one another, even if they are often distinctly delineated from one another within the field of subjective perception. In the perception of the so-called *inherent patterns* it is possible during the perception process for fragments of a pattern to break away and attach themselves to another pattern, so that the overall complex during the course of several repetitions is perceived sometimes in this way and sometimes in that, rather like a picture puzzle (Kubik 1960, 1970).

The perception of auditory complexes takes place on this plane of fluctuating, interlocking, superimposed, displacing, combining, conflicting patterns. It is impossible to hear a piece of music "panoramically", even if it only lasts for a few seconds. During auditive perception a musical passage breaks down into a set of *ensembles which can be grasped*, into a number of conflicting patterns which when placed together once again form more complex units.

In this connection there is an important question which arises: Is pattern perception subject to general human prerequisites? Is it determined by these alone or is it also influenced by the specific culture to which one belongs, in the present instance by the fact that one subscribes to a certain musical culture?

In this contribution it is only possible to pose the question, but not to answer it. In a few areas, such as in the case of the so-called inherent patterns, however, it seems to have been proved that pattern perception is not bound to a given culture. It would appear to be otherwise in the case of pattern recognition. Here cultural influence can be detected. Nevertheless, Corcoran (1971) emphasized how much these phenomena, pattern perception and recognition, are linked with one another.

In auditory perception there are various structured numerical relations which are probably a representation of such an "original form of pattern perception". In the field of Black African music there are the significant *form numbers*: 6, 8, 9, 12, 16, 18, 24, 36 (Kubik 1961). Pattern 24, for example, is structured as a multiple of 2, 3, 4, 6, and 12.

Dauer (1966) intimated that the "rhythmic complexity" of African music which is so highly praised throughout the world could be based on *unnamed numerical experiences* on the part of African musicians. In this way Dauer gave expression to the possibility that such an "original form of pattern perception" transcended the conscious range. Creative formation in African music, as indeed in other types of music in the world, is to a large extent guided by unconscious patterns, in the event by archetypes on a numerical basis (cf. the importance of trinity, quaternity and also of the numbers 6, 8, and 12 in C. G. Jung's archetypes), especially in the motional range taking place over a period of time.

Patterns are often sharply delineated. In types of African music motional patterns are usually defined by a *starting point*, an insertion point (in relation to other patterns); by their *length* and *internal* structure (both expressed numerically in nominal values: elementary pulses, fastest pulses); and by *their relation to other patterns*, to give the uniform imperious *pulsation of the nominal values* and sometimes to give a *beat or gross pulse*.

Metric patterns as a basis for motional form are usually not a feature of African music or are of subordinate importance. Accordingly, when learning to play African musical instruments, unlike the custom in Western music schools, one does not beat time. The nominal values are the foundation of the motional form, but they are not a pattern. On the other hand, the beat or gross pulse (Koetting 1970) is to be regarded entirely as a pattern because, just like the types of time in European music, it indicates an internal structure even if it is one which is different from the European. The nominal value pulsation, on the other hand, is completely unstructured. It has no beginning and no end.

In African music patterns are understood as "themselves" and in conjunction with one another. Regarding rhythm formulas Koetting writes, with special reference to music in Ghana: "For the performers any one pattern has little meaning out of that context; indeed members of an ensemble often experience difficulty in performing their pattern alone, their success in doing so being dependent on their ability to reconstruct mentally the other patterns of the piece" (1970:120).

In the case of the performer of the *okukoonera* part in the *amadinda* [xylophone] music of Buganda I have long been struck by the fact that playing this part in isolation (for instance at the request of an ethnomusicologist) leads to a severe deformation of the rhythmic infrastructure (cf. Kubik 1970). This is explained by the fact that the okukoonera formulas, which are frequently very long, are defined by a congruence relationship with other parts of the musical passage and not by their own intrinsic rhythm structure. The latter is often so complicated in its time relations that it cannot be pattern-forming. Since okukoonera formulas are also often very long they break down into sections which cannot be kept in mind with reference to a beat or a meter.

Just like linguistic formulas or the rhythm of a spoken sentence, it is true that the okukoonera formulas have a quality of form, but in their temporal organization they have a marked width of variation or breadth of tolerance. But the crudest rhythmic distortion, from the point of view of a metrically oriented Western observer, is not interpreted, certainly not perceived, by the performing musician as a distortion of this pattern, so long as he plays the pattern in isolation — just as when talking on various occasions one can alter the rhythm of a sentence to a certain degree or one can extend it or compress it and yet at the same time it can

still be recognized as an identical form. The amadinda musician reproduces the okukoonera formulas from his conception as an *autonomous*
pattern which is determined very accurately melodically but only vaguely
from the point of view of rhythm, in relation to the twenty-four or more
nominal values at which he has to aim. In no way are the okukoonera
formulas imagined by the musicians to be in a fixed relationship to a
controlling pulse or meter.

The guiding factor when playing together is the congruence relationship of the okukoonera pattern with an inherent melody which is perceived on what are known as the *entengezzi*, the two lowest slats of an
amadinda instrument. When the musician is playing, every stroke must
coincide with the corresponding note on the entengezzi in *absolute
rhythmic* congruence. In other types of African music there is often also a
partial congruence (Kubik 1970).

The case described shows that particularly long rhythmic patterns in
some types of African music are defined *in isolation* with a comparatively
wide breadth of rhythmic variation without thereby losing their quality
and identity. Despite this breadth of variation they are recognized by the
musicians as *this* and no other pattern. Such cases also show the inadequ-
acy of one method of "analytical tape recording", where one allows each
musician taking part to play his part in isolation. Rhythmic inaccuracy in
the execution of the pattern can lead to errors in subsequent attempts at
transcription. In any case stereophonic recordings and film documentation have already superseded "analytical tape recordings" as a method of
field research where transcription is intended.

The determination of intraculturally accepted tolerance in the perception and recognition of patterns of all kinds is a prerequisite for attempts
at defining the organization of a musical culture. The intracultural significance of patterns can be defined only in the light of such tolerances (cf.
also the section on tuning patterns below). As everywhere else, one has to
make sure that sufficient intracultural evidence (statements by people
belonging to the musical cultures in question or observations of their
behavior) is found so as to prevent speculation in terms of the point of
view of a different culture.

Below, three partial aspects of the structure of African music will be
dealt with separately, in which the perception, recognition, interpretation, and understanding of patterns are the paramount requirement and
foundation of any musical organization.

MOVEMENT PATTERNS

What is still frequently described in the ethnomusicology of Africa under
the term *rhythm*, which originates from the Greek, can be explained

under the main heading of *movement patterns*. The difference between *rhythm pattern* and *movement pattern* is that the former term implies something which sounds whilst the latter also includes musical phenomena which are completely without sound.

Investigations which have been going on for several years based on a careful evaluation of film material show that behind the so-called rhythm patterns of African music there are movement patterns which have both a sonic and a nonsonic dimension. This only reinforces an old view, namely, that African music is not sound alone. The Western distinction between music and dance helps but little in understanding African music because in African musical cultures it is irrelevant. Movement patterns transcend these two spheres, which are regarded as separate in Western cultures. The same movement patterns are to be found both in the dance and in the musical aspects of the phenomenon which is African music.

There is a wide degree of congruence between the movement patterns of the music and those of dancers. One can define African music in one of its fundamental structural aspects as *a system of movement patterns*. Consequently, in the situations which arise when teaching African music one emphasizes in many cases not only the sonic auditory aspect but primarily the motional production process. According to an informant in Baturi in December 1969, for the player of a "mendzaŋ", a xylophone in southern Cameroon, it is in the first place important to know at what point of time he must *strike* which key, and this is what he learns (see also Ngumu 1976).

On by no means rare occasions during the teaching process patterns of movement are imparted "physically" by the teacher to the pupil, for instance by a xylophonist holding his pupil's hands and imparting direct impulses to them until the pupil has absorbed the movement pattern and his hands holding the sticks act at the correct instant. James Koetting writes regarding his experiences with a Ghanaian who was asked to teach drum-playing at the University College of Los Angeles: "The drum ensemble players, for example, learn and even perform their music — from single sounds to pattern sequences — largely in terms of the physical movements required to produce it" (1970:119).

African instrument playing is motionally organized throughout in a characteristic manner. This is true both of what are known as traditional instruments as well as those of recent importation. On occasions the organization is so all-pervasive that a musician like Daniel J. Kachamba from Malawi (cf. Kubik 1972b, 1973) is able to play three instruments simultaneously: mouth organ (bound on to a support), guitar, and rattle. His right hand holds the rattle, a pear-shaped or spherical rattle with a handle, and shakes it up and down. At the same time he plays separate patterns with his index fingers on the three top strings and with his thumbs on the bass strings. They are figures which are motionally congruent in their overall picture with the upward and downward movement of the rattle, but not with a result which is auditively perceptible. The auditory picture and the playing picture are different. In relation to this the mouth organ plays a lead voice which is motionally different.

A rigorous but nonetheless comparatively elementary organization of the total movement forms the foundation of an apparently unheard rhythmic multiplicity in the range of auditory perception. This multiplicity is produced indirectly: the movement patterns which form the basis of African music are usually simpler than the sonic result, which often confuses the outside observer. The mental, or even physical, absorption of patterns of movement in the learning process is one of the secrets of understanding African music as a musician or as a participating dancer. The *body* of the musician or dancer absorbs these patterns until they act as conditioned reflexes, and when they occur externally they immediately produce an inner response just like a reflex. If one has learned to know African music in this way it is very difficult to sit still when one hears it and to suppress an inner response in the sense described. The affective response to the perception of such patterns takes place after the fashion of a reflex. One starts spontaneously to dance.

The organization of African music is motionally rigorous, right down to the tiniest areas. Whereas in Western music the movements of a musician playing his instrument generally have meaning only in terms of the sonic result, in African music patterns of movement are in themselves a source of pleasure, regardless of whether they come to life in sound in their entirety, partly, or not at all. In Western music movement is a means for producing auditory complexes, whereas in African music it can be self-sufficient. In such music auditory complexes may even only be an, albeit important, by-product of motional process.

In the case of guitarists of the Congo region, for instance, the overriding motional organization is dominant. Not only do the movements of the thumb and forefinger of the right hand, which strike the strings in the typically Central African two-finger guitar technique, form organized movement patterns, but also do the finger movements of the left hand in front of the joints. Motional formulas of the right and left hands when combined give an overall picture, a substructure, which is not audible but exists behind the music as a formative foundation.

The nature of the patterns of movement has a direct influence on the audible "music" — see the example of a motional formula on drums of the Vatumbuka in northern Malawi in Kubik (1962). Although certain melodically sonic complexes can be produced in many different ways with a practically identical result, complete accuracy is dependent upon the correct pattern of movement. The imitation of African music by adherents to other musical cultures on the basis of gramophone records is frequently doomed to failure because the movement patterns on which the audible result is based are not included. This is also true of imitations of Afro-American music (jazz, and so on) throughout the world. Only the "sound" is reproduced, but that foundation, of a musical, motional, and even an extramusical nature, which produces this "sound", is often not included. The movement patterns are seldom recognized. An example is also to be found in the imitation of so-called Congo guitar music by Western concert guitarists, such as the music of Mwenda Jean Bosco as accessible in the transcriptions of David Rycroft (1961, 1962). Bosco and other guitarists from the Congo region understood their music not only auditively, but auditively *and* motionally. The movement pictures of Bosco's music are built up in such a way that certain notes are only produced in a certain manner. For instance the right hand only uses the forefinger and thumb for plucking the strings. As a rule the forefinger deals with the three top strings of the guitar and the thumb with the three bottom. Overlapping is possible. Western concert guitarists play Bosco's music using more fingers according to the "classic" techniques of guitar playing to which they are accustomed. The consequence is that the motional pictures of Bosco's music are lost.

The nonrecognition of movement patterns in African music and the attempt at reproduction on the basis of auditory perception by means of other motional formulas has an important effect. The change in the motional pictures brings about a change, even if only slight, in the exact "spacing" of the notes to be struck. This leads to delays, anticipations, slight fluctuations in tempo, and a sense of lack of *drive*. The changing of the motional picture also destroys the original accentuation and the change in the mode of striking the individual notes also exerts an influence on their sound spectrum.

On the other hand it is a striking fact that adherents to the same or related musical cultures, even from purely auditory representations (gramophone records, radio broadcasts) spontaneously comprehend the movement formulas on which a given piece of African instrumental music is based. This led to a series of experiments which I carried out with Donald Kachamba, a guitarist and flautist from Malawi. His guitar playing is close in some ways to that of the copper belt of Zambia and Zaire. Donald Kachamba was confronted with the recording *Tambala moja* (Bosco 1952) transcribed by Rycroft (1962) and was requested to reconstruct Bosco's guitar-playing technique from the gramophone recording. Donald immediately recognized certain movement patterns and played with the two-finger technique. What was particularly interesting was that he also came to the conclusion that Bosco did not use the standard tuning of the guitar. Donald tuned the sixth (bottom) string of the guitar at such a high pitch that Bosco's bass formula could be played on the three open bottom strings (that is, without fingering).

For an adherent of the same or related musical cultures it is possible to recognize the patterns of movement merely from their auditory outcrop, because he knows from his previous experience how these auditory complexes come into being. From the way the auditory complexes make their appearance he *recognizes* the movement patterns and can then execute them, for example by casting them into the mold of dance movements, or by associating with them syllabic or verbal formulas, or again by reproducing the music as an instrumentalist.

Because African music is not solely sonic, it is possible for various types of music to be transcribed by the evaluation of *silent* films (Kubik 1965, 1972a). In silent films movement patterns become visible without any disturbance. In a silent film sequence of a clapping formula of a girl of the Fō of Togo the "silent" and "sonic" sections of the movement were formative (Kubik 1972a). The complete motional pattern consisted of both portions. From the sound recording it was possible to deduce the sonic aspect. From that alone, however, it was impossible to understand the girl's clapping formula. It was not until one had the analysis of the silent film, which took into account the nonsonic parts of this clapping formula (the opening of the clapping hands and so on), that it became possible to understand what the Fō girl was in reality performing.

In this series of investigations of movement patterns I introduced by way of experiment a concept of movement analysis which differs from conceptions such as are implied, say, in Laban dance notation or in Pantaleoni's transcriptions (Serwadda and Pantaleoni 1968). I subdivided a piece of movement first of all into corner or turning points. These are those points in a pattern of movement where the kinetic energy reaches zero intensity and, consequently, where fresh energy has to be provided by the performer in order to bring about a change in the motional direction. The corner or turning points appear to be particularly important formative components of a movement pattern.

As soon as one has discovered them and determined them by film evaluation, one is in possession of an important key for transcription. Movement patterns are transcribed here according to the energy employed by the performer. These cycles of the use of physical energy are experienced with intensiveness by the performer. Together with the sonic result they are a source of pleasure. Joy and pleasure in movement formulas arise from the actions and from the response after the perception of the successful result.

Cultures are to a large extent characterized and distinguished from one another by the movement patterns which are usually found in them (in this connection compare the works of Alan Lomax and his choreometrics project). Even a single stroke can possess a different inner organization in different cultures. I first of all discovered this to my amazement in 1965 in southeastern Angola. By the film evaluation of a recording of the bast beating in a *mukanda* initiation school among the Mbwela it was possible to see that each stroke possessed from the motional point of view a tripartite organization. The low point (impact of the hammer on the bast) was reached on the first elementary pulse, and the high point (highest position of the raised hammer) was reached on the third elementary pulse of a fundamental nominal value pulsation. The action on the first elementary pulse was sonic, that on the third was silent. An individual stroke can thus possess a pattern structure. Similarly the striking of xylophone slats or the bars of a *likembe*, and so on, in African music, is often internally structured.

The motional patterns in African music are usually immediately recognized by those taking part and the dancers respond with the corresponding movements. Frequently such patterns are *named*, for instance by means of syllabic or verbal formulas, which are used as a means of communication between teachers and pupils in dance instruction.

How are patterns of movement perceived and recognized? Some information on this point is provided by the careful observation of teaching and learning situations. Movement patterns in their various *possible visible* forms, for instance in the form of dance steps, can be observed by the pupil, imitated, and in this way absorbed by him (learning by slow absorption). The characteristic feature, however, is that anyone who has grasped a movement pattern, such as the famous two against three relationship in widely differing forms of African music, in *one* visible form, is able of himself to recast it into other visible forms. Anyone who has learned the pattern can, instead of dancing it with his legs, also play it on a xylophone.

What is recognized in such learning processes? A complex stimulus is perceived, or rather *interpreted*, as something coherent. What is recognized in the event is the pattern not in its manifest visible form alone, but in its *abstract content*, and this is a *numerical relationship*. Movement patterns are based on numerical relationships and are determined by them. These numerical relationships can assume an expression in terms of space or time. The extent to which this process of the perception and recognition of such number patterns takes place within the unconscious range (cf. Dauer 1966) is an interesting subject for future investigations. Moreover the convertibility of forms of occurrence of movement patterns is only possible if these possess an abstract foundation which remains unchangeable: unnamed numerical experiences.

INHERENT PATTERNS

In the xylophone music of southern Uganda (Buganda, Busoga, and so on), in the *timbrh* [lamellaphone] music of central Cameroon (cf. Kubik 1966) and numerous other types of music, especially in Central Africa, there exist phenomena which are of particular interest in research into patterns: what are known as *inherent patterns*.

Inherent patterns are auditory patterns which stand out from the overall complex of the melodic/rhythmic models of a musical passage, just as though they were appearing from a picture puzzle. They are not produced directly by any musician, but are a perceptive phenomenon. Nonetheless they are provided as part of the composition, the composers of the relevant types of African music making skillful use of the characteristics of human auditory perception.

The total melodic/rhythmic models of a composition are constructed in such a way that the notes of different pitch layers form subpatterns with one another. These subpatterns are located in the total complex; they are inherent in it. That is why we talk of inherent patterns. In this field, too, we can see the total, all-embracing, organization of African music. The notes of a melodic/rhythmic complex are related to one another to the very tiniest detail both as regards motion (rhythm) and as regards pitch (melody), possible variations also being provided for organizationally.

In African music inherent patterns are usually the carriers of textual phrases. These are picked up by the ears of listeners from the respective linguistic areas for purely instrumental representations, or else new texts, phrases, and so on, are associated with them (Kubik 1966–1967; Cooke 1970).

These phenomena, which are of interest from the point of view of pattern psychology, struck me first of all in 1959 in the case of the amadinda and *akadinda* music of Buganda. They were described by me under the terms "inherent rhythms", "inherent melodies" in 1960 (Kubik 1960) and later (Kubik 1961, 1962, 1964a, 1966–1967) and in greater detail in 1970 (Kubik 1970). Since these are phenomena which involve both the motional sphere and the pitch (melodic) sphere, I finally proposed the expression "inherent patterns" as a neutral term (Kubik 1969, 1972a, 1972b).

Amadinda compositions and timbrh pieces (Kubik 1966) consist primarily of the combination of two basic series of punctual sequences of strokes, of exactly the same rhythmic value, which are determined by the technique of playing. These basic series are not constituent elements of a piece of music which is to be built up. Instead one must regard the process as the reverse of this. A musical total complex, such as it also sounds on other instruments, for instance on the harp, was for reasons of technical execution split into two halves, the basic series, which are now played separately on the xylophone by two musicians. What is now being combined was therefore originally a single whole in the first place.

The two basic series are played together like the fingers of a folded hand interlocking with one another. Their combination produces (or rather, *re*produces) that frantic chain of pulsations of about 600 M.M. (Maelzel's metronome) for the nominal values from jerky intervals which represent the total picture of the piece of music.

Human auditive perception reacts in a characteristic manner to such a frantically occurring form consisting of forty-eight, ninety-six and more successive notes. One hears neither the basic series which are played by the individual musicians or, in the case of the timbrh music of the Cameroon by each thumb of a musician, nor their combination, the overall picture. In place of the perception of a "total pattern" or "resultant pattern" (cf. Jones 1949) a series of obtrusive rhythmic/melodic forms at different pitch levels suddenly enter the field of perception. These are not played by any musician. They are purely and simply a pattern effect.

Inherent patterns are auditory phenomena. Nevertheless, they are structurally contained in the overall picture of the composition in question. Auditory perception does not conjure up any notes, but only note material which actually sounds is perceived. In a transcription, therefore, inherent patterns can be made visible by underlining, marking in red, or by using other methods of emphasizing them out of the total complex (cf. Kubik 1960).

What happens here as regards criteria for pattern perception? The melody which is provided from the two interlocking series is no longer continuously grasped by auditive perception, but is split into individual *melodic pitch layers* which continue to exist as autonomic melody complexes. One suddenly hears several separate melodic/rhythmic structures which conflict rhythmically with one another: one in the bass, one in the middle pitch range, and others in the higher range.

Although they are a pure perception phenomenon, such inherent patterns are provided by the producers of the music, the composers. They are by no means fortuitous products, as has been assumed by some people (Cooke 1970). On the contrary, they constitute one of the most important composition techniques in the amadinda, akadinda, *embaire* and *budongo* music of southern Uganda, as well as in the timbrh music of the Vute of central Cameroon. In the *likembe* music of the Congo area, in guitar playing of Shaba, and numerous other Central African types of music, composition is carried out on the same basic principle. The African musics of this large zone have long since discovered important bases and properties of auditory pattern perception in man and they have recognized these and subsequently utilized them for purposes of composition. African musicians play with the reactions of human perception with an intuitive insight into the nature of its psychology which puts the knowledge of Western science in the shade. Those "laws of organization" (Koffka 1935) have long been recognized intuitively by the creative musicians of Africa. And in the course of time they learned by trial and error to utilize these discoveries in practice without providing a theoretical foundation for them in the Western sense.

The systematic research of the phenomenon of what is known as inherent patterns in African music is therefore of the same importance to perception psychology as it is to the musical ethnology of Africa. However, musical science is still right at the beginning in regard to this matter. How does it happen that listeners and participants manage to extract in their hearing precisely such patterns and none other from an amadinda composition? How does a complex auditory stimulus become an inherent pattern?

Up to now it has been possible to establish that the following prerequisites exist: (1) the piece of music must consist of series of notes which take place as quickly as possible; (2) the intervals are for the most part jerky, so that the splitting into pitch layers occurs; and (3) the internal structure of the entire passage is regular, so that all the high, all the middle, and all low notes form distinctly delineated and independent rhythmic melodic patterns. Further points will still have to be defined.

The discovery of the capacity of human perception to hear inherent patterns should have been possible to practitioners of African musical cultures as a result of their full use of irregular melody and rhythm, because an irregular nonmetric series of elementary parts seems to favor such pattern effects.

The perception of inherent patterns seems finally to be based on a *compensatory reaction* of the perceptive capacity; there may be compensation for a transient loss of order in the perceptive material. Perception itself takes place within the framework of a subjective system of reference points with which perceptive material is confronted and brought into congruence. When congruence is achieved, a pattern is perceived and experienced. This means that certain *elementary patterns* are already provided mentally in advance. Such "fields" form a type of picture screen or *scanning pattern* and are projected onto every new complex stimulus. Then a selection process takes place. Those components of the multidimensional stimulus which fit into the structure of this inner "field" or *scanning pattern* are released and brought into congruence with it. At this moment a pattern is perceived. Any parts of the multidimensional stimulus which do not fit in are suppressed, pushed aside.

Perception itself can be imagined as a sort of "focusing". If an external stimulus impinges on the inner picture screen, the inner structural properties of the picture screen are sharply focused to the external material.

If something unexpected now takes place, such as a vigorous confrontation with perceptive contents whose own structuring runs *against* these inner scanning patterns, against this inner system of orientation points, then in the first place there occurs a disorientation of perception. A chain of ninety-six notes succeeding one another rapidly and in jerky intervals already exceeds in its length the capacity of all inner scanning patterns. One can also say that the perceptive capacity is *overmodulated*. The needle is deflected, the picture screen becomes confused like a radar screen. If this disorientation cannot be overcome, the hearer only perceives a chaos of notes.

The irregular rhythmic sequences or movement patterns of irregular internal structure first of all bring about a marked disorientation of the control impulse on which rhythmic perception is based (nominal value pulsation in African music). This confusion effect is enhanced to an extraordinary extent if such irregular rhythm is melodic at the same time and the melody occurs in jerky intervals.

In the amadinda music of Buganda and the timbrh music of the Cameroon jerky melodies follow one another at a rapid tempo with a distribution of accents which is for the most part irregular. This brings about a loss of reliable reference points in the perception capacity, a confusion of the inner scanning patterns. The overall melody of such a structure lacks any pattern. It consists apparently in the first place of unordered chaotic components. However, in the next fraction of an instant this loss of pattern leads to a perceptory compensation in which the note material which breaks up into its components *is organized in a new way* in the perception.

This new grouping follows a definite scheme and takes place within the framework of the capacity of the inner scanning picture. The auditory perceptive capacity now forms patterns *by associating into groups the notes which are of the same or neighboring pitches* and simply jumps over whatever lies in between in this selection operation. All the "nonpatternable" material located in between is simply set aside from the point of view of perception, jumped over, because it is not possible to bring it into congruence with any inner scanning pattern.

In this way there suddenly occur several inherent melody lines in different pitch ranges which are in conflict with one another. As a rule they are two-note or three-note melodies, strongly structured rhythmically. Irregular melodies consisting of several notes break down in this way in perception into their internal structural parts; into inherent melody.

The occurrence of inherent patterns is not dependent upon the instruments used. Corresponding phenomena have been observed with most widely differing African instruments: xylophones, lamellaphones, zithers, harps, flutes, drums, and so on. They are also not dependent upon the note system employed. Similar pattern effects can be produced in pentatonic or heptatonic modes, also in the Western note system, as the playing of Congo guitarists shows.

The *accentuation* of individual notes can certainly influence the occurrence of inherent patterns since as a result of particularly marked accentuation marginal tones can break away from an inherent pattern and join on to one another (Kubic 1960). However, accentuation does not create any inherent patterns. In African instrument playing accentuation is often used in order to render already existing inherent patterns more distinctly audible, to push them into the foreground, say, immediately in front of singing with textual phrases which are identical with such patterns. It was possible to prove this some time ago in the harp playing of the erstwhile court musician of Uganda, Evaristo Muyinda (Kubik 1966–1967).

Inherent patterns always arise from a given *structural* arrangement of the note material. A machine which is "fed" with the corresponding sequences of notes produces the same effect. This naturally does not mean that African music can be reduced to a "machine". Still less are inherent patterns created by differences in the sound spectrum of individual xylophone slats. Such differences can only exert an influence on already existing inherent patterns by rendering individual parts of the structure more prominent (cf. Kubik 1960).

Structurally, inherent patterns arc determined in such a way that in the event of a change in an individual note something different immediately comes out, such as any performer on the amadinda can show clearly by experiment.

Amongst African musicians or those well acquainted with the musical culture there are numerous direct witnesses to the existence of inherent patterns in African music. In amadinda music, for example, it is the job of a third musician to pick out such an inherent pattern from the total picture of the two basic voices which interlock with one another and to play them two octaves higher on the two highest xylophone slats, the *amakoonezi*. This constitutes direct proof that inherent patterns are perceived and recognized by the musicians concerned and are not, for instance, a subjective impression gathered by contemplative Western ethnomusicologists.

Evaristo Muyinda defined as follows the task of an *omukoonezi*, the third player of an amadinda: "The omukoonezi listens for the *entengezzi* [that is to say, the two lowest slats of the xylophone] and plays what he hears there on the amakoonezi" (personal communication 1962).

The inherent melody and the important entengezzi can be heard exceedingly loud. Music students from other cultures only have difficulty in perceiving it at the beginning, because their attention is otherwise adjusted. However, this important dimension of East African xylophone music is soon opened up to them.

Maurice Djenda, from the Central African Republic, who worked on the music of the Pygmies, the Gbaya, and the Mpyemo, is well acquainted with similar phenomena arising from his cultural area. On one occasion he called my attention to an inherent pattern in the playing of the *bio* flute of a member of the Bambenjele, Upper Sangha (personal communication, 1966). This inherent melody in the low register had escaped me.

Daniel Kachamba, guitarist from Malawi, took delight in a certain inherent pattern which he discovered after a sound film recording in the Institute of Film Sciences Göttingen, October 1972, when he listened to the solo guitar composition *Maliro aKachamba*. On his way home he constantly repeated this piece on his cassette recorder, and continuously pointed out this inherent pattern which was composed of the notes of the third guitar string. He said that it sounded like *ulimba*, a xylophone of the Sena and neighboring tribes in southern Malawi. He began to dance a sort of tap dance, the steps of which followed this inherent pattern.

The perception of inherent patterns is not a cultural trait. During my numerous lecture tours in Europe and Africa experiments with Kiganda xylophone music have shown Europeans and West Africans that the perception of inherent patterns is not bound up with belonging to certain musical cultures. In the akadinda composition *Basiibira malayika* (Kubik 1964a:154) all the persons tested, regardless of their ethnic or cultural relationship perceived in an identical manner the obtrusive inherent pattern in the lowest notes of the xylophone.

The prerequisite for the perception of inherent patterns is an at least average receptivity for music. A completely "unmusical" person probably hears nothing.

In a piece of music from southern Uganda several inherent lines are perceptible at the same time. Some of these are very distinctly emphasized, some are even obtrusive, whilst others are only discovered after intensive exposure to such sound material, in just the same way as it can take some time with a puzzle picture before the picture tips over and a different one is seen. During tests in West Africa, with students of the University of Ghana, at Legon, and at the University of Nigeria, at Nsukka, in 1973, I was able to show that at first all the persons under test do not hear the same inherent pattern. They were asked to sing or to whistle at the same time inherent patterns in the akadinda composition *Basiibira malayika*. It was then found that some students first of all imitated the high patterns, others the low patterns. The *direction* of perception or the direction of attention can differ between individual persons either at given intervals of time or at any time. Some concentrate their attention more on the low register, some on the high. It was also possible to observe small individual discrepancies in the recognition and comprehension of inherent patterns with West African students.

According to the results obtained it may be assumed that the perception of inherent patterns is a general human feature. Such phenomena therefore are not only the subject of musical ethnology and ethnological psychology, but of perception psychology itself. The perception of inherent patterns belongs in the most basic mental stratum, which certainly easily transcends ethnic and cultural differences.

The systematic exploitation of these properties of the human mind, namely the composing of structural models which produce such pattern effects, is nevertheless bound up with culture. In Western music inherent patterns are either not present at all or only in rudimentary form.

Inherent patterns and their composition are a special feature of numerous Black African musical cultures, whereas in other areas of the world they either do not occur or are less pronounced. Comparative investigations have, however, not yet been carried out in this field, and therefore it is hardly possible at this stage to make any definitive pronouncements on the subject.

In Black Africa the principle of the creation of inherent patterns is known almost everywhere, but in some musical cultures it is pronounced particularly intensively. Such areas include: (1) southern Uganda (Buganda, Busoga, and so on), and northern Uganda (Acholi); (2) southern and western Zaire; (3) central Cameroon (Vute and so on); and (4) the area of Zimbabwe and the lower Zambezi valley.

TUNING PATTERNS

Of special interest in the psychology of the perception and recognition of auditory patterns in African music are the operations of tuning musical instruments. Some authors assume that there is an absolute reference note for the tuning of some instruments (cf. Jones 1964). Aids such as tuning forks do not seem to be usual at all in Africa. However, a new instrument, such as a new xylophone, can be tuned from an old one. The basic note of an instrument, for instance a flute, can also be used as the starting point for tuning other instruments with a nonfixed tuning, for example stringed instruments (zithers, guitars, and so on).

Pie-Claude Ngumu reports as follows in an article regarding the *mendzaŋ* [carrier-strap xylophone] in southern Cameroon as to how they were tuned by his informant Ambasa:

In his technique of manufacture, Ambasa starts by fixing empirically the tone of an *omvɔk* slat. The position of this slat is a double one. It is the first to be made, but it is also the middle slat of the instrument. I think this is justified by the *beti* tradition. The head of the family, in his responsibility for the life of those who claim kinship to him, is always to be found at the middle of his people at traditional gatherings. The musicians have also found it right to parallel this to underline the importance of this first wooden slat of the mendzaŋ. They have given a central position to this initial slat. All the tones originate here. This is a very original method of underlining this slat's importance. From now onwards I shall designate it by the number "1" (Ngumu 1976:35; my translation).

As in many other musical cultures of Africa, there is here a hierarchic arrangement of the notes analogous to a social pattern. Something similar is reported by Maurice Djenda regarding the Mpyemo in the Central African Republic, where the notes of musical instruments are named like the members of a family — mother, children, and so on (personal communication, 1966). Obama, a musical ethnologist from the Cameroon, reported a "polygamous *mvet*" (mvet is the Cameroon harp zither).

The further process of the tuning of a mendzaŋ is carried out, according to Ngumu, as follows: starting from note 1 of this ten-slat xylophone, the musician tunes step by step downward: 1, 2, 3, 4, 5, 6, and with note 6 he reaches the lowest note of the instrument. Then for 6, 5, and 4 he finds the upper octaves 6́, 5́, 4́, by tuning them one after the other in an upward movement. What is then left is the tuning of the note 7̄, which falls between 6́ and 1. On this Ngumu reports as follows:

After tuning these nine notes, . . . Ambasa does not hide his embarrassment with regard to fixing the note of the last slat. The xylophone which he had known and used in his infancy only had the nine slats which we have just seen. But subsequently he had observed, especially on his stay in Etenga country, that there were mendzaŋ groups who had introduced a new note betwecn 1 and 6. This slat was named *Esandi*. . . . The word *esandi*, in Ewondo, comes from *asanda* which means "bad luck." The change of the initial *a* into *e* and of the final *a* into *i* creates a new word which designates the action of casting bad luck and trouble. This is the word *esandi*. An object which bears this name . . . is regarded as a spoilsport. This wooden mendzaŋ plate, known as esandi, is therefore rcgarded, by those who introduced it, as a purely foreign invention in the system, introducing an unaccustomed sound into the beti xylophone . . . higher than 1 and lower than 6́. I will designate it by the number 7 (Ngumu 1976:37; my translation).

According to Ngumu the complete tuning pattern for the omvək runs as follows (numbered from the point of view of the performing musician): 6, 5, 4, 3, 2, 1, 7, 6́, 5́, 4́.

Ngumu's interesting description of the tuning of his informant Ambasa throws light on the process which is behind this. Ambasa possessed no aids such as tuning forks or an old xylophone. He had a tuning pattern in his mind with the following features: (1) it had a starting point like the social standard of a chieftainship or a family, a head man, a One: the starting point of the pattern was at the same time the most important point; (2) from there onward the tuning pattern proceeded six steps downwards; and (3) after reaching the sixth step the musician regards the pattern as proceeding further in an upward movement (traveling backward), but only for three steps, and he tunes the higher octaves to this.

In this way the tuning process of this basic hexatonic pattern reached its end. To this there is then added an appendix. Some time ago, in fact, a seventh note was inserted into this xylophone music of southern Uganda. Where it came from, no one knows. From German missionary songs and school songs? From Western instruments such as mouth organs which, according to reports known to me were already played in German times in the Cameroon?

This seventh note is foreign; it stands in isolation and is found to be difficult and is therefore designated as a "spoilsport". Ambasa now inserts this in between.

The measurements of several xylophones and other musical instruments recorded by me in southern Cameroon in 1964 gave Cent figures which often come close to an equiheptatonic division of the octave. The process of tuning by Ngumu's informant, however, does not seem to confirm very much this result obtained a long way away from the Beti culture. It is not possible to detect the principle of a division of the octave into seven equal steps in Ambasa's tuning pattern, even if the intervals which are heard do in fact come surprisingly close to the equiheptatonic Cent values (171.4 Cents). Stroboconn results are valuable. But we must first of all keep to what the musician does and what he himself says about it.

Are *fixed* intervals a component of Ambasa's tuning pattern? What takes place in his head when he tunes downwards the six notes starting from 1, the "head of family"? Has he a constant interval in mind or changing intervals? Pie-Claude Ngumu expressed himself as follows on this point:

Up to now I am still persuaded that, among the Beti, there is no common measure for the tuning of the seven tones of the mendzaŋ. I think that every ethnic group tunes the notes of the instruments according to the music of the area, the traditional music and the most recent music of present musicians, music whose particular inflections are not necessarily identical everywhere (1976:65; my translation).

It is true that there is no proof that Ambasa when tuning his first six notes has any fixed intervals in his head. Still less are there any indications that he aims at different intervals, such as major and minor thirds.

In the traditional xylophone music of southern Cameroon thirds and octaves are struck simultaneously (harmonically) on the xylophone. If one observes not only the Cent numbers of the intervals between successive stages but also those of the thirds, it is found with striking regularity that one is dealing with constant *neutral thirds*. It is probable that Ambasa when carrying out his tuning has impressed upon him *an interval magnitude* which he realizes stage by stage in a downward movement and the double value of which gives those neutral thirds, that is to say thirds which sound as similar as possible. These are regularly immediately tested by musicians of southern Cameroon after they have tuned an instrument.

During a joint lecture tour in West Africa the Malawi flautist and guitarist Donald Kachamba, when asked by Ben Aning, of the Institute of

African Studies at Legon, what was the concept he used for tuning the guitar, thought for a moment and said: "I am thinking like playing, I hear the tune [he meant 'tuning']". As soon as he had "heard" the tuning inside, he tuned. Therefore by means of action (turning the pegs upward or downward) he brings the notes of the individual strings into congruence with an inner tuning pattern which is embossed in his memory. He has the tuning "in his ear".

Donald Kachamba's music belongs to the so-called acculturated music forms of Malawi which are dependent upon the South African *kwela* and *simanjemanje* music. In their conceptions, however, teaching and learning techniques fit them into the system of the traditional musical culture in this Malawi area (Kachamba Brothers' Band 1972; Kubik 1972a, 1973).

Donald remembers the notes of a tuning pattern and the basic chords which are possible when the instrument has been correctly tuned according to this pattern. As soon as the strings have been tuned, he checks these chords.

Donald certainly does not tune according to an "inner" *scale*, but he has in his ear a *major triad*, the first position of fingering in his guitar playing. This can be observed very distinctly if one watches his actions when tuning. He turns the strings up and down, but when he is checking them he does not merely strike the strings whilst open, but time and again fingers the strings with his left hand.

Donald's tuning pattern is a chord, a major triad, a "cluster" of five notes one over the other, because he plays the five-stringed guitar. These are determined not only by their relationship with one another, but also in regard to their absolute pitch. The interval relations of these five notes are completely pure. His most important guitar tuning he refers to as LG. This goes in the relative notation with open strings: E, B, G, D, G. However, it is not the notes of the open strings but the tonic chords F sharp, D, A, D, A (relative notation) which are his tuning pattern. There is no idea of a scale with him, but this does not mean that scale melodies are not manifest in the music. When the first chord (tonic) has been established, he then immediately tests further fingering positions (dominant, subdominant) and other chords. After each tuning operation he checks them by carrying out the progressive use of further fingering positions, starting with the tonic position, and then he uses musical fragments for testing out his tuning system.

Tuning according to a major triad, usually in a certain reversal (as a fourth/sixth chord) is by no means a feature of acculturation. Major triads are important tuning patterns in many areas of Africa and are the basis of consonant chains in harmony. Their recognition is based on the experience of overtone structures, and therefore the inversion as a fourth/sixth chord plays so great a part in African music, because this inversion represents the order of sequence third, fourth, and fifth partial note. In the traditionally heptatonic areas of Africa, especially in a huge area which embraces parts of Zaire, Zambia, Angola and Malawi, there are two principles, the *consonance principle* (major triads) and *equidistance principle*, which work together as two conflicting patterns and produce that characteristic harmony of this area which is characterized by major triads and neutral triads (the latter as a compromise with equiheptatonics). Minor triads as a counterpart to major triads are completely absent in these African musical cultures.

One can imagine the tuning operation of an instrument rather as follows: a tuning pattern, learned by the musician and finally internalized, which is determined by certain note relationships and which can be either relative or absolute in regard to pitch, is projected onto chaotic stimuli (an instrument out of tune). By various interventions and actions on the part of the musician these chaotic stimuli are modified in such a way that they are brought into congruence with the inner tuning pattern. The instrument is now in tune.

The inner tuning pattern is culturally determined. In some musical cultures it is possible for purely physical features, for example rational vibration ratios, overtones, and so on, to play a part in the coming into being of the inner note system pattern. Stimuli for this purpose are received from strings or other sound-producing objects.

Such inner note system patterns form the basis of the tuning and the hearing of music and are extremely resistant to change. Hearing habits in the field of the recognition of note systems, once learned, are apparently irreversible. Someone who has "grown up" into a given note system from childhood onward perceives the note material of a foreign musical culture always in relation to his own patterns. Musicians brought up in Western musical culture, for example, hear the equiheptatonic scales of Africa instinctively in relation to the known diatonic scale, and equipentatonic systems as C, D, E, G, A. Even a major effort of will cannot change this perception process.

The ingrained inner note system pattern is embossed so deeply that it *must* be projected reflex-fashion on external stimuli. By the immense power of this inner pattern the outer stimuli are unbent, "heard as they should be". In the most favorable instance the observer is conscious of this process. He is aware that something is not right, that the notes of the foreign note system do not quite coincide with the notes to which he is accustomed, and in fact that some notes do so less than others. Nevertheless, he hears these nonconforming notes as *deviations* from his own note system pattern. He does not hear them as a component of the pattern, for example equiheptatonic, which transcends his own sphere of experience.

There are numerous indications that the members of African musical cultures with approximately equiheptatonic scales also "unbend" the

European diatonic scale from their own standpoint, that is to say, hear it "as it should have been". From the standpoint of some African musical cultures, however, the diatonic Western scale falls within the *tolerance range* of an approximately equiheptatonic system. The European scale is then nothing other than *one* out of many possibilities within an amply extendable approximately equiheptatonic scale. This also explains why precisely in the equiheptatonic zones of Africa the European note system was absorbed without trouble. The more recent music of Africa (highlife, Congo guitar music, and so on) had its birth almost entirely in heptatonic zones.

The tolerance range of an equiheptatonic system would appear to differ from region to region. Under foreign influence it can evidently be stretched to such an extent that the seven notes of the European system find a place therein without trouble and finally the old scale may even gradually be forgotten in favor of this narrower definition of a heptatonic scale in whole and half tones. Historically this would seem to be the case, say, with southern Cameroon. Here, during the last few decades, it has been possible to observe several stages in the adaptation of the old African scale with its neutral thirds to the Western scale. A similar case is to be found in the songs of Nkangela-speaking groups on both sides of the boundary between Angola and Zambia. In southeastern Angola I was able to observe in 1965 in the harmony of Nkangela-speaking groups an intonation in the traditional tone system of this area. This can be regarded as a compromise between the ideal continuingly pure major triads and an equiheptatonic octave division (Kubik 1968). On the Zambian side of this zone, however, there has occurred a far-reaching adaptation to the diatonic Western pattern, evidenced in field recordings among the Luchazi in 1972. During my stay in Zambia I did not find any indication that these populations were conscious of any change. Equiheptatonic scales and their adaptation to the Western diatonic system are regarded by the populations concerned as identical patterns.

Regarding this identity of *pattern* between equidistant and certain Western note series there have been several interesting statements by African musicians.

"Equiheptatonic" and "equipentatonic" relate to very flexible phenomena. Therefore Wachsmann (1957) suggested the expression "pen-equidistant". What he meant was approximate division of the octave into seven or five equal stages. In some areas this division of the octave may have been conceived approximately in this way from time immemorial, so that the diatonic scale of European origin was perceived within this system and was in no case felt as running counter to it. A Western observer may be astonished that African musicians tell him that it is all the same, when *he* feels distinct differences or thinks he can prove them by stroboconn results.

In 1959, during my first stay in Africa I was extremely astonished when George Kakoma from Kampala once invited me to his house and demonstrated the amadinda composition *Olutalo olw'e Nsinsi* on the black keys of the piano. In all seriousness he explained to me that the Kiganda scale is "the same" as the black notes on the piano. Even when a Western musical ethnologist researching African note systems is glad to dissociate himself from such remarks and to regard them as unscientific, they do nevertheless represent a reality from the *mental* point of view. I do not know what George Kakoma would say today, but in 1959 he evidently felt the frequency pattern of an amadinda to be identical with the black notes on the piano. The fact that one pattern had its place in another was evidently not regarded as troublesome.

As far as a range of tolerance is concerned, the notes of the white keys on the piano (in the case of the heptatonic scale) or those of the black keys (in the case of the pentatonic scale) must nevertheless be just acceptable to the musicians of the relevant African musical cultures. Pie-Claude Ngumu gives vigorous testimony to the way he feels this:

For the moment I think that the essential feature of the Beti mendzaŋ is that it is built up on a scale of seven different tones. . . . I allowed myself to take advantage of this margin of tolerance. I aligned the seven tones of the mendzaŋ of the music school to the tuning fork using the diatonic system of the European scale. But the traditional method, obviously much tarnished by this alignment to the tuning fork, was by no means influenced by a predetermined sound. Accordingly its scale was much greater . . . (Ngumu 1976:65; my translation).

Atta A. Mensah writes regarding the tuning of the *gyilgo*, a lamellaphone of the Gonja in Ghana:

Some variation indeed exists in the tuning of *gyilgo* in Gonja; but the more striking aspect of these tunings is the overwhelming consensus on an anhemitonic pentatonic scale used by Gonja singers. This is so near the scale obtained from the black notes of the pianoforte that the ear trained in European classical traditions tends to equate the two. But insistent minute intervallic differences indicate that the Gonja penta scale is not to be identified with any Western penta forms (Mensah, n.d).

How wide are tolerance margins when expressed in Cents? Certainly not uniformly wide. It is feasible that they are wider where the old system has been broken open by the influence of Western or other influences, where a certain bimusicality has come into being, such as is probably the case in the Beti-Buli region of the southern Cameroon.

How would a traditional musician of the mendzaŋ fifty to sixty years ago have reacted if one had placed before him for approval a xylophone tuned after the Western fashion? Would he have accepted the tuning or would he have immediately started the tedious process of retuning?

Andrew Tracey provides interesting information regarding the reactions of his teacher Jege A. Tapera when tuning the *mbira* (Tracey 1961).

Concepts of tuning differ widely in Africa. In Buganda and Busoga *scale* concepts seem to be present, and a scale is conceived as starting from the highest frequency. In southwestern Angola among the Humbi and the Handa, when tuning a *chihumba* they usually tune two tones in pairs in neutral thirds. The musician begins his tuning pattern with the lowest note and tunes upward in thirds, his fingers always jumping over one note (*Humbi en Handa* 1973, Kubik 1975–1976).

Tuning patterns are sometimes *named* and identified in this way. Such verbal or syllabic tuning formulas can often provide information regarding the structure of tuning. With the Azande in the Central African Republic (Kubik 1964b) the *kundi* [harp] is tuned according to the verbal formula: *Vili pai sa sunge*. The scale begins with the highest notes and comes downward step by step. This verbal formula is impressed in the memory of the musician. It is also a sort of name of the tuning pattern which is in his mind.

Not seldom are Western ethnomusicologists struck by the observation that an African instrumentalist when newly tuning his instrument only reproduces *approximately* those note relationships which he had, say, the day before. Ethnomusicologists have therefore recorded on tape such "unheard" variations, say, the tuning of a harp by the same musician at an interval of several days. In reply to questions the musician answered the doubting observer by saying that this was the same tuning and he also quickly played the same pieces on it with the same gusto. The observer is then faced with the difficult problem of deciding whether the instrument was on one occasion wrongly tuned or whether a certain amount of freedom is allowed in the tuning within a scale which is only approximately determined (cf. Kubik 1961).

In 1965 my friend Kufuna Kandonga, a *likemba* [lamellaphone] player from the Longa area of southeastern Angola, in the Cuando-Cubango district, tuned his instrument, to my ear, practically every day slightly differently. This was unpleasant for me because I had become accustomed to a certain tone sequence which I heard in terms of my own tone system.

Such was the typical reaction of an external observer who was not yet accustomed to the relevant problems of the perception and recognition of patterns. What can be done with such phenomena? The only reliable yardstick is what the particular musician says himself, and the ethnomusicologist must first of all keep to this. Kufuna's tuning seemed to me once to be C, D, E, F sharp (minus), G, A (minus) and it would have been nicest for me if Kufuna had always tuned exactly like this, so that these tone relationships would have become established in my ear. That would have done away with a problem which was very unpleasant to me. But, to my great disappointment, another time it sounded to me like C, D flat, E, F, G, A flat (plus), and the next time something different again.

Likewise, the impression often arises that African choirs, for example in the Congo/Angola area as reported by Pechuel Lösche (cf. Kubik 1968), sing the same song on different days with different "sorts of notes", on the one hand major, on the other hand minor, but in any case with curiously deviant intervals.

African choirs, likembe players, and so on, however, have themselves no approximate view of the tonal material, no "approximate scale". To the musician carrying out the tuning his tuning pattern is something very certain, which is branded into his memory, not something approximate. He knows what he wants. When newly tuning his instrument, it does not produce *his* note system pattern approximately, but that note scale which the external observer hears in it. He reproduces approximately not his scale, by *my* scale projected on to his music. As my Western note system pattern does not coincide with his, *I alone perceive deviations in the manifestations of his inner tuning pattern, which are irrelevant to him*. For the African musician it is the same pattern.

The outside observer projects his own note system pattern on the foreign music which is otherwise delineated. Certain objective deviations from culture-impressed patterns are tolerated in all cultures. Also in the tuning of European musical instruments there is often a considerable tolerance range, for example in the case of recorders. In the case of intercultural projection, however, deviations which from the standpoint of the one culture are regarded as completely normal and are tolerated, are found to be so divergent from the standpoint of another that those belonging to the latter culture suddenly recognize in it a different pattern (their own musical culture). Tiny fluctuations of intervals in the tuning of an equiheptatonic system in Africa are heard by Western observers as approximately major and then once again as approximately minor patterns. The oscillation range of the African tuning pattern, one could say, transcends the range of tolerance in the perception of Western tone system patterns by the Western observer.

An interesting field of investigation is what breadth of tolerance is effective in this adapted hearing from one musical culture to another. In a series of investigations, persons to be tested were confronted with an instrumental tuning played back from a tape recording and were asked to give their impression graphically in some way or other. At the same time any reference points which were felt as central (key note, tonic notes, and so on) were also to be marked. This series of tests on the intercultural projection of tuning patterns, however, is still in its early stages because there are numerous problems which have not yet been solved. For example the nature of the representation of the tone material can favor a certain way of hearing. The person being tested can acquire a completely different impression of tone system if one plays the scale upward or in the reverse order, or again if one plays the tones in an irregular sequence.

In 1960 I reported on a self-experiment on the amadinda of Uganda.

The "sound" of each xylophone key is extremely complex and rich in overtones. . . . Quite a number of notes can be found out by measuring for instance the vibrations of our Fig. 1 [illustrating the sound of amadinda key XII], . . . The three greatest notes (keys X, XI, and XII) *often* sound a third smaller to the ear of a listener. . . . When I was playing the *amadinda* in Kampala the three keys always sounded to my ears as C, D and E+. But listening to the tape-recording of the scale now, most people, including myself, seem to hear instead of these pitches, E, F and G . . .; when it was played downwards most of them heard the basic notes C, D and E. This is musically and psychologically very interesting (Kubik 1960:7–8).

What had happened here was not elucidated until much later on. As I could see on sonagrams of the tones of the corresponding slats, the lowest tones of the relevant xylophone recorded in Uganda were tuned not to the basic tone of the slat, the first partial — the C, D and E was already the fourth partial, which stood out particularly strongly. The musician had cut the xylophone slats in such a way that this partial, together with the other tones of the scale, formed the tuning pattern.

When tuning, the musicians listen for the tone which they want. Here the fourth partial impressed itself on the ear as that tone. The tuning pattern uses those tones which impress themselves on the ear, regardless of whether it is the key note or a higher partial which is not of interest to the musician. Andrew Tracey reports that often something similar occurred when tuning the mbira.

The noteworthy "third effect" on that amadinda (Kubik 1960) occurred because in the case of the lowest notes the fifth partials always penetrated particularly loudly. If one is confronted with the sound of a xylophone slat in isolation, one hears the loud fifth partial (that is to say for, C, D and E the notes E, F sharp and G sharp, relative notation) as the dominant feature. But they are not exactly these intervals.

If the scale is played upward, beginning from the bottom, then the ear perceives first of all the fifth partials until after the third note of the xylophone from the bottom the fifth partials become so weak that the hearer is now thrown back to the basic tones and he continues to hear the fourth or second partials. This is distinctly visible in the sonagram.

It is different if one listens to the scale in a downward sequence. Then the basic pentatonic tones have so strong a coherence as a pattern that one automatically hears the pentatonic pattern *right to the end*, even if the fifth partials which destroy this pattern are stronger in the lowest register.

This is a further example which shows how the coherence of patterns as a perception-determining force can be stronger than physical facts.

REFERENCES

COOKE, PETER
1970   Ganda xylophone music: another approach. *African Music* 4(4):62–80.
CORCORAN, DEREK W. J.
1971   *Pattern recognition*. Harmondsworth: Penguin.
DAUER, A. M.
1966   Musik-Landschaften in Afrika. *Afrika Heute* 23, special supplement. December 1.
DJENDA, MAURICE
1968   L'Arc-en-terre des Gbaya-Bokoto. *African Music* 4(2):44–46.
1969   Les Pygmées de la Haute Sangha. *Geographica*. April. Ile-Ife, Nigeria.
JONES, ARTHUR M.
1949   *African music in Northern Rhodesia and some other places*. Livingstone, Zambia (Northern Rhodesia): Rhodes-Livingstone Museum.
1959   *Studies in African music*, two volumes. London: Oxford University Press.
1964   *Africa and Indonesia: the evidence of the xylophone and other musical and cultural factors*. Leiden: Brill.
KOETTING, JAMES
1970   Analysis and notation of West African drum ensemble music. *Selected Reports of the Institute of Ethnomusicology of the University of California* 1(3):115–146.
KOFFKA, KURT
1935   *Principles of gestalt psychology*. New York: Harcourt, Brace.
KUBIK, GERHARD
1960   The structure of Kiganda xylophone music. *African Music* 2(3):6–30.
1961   Musikgestaltung in Afrika. *Neues Afrika* 3(5).
1962   The phenomenon of inherent rhythms in East and Central African instrumental music. *African Music* 3(1):33–42.
1964a Xylophone playing in southern Uganda. *Journal of the Royal Anthropological Institute* 94(2):138–159.
1964b Harp music of the Azande and related peoples in the Central African Republic. *African Music* 3(3):37–76.
1965   Transcription of Mangwilo xylophone music from film strips. *African Music* 3(4):35–51.
1966   Musique camerounaise: les timbili des Vute. *Abbia* 14, 15. Yaoundé.
1966–1967   Ennanga music. *African Music* 4(1):21–24.
1968   *Mehrstimmigkeit und Tonsysteme in Zentral- und Ostafrika*. Vienna: Hermann Böhlaus.
1969   Composition techniques in Kiganda xylophone music. *African Music* 4(3):22–72.
1970   "Aufbau und Struktur der Amadinda-Musik von Buganda," in *Musik als Gestalt und Erlebnis*. In honor of Walter Graf. Vienna: Hermann Böhlaus.
1972a Transcription of African music from silent film: theory and methods. *African Music* 5(2):28–39.
1972b *The Kachamba Brothers' Band*. Acta Ethnologica et Linguistica 27. Vienna: Institut für Völkerkunde der Universität Wien. (Translated 1974 as *The Kachamba Brothers' Band: a study of neo-traditional music in Malawi*. Manchester: University Press for the University of Zambia Institute for African Studies.)

1973   Der Verarbeitung von Kwela, Jazz und Pop in der modernen Musik von Malawi. *Jazzforschung/Jazz Research* 3, 4. Graz.

1974   "Verstehen in afrikanischen Musikkulturen," in *Music und Verstehen: Aufsätze zur semantischen Theorie, Ästhetik und Soziologie der musikalischen Kommunikation*. Edited by Peter Faltin and Hans-Peter Reinecke. Cologne: Arno Volk.

1975–1976   Musical bows of south-western Angola, 1965. *African Music* 5(4):98–104.

MENSAH, ATTA A.

n.d.   *The gyilgo, a Gonja sansa.* Papers in African Studies 3. Legon, Ghana: Institute of African Studies.

NGUMU, PIE-CLAUDE

1976   *Les Mendzaŋ des chanteurs de Yaoundé.* Acta Ethnologica et Linguistica 34. Vienna: Institut für Völkerkunde der Universität Wien.

NKETIA, J. H. KWABENA

1962   *African music in Ghana: a survey of traditional forms.* Accra: Longman's.

1963   *Folk songs of Ghana.* Legon: University of Ghana.

RYCROFT, DAVID

1961   The guitar improvisations of Mwenda Jean Bosco. *African Music* 2(4):81–98.

1962   The guitar improvisation of Mwenda Jean Bosco. *African Music* 3(1):86–102.

SERWADDA, MOSES, HEWITT PANTALEONI

1968   A possible notation for African dance drumming. *African Music* 4(2):47–52.

STIGLMAYR, ENGELBERT

1970   *Ganzheitliche Ethnologie: Ethnologie als integrale Kulturwissenschaft.* Acta Ethnologica et Linguistica 18. Vienna: Institut für Völkerkunde der Universität Wien.

TRACEY, ANDREW

1961   Mbira music of Jege A. Tapera. *African Music* 2(4):44–63.

WACHSMANN, K. P.

1950   An equal-stepped tuning in a Ganda harp. *Nature* 165(4184):40–41.

1957   A study of norms in the tribal music of Uganda. *Ethnomusicology* 1(11):9–16.

Music

BOSCO, MWENDA JEAN

1952   *Masanga/Tambala moja.* Gallotone GB1586.

Humbi en Handa

1973   *Humbi en Handa–Angola.* Recorded and annotated by Gerhard Kubik. Belgisches Radio en Televisie 6803 044. Tervuren: Koninklijk Museum voor Midden-Afrika.

KACHAMBA BROTHERS' BAND

1972   *The Kachamba Brothers' Band.* Acta Ethnologica et Linguistica Series Phonographica 1.

Tactility as an Aesthetic Consideration in African Music

ROBERT KAUFFMAN

The *mbira* or *sanza*, a plucked lamellaphone (hand-piano) unique to Africa and African-related areas, presents some unique challenges to those interested in assessing the aesthetic characteristics of African music. Several factors indicate that the mbira is an instrument meant more for personal enjoyment than for public presentation. The resonating gourd in which the instrument is often played completely obscures the keys from everyone except the performer. Instruments are often imbued with personality, thus giving a special personal relationship between the performer and his instrument.

I have seen so many mbira players who give names to their instruments. Mbira is not enough, but names like *chido* [lover], *mwana umwe* [the only child], *munanzi* [the beautiful music producer], *murombo* [the powerful one] are given to the instruments. The mbira is especially important to men who have difficulties in the running of their families. Say, if a man is married but has no child, his children die, his wife dies, or he is so poor that he becomes a beggar. If the player has these difficulties, then mbira will always be there to comfort him. . . . Nearly all mbira players can play alone for the whole night. . . . When the mbira player plays his instrument, he is not playing it for the world . . . what he will be doing is to communicate with a friend (Maraire 1971).

The personal quality of mbira playing is especially apparent in ritual situations where it is played together with gourd rattles for the purpose of inducing a trance. In such cases, the mbira is rarely heard, since its sound is so strongly dominated by the percussive sound of the accompanying gourd rattles. People who attend these rituals see the resonators in which the mbiras are being played, but they hear only the gourd rattles, the strong and persistent sound of which seems to be necessary for inducing the trance. If the mbiras cannot be heard, then why are they used? Are they considered as ritual objects more important for maintaining tradition and as visual symbols rather than as musical instruments? However, on close examination, the musical patterns played on the mbira are shown to be extremely intricate and involved. If the instruments were not important musically, and were merely retained as traditional symbols, less attention would probably be given to the skillful playing of them. Two reasonable explanations can be given for the presence of the mbira in these ritual situations: (1) the mbira is a personal instrument which is played mainly for the enjoyment of the performer rather than for the aural benefit of others involved in the ritual; or (2) at least a large proportion of the enjoyment of playing the mbira must come from its tactility rather than from its sound-producing characteristics, in other words, the vibration complex of the mbira keys can be enjoyed as a pleasant sensation. John Blacking (1961:29, 34–35) indicates that in the Nsenga *kalimba* (mbira) music of Zambia, there may be intervallic similarity from one piece to another, but the similarity in the physical pattern of thumb movement is very great.

The personal aspect of music making is not difficult to understand in our current way of assessing musical significance, but tactile aspects of music making have been ignored, particularly in Western studies of aesthetics, even though tactility is probably one of the most important aspects of artistic consciousness in Africa. For example, a musical mouth bow, like the mbira, is probably experienced tactilely more than aurally. The external plucking of the bow emits a very soft sound, but internal resonating of the string inside the mouth cavity is felt quite intensely and is mainly transmitted tactilely through the bones of the head rather than aurally through the ears. Bow players do not refer to the melody in terms of the plucked sounds, but in terms of the mouth-resonated sounds.

The extensive use of dance as a major art form is another example of the emphasis placed upon feeling rather than sound. In the Shona cultures of Rhodesia, dance and drum terminology are often identical, indicating that in some ways at least dancing is considered similar to drumming.

The tactile aspect of music making has been one of the principal stumbling blocks in Western attempts to understand African music in aesthetic terms. Berleant reminds us that sight and hearing have been considered the only aesthetic senses from the time of Plato and Aristotle, because these are the senses that are "most closely related to the operations of reason" (1964:186–187). Moral justification was later given for the exclusion of the tactile since it was so closely related to eroticism. Berleant believes that this exclusion of the tactile sense has become "a fissure in the rock of aesthetic respectability" (1964:187). It seems that tactility is crucial to our understanding of aesthetics in African terms. It is also a factor in attempting to cope with the aesthetic content of much Western music.

The strong emphasis upon tactility would seem to indicate that different cultures can use different combinations and emphases of the basic sense phenomena. Hornbostel showed unusual insight into this aspect of aesthetics when he wrote that "movement can be seen, heard, or touched. Hearing through the skin is not an unusual phenomenon" (Hornbostel 1927:87). The meaning of the various sense verbs in Shona throws considerable light upon the way that the Shona people respond to the various sense phenomena. The verb *kuona* means "to see"; *kubata*, "to touch"; *kuravira*, "to taste"; and *kunuhwa*, "to smell". The verb that means "to hear" is much more comprehensive in its meaning than the other sense verbs. It is *kunzwa* and it means "to perceive by touch, sight, or hearing; to understand." Its meaning involves perception in terms of a unity of the senses, and cognition in terms of understanding. This assessment of the meaning of the sense verbs, together with the apparent emphasis that Shona musicians place upon the tactile phenomenon, would tend to indicate that the hearing and tactile senses are primary in Shona culture, in contrast to the seeing and hearing senses that are primary in Western culture. Understanding this should make a tremendous difference to the study of aesthetics in Africa.

The nature of perception has generally been avoided as an aspect of aesthetic study. If we look at one of the meanings of the word *aesthetics* as "the science whose subject matter is the description and explanation of the arts" (*Webster's third new international dictionary*, s.v.) then aesthetics means more than just "philosophy of the beautiful". The real meaning of aesthetics comes into bold relief when we contrast it with its negative form "anesthetic". The cognitive processes to which the perceptive phenomenon is directed are indeed an important part of aesthetic considerations. But in Western studies too much emphasis has been placed on cognitive aspects at the expense of the sensual. A balance between the two must be restored for an accurate picture of the aesthetic creativity of Africa to be drawn.

REFERENCES

BERLEANT, ARNOLD
  1964   The sensuous and the sensual in aesthetics. *Journal of Aesthetics and Art Criticism* 23(2):185–192.
BLACKING, JOHN
  1961   Patterns of Nsenga *kalimba* music. *African Music* 2(4):26–43.
HORNBOSTEL, ERICH M. VON
  1927   The unity of the senses. *Psyche* 7(4):85–89.
MARAIRE, ABRAHAM
  1971   *Mbira music of Rhodesia*. Notes to long-playing record. Seattle: University of Washington Press.

Stress Behavior in Musicolinguistics

ANOOP C. CHANDOLA

By the term "musicolinguistics" is meant the study of the interaction of music and language from the standpoint of linguistics. In the context of South Asian music such an approach can be seen in Bright (1963) and Chandola (1969, 1970). The aim of this paper is to see some aspects of stress in the context of various verbal and nonverbal devices of human organs that are employed in measuring the rhythms of the Hindustani musical system of South Asia.

In the Hindustani (referred to also as "North Indian") system of rhythms, the first beat of a rhythm is called *sam* in Hindi-Urdu, from Sanskrit *sama* [even, equal, same].[1] In theory the first beat must be the loudest beat. We will therefore say that the first beat receives the highest stress. This stress serves as a reference point for the beginning of the rhythmic cycle. Rhythms vary in terms of the quality, quantity, and distribution of beats. Quality refers to their phonetic timbre; quantity to their number; and distribution to their division in terms of measures or bars. In this paper the quality aspect is not dealt with.

The following two rhythms illustrate the differences of quantity and distribution.

Rhythm A   1   2   3   4 | 5   6   7   8

Rhythm B   1   2   3 | 4   5 | 6   7

The Indo-Arabic numerals are for beats and the bars indicate the divisions or measures. Rhythm A has a total of eight beats and has two divisions with an equal number, that is, four beats in each. Rhythm B has

---

[1] The Sanskrit and Hindi-Urdu terms in this paper are transcribed here in the international Romanized phonemic convention.

seven beats with three divisions where the first division has three beats and the other two have two beats in each of them. These two rhythms imply that it is not necessary to have equal and even numbers of beats in each division. Rhythm A can be exemplified by the *kaharvā* rhythm and Rhythm B by the *rūpak* rhythm of the Hindustani music.

The stroke on Beat 1 is supposed to be the loudest, not only on a percussion instrument (for example the tabla) but also on any other tonal instrument (for example the sitar). The human vocal apparatus producing tones is also a tonal instrument in this respect, that is, the singer who is using language is also supposed to stress that linguistic syllable which falls on Beat 1. There are, however, other body parts which are used as non-tonal and nonverbal markers of rhythmic structure only in terms of the quantity of beats and their distribution. These parts are the hands, feet, and head. Hands and feet are employed in more than one way, but we will give only one example of each below.

One use of the hands is clapping, which indicates the divisions of a rhythm. Clapping is the most important measuring device among all nontonal or nonverbal uses of body parts. In written convention the presence or absence of clapping is indicated by these symbols — zero, cross, and Indo-Arabic numerals over or above the first beat of a division of a rhythm. Since in this paper, Indo-Arabic numerals are used for beats, Roman numerals have been used instead for marking the first beat of a division. Thus, Rhythms A and B would be rewritten as below:

```
              ×               0
Rhythm A      1   2   3   4 | 5   6   7   8

              ×           |  II      |  III
Rhythm B      1   2   3   |  4   5   |  6   7
```

The cross occurs on the first beat of the first division of a rhythm and as a principle, therefore, this first beat which is Beat 1 of the entire rhythm, receives the loudest clap. Zero indicates the absence of any clap. The Roman numerals are also for claps, but are weak in loudness compared with the first beat of the first division. Thus "×" means first division, "II" means second division, "III" means third division, and so on. It should be mentioned here that it is highly uncommon to have no zero, that is, the absence of a clap, in a rhythm. At zero the hand is simply waved in the air. The Hindi-Urdu term *tālī* [clap] is used for clapping, and *khālī* [empty, blank] for zero.

Either foot can be employed to mark rhythms, and parallels the pattern of clapping. The foot is moved down against the ground or moved upward, or rather sideways. The downward movement occurs on the cross and numerals. The upward or sideways movement occurs on the zero. The movement on Beat 1 of the rhythm is wider and more forceful, so much so that it reaches the level of a mild kick; and the head is generally nodded. However, infrequently, the nodding of the head can parallel the pattern of clapping: on the cross and numerals, but not on the zero. In such a case the nodding is more forceful on Beat 1.

At a performance the players can use feet and head devices, but not clapping (as their hands are busy playing an instrument). The singer, and the listeners, may use any of these devices. In a concert the head is the most conspicuous device to be noticed: others play little part.

In order to observe the interaction of various stress devices, consider the song text (Table 1) composed by Bhatkhande (1920) in the Braj dialect of Hindi.[2] From the standpoint of musical rhythm this entire poem

Table 1. Composition of the song text (Bhatkhande 1920)

0				III				×				II			
9	10	11	12	13	14	15	16	1	2	3	4	5	6	7	8
1.														C	B♭
														pra	*bhu*
2. C	D	D	ᶠE♭	–	F	–	F	G	–	–	F	G	A	B♭	Ċ
te	*rī*	*da*	*yā*	–	*hai*	–	*a*	*pā*	–	–	*rtu*	*a*	*ga*	*ma*	*a*
3. B♭	A	G	F	ᶠE♭	E♭	D	D	D	B♭	A	B♭	G	A	F	G
go	–	*ca*	*ra*	*a*	*vi*	*ka*	*la*	*ca*	*ra*	*a*	*ca*	*ra*	*sa*	*ka*	*la*
4. F	E	F	G	F	–	C	B♭	C	E♭	D	F	E♭	–	D	B♭
ko	–	*tu*	*a*	*dhā*	–	*rpa*	*ti*	*ta*	*na*	*ko*	*u*	*ddhā*	–	*pra*	*bhu*
5. G	–	G	A	F	G	B	Ċ	ᶠ̇D	Ėb	Ḋ	Ċ	Ḋ	B	Ċ	Ċ
dī	–	*na*	*a*	*nā*	–	*tha*	*pa*	*tī*	–	*ta*	*ru*	*du*	*ra*	*ba*	*la*
6. E♭	E♭	A	G	ᶠE♭	–	D	–	D	B♭	A	B♭	G	A	F	G
ma	*ha*	*da*	*ba*	*rā*	–	*dhī*	–	*śa*	*ra*	*ṇā*	–	*ga*	*to*	*hū*	–
7. F	E	F	G	F	–	C	B♭	C	E♭	D	F	ᶠE♭	–	D	B♭
ca	*tu*	*ra*	*ti*	*hā*	–	*rmo*	*he*	*pā*	–	*ra*	*u*	*tā*	–	*rpra*	*bhu*

[2] This song text is considered to be a classical composition in the *rāga* called *kāfī* or *kāphī*. The rhythm of this text has sixteen beats divided into four measures where the first, second and fourth occur with claps and the third occurs with zero (as shown by ×, II, III, and 0 respectively on the top of the song text). I have replaced the Indic names of the twelve tones by C, D♭, D, E♭, E, F, F#, G, A♭, A, B♭, and B. The dot below a tone indicates a lower octave tone and the dot above a tone is for the higher octave. The undotted tone belongs to the middle octave. A superscript tone is a grace note that occurs before the tone written below it. The dash after a tone or a vowel means "continuity" of it to the next beat or beats. The numbering of the lines is just for convenient reference and does not occur in the original song text.

The natural breakdown of these poetic sentences in this text would be as follows:

a. *prabhu   terī   dayā   hai   apāra.*
   lord   your   mercy   is   boundless
   Lord, your mercy is boundless.

b. *tū   agama   agocara   avikala.*
   you   inaccessible   invisible   painless
   You are inaccessible, invisible and painless.

c. *cara   acara   sakala   ko   tū   ādhāra.*
   movable   immovable   all   of   you   support
   You are the support of all movable and immovable ones.

d. *patitana   ko   uddhāra.*
   fallen-ones   of   redeemer
   You are the redeemer of the fallen.

e. *dīna   anātha   patita   aru   durbala   mahad   aparādhī.*
   poor   masterless   fallen   and   weak   big   criminal
   I am poor, masterless, fallen, weak and a great sinner.

f. *śaraṇāgata   hū̃   catura   tihāra.*
   refuge   I/am   smart   your
   I am now smart as I take refuge in you.
   (I, whose name is *Catura*,[3] take refuge in you.)

g. *mohe   pāra   utāra*
   me   across   drop
   Take me across.

is measured in terms of sixteen beats, which differs from its linguistic metrical measurements. The linguistic and musical meters may or may not be parallel in terms of their individual metrical units (such as stress, mora, syllable, tone, beat, and so on). Since our focus is on stress, brief information about general stress rules in Hindi-Urdu is provided in the following paragraph.

The stress pattern may vary in the Hindi-Urdu area from the point of view of dialectology. Nevertheless, one thing is definite — linguistic stress is predictable in every dialect of Hindi-Urdu. One simple description of Hindi-Urdu stress would be that it always falls on the first long syllable of a word. If there are all short syllables in a word, the stress would fall on the first short syllable. A short vowel followed by two or more consonants is also like a long vowel from the point of view of stress and meter. A short vowel, namely, *a*, *i* and *u* plus two or more consonants, and all natural long vowels, namely, *ā*, *ī*, *ū*, *e*, *ai*, *o* and *au*, can be called "heavy" syllables also. The linguistic stress may be referred to as natural stress in this paper.

The singer starts singing with the word *prabhu* of Line 1 of the song text, but the highest stress occurs on *apār* for the first time as indicated by × and Beat 1. All the rhythmic devices mentioned above start counting or measuring from the syllable *pā* of the word *apār*. The first long and

---

[3] Bhatkhande wrote many song poems with his pen name *Catura* which means "smart". There is a pun in this word shown by the two translations of this sentence.

therefore stressed syllable in this word is *pā* because of the long vowel *ā*. Thus the natural word stress coincides in this line with the loudest, or Beat 1, of the rhythm. The drummer might start his drumming even before the occurrence of the word *apār* of Line 2, but the loudest stroke of the drum would occur first on this syllable. Similarly, in Line 3, Beat 1 falls on the first syllable *ca* of the word *cara* which again coincides with the natural stress of this word. Beat 1 in Lines 4, 5, and 6 falls upon those syllables which do not have the highest stress linguistically. That is, in the word *patita*, the first syllable *pa* has the natural word stress.[4] But Beat 1 occurs on the syllable *ta* in Line 4 and on *ti*, lengthened as *tī*, in Line 5. In Line 6 the natural stress of the word *saraṇāgata* occurs on the first long syllable *ā*, but Beat 1 occurs on the syllable *śa*, which has a short vowel, *a*. In Line 7 the natural word stress of *pār* and Beat 1 coincide.

Thus, we notice that the natural word stress may or may not coincide with Beat 1. Note that Beat 1 has to receive the highest stress, except in stress switch. The stress switch is of a temporary nature. The drummer or a musician can switch the highest stress to a neighboring beat for a few cycles of a rhythm. He has to restore the highest stress back to Beat 1 as soon as possible. The stress switch is possible only in terms of the drum strokes, tones, or word syllables. The nonverbal and nontonal devices of body parts put the highest stress always on Beat 1 of every rhythmic cycle.

The place of highest stress on Beat 1 of a rhythmic cycle is fixed. But the stress switch cannot be predicted in terms of already known fixed places. Such a distinction can be indicated by the terms "stress" and "accent" as Bolinger did in the case of English stress and concluded that "Stress belongs to the lexicon. Accent belongs to the utterance" (1972:644). To put it simply, the stress on Beat 1 is fixed and the stress switch on some other beat in a rhythmic cycle, which is like an utterance, is for the sake of emphasis. It could be said that "stress" is a phonetic phenomenon whereas "accent" is "unexpected stress plus emphasis" and therefore can be considered as a semantic phenomenon. However, what may be the stressed position from the rhythmic point of view may turn out to be in an unexpected position in a word. For example, the highest linguistic stress in the word *saraṇāgata* falls on the vowel *ā*, but in the song text the stress occurs on the first vowel *a* of the same word because of the Beat 1 superimposed on it. From the linguistic standpoint there is a switch of stress in the word *saraṇāgata*. That is, we have two stress versions of this word now as: (1) *saraṇā́gata*, and (2) *sáraṇāgata*. Thus, from a linguistic point of view as suggested above, the first version is with "stress"

---

[4]   The words *patita* in Line 5 and *patitana* in Line 4 are singular and plural forms of one and the same word *patita* (or *patit*). The final vowel *a* can be dropped (except in verse meter). Thus, *patita* can occur as *patit*, *apāra* as *apār*, *tihāra* as *tihār*, and so on, as can be seen from the versions that appear in the song text on the one hand and in its natural breakdown into poetic sentences on the other.

and the second version is with "accent". That is, the second version has "unexpected stress plus emphasis". The emphasis is for the sake of expressing a musical meaning, namely, the "beginning of a rhythmic cycle".

In the case of words like *apār* in Line 2 and *cara* in Line 3 the linguistic "stress" as well as the linguistic "accent" coincide with the rhythmic "stress". If the rhythmic "stress" is switched to a beat other than Beat 1, it would be considered as a rhythmic "accent" which may or may not coincide with linguistic stress.

The notion associated with stress seems to be the size or extension of the force that is exerted in the articulation of a particular segment. In this sense, stress is roughly the same thing as "amplitude". Here stress and length seem to be correlated to a great extent as the stress occurs on the first long vowel whenever there are two or more vowels in a word. It could be expected that the length of a short vowel in stressed position is relatively extended. For example, in the case of the word *patitana* the first short vowel is stressed from a linguistic point of view and the first vowel should be relatively longer than the following short vowels *i* and *a*. From the musical point of view, the stress, or Beat 1, falls on the third short vowel, namely the second *a* of *patitana*. Can we say that the tone, C, and the beat on it would be slightly longer than the tone and beats on other vowels of this word? Our case is worth considering because we notice that the word *patita* appears as *patīt* in Line 5 where the stress occurs on *i* because of the Beat 1 and is changed to a long vowel as *ī*. This *ī* is continued to the next beat. Perhaps the overt change from short to long may have been motivated by the fact that the short vowel *i* was stressed as Beat 1. It should not be understood, however, that long vowels are usually extended to two beats or tones. For example, the long vowels like *e* and *ī* in the word *terī* of Line 2 have one beat and one tone each. In the case of *patīt* in Line 5 the lengthening is clearly perceptible because of one extra beat added to the vowel *ī*. That is, the change is clearly phonemic. We do not have such a situation in the case of *patitana* of Line 4. Nevertheless the point is that the stressed short vowel is slightly longer than the unstressed vowel even though such a change of length may not be perceived as clearly phonemic. This nonphonemic lengthening, however, must be verified by acoustic machines before considering our argument really valid. Perhaps machines can also answer the question whether the pitch of the stressed vowel has relatively more frequencies than the unstressed vowel in singing. Most probably pitch and length of a vowel grow more in size (quantity) when stressed.

Finally, stress is not necessarily expressed through sound systems. The device of the head, for example, does not have any system of sounds. Nevertheless, we could say that the movement or nod of head has the largest size or force quantity at Beat 1, just as other measuring devices which employ sound systems produce the loudest sound at Beat 1.

REFERENCES

BHATKHANDE, V. N.
1920   *Hindusthānī sangīt paddhati* [Hindustani musical poems], volume
one. Bombay: B. S. Sukhtankar.

BOLINGER, DWIGHT
1972   Accent is predictable (if you're a mind-reader). *Language*
48(3):633–644.

BRIGHT, WILLIAM
1963   Language and music: areas for cooperation. *Ethnomusicology* 7:26–32.

CHANDOLA, ANOOP C.
1969   Metalinguistic structure of Indian drumming: a study of musicolinguistics. *Language and Style* 2:288–295.
1970   Some systems of musical scales and linguistic principles. *Semiotica*
2:135–150.

PART SIX

Music and Dance in Africa and The New World

Igeri Ututu: *An Igbo Folk Requiem Music Dance Ritual*

C. O. OKOREAFFIA

Ututu is an Igbo clan in the Arochuku division of the East Central state of Nigeria. It is made up of nineteen villages: Amaasa, Amaeke, Amankwu, Mkpakpi, Obiagwulu, and Amodu, which make up the Eleoha section of the clan; and Amakofia, Obijoma, Ugwuogo, Ohomja, Eziama, Amaeben, Obiakang, Ukwuakwu, Obialoko, Abuma, Obiene, Amaetiti, and Ubila, which constitute the clan's Umuiwe section.

Each of the nineteen villages has a village head, and the entire clan has a clan head. The functions of the village heads and clan head are political and judicial. At the time when the folk requiem music dance ritual was important culturally, the village heads together with the clan head executed the policies agreed upon by the elders in council. They adjudicated between disputing parties and interpreted the laws and customs of the clan.

Ututu has a clan deity, called *Obasi Ututu*, whose main habitat is a grove by the side of the Cross river, but whose shrines are in the holy groves near Amaeke village. Obasi Ututu is served by a priest. Both the clan head and the clan priest reside at Amaeke.

The economy has always been mainly agricultural, the people being hard-working farmers who also keep domestic animals and have established large cash crop plantations. The farmers plant yams and cocoyams, cassava, peas, beans, corn, okra, peppers, spices, and so on. Plantains, bananas, cocoa, rubber, oranges, mangoes, coconuts, the oil palm, the raffia palm, and pears, are some of the cash crops. Palm wine is always available. The animals kept are goats, sheep, chickens, dogs and cats, the duck being not very popular.

Afo-ebi is the clan market and is held every *afo* day. Traders come from all over the Arochuku division, from Ohafia division, and from Itu and Biase divisions in the South Eastern state. Yams, plantains, cassava, fish, vegetables, textiles, footwear, hats, mattresses, lamps, machetes, hoes, ropes, mats, meat, and chickens are the chief articles of trade. About three cows are slaughtered every *afo* day to supplement the protein content of the fish and bush meat (meat from wild animals) in the people's food. The Ututu clan is rich in feasts and festivals. The festival calendar begins with the *Ikeji*, the new yam festival around August and September of each year. This particular festival is made up of numerous feasts, such as *Ibo uzo* (the clearing of the roads) and *ichu afo* (the expulsion of the old year). Another feast is the *Izu*, which is held at the end of the planting of yams to prepare the people physically and spiritually for the subsequent period of scarcity.

Ila asaa [ranking seven] and *ila ano* [ranking four] were once the most important ritual feasts, being for the repose of the souls of the wealthy dead. *Igeri* was the climax of such feasts and featured most prominently in such a way that it gave its name to the entire festival. The Igeri was, then, a folk requiem music dance ritual for the good of the souls of wealthy Ututu men.

The Igeri troupe, made up of professional musicians and artists, is usually invited, at considerable expense, to perform during funeral ceremonies in honor of the dead. The troupe would perform for four days for those who were well off in their lifetimes, or for seven days for those who were very wealthy.

The emphasis which the people of Ututu used to place on the Igeri as an entertainment ritual in honor of the dead resulted in an African art form of thematic variety worthy of deeper appreciation and exhibition. Wealthy Ututu men determined, during their lifetime, the form of burial that would be accorded them upon their death, entrusting two independent confidants with this information. They set aside considerable wealth: in money, clothing, ornaments, food, and domestic animals, which would be necessary for the funeral ceremonies. It has been observed that the two confidants do not communicate the confidence to each other until after the death of the rich man, whose burial would become their principal concern.

When the great man who was to be honored finally died, a very deep grave was dug in his house. Pillars were driven into the grave, upon which, close to the surface, was constructed a strong scaffolding to support the body in its leopardskin shroud. The whole was then covered with a mound of earth. The top of the grave was thereafter regularly set on fire. During the burning, and as the corpse dried up, liquid from it dripped into the hollow grave below. The firing and drying-preservation of the corpse went on for as long as the required preparations for burial continued. As soon as these preparations for the repose of the soul were completed, the Igeri troupe was invited to announce, conduct, and orchestrate the rituals.

In the nineteenth and early twentieth centuries, the Igeri consisted of twelve drums with five professional drummers. Usually there were some seven assistant drummers around. The drums themselves are interesting specimens of accomplished woodcraftsmanship. The twelve drums were arranged in a single row (see Plate 1 for examples of the drums used) with the high-pitched sounding drum called *nwekwe* at the extreme right; four drums of various sounds, called *isi nkwa*, next to nwekwe; three drums called *ike nkwa* next to isi nkwa; at the extreme left a small drum called *abia*; and three other drums called *mkputu* with the abia.

Plate 1.   Some of the Igeri drums

THE MUSIC

The Igeri troupe is a most emotionally charged traditional musical ensemble. The ike nkwa drummer calls the tune, which is picked up by the nwekwe drummer, who is then joined by the abia and mkputu drummers, harmonizing the ike nkwa and nwekwe melorhythms respectively. Finally, the drummer at isi nkwa completes the rich texture of Igeri music (see Plate 2).

The Igeri drums were usually held together in a long basket called *abo igeri*, and carried solemnly and gracefully from their home to the entertainment venue. At its home the basket was stored suspended. A fee was paid to bring it down; another fee was paid to invite it; and yet another fee was paid to set it to play. The troupe, camped for the duration of the Festival, was paid, fed, and properly entertained with wine and various gifts.

The chief dancer was the *Ada*, the first or eldest daughter of the deceased. She was gorgeously attired. Her head gear was called *okpu okoko*, and from her shoulders to her knees fathoms of *georgey* cloth were plaited into what was called *uwo*. Around her neck she wore a

Plate 2.   Igeri drummers

necklace of leopard teeth. In her right hand she carried a short white-painted sword and around her ankles she wore decorated bangles and jingles. She danced to the drums and recited the glorious achievements of her late father. Other dancers in her troupe included her late father's wives and his female relations, all attired in a manner similar to that of the Ada (see Plate 3). They danced in short steps, with raised painted short swords with which, from time to time, they smote at bad spirits that were thought to molest the soul of the dead man about to be ancestralized. The dancing steps were measured: a forward and a backward step on one foot followed by similar movements of the other foot.

As these female dancers performed to the rhythm of the solemn Igeri music, and as they recited the noble achievements of their dead hero, their well-wishers showed appreciation by presenting gifts to the dancers they admired.

The chief celebrants of the occasion, the principals in the ritualistic festival, were the *umu nna* or paternal relatives and the children of the deceased. The ceremonies provided for them an occasion to demonstrate their affluence and the legacy of the deceased. After all, they brought all the people together to feast and witness the honor they were giving to their dead relative and father.

Plate 3. The *Ada*, eldest daughter of the deceased, dressed for the ceremony

COMMENCEMENT AND PROCEEDINGS

The Igeri troupe is housed in a booth constructed with raffia palm mats in front of the thatched house of the deceased under the cover of the eaves. The interior, where the leopardskin-shrouded body lies in state, is well decorated. Important in the festival are the rituals performed to guide the spirit or soul of the deceased safely on its way to the other world. The Igeri was a four-day four-act, or seven-day seven-act, ritualistic scenario evolving around the Igeri music. The proceedings are described below.

First Day

The first day was always an afo market day. When the troupe had assembled, the commencement of the requiem music dance ritual was announced by two drummers from a warrior dance troupe (see Plate 4). The first drummer beat his leather drum to the music of the warrior dance, and the second drummer beat his *ikoro*, the talking slit drum, to signal the beginning of events. Then an elder, who makes sacrifices, emerged from the house of the deceased to offer gifts of kola nuts, peppers, and palm wine to Chi-ukwu to seek his presence at the cere-

Plate 4.   The drummers alert the local people. The significance of this first act is to herald a great event, to bring as many people as possible together to witness the ritual honor about to be accorded the dead hero

monies and his protection of those who have come from far and near to take part in the various rituals (Plate 5). He pleaded as follows:

Obasi above
You gave us life
You gave us joy
We your children
Are gathered together
To return to you
What is yours

Obasi above
We bring your kola nuts
We offer your peppers
We pour out your wine

Obasi above
It is in your power
It is not our strength
That we celebrate and rejoice

Plate 5. The elder, making sacrifices to Chi-ukwu

Obasi above
Please be with us
Protect all the people
And lead them safely home.

The Igeri troupe then announced their presence with a rallying dirge, and their drums spoke as follows:

We come, we come, we come
Wey di people dey?
We come, we come,
Wey di people dey?
We come come, we come come
We come, we come, we come

Wey di people dey-o-o?
We come come, we come come
We come, we come, we come
Wey di people dey-o-o?

We come come, we come come
We come, we come, we come
Wey de dey-o-o-o?
Wey de dey, de dey, de dey-o-o-o?

We come, we come, we come-o
We come, we come, we come-o

We come come, we come come, we come come
We come come, we come come, we come come.

As this rallying dirge proceeded, the local people trooped out from their homes to the place of the ritual burial. And when the number of those assembled had grown into several hundreds, the drums thanked them for the response in the following notes:

We see, we see, we see
Una dey, una dey, una dey
The daughter, the mother, the brother
We see, we see, una dey
The sister, the uncle, the aunt-o
We see, we see, una dey-o
We see, we see, we see-o
We see, we see, una dey-o.

And throughout the rest of the first day, the drums roll out their dirge to rally the people together for the great event.

Second Day

On the second day, which was an *nkwo* market day, the Igeri drums aroused the local people from bed to say good morning to them, and to thank them for the hospitality of the first day. The drums sounded as follows:

Good morning, good morning to you-o-o
Good morning, good morning, good morning-o-o
For the kola, the chop, the wine-o-o
Una dey, una dey, una dey-o-o

The daughter, the mother, the sister-o-o
For the chop, for the chop, una dey-o-o
The uncle, the brother, the aunt-o-o
For the kola, for the wine, una dey-o-o

Ti kon kon, ti kon kon, ti kon kon-o-o
Ti ñko ño, ti ñko ño, ti ñko ño-o-o
Ti kon kon, ti kon kon, ti kon kon-o-o
Ti ñko ño, ti ñko ño, ti ñko ño-o-o.

Then the troupe proceeded to play four pieces, to accompany the second act, dedicated to the life history of the deceased, his achievements and the lessons to be learned from his example.

Third Day

On the third day, an *Eke* market day, the Igeri troupe repeated the rallying dirge of the first day to accompany the third act. And, when the stage was fully set, the first or eldest daughter led a group of dancers (see Plate 6) to do final homage to her late father. She danced and recited as follows:

Plate 6.   A female Igeri dancer on the third day

First daughter: My great father
I am your eldest daughter
I have come to perform my duty
I have brought all the people together

My great father,
You were indeed very dear
You loved your family
You served your people

My great father,
You were a great farmer
You farmed several acres of land
You planted from the bank of brook to brook

Therefore you were able, great father,
To feed the poor,
To help the needy,
To serve the people.

Chorus: Dutiful daughter,
Your statements are correct,
Let the proceedings go ahead.

First daughter: My eminent father,
Your wishes have been fulfilled,
Umu nna have taken their shares,
Umu nne have been satisfied,
Ikwu na ibe are happy
The men are full of action
The women are gay and merry
The visitors are pleased with us
The entire community is lively

My great father
Your market is in full session
The people have come to buy and sell your name
Your name was great
You fed the poor
You helped the needy
You served the people.

Chorus: It is it,
Let the proceedings go ahead.

First daughter: Let the men rejoice!

Chorus: Ohororororo–o–o–o!

First daughter: Let the women confirm!

Chorus: Ohororororo-o-o-o!

First daughter: Ikwu na ibe give assent.

Chorus: Ohororororo-o-o-o!

First daughter: Let the visitors testify!

Chorus: Ohororororo-o-o-o

First daughter: All is set, the people are here
My great father is ready
He has done his assignment
He returns to his creator.

THE JOURNEY TO THE NETHER WORLD. The dried corpse was placed in a sewn leopard or tigerskin shroud. It was borne high by very strong men. These men carried their burden and ran round the compound four or seven times as the case may have been.

Thereafter, the burial took place in utmost secrecy. But here is an account of what went on as observed by the elders. Four or seven white pieces of chalk were placed near the dried corpse to signify the rank in the ritualistic burial. The coffin was then lowered into the deep grave where the servants who went to serve the dead in the nether world were already seated. The final rites were performed as follows by an elder who offered sacrifces:

Elder: Obasi who lives above
We present your kola nuts
We offer your peppers
We pour out your wine

Chineke who creates
We rejoice with white chalk
We hallow with yellow chalk
We demarcate with black charcoal

Here comes [name of the deceased]
He lived according to his *chi*
He died according to his *chi*
Now receive back his spirit.

The high pitched drummer then struck his drum very hard. Then the warrior dancers performed for some time, after which the grave was covered.

Fourth Day

On the fourth day, *orie* market day, the Igeri troupe and the local people took it easy. The troupe played four pieces in the morning and four other pieces in the evening to accompany the final act. After the morning session, the members of the Igeri troupe dispersed to visit friends and relatives, and to receive private hospitality from the people of the locality.

The troupe then departed for their homes on the morning of the fifth day or on the morning of the eighth day, as the case may be.

SUMMARY

1. The Igeri represented the most expensive ritualistic folk requiem music dance entertainment among the people of Ututu in the Arochuku division up to the beginning of the Second World War. When the Igeri troupe was invited to the final burial ceremonies, it was the signal for a general invitation to everyone in the community. The people came purposely to consume the wealth of the deceased, and sometimes by a combination of circumstances they also consumed the wealth of those who brought them together to witness the honor they were doing to their departed hero.

2. This cultural festival emphasized the perishability of all material things. When a man died, everything was done to consume his wealth. The movable property was consumed by the community, the immovables were distributed according to custom. The children received minimal shares, and therefore could not speak of a foundation laid down by their father upon which they only needed to make their own contributions for the continued progress of the family.

3. The once successful man soon became legendary, and when there were no physical objects around with which his name was associated, his life and times soon disappeared into the remote past.

4. If the hero had killed a buffalo or a leopard or a tiger singlehanded, he received the appellation of buffalo killer or tiger killer and the carcass belonged to the entire community. The umu nna took away their traditional shares; the ikwu received their own portions; the village stalwarts had absolute rights over certain portions of the meat. After all, they had sweated to bring the carcass to the village square, or had suffered in cutting up the meat in the bush. The killer kept the skull of the animal; his eldest son and eldest daughter received their traditional shares. His wives collected what was their due. The community rejoiced over the heroism of the buffalo killer, while the buffalo killer alone nursed his bruises during the encounter.

5. The conflict and struggle of the individual with his own community is manifested by the various acts of the community against the individual when he is down.

6. The individual tries to escape from the tyranny of the community which pursues and chases him to his death, and then grabs all that he had kept from them.

Ngoma *Music Among the Zulu*

ELKIN THAMSANQA SITHOLE

The Zulu have a strong sense of division of labor according to sex, a division evident even in their arts and crafts, and especially in their songs.

Songs of a national character, such as anthems, were traditionally referred to as *izingoma, ingoma kaZulu* being a song of the Zulu people, just as *ingoma kaBaba* is "father's song". Respect for the father as head of the family is reflected in respect for his songs in the same way as the Zulu respect *ingoma kaShaka*, "the song of King Shaka". Because the boys sang more of the father's songs than the girls, who often sang *ingoma kaMama*, "mother's song", boys' songs tended to fit the male character as conceived by the Zulu.

CLASSIFICATION

The Zulu classify *Ngoma* choirs and their songs according to style of singing, dance forms, and the influence of school music.

Style of Singing

UMBHOLOHO OR "BOMBING". One of the most popular style of presentation is that heard in *umbholoho* or "bombing" songs. Since emphasis is on the volume of sound, the higher the pitch the better. The addition of more voices to the lowest part increases the distance over which the sound can be heard.

Although there are four parts, characterized by harmonies of consecutive fourths or fifths, the lower voice, or bass, is reinforced. If the choir has eight members, for example, the distribution of voices would be: first part (leader), one voice; second part (alto), one voice; third part (tenor), one voice; and fourth part (bass), five voices. If there are ten or more members, the next to be reinforced would be the third part, or tenor, for example: first part, one voice; second part, one voice; third part, two voices; and fourth part, six or more voices.

In order that every singer may listen to himself as he sings, the hand is placed or pressed against the cheek, especially at the beginning or end of each song. Another technique used by "bombing" choirs is to form a circle and bring heads together in order to listen to other members.

SIKWELA JO. The term *sikwela Jo* is the most foreign and urban of all the terms which refer to this music. Just as bebop in America got its name from the short staccato cadence which was popular with Charlie Parker, so *sikwela Jo* originates from the last phrase, *Kwela*! [attack!], given by the leader of the group, who, as David Rycroft maintains, "demands of each of his seven or eight choristers an unflinching hypnotic gaze and executes vigorous and precisely timed signals, both manual and vocal, for the attack of each choral yell" (Rycroft 1957:33).

In order for the leader to obtain the explosive fortissimo chord result, he must make a distinct contrast between his casual melodic or spoken phrase, and the sharp, forceful "Kwela!" which he used to elicit the loud chordal response from the group. The mention of the names of individual singers after "Kwela", such as "Kwela James!", "Kwela John!", "Kwela Tom!", in effect recognizes some while discouraging others, who for some reason are not frequently mentioned by the leader. Hence, "Jo" (Joseph) is used generally, to apply to each individual singer and to encourage everyone to give their utmost, so that a thunderous attack results.

Interchangeably with kwela, the term *khala* [cry] is frequently used, not only for its rhyme and similar effect, but also for its meaning. The most intense emotional state is expressed by crying or laughter, as when some people can be seen wiping their eyes after a joke.

Dance Form

SIKHUNZI OR "GRUMBLING". In *sikhunzi* dancing becomes more important than singing. The choristers display individual variations of dance steps, unified only by turns to the right or left, and even turning their back to the audience. Untranslatable phrases, such as *Hololo mama*, *Helele mama*, *Hululu mama*, and *Heya Yeya*, are frequently used, since direct meaning is not a priority. In uncemented halls, dancing raises so much dust that by the end of each song singers are barely visible. The bass part does indeed sound like grumbling, as they repeat the nonsensical syllables over and over again, embellished only by minimal melodic lines from the leader, alto, and tenor.

Sikhunzi singers prefer very deep bass voices, which they call *mbambatoni*, a voice level lower than that of the bass. Since every young boy wishes to have the *mbambatoni* when he is older, this is often their justification for smoking at an early age. To have *mbamba* is proof of masculinity, since a light male voice sounds feminine.

COTHOZA MFANA OR ZICATHAMIYA. Although dance is also a priority in this case, the steps in *cothoza mfana* [walk with shod feet young men] have to be gentle, as if stepping on eggs or tiptoeing on forbidden ground. Unlike the postures in "grumbling", where the body bends in all directions, in cothoza mfana an upright posture is desired. Legs are stretched or kicked out as gently as possible. Even if the halls are uncemented, there is little or no dust at the end of the dance. Since cothoza mfana combines singing and dancing in almost equal proportions, choirs are very exciting to watch, as well as to listen to, when this form is presented.

The South African Broadcasting Corporation has adopted the name *Cothoza mfana* for its Radio Bantu program. Sometimes these choirs are referred to as *mbube* choirs, after a popular song, "Mbube," known in America as "Wimoweh" or "The lion sleeps tonight."

School Influence; Mnyuziki

School choral music has had a profound influence on the ngoma male choir, not only through its Western choral arrangements, but also in the suspension or elimination of action and dance. Singers stand upright, sometimes with their hands behind them and their heads slightly raised, so that their eyes face upwards.

Narrative songs, known as *mnyuziki*, may be about biblical subjects, such as Moses and Joshua, or about legends of King Shaka, Dingane, Ngqika, and Nongqawuza. In one evening concert, however, a choir will sing only one or two such songs, and even in an all-night performance, such as given by the Newcastle Humming Bees, only one in twenty would be a mnyuziki song, for such songs are usually reserved for special competitions among the choirs, as the writer discovered when he served as a judge in a competition of the *Ngonyameni* male choirs (Sithole 1968).

The music itself is composed by Western-trained Zulu and Xhosa musicians, such as R. T. Caluza, A. A. Khumalo, the Sitholes, and the Sidyiyos (Huskisson 1969:23–26, 62–65). Note-perfect accuracy is sacrificed in favor of extemporary additions by any member of the group, especially the leader. Like all Zulu music, mnyuziki songs are learned by imitation. A member hears a song performed by another choir or community, and commits all parts to memory; he then teaches the song to his own group, beginning with the voice that carries the basic rhythms and melody. None of this music has been written down, nor is there any desire on the part of the musicians to do so in the future.

Ngoma and Zulu Praise-Poetry: Ukubingelela

The leader, usually the founder of the male choir, improvises more than any other member of the group. Apart from his musical talent, he is also expected by the group and the audience to be able to include Zulu praise-poetry in his improvisation. One class of songs in which he may display his knowledge of Zulu praise-poetry is the introductory song, *ukubingelela*.

The introductory song may either tell about the home of each individual singer, or introduce his family tree or lineage. An abbreviated translation of one northern Natal ukubingelela song follows:

Leader (spoken): Could you estimate for me how big our audience is tonight?
Choir (sung): They are as many as *bangangotshani* [grass]. They are as many as *bangangoboya benkomo* [ox hair].
Leader (half-spoken, half-sung): Tell them where you come from, boys. *Kwela!* [Attack].
Choir (sung): We come across Mzinyathi river *Kwela kithi e Dundee* [from our home near Dundee]. If you ever come to Mzinyathi, inquire or ask about us *inzinyoni exidla ezinye* [birds which feed on other birds].
Leader (sung): Now I want to tell you who my colleagues are. This is the young man from *Sibiya* clan, who milk the cow in the mountain cliffs; if they milk it in the barn, it has been stolen (the choir hums).

The leader will continue down the line, introducing every member of the choir, as each steps forward in turn. He may choose at random what praise or what negative comment he wishes to include on that particular night or day. For this he will need to have done prior research into the achievements or failures of each clan represented in his choir. The leader may end by introducing himself or sometimes the choir will introduce him in a final coda and cadence.

Such an introductory song creates rapport between the musicians and the audience, since in the audience there are kinsmen of the singers, including affinal kin, who will identify not only with their own relatives in the choir, but also with the entire group. As the choir sings, any older man or woman may stand up and recite the praises of any member whose praises have fallen short of expectation.

When choirs sing about Shaka, Dingane, Cetshwayo, or any other Zulu king or leader, they use extracts from traditional praise-poetry, such as

Ilembe Eleqa Amanye Amlembe for Shaka, or *UVezi uNonyanda* for Dingane.

TIMES OF REHEARSAL AND PERFORMANCE: *NGOMA BUSUKU*

The male choirs find the convenient time for both rehearsal and performance to be the night, hence the name *ngoma busuku* [night singers]. In the country, during the day, young men plow and cultivate the soil, or attend *ibandla* [male gatherings] with other young men. In the city they are at work during the day, hence:

any evening of the week in Johannesburg, small groups of Bombing enthusiasts are to be heard rehearsing in hostel rooms, on balconies, in backyards or in the servants' quarters at the top of luxury blocks of flats [nicknamed "locations in the sky"] (Rycroft 1957:33).

In the country, boys and young men rehearse near the cattle *kraal* every night, since every boy between ten and twenty belongs to some ngoma busuku choir. Rehearsals are very much an evening social event, and some choirs never perform anywhere except when asked by parents to rehearse or sing in the *endlini enkulu* [big house] for their own amusement.

Singing or rehearsing in the big house rather than behind houses is already a measure of success, since boys are judged by parents or passers-by as they rehearse in the open. Compliments from the community are expressed casually in conversation, for example, "Bayayishaya ingoma abafana bakwa Twala" [The Twala boys sing very well]. Invitations to younger boys to join famous and successful ngoma busuku choirs result from the spreading reputations of the best altos, tenors, basses, or leaders. Younger ngoma choirs keep losing their best individuals to older groups. Even if they move to the cities, boys continue singing in the choirs with which they sang in the country, except when promoted or invited by famous choirs, but those who grew up in the cities do not sing ngoma, since they are influenced by jazz. Radio Bantu disc jockeys generally shun assignment to ngoma busuku programs but one exception is Alexius Buthelezi, one of the best Western-trained African musicians in Johannesburg, who is always proud to present ngoma busuku choirs, perhaps because "At Pomeroy Buthelezi also came into contact with Zulu *mbube*, introduced there by an exponent of *mbube* singing, Solomon Linda, a Pomeroy man who used to bring the *mbube* group Evening Birds from Johannesburg on holidays" and conducted gigantic *mbube* concerts (Huskisson 1969:17).

OCCASIONS OF PERFORMANCE

Year-round Occasions ·

In the country, apart from school concerts and church activities, the ngoma singers provide the only regular and reliable entertainment for the community. Weddings depend on the season, as well as on the availability of young men and women who are prepared to marry. It is in the interest of male singers to sing when the opportunity avails itself. Hence, they accept invitations from relatives, friends, unrelated families, or girlfriends, to sing at birthday parties, tombstone unveilings, and so on.

The choirs are founded for social rather than financial reasons, so there is no charge except when there are special concerts, advertised as such long beforehand. In the townships, ngoma groups compete with jazz groups or bands to perform in the *stokfelas* [meetings of rotating credit associations]. The stokfelas vary according to purpose: some are for entertainment, while others are for fundraising. Selected families and individuals are invited to one of the homes, where they pay to take part, and pay for food as well as entertainment. Where people are charged money to take part in a stokfela, the ngoma singers are also paid for providing entertainment.

Christmas and New Year Celebrations

Normally Christmas and New Year celebrations are church or school activities, and are organized in both rural and urban areas by teachers and similar individuals. Ngoma male choirs either ask to perform at Christmas celebrations, or are included by public or community demand, since missionaries have not accepted their music as legitimate, especially in areas under strong missionary influence.

Competitions

One of the most regular activities among the ngoma male choirs is the weekly, fortnightly, or monthly competition held to establish the best choir in the area. In the urban areas, there may be as many as twenty-five choirs competing on any one night, while in the country between ten and fifteen is normal. Competitions for trophies are not as popular as those where a live goat is the first prize. In one competition, in which the writer served as a judge, there was a curious reversal of values, for the winners' live goat was worth less than the cash prize for second prize. The singers place a higher value on the opportunity to spill blood (*ukucitha igazi*) as a ritual following a successful undertaking than they do on cash.

CLOTHING: *JAZIBHANTSHI*

In the cities during the 1920's six- or eight-button coats were popular among the ngoma busuku. Upon return from Durban or Johannesburg to the country, they were named *jazibhantshi*, after the long coats, which were neither overcoats nor jackets. Even when they changed to newer styles, such as zoot-suit jackets, or "open shirt with a black or multi-coloured muffler [*izimamfula*] tied into a knot around the neck; and pants which were tied just under the knee in imitation of breeches" (Vilakazi 1962:76), male singers retained the name jazibhantshi. Their present-day uniform is a college blazer with colorful trimming or lining.

AGE DISTINCTION: *BAFANA BENGOMA*

Although male singers continue singing even at the age of forty-five or more, they are always referred to as *bafana bengoma* [boys who sing]. The term "cothoza mfana" denotes the style of dancing, as well as an age distinction, while *bafana bebhantshi* [boys of the coat] denotes both age level and clothing. Perhaps adherence to the notion of "boys" or "young men" is related to the fact that ingoma was a sacred king's song, sung by the nation at the ceremony of the first fruits (Krige 1957:339), so that as long as young men sing in the new "Zulu male traditional singing" style, it is felt that the original dignity of the ngoma is still preserved, even though the songs now extend beyond first fruits ceremonies.

MASCULINITY

Ngoma musicians have managed to keep their music male-oriented, not only by excluding women from participating, but also by reinforcing masculinity through various means, such as:

Name of the Group

The group selects a strong fearsome animal, bird or insect as a symbol, and calls itself by that name or its English equivalent, for example: Brave Lions, Morning Tigers, Happy Dogs (after a successful hunting expedition), Humming Bees, Evening Birds, and even Lion Bees, where the strength of the lion is combined with the sting of the bee. Such names as Phumasilwe [come, let's fight], or Thathezakho [get your weapons] imply personality traits that could make the group "Zululand home defenders, and even the American Home Defenders" (Rycroft 1957:33). From the Bible have come such names as Nebuchadnezzar, Daniel, the Philistines, Pharaoh, and Beelzebub, rather than names of meek, gentle characters.

As the groups have tried to emulate and live by their symbols, some of them have become aggressive. For example, they have sometimes entered the stage with sticks or thick hippo whips (*imvumbu*), which, the writer recalls (as a boy in northern Natal in the early 1940's), they readily used against members of the audience who were seated so close to the front as to reduce the space for dancing.

Relationship with Women

Although they did not include women singers, the ngoma groups were very popular with women, who referred to them as *amadoda ethu* [our husbands to be]. Often, in the middle of a well-presented song, some women would shout *Yeka amadoda ethu!*" [Oh! Our husbands to be], as an immediate compliment to the singers. From this general behavior pattern, the groups are also known as *amasoka ezintombi* [young men popular with the girls]. As a result singers would first introduce themselves to a new community by offering to give concerts there, and would return at a later date to propose love and later marriage to girls of their fancy. One of the reasons for preferring night performances is the convenience of the night for dates or appointments with women. In some cultures it is common knowledge among young men, though it still remains to be proved scientifically, that women are easier to win in a love proposal at night than they are during the day.

CONCLUSION

Since ngoma musicians have survived nonacceptance in Christian mission stations, and have turned migratory labor patterns to their advantage, it is more than mere speculation that their music has achieved a state of permanence that no history of African music can overlook, with their versatile musicianship covering a period of more than fifty years of music making. Already, whether commercially or otherwise, ngoma music dominates the international scene as no other music from southern Africa does. "Mbube," for example, has been imitated throughout the world, while another ngoma song, "Shosholoza," has appeared in several plays and films, including, for example, *Dingaka*. Ngoma has not been discussed since David Rycroft's article written in 1957. It is time we looked at the development of this type of music, whose composers' and performers' chief interest is to please their families, neighbors, and fellow workers, and at most to win a live goat on a Saturday night to be killed off in the early hours of Sunday morning.

REFERENCES

HUSKISSON, YVONNE
  1969 *The Bantu composers of southern Africa*. Johannesburg: South African Broadcasting Corporation.

KRIGE, EILEEN
  1957 *The social system of the Zulus*. Pietermaritzburg: Shuter and Shooter.

RYCROFT, DAVID
  1957 Zulu male traditional singing. *African Music* 1(4):33–35.

SITHOLE, ELKIN THAMSANQA
  1968 "Zulu music as a reflection of social change." Unpublished master's dissertation, Wesleyan University, Middletown, Connecticut.

VILAKAZI, ABSOLOM
  1962 *Zulu transformations*. Pietermaritzburg: Natal University Press.

The Possibility of Objective Rhythmic Evidence for African Influence in Afro-American Music

HEWITT PANTALEONI

Ensemble drumming among the Anlo-Ewe of southeastern Ghana is an old and indigenous art. Technical objective analysis of the rhythmic structure typical of this art form reveals two features striking in their divergence from Western European tradition. Should it be possible to establish these features as typical of West African ensemble drumming as a whole, their presence in the music of Afro-American groups, combined with their absence from other music influencing these groups, would be evidence as convincing as lexical identities of African cultural survival in the Western hemisphere.

The instruments of Anlo ensemble drumming owe nothing to white colonial intervention. The drums are essentially conical: an instrument with one open end will have at its other end a playing head distinctly larger than this opening; an instrument with a closed end will have a playing head distinctly smaller. Double-headed drums and kettle drums are not indigenous. The rattles are netted beads, shells, or bamboo sections draped around the globular head of a smooth-shelled, hollow gourd whose shape provides a natural handle and rarely exceeds one foot in length. There are also clapperless iron bells that take the form of either single open pods, or cups joined at their stems like a spray of flowers.

Some of the music played by these instruments (with the addition of handclapping, singing, dancing, and — recently — the striking together of wooden blocks) entered Anlo culture relatively recently: *Gahū*, for example, which Anlo fishermen learned in the present century while resident at Badagry on the western coast of Nigeria. But there are also "ancient drums" — musical styles that go back, according to tradition, as far as Anlo migration from Togo at the end of the sixteenth century. Though such musical tradition cannot be verified, it does indicate as well as any other test that rhythmic structures presently to be discussed are, in the view of their practitioners, both old and indigenous.

Musical analysis, especially rhythmic analysis, is always in danger of being subjective and therefore insubstantial as proof. For this very good reason research concerning African musical influence in the Western hemisphere has had to emphasize the more tangible evidence of dance styles, social organization, or instrumental names and shapes; aural observations have had the force of peripheral comment, not of data.

One problem is notation. Our only script, the familiar five-line staff and its symbols, was developed in a specific Western European context of medieval and renaissance art music. Other musics are served by this notation only to the extent that basic assumptions are shared — for example the assumption that the lines, spaces, sharps, and flats cue that certain set of pitch distinctions we find in the notes of a piano. Western art musicians now agree fairly well about pitch (there was a time when the same written notes stood for different pitch relationships in different systems). Musicians of another culture are apt to have their own pitch system, however, and also their own rhythmic system.

To turn aural observation into tangible and objective evidence more is needed than a suitable notation: the mind of the observer must also be suitable. The cultural assumptions embedded in Western musical notation are also embedded in Western minds, and they have to be overcome as much as possible. This is difficult to do — surprisingly so, since we are not used to thinking of our normal musical responses as the peculiar evidence of a particular cultural training (note, for instance, that the flurry of interest in measuring human perception of rhythm during the first years of this century produced several ingenious devices and precise results without *ever* considering the cultural background of the subjects measured).

If we hear an American folk fiddler consistently sharpen a certain pitch during the performance of a tune, it is not accurate to report that he "raises" this note: he plays it normally with regard to the pitch system of that piece. And if the strokes of a West African drummer consistently deny our sense of regular pulse, it is not accurate for us to report that he "syncopates": syncopation requires a steady pulse against which the musician makes emphatic sounds, and in fact there may be no such pulse operating in this case. Steady pulse is an embedded cultural assumption.

To avoid rhythmic assumptions in my analysis of Anlo drumming I combined two approaches: (1) I tried to learn to drum acceptably in Anlo ensembles, in order to give my mind a chance to entertain new assumptions and discard old ones; and (2) I tried to develop a notation free of rhythmic implications. Both efforts have been successful to the extent that two rhythmic features have emerged which run directly counter to Western practice.

The first of these features is the use of the high range of the ensemble for the placement of regular and predictable cues that govern the timing of musical events. The high range of a Western ensemble is for decoration and divergence, the *low* range for fundamental timing. To the appreciation of Anlo ensemble drumming we bring a thoroughly mistrained mind.

The proof of the existence of this feature is simple and clear. A full score of an Anlo performance shows among the lower-sounding instruments continual changes of pattern and shifts of pulse, while among certain of the highest instruments there is no change at all. Furthermore, the various conflicting rhythms of the lower voices all relate rigidly, each in their own way, to the steady, repeating pattern of the iron bell. Anlo drummers consistently point this out, and it is plain to hear and to see in a score — see, for instance Jones (1959), where the alignment of events is accurate, though misinterpreted. High-voiced instruments other than the bell, though carrying unchanging patterns in the ensemble, fail to give the lower voices the needed guidance because they are not precise enough (the rattles), or not dependable (the handclapping of onlookers), or carry too short a pattern to provide a distinct enough relationship (the highest-sounding drum, *kaganu*).

This last point, the need for a long enough guiding pattern, can be illustrated with a decorative exchange between lower drums in a music called *Atsiā*. One of these drums, *sogo*, is playing sounds that drummer Kofi Kpeglo Ladzekpo represents with the following syllables (italics indicate emphasis, height on the page corresponds to pitch level, and vertical lines mark off equidistant moments in time):

	TSIA,	TSIA		TSIA,		
DE-*RĒN*,			*KPIM*,			GE-*RĒN* ...
					GE-RA,	

At the same time a drum with a higher voice, *kidi*, makes the following play:

		SH–	K–	T$H–SH,		SH–	K–	T$H–SH,		
KI– *DI*–					*KI*– *DI*–				*KI*– *DI* ...	

The two drums must interlock this way:

				SH, TSIA,	T$H			
DE– *RĒN*– *KI*– *DI*–						*KPIM*– *KI*– *DI* ...		

Clearly the guiding pattern — what African musicologist J. H. Kwabena Nketia has called the "time-line" — must be at least as long as one statement of this interlocking drum rhythm if the entry points for each instrument are to be clearly placed. But the highest-sounding drum, *kaganu*, has a pattern only as long as it takes to sound "RĒN–KI–DI". Though *kaganu* repeats its pattern steadily throughout *Atsiā*, this part cannot be used for a time-line, since it does not distinguish the musical space "RĒN–KI–DI" from the musical space "SH, TSIA, TSH".

It is not enough to have a long time-line: the pattern must be distinctive so that the correct placement of a musical idea against it will have a unique effect. The *Atsiā* time-line has such a pattern, an asymmetrical one here shown twice in succession:

K♪ | K♪ | K♪K♪ | K♪ | K♪ | K♪K♪ | K♪ | K♪K♪ | K♪ | K♪ | K♪

Against this distinct arrangement of strokes the simple part played on the smallest drum, *kaganu*, creates a very different overall effect in each of its three possible placements:

K♪ | K♪ | K♪K♪ | K♪ | K♪ | K♪K♪ | K♪ | K♪K♪ | K♪ | K♪ | K♪
KA-GAN | KA-GAN | KA-GAN | KA-GAN | KA-GAN | KA-GAN | KA-GAN | KA-GAN

K♪ | K♪ | K♪K♪ | K♪ | K♪ | K♪K♪ | K♪ | K♪K♪ | K♪ | K♪ | K♪
KA-GAN | KA-GAN | KA-GAN | KA-GAN | KA-GAN | KA-GAN | KA-GAN | KA-GAN

K♪ | K♪ | K♪K♪ | K♪ | K♪ | K♪K♪ | K♪ | K♪K♪ | K♪ | K♪ | K♪
-GAN | KA-GAN | KA-GAN | KA-GAN | KA-GAN | KA-GAN | KA-GAN | KA-GAN | KA-

The first of these is correct in many Anlo musical styles. The other two sound quite different, and are wrong.

The asymmetry of Anlo time-lines — not just the one shown but all of them — is the second major feature of this music which differs markedly from Western rhythmic practice. Our Western time-line is a string of equidistant pulses given the effect of a repeating pattern by changes of harmony, pitch, and stress. Without these changes supporting them, the pulses fail to tell us whether we are listening to a waltz or a march. It is these supporting changes that condition our minds to hear the rhythms of other cultures in terms of loud beats and low beats.

It has not yet been established that Anlo practice is typical of West Africa. From The Gambia to Nigeria there are some indications that such will turn out to be the case, but study of the question is not yet sufficient. Indeed, the explication of Anlo rhythmic principles just given cannot yet claim acceptance among specialists, though I would venture to speculate that the delay stems more from the heavy hand of preconditioned response than from any failure of this explication to weather close examination.

We have, then, the possibility — and I believe it to be a strong one — that a high-pitched, asymmetrical time-line in the ensemble music of Afro-Americans can be used as tangible evidence of African roots.

REFERENCE

JONES, ARTHUR M.
1959 *Studies in African music*, volume two. London: Oxford University Press.

Music and Dance as Expressions
Religious Worship in Jamaica

JOSEPH G. MOORE

*whether it be a
tribe or christian
method of service*

Music and dance are the dominant tools or modes of religious expression of the major cult groups in eastern Jamaica. They are the bones and sinews of the ceremonies of these groups.

The two major cult groups to be considered here were active throughout the 1950's and 1960's in St. Thomas parish in the eastern part of Jamaica, which stretches from Kingston through Port Morant to Port Antonio. The cult involving the largest number of people attending ceremonies is called Cumina, sometimes referred to as African Dance. While it is difficult to estimate the total number of people involved in one way or another, it seems probable that as many persons attended Cumina as attended all the established Christian churches together in this area. It is difficult, too, to estimate how many Cumina ceremonies are held within this region. One drummer, who plays at Cumina ceremonies, indicated that in the course of eight months he attended or played in sixty-seven ceremonies. The largest ceremony I attended was held in Morant Bay, where approximately four hundred men, women, and children were present. These dancing ceremonies are always held for a specific purpose, such as a death in a family, an entombment ceremony a year after death, or a festival at the time of a marriage or a christening.

The second major cult group, Revival, is a syncretistic group, drawing characteristics from Western Christian and African beliefs and practices. Within Revival groups there are sectarian differences; descriptions here will be concerned with three types — Revival, Revival Zion, and Pocomania.

The Jamaicans we are concerned with live in St. Thomas parish where the highest percentage of blacks in the population is recorded. Most of their ancestors were brought to the island as slaves, from 1655 to the abolition of slavery in 1834. They came from West Africa and the Congo.

In the latter half of the nineteenth century a considerable number of indentured West African agricultural workers were brought to Jamaica.

It will be necessary to define some of the underlying concepts and beliefs which are expressed through music and dance. For instance, it is important to clear away some of the ambiguities attached to the terms "duppy" and "zombie". Cumina informants explain that when a man is born, he has a personal spirit and a duppy spirit. The personal spirit is regarded as a man's personality, whereas the duppy spirit is the shadow of an individual. At death, the personal spirit is believed to go directly to Oto, King Zombie, never to return to earth if in life the personal spirit has never experienced possession by a zombie. If a person has been possessed by a zombie, his own spirit then takes on a new quality and, at death, joins all ancestral zombie spirits who can return to earth for various kinds of duties. These include attending cult ceremonies and possessing living persons. The duppy spirit, or shadow, remains with the corpse in the grave and comes out of the grave if it wishes; it is especially dangerous if it belongs to the body of a man who had never been a zombie. When the duppy feels that his body has not been buried properly, it is believed that he becomes restless and dissatisfied. He may then leave the grave to walk the face of the earth for any evil purpose that may occur to him. It is for this reason that the duppy is to be feared and guarded against.

A person, then, is made up of flesh, blood, and spirit. The spirit has two parts: a personal spirit that always lives within the man or woman as long as he or she is alive, and a spirit that "walks along beside him", described as one's shadow. A zombie is either (1) a god, or (2) an ancestor who was once possessed by a god or another ancestral zombie, or (3) a living being who has been possessed by one of these. There are two classes of zombies who are gods — skybound and earthbound.

Living dancers and drummers who have been possessed are described as people who have had their "heads turned", at which time they join the ranks of the zombie world. It is clear that what is considered to happen in possession is a phenomenal change of the personal spirit; it is described as being like an electric shock, and once accomplished, is indelible.

The elements of drum, song, and dance are so predominant a characteristic in Cumina that it is easy to understand why ceremonies are commonly referred to as African Dances in Jamaica. In Revival, Revival Zion or Pocomania, no ceremony can be carried out without its own form of music and dance. At all of these ceremonies the zombies in Cumina and the saints and ancestral spirits in Revival are identified through the musical rhythms and dance patterns in each possession. In private ceremonies, called "workings", the Cumina *obeah* man,[1] or the Revival shepherd, uses music to invoke the spirit and then identify the possessing spirit by its dance movements.

[1] *Obeah* is a spirit power used in Cumina, referred to as *African* (Cassidy 1961:232).

The importance of dancing has been generally reported by students of negro culture in the New World (Herskovits 1941:269). Although many hundreds of people attend cult gatherings, most of them may not be initiated members of the group. Yet they are familiar with the songs and the basic dance patterns and enjoy taking part. When possessions begin to come thick and fast, many participants in the earlier period of dancing drop out to become observers. Children, too, dance in the early hours of a ceremony, but by eight o'clock in the evening they are no longer in the dancing area.

There are several kinds of dancing which can be distinguished at a Cumina ceremony. The basic dance, participated in by everyone in the ring, is a walking step in time with the beat of the *banda* drum. The body is held erect but responds to the polyrhythms of the *playing drum*, the *shaker* and the *scraper* (see Figure 1). Because of the multiple rhythms, the hips, shoulders, arms, and head are presented with infinite variation in posture and movement. With few exceptions, dancing is counterclockwise around the ring, done solo or with partner. To a casual observer, this ring dancing looks somewhat like a group of people anywhere in the Western world moving freely to North American jazz or South American rhythms, but in spite of the great deal of freedom and variety of movement, the behavior of the Cumina group is orderly. There is a good reason for this friendly and considerate spirit as a group. These dances are most

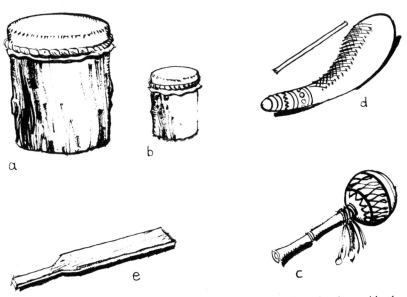

Figure 1. Cumina musical instruments: (a) the *banda* drum, a large log drum with a low tone; (b) the *playing drum*, a smaller log drum with a higher tone; (c) the *shaker*, a simple rattle; (d) the *scraper*, a gourd with notches filed in its neck, which is stroked by a metal stick; and (e) the *catatic*, a thin piece of wood hit against the center pole

likely to be memorial or entombment ceremonies conducted and paid for by a family for its own dead and held in the family's yard. Even though all those in attendance are not dancing zombies, and therefore, limit themselves to the social aspect of the dancing, they respect the purpose of the ceremony and conduct themselves accordingly.

Skybound and earthbound gods, who possess dancing zombies, differ widely in pattern and style of movement. Also, each ancestral zombie who comes to possess and dance has a distinct style. The essential quality of the possessed dancer is total absorption in the dance of the controlling god or ancestor, completely unaware of the people around him or her.

Music and dance, then, are used for calling and for possession by zombie spirits in Cumina, and for invocation and for possession by saints and ancestral spirits in Revival cults. Infants are carried in the ring; children dance in the early periods of the ceremony; after growing up in these experiences, a person is rarely aware of the vast accumulation of knowledge he has acquired of the variety of music and dance patterns he so thoroughly enjoys and understands.

In this form of animism, including ancestral spiritism, proper controls cannot be achieved without the development of a balance between music, rhythm, and dance patterns, which is both complex and flexible. Differences may be slight, but must be recognized in order to know each zombie or spirit. The situation is compounded when, in a single possession, several spirits may be represented and therefore administered to. As this phenomenon occurs mainly in ancestral zombie possession, the cumulative pattern is established in the latest ancestor. Complexity remains a very high factor, however, for human memory can cause a variation and neither Cumina nor Revival has an institutional structure where forms of worship can be recorded.

MUSIC AND DANCE IN CUMINA

Unlike Trinidad, Haiti, or Bahia, Brazil there are no formal cult houses, as such, in the eastern part of Jamaica. An obeah man sets up a dancing booth, similar to the kind for public dances, in his yard, but for public ceremonies a new booth is built in the yard of the family holding the dance. This is done for each ceremony and the entire event is supervised by the host family. The construction entails setting a center post and four corner posts, on top of which is laid a thatched roof.

The center of the booth is sprayed with rum. The banda drum (heavy) and the playing drum (treble) are set with their heads facing one another south of the center pole. The other instruments, the *catatic*, the shaker and the scraper, are placed north of the two drums in line with the center pole. The singer stands facing the two drums during the first part of the ceremony.

Greatly respected are the skilled drummers who play for the god-zombies, and who, in almost every instance, are zombie dancers as well as drummers. The outstanding drummer in each neighborhood is known and recognized as such throughout the region. There are at least ten of these and dozens of less outstanding but capable drummers on the playing drum, which is the lead drum. Several hundred men are capable of playing the banda and, also, the other instruments.

Two or three drummers are used at a dance, although at a very large dance there may be as many as six lead drummers together with many who play the less important instruments. Normally, not more than four men comprise the instrument section at any one time; this is occasionally augmented by extra players and a singer.

For the first five years that a drummer plays the banda, which is the larger drum, he is exposed to and learns many of the beats of the possessing spirits. It is claimed that he does not know as many gods as may come to him and, therefore, he must wait before playing the lead drum, the playing drum. His training comes from working with other drummers at Cumina and from helping obeah men in private workings. Sometimes, the drummers get together to practice by themselves. At such times they observe the ceremonial use of rum, for they say:

It is just a rule that you keep that way now [using rum] for any time we punch a drum. The gods come down sometime when you practice. They come by and come right into the drums. You feel them when they come. You have a different song come from the drum and you feel them with your fingers. It feel like something that come in and run around the drum, like playing a guitar when the string bursts — you get a different sound.

The drummers also say, in connection with the learning period, "It depends upon your brain. You can have a quick brain, you only have to play for a god one time, next time you can play him."

To become a playing drummer, then, is a goal to which many young men aspire, but few achieve. There are hundreds of dancing zombies but only a few dozen good drummers capable of handling the playing drum. The playing drum is also referred to as the *playing case*, or *treble drum*, as it is the smaller of the two drums and plays the higher notes. Drummers range in age from boys of seventeen to men in their fifties. It is a position of honor held by men of strong personality. Obeah men have all been drummers, for only by this method can they learn to invoke the spirits. The drummer's art is solely practiced by men, while women can be seen, on occasion, handling the shaker or catatic.

All zombies are invoked through the use of drum and song. There are two classes of songs, *bilah* and *country* songs (see Appendix 1). The term *myal* is used to describe some country songs that are used in the strongest possessions. Although all songs fall into these two classes, they are similar in type. The country songs, more often than not, have a lower percentage of English words. Both types of song are sung by a singer whose role is given prestige by the cult because of the importance of the songs to the ceremony. The singer, who stands in the center of the dancing booth together with the drummers and other players sings the verses and the people respond in chorus after each line. Male singers are drummers or obeah men, but female singers are strong dancing zombies.

The basic Cumina dance step is begun by all participants and continued throughout the ceremony by the unpossessed. It is a simple walking stamp in time with the banda drum which always plays the first and fourth beats of the six-eight time; this is the rhythm of Oto, the top sky god. This basic beat underlies all the many rhythms which are introduced almost immediately in the ceremony. Later, the counterrhythms introduced may be the specific beat of a god or ancestor who comes to possess a dancer. All through the night and the next morning the dance goes on. It is loose, easy, solo or partnered, and moves counterclockwise around the booth.

Under possession there comes a drastic change. Since it is believed that the zombies come down the center post, or other posts, into the ground, then into the drums, the first sign of this comes from the playing drum as it begins to play rim beats high, hard, and fast. It is believed that the zombie spirit goes into the ground from the center post and then into the dancing person starting at the heels, going up the spinal column into the shoulders and head. Then, in possession, the person so seized becomes a dancing zombie. This is always a dramatic moment and it is clear to all present that a possession is taking place.

There are usually three phases in a possession: the opening phase at which time the possessed person may fall to the ground or stand rooted as with an electric shock; the second phase when the dance patterns call for strenuous dancing, more in some possessions than others, and the dancer must be attended, supported, or gently restrained; and the third phase when the dancing zombie can dance alone, unattended, executing the patterned dance of a specific zombie.

Combinations and variations of zombie dances make generalized descriptions unsatisfactory. To give a clearer picture, the following eight descriptions, based on specific and frequent repetitions at a number of Cumina ceremonies can stand as types:

1. At least eight variations have been observed in the general classification of this first type, which is characterized by an upright dancer who sometimes holds his arms up and sometimes shakes hands with people as he dances or moves his hands in other ways. The eight variations are illustrated in Figure 2, but the fluidity of the dances argues against such rigid classification.

Figure 2. Zombie dances at Cumina ceremonies 1: the upright dancer: (a) arms extended even with the shoulders, palms up, sometimes snatching thatch from the roof; (b) bent elbows, palms up, sometimes carrying a glass of water on each hand, dancing with a swinging motion from side to side, sometimes dipping in a two-step; (c) arms bent and hands on head, a bobbing dance, torso turning slightly from side to side, bending knees in a slight dip; (d) hands behind the neck and chest pushed forward, dancing in a two-step with mid-torso moving back and forward in a kind of grind; (e) shoulders, back and knees bent so that the midsection can be pushed forward, calling for a towel and pulling it tight around the buttocks while stamping and swinging hips from side to side; (f) hands on hips, tramping forward with a slight sway and swing to the right and then to the left; (g) knees bent slightly, hands on belly, tramping with emphasis on first and third beats and a slight grinding motion in the torso; and (h) front of foot supporting the body, arms hanging relaxed from the shoulders, dancing swinging slowly from side to side

2. The possessed spins in a manner unlike that in any other Cumina dance form. The spin is clockwise, in four-four time, and the dance, for all its spinning, is quite controlled. Other dancing zombies add a dipping swing to their spinning; these are associated with a sky god, two earth-bound gods and two ancestors (see Figure 3).

3. This is a violent form of possession, frequently part of the dance experience of Cumina. After the spirit hits, the dancing zombie hurls himself through the dancing crowd blindly, yet not knocking others down (Figure 4). Attending dancers, who are dancing zombies, are alert to this

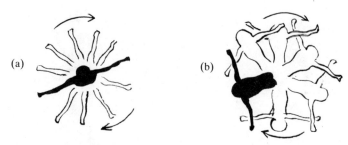

Figure 3.   Zombie dances at Cumina ceremonies 2: spinning: (a) upright throughout, and (b) dipping

Figure 4.   Zombie dances at Cumina ceremonies 3: the possessed hurling himself through the dancing crowd blindly

behavior and spring to the aid of the possessed person. This possession is characteristic of Obei, a sky god.

4. This is a possession by the ancestral spirit named William Bailey. The possessed dances around the ring head first on his back with a jerky movement, propelled by his heels and elbows (Figure 5). An ancestral spirit, or zombie, is generally believed to walk into the booth, much as he did in his lifetime, rather than come down through the center post. It circles the dancing ring, chooses a zombie partner, hits the dancer on the shoulders and head directly, and then proceeds to dance with the chosen dancer. The exceptions to this are those instances in which an ancestor danced to an older ancestral or earthbound god.

5. This is a form of possession which occurs often to drummers, and includes one sky god and one earthbound god. The drummers fall from their drums and lie on the ground on their sides, arms stretched out around their heads. After several minutes lying quietly on their sides, their torsos contract, they roll over on their stomachs, wriggle rapidly like a snake, and travel directly out of the dancing booth unless restrained (Figure 6).

6. This dance, easily recognizable, which brings the possessed dancer to his knees, arms folded behind the back. At first, there is no movement, then the body begins to pulsate to the beat of the music. Slowly, the head is raised off the ground and the dance begins in a kneeling position. It continues on the knees until the dancer is raised to his feet and goes into a stomp step. A variation of this is worked from a sitting, rather than a kneeling, position (Figure 7).

Figure 5. Zombie dances at Cumina ceremonies 4: the possessed dancing on his back, propelled by heels and elbows

Figure 6. Zombie dances at Cumina ceremonies 5: possession which occurs often to drummers: (a) contraction of torso, and subsequently (b) wriggling rapidly like a snake toward the outside

Figure 7. Zombie dances at Cumina ceremonies 6: (a) the kneeling dancer, and (b) the sitting dancer

7. This is the dance of Singquess, an earthbound god who seldom dances. When he does, the possessed dancer is knocked to the ground, rises and forms a wrestler's bridge with the back of his head touching the ground, the body supported by the hands and feet, while the torso begins a grinding rhythmic motion. The second phase of this dance comes after the attendants bring him to his feet and dance with the possessed dancer who now moves with hands on hips, abdomen extended and pulsating in a grinding motion. The third phase of the dance is the grinding motion while dancing alone, a slower, easier pulsation of the abdominal region of the body. Other possessions in this type can cause the dancer to move sideways in a crab motion, the body in the same wrestler's bridge, resting on head, elbows, and hands (Figure 8).

8. The choreography is completed in this last type, the form in which most possessions come. It is the basic step and position of Cumina, and forms the holding pattern against which the more exotic types play out their figures. In this type, most of the dancers are moving with an erect body, dancing on the heels, arms loose, head carried easily, and either a one-step or a two-step swinging them along with a slight side to side motion. From this basic movement, which gives the dancing ring its

Figure 8.   Zombie dances at Cumina ceremonies 7: two phases of the dance of Singquess

substance, some go into second and third phases of their possessions, some turn and dance backwards, always maintaining the clockwise direction (Figure 9).

These are some, but by no means all, of the basic patterns of possession dances that were observed at Cumina dances in St. Thomas parish, Jamaica. They, and many others, are recognized throughout the region, indicating that their style is constant, their spirit personalities familiar (see Appendix 2).

Those who are experienced dancing zombies rarely have difficulty attending and dancing with the possessed dancers. In turn, those who are possessed respond easily to the ministrations of the attendants. The seasoned dancing zombie becomes very skillful in caring for the possessed dancer, especially during a first possession, which can be awkward and sometimes dangerous to the newly possessed person.

As for the music in Cumina, the drums establish the basic beat for the rhythms used in the zombie possessions — a basic beat from the heavy banda drum, and from the higher playing drum a variety of counter-rhythms related to a variety of possession dances. This is augmented by the catatic, scraper, and shaker. The basic beats in all the music at these Cumina dances are two-two, four-four, and six-eight time, with the underlying constant six-eight beat of the top sky god. High rim beats indicate the presence of a zombie in the drum.

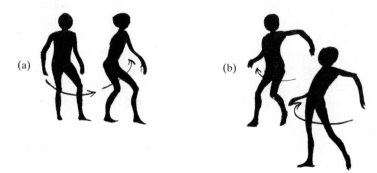

Figure 9.   Zombie dances at Cumina ceremonies 8: (a) the basic step and position of Cumina; (b) the basic step in reverse

It was mentioned before that two types of songs are used, both types being folk songs, and both being used in possessions. It appears that bilah songs are principally in Jamaican English dialect, while country songs are sometimes in this dialect and sometimes in a language locally called African. This reinforces the local reference to Cumina as African Dance. Preliminary study indicates a Bantu base to the "African" words collected and their meanings.

Cumina ceremonies are prepared in the afternoon, start in early evening, and continue until the next afternoon. From afar, the ear will pick up the overall beats, the repetitious sounds of the songs. At ringside, the polyrhythms, the complexity of visual movements, and the leader and response type of singing will come across in wide variety. Each sequence of song and the subsequent possessions, as they take place, play themselves out in a long arch of enduring time during the night. A perspective on Cumina music would not be available to anyone visiting a ceremony briefly. A minimal stay would be all night and into the light of morning in order to hear the scope of the songs and to gain some understanding of their use at certain points. The words and music of some of these songs are in Appendix 1.[2]

REVIVAL CULTS

Members of the Revival cult believe that it originated in the Middle East, with Revival Zion members asserting Mount Zion to be their origin. Pocomania cult members say the same and often call themselves Black Israelites. There is a marked difference here between the beliefs of origin of these and the Cumina cults. The great difference, however, is that all of the Revival groups are syncretistic, blending African and European Christian elements and traditions, while Cumina is African with New World negro inventions. Their similarities are in their animism and their ancestral worship.

There are other similarities. The Revival dancing booth is not unlike the booths built for Cumina — with five upright bamboo poles, one in each corner and one in the center. But in Revival, the four corner poles represent the four Evangelists, Matthew, Mark, Luke and John, who control the four points of the compass, north, south, east and west. The center pole represents the central power of God, particularly the third person of the Trinity, the Holy Ghost. Again, like the Cumina booth, the four poles are tied around by thinner poles latched from one to the other to make a base for what constitutes the top of the booth. On the top, across from side to side, are stretched more poles and upon these are laid

---

[2]   In addition the music of 38 skybound, 62 earthbound, and 21 ancestral zombies has been recorded with data on all of them (Moore 1953).

palm and banana leaves which make a fairly good protection from any weather but the heaviest downpour. As in Cumina, the booth is always placed inside the yard of a family so that guards may be stationed at the entrance, thereby controlling both the living persons who come to the ceremony, as well as the spirits of the dead who come through. At the time of a ceremony there is always a lantern or a torch burning at this entrance.

However, there are major differences between Revival and Cumina. In Revival, there is an altar, a table set so that it touches the center pole near its own center; it may be on any side of the pole as long as it touches it. The altar may be variously dressed with an arrangement of candles, flowers, food, and drink laid on a white cloth. In Cumina, there are only the drums at the center pole.

After the Revival altar table is completely laid out, a glass of water is placed on the table near the center pole and an ordinary two-gallon pail of water, covered by a white cloth, is placed under the table, just across from the center pole. At this point, the preparations are complete.

At sunset, the ceremony is begun with gospel hymns interspersed with psalms and prayers read by some of the leaders. During the singing of the hymns, the group begins a mild *trumping and laboring*, a phrase which describes the basic body movements of this cult's groups. It is a dance which bends on each two steps (laboring) with air released and sucked in vocally (trumping). As the dance proceeds past its opening phase of invoking the spirits, the drums and shakers stop and the only percussion comes from the beat of the feet and the intake and release of the breath in four-four rhythm. The combined effect of this sound is completely unlike any other sound made with instruments or song. There are some minor differences among the three Revival groups: in Pocomania the air is released on the down bend, while in Revival and Revival Zion it is released on the upward movement.

The group moves in a counterclockwise direction around the altar table. This is the sign that the ceremony has really begun, for the trumping and laboring is to invite the Holy Ghost and the other spirits to come down and join the Revival band. Specifically, the first period of trumping and laboring is to bring the Holy Ghost down the center pole of the booth and into the pail of water under the altar table. At the same time, it is to bring the Evangelists who control the corner poles of the booth. After this, the ceremony is set, the ground around the altar and inside the booth is consecrated, and the ceremony can proceed; all other spirits can come as they will. The process is always the same: down the center pole, into the water in the pail, and then into the bodies of the faithful members of the band. Water is the important element in Revival for the transmission of spirits. The glass of water on the altar table, the pail of water under the table, the drinking of water during the ceremony — these are all vehicles through which the spirits gain entrance and possession of the bodies of Revival members.

To appreciate the body movements, or the dance of Revival, it is necessary to understand this origin through water of the power and the spirits which come. It is also important to know the mood of the spirit as it is revealed in the dance of a possessed person. Revivalists feel that they are used by the spirits who possess them in order for these spirits to rejoice. The spirit is described as coming down in the booth through the center pole into the water, then into the ground, and from there into the feet of the person to be possessed, up his legs to his spine, up his spine to his shoulders, and from his shoulders to his head.

Who comes to possess the bodies of the faithful in dance? Not God the Father, who stays in high heaven; not God the son, who comes but does not dance; but God the Holy Ghost, who is the chief energizing spirit in Revival, the force behind Revival's power. Others who come are the archangels and prophets: archangels Michael and Gabriel; the prophets Elija, Daniel, Moses, Amos, Joshua, Isaiah, Ezekiel, and Nehemiah. The four Evangelists come to dance. Next come the disciples Peter and Paul, and some of the others. Finally, ancestral spirits, great leaders of the Revival flock, called shepherds and shepherdesses, who have died, come to dance (the officers in charge of Revival are shepherds and shepherdesses: in large bands there may be males and females for each office). Many former shepherds, when they come, have certain hymns which are sung for them, and certain colors are placed upon the persons who are possessed by them.

A characteristic of the dance of the shepherds is that of the *wheeling shepherd*. Of the seven kinds of shepherds,[3] the wheeling shepherd is the principal officer in charge of ceremonies. At various times during the ceremonies, he wheels about the altar, always counterclockwise. He has other duties to perform but his dancing qualifications are essential so that his wheeling will attract the Holy Ghost and draw him to the service.

Another officer who affects the ritual dance and music is the *rambling shepherd*, who whips up the tempo of the ceremony and leads the procession when it leaves the booth. He travels from one end of the procession to the other in order to keep in touch with the group all the time. He will also ramble in and out of the group and in and out of the crowd.

The music of Revival is drawn from hymns by Ira David Sankey and other gospel songs in English (Sankey 1878). The beat is mainly in four-four or six-eight time, and the tempo is slow to begin with, shepherds and shepherdesses leading the singing. No hymn books are used as

[3] The ranks of officers in Revival cults, downward from the crowned shepherd or shepherdess, also called governor or governess, are wheeling shepherd(ess), and then rambling, warrior, hunting, spying, cutting, and water shepherd(esses). Assistants to these are called *wheeling man* (or woman), and so on. There are bearers who are simply members.

everyone knows the words. The ceremony proceeds through the "first table", the "smashing of the table", and the "second table", which will be explained. The music and sounds of the ceremony consist of an early period of instrument accompaniment, hymn singing, psalm reading, other Bible reading, trumping and laboring, and singing without words.

The foregoing comments are generalized from observations of many groups and ceremonies. It may be helpful to place these elements in context by describing a ceremony which took place in a private yard beside the sea in a small fishing village outside the town of Morant Bay.

There was a lantern at the gate leading into the yard and a guard charged all guests threepence to enter. By the time the opening part of the ceremony was under way there were almost four hundred people in attendance.

The shepherd and shepherdess wore white headdresses and stoles, the warrior and governess wore red headdresses, the bearers and bellringers wore white on their heads. At this particular ceremony there were mixed colors present because the occasion was a combination memorial dance and crowning ceremony, the latter being the term used for an investiture of office. The woman to become a crowned governess served also as the queen, or sponsor, of the ceremony. It was her mother for whom the memorial aspect of the ceremony was being held. The center post of the dancing booth was wrapped in black and white, the conventional colors for a "memorial table", but the participants wore bands of blue in honor of the crowning aspect of the occasion. The queen was dressed in white with a bridal veil and was attended by a man and a bridesmaid.

The altar table was beautifully set with Coca-Cola, bread, and star apples and other fruits, with also the glass of water covered with a white cloth and the pail of water, covered the same way, under it.

As the first part of the ceremony proceeded, the queen who was to be crowned governess trumped and labored along with the other participants. Then the possessions began. The Holy Ghost, the apostles, various saints, ancestral shepherds and shepherdesses came down and possessed many of the Revival band. During all this period of trumping and laboring and possession, verse after verse of gospel hymns were sung.

At midnight, the "smashing of the table" took place, which simply means that all the food was distributed to the people present and everyone partook of the "love feast". The feeling was friendly and warm; there were many possessions and everyone seemed relaxed and happy. After the "smashing of the table" there was a break in the service until about 1:30 A.M. when the regular presiding officers took over and the second ring was started. The signal for the "second table" was the singing of hymns as before and the beginning of trumping and laboring. The shepherd led the group out into the yard outside the dancing booth, and for the next hour the group danced in the yard around the booth.

At 3 A.M. the procession danced through the gate toward the grave of the mother of the queen of the ceremony. The queen was, by now, acknowledged as having become a crowned governess. The procession was led by a *rambling man*, a bearer, and the leading shepherd himself, with the rest of the officers of the band close behind. The queen and her attendants, her immediate family and friends, brought up the rear. As the procession reached the grave, the participants mounted it, and it was abundantly clear in the body movements of the worshippers that many powerful spirit possessions were taking place. Especially was it evident that the mother, whose grave it was, had been successfully invoked and was dancing in the body of her daughter, the queen. The trumping and laboring at the graveside continued until 9 A.M., at which time the group proceeded back to the yard where the ceremony concluded. One of those present that night, not a member of the group, described it this way:

At the part of the day when they are about to go home, they make a circle, they start to sing a chorus and sing a hymn, and they read a psalm, and after the psalm, the Mother pray, and the governess pray, and the wheeler girl pray, and the dove pray; and after the dove, the bellringer and the Bible pointer pray, and the hunter boy . . . and the whole company read the twenty-third psalm and they read a Sankey; and after that Sankey they sing, and during the singing they trump, and after trumping they break away and went home to their several abodes.

Culturally the Revival cult is closely connected to the non-Christian Cumina cult. In Revival, the spirits are Christian, but they respond in a manner which is completely understandable to the members of Cumina, whose gods are non-Christian. It should be pointed out that an occasional feature of a Revival ceremony will be the River Maid and the river gods, who appear in Cumina as well. Quite apart from the regular officers of Revival, the River Maid, under certain circumstances, will appear and function as the most important officiant. During storm or rain, or when there is some particular aspect of a ceremony which invokes the river gods, the River Maid takes over and is the primary functionary of the band. Serving her are a water shepherd and shepherdess, a water boy and girl. At times it is believed that she is stronger than the top shepherd or shepherdess because it is said of her that she rules the ocean and the seas. Significant also is that two of the Trinity use water coming down into Revival and because water is used by "all the heavenly and earthly host". The importance of water cannot be overemphasized, for it is the lifeline of the spirit. It is described this way by one person:

The River Maid and her assistants labor in the water . . . even if the rain is downpouring, it won't hurt them. . . . They don't have to be afraid of pneumonia, nor have they any fear of ailments, because directly the water becomes a potion which guards and supports the River Maid and her assistants.

These are some of the roles, the dance movements, the music, and possession types which characterize one or another of the Revival groups. Some of the specific ancestral spirits who return and dance frequently in Revival ceremonies are described in Appendix 2.

CONCLUSION

During the period studied, Cumina and Revival cults were providing expression in music and dance to many persons in the lower economic segment of the area. Despite their enforced separation, artistic and religious acts seem to emerge from the same source, the vision of the inner man, the spirit, the undefinable. These acts, expressed in nonverbal forms, give social, recreational, and psychological satisfaction.

Each dance or ceremony reviewed in this paper is carefully structured and a unity within itself. The musicians and dancers are skillful in their performance because of their long training. Years of practice go into trumping and laboring. No one could withstand the rigors of this intensive physical activity unless his or her body was conditioned over a long period to it. The physical setting, the engaging of the musicians, the informing of the community, the preparation of food, the costumes to be worn — these are all part of a carefully planned event. In this sense the religious function is also a production of a spectacle consisting of pageantry, music, and dance (see Herskovits 1948:429; Kerr 1952).

The audience is both observer and participant; it is also highly sophisti-cated regarding the ritual content of these ceremonies because of its acquaintance with the elements of music and the possession dances of local ancestors and other spirits.

The role that these two cults play in the lives of the people is one that helps them to be integrated into their own culture. Unemployment and poverty make the lives of most of these people very difficult. Participation in Cumina or Revival helps to make life tolerable and brings to its followers a sense of security.

To an observer, an art form brings stimulation and, perhaps, a deepen-ing insight, but to a participant it is a vehicle for self-expression and a release of inner tensions. This psychic outpouring restores vitality and refreshes the whole person. This effect was evident in the behavior of people after a ceremony was over. The completed event had a psycho-logical effect on all present and there was a prevailing sense of deep satisfaction.

APPENDIX 1: SONGS

Bilah Song Titles

Ricketa
Maneno Cuban
Finger nail Oh!
Manuka de lan gal
Three days three nights
Bad mother-in-law
Nina malua tu noa
Mighty clever (Marty Clever)
Wan go hom tangala
Grave yard don't bother me
Oh ya gal of Sininine
Shay shay Murray
Want to go home Cudjo
Vida tell me
Poor stranger
Simea simea
Alanda Cumina
Kisalea Mama
Daylight Mama
Landeman he lied though
Mona mona, gal, don't mona me
Don't care what dem say
Oh Maloche am Bombala
We walk all the night, Mondumbay
Cymbal, Oh!
One quarter guma
Bakine tumbay
Geng geng geng
Oh gal oh me cum
My yea, my yea
Oh de belly of a femme
Tangoona
Sally Water
Sakoolande
Rundudungadu, dilly dilly Sally
Fire like to burn me
Follow the niger gal, Mama
Wonder what me do
Oh Pilar name in the day
Sevenyear a coolie come

Country Song Titles

Wansuka, King Kongo mama
Oh de lang gang tang la
Vumala cacate

Wan Makenzie gone
Way O poor Megiliard gone
Hand a born a knife a troat
Mona Kongala wan de la
Wakee, wakee, cum kill me dead
Run go down a dilly dilly
Tanga langa Jennie

Some Songs Transcribed

LONG BAG OF MONEY

Bilah

Drum Rhythm

Long bag of money oh
  Long bag of money
Long bag of money oh
  Long bag of money
Habe, habe, no want to you
Long bag of money
Getee, getee, can't manage you
Long bag of money
Long bag of money oh, Long bag of money
Long bag of money oh, Long bag of money
Wala, wala what to do Mama
Long bag of money
Habe, habe, no want tee you
Long bag of money
Getee getee can't manage you
Long bag of money
Oh call ee money oh
Long bag of money
Oh talkee with the dead
Long bag of money
Duppy dug a do
Long bag of money
Let me dug a tomb
Ah wan go home
Long bag of money
Daylight may not get to you
Long bag of money
Why oh money oh
Long bag of money
Why oh money oh
Long bag of money
Den I want teh want teh
Can't get to you
Long bag of money
Want teh, want teh
Can't get to you
Long bag of money
Habe, habe no want tee you
Long bag of money
Getee, getee can't manage you
Long bag of money
Why oh money oh
Long bag of money
Why oh money oh
Long bag of money
Why oh daylight Mama
Long bag of money
Let me dug a tomb

Ah wan go home
Long bag of money
Habe habe no want tee you
Long bag of money

MAROON GONE

Bilah

Drum Rhythms

Maroon gone, oh why oh, Maroon gone
Maroon gone, oh why oh, Maroon gone
Gal I wonder what my do you
Maroon gone go down go long go see

Maroon gone oh for Hayfield above
Maroon gone, oh Maroon gone
Maroon gone, oh gal oh, Maroon gone
Gal I wonder when me do you, Maroon gone
Maroon gone, oh by a Maroon gone
Maroon gone, oh gal oh, Maroon gone
Gal I wonder what my do you, Maroon gone
Maroon gone, oh Maroon gone
Down Boss Pen, Maroon gone
Darky Nation, why oh, Maroon gone
An we gone down Seaforth Road, Maroon gone, go down go see
Maroon gone oh for Jasmino Road
Maroon gone oh Maroon gone
Maroon gone oh why oh Maroon gone
Maroon gone, oh why oh, Maroon gone
Justine Miller, oh why oh, Maroon gone
Maroon gone, oh why oh, Maroon gone
Maroon gone, oh why oh, Maroon gone
Maroon gone, oh, Maroon gone
Maroon gone, oh why oh, Maroon gone
Maroon gone, oh why oh, Maroon gone,
Gal I wonder what my do you
Maroon gone go down go long go see
Maroon gone oh Maroon gone

"Seek a place for thy labor" and "A pillar of salt": Drum Rhythms

SEEK A PLACE FOR THY LABOR   Revival

Seek a place for thy labor
Get a hold of thy Lord
Seek a place for thy labor
Get a hold of thy Lord
Seek a place for thy labor
Get a hold of thy Lord
In the name of Jesus Christ the Lord
The Son of God

A PILLAR OF SALT   Revival

A life in a pillar of salt
A life in a pillar of salt
All for the need of a word of God
A life in a pillar of salt

DOWN BY A BEAUTIFUL RIVER   Revival

Drum Rhythms

Down by a beautiful river
Meet me there you shall meet me there
Right down the way
On the banks of the beautiful river
We meet again at our journey's end

WHEN YOU PLACE YOUR FAITH IN THE LORD   Revival

Drum Rhythms

When you place your faith in the Lord
And when you place your faith in the Lord
And when you place your faith in the Lord
And when the Lord God's angels kindles the fire
When you place your faith in the Lord

TANGA LANGA JENIE   Cumina

DANCING TALL JENNIE	TƆNGE LƆNGE JENI
Dancing tall Jennie	TƆNGE LƆNGE JENi
The girl always greeted by	Di GAL Ev Ɔ DiLƆ CU
The dead spirits	MƆRTi PƆNG Ɔ LƆ
The girl waiting to	GƆL EM WƆTTO
Greet her dead mother	PƆNGA MƆMƆ LƆ
All dead spirits greet her	DE LƆ CUWiDi PƆNGO LƆ
Dancing tall Jennie	TƆNGE LƆNGE JENi
The girl who walks straight and tall	Di GAL EVƆWƆNGƆ LƆNƆ
Dead mama	MƆMƆ O
Whom dead spirits greet	Di LƆ COWiDi PƆNGƆ LƆ
The girl like clear water	SO SO LƆNGƆ WiDi
To the spirits	Ă GƆL
Clear water, dead mother	O SO SO LƆNGƆ MƆMƆO
Oh what a day for zombies	O WƆT KOQUALƆ ZƆMBi
And the girl the dead like	Di GƆL ƆLƆK O WiDi
The girl greeted by the	WiDi PƆNGƆ LA
Dead who love her	

APPENDIX 2: POSSESSING SPIRITS AND THEIR DANCES

Cumina Sky Gods

Obei seldom comes to a dance to possess an individual, but when he does come it is very dangerous, and his beats are handled by the strongest drummers. At certain times, when he is called upon or feels the need to dance and does possess an individual, it is considered to be a very fearful occasion and often the possessed person dies. When he first comes into an individual the force of his possession knocks the individual flat to the ground for seconds. Then the individual breaks for the nearest pole or tree and climbs up backwards, feet first.

Batoon is an agricultural god who lives in the fields of the plantation. He works in the fields doing most of the types of work that the people do. He likes to dance, and occasionally, in the evening, he comes to dances. His dance is a simple, erect *myal* dance around the ring.

Abro is a god of the Cumina. He lives in the center post in the middle of the dancing booth. He goes up and down the post throughout the dance, and his duty is to bring the gods up and down the post into the drums. He loves to dance on his back and has a wriggling motion, similar to that of a snake, taking the possessed dancing zombie and wriggling straight out from the post to the edge of the dancing booth. He loves the beat of the catatic and becomes more active in his work when these sticks are being used against the center post. His song is "Congo, hear ye, Congo".

Mandoonbay is a dancer who loves to be with dancing zombies and drummers.

He lives in the most African part of town, visiting obeah men and drummers' homes. He dances many times during the evening, doing a belly-rubbing type of dance. His color is black and his song is "Long bag of money".

Cumina Earthbound Gods

Macoo begins his possession dance as illustrated in Figure 3. The possessed dancer staggers but does not fall and immediately goes into a spinning dance with wide circles, which must be controlled or the dancer flies out of the dancing ring. During the second section of his dance, the spins are controlled and the dancer spins as he travels the ring. The third part of this dance comes when the dancer stops the spins, straightens up, and dances around the ring, stopping to shake hands with people watching the ceremony, sometimes trying to drag the people into the ring.

Appei hits hard and suddenly, and the dancer falls to the ground, completely unconscious. When he comes to, the dancer springs up, hops in strict time to the beat of the *banda* to the nearest tree or post, where he climbs to the highest spot possible. In the second phase, he breaks away many times and tries to climb one of the posts which hold up the corners of the dancing booth.

Matee begins his possession dance as illustrated in Figure 2, riding the shoulders of the dancer. It is a dignified erect posture, with the head moving slowly from side to side, the arms stretched up with the palms of the hands facing upward, shoulder high. Very slowly majestic turns are made and the face is happy and peaceful. The attendant induces the god to leave by holding the waist of the man or woman dancer, and turning the body in a clockwise direction. The turns are faster and faster until the god leaves the body.

Seeco dances with arms outstretched, even with the armpits, hands up to the sky. The dancer immediately calls for two glasses of water, one for each palm. The second phase of the dance is a slow majestic wheeling with arms outstretched, which is broken, and the walking step continued, turning the body from the waist up, first left, and then right, in time with the first note of the *banda*. The fact that the water in the glasses is never spilled is indicative of the balance of this dance.

Cumina Ancestral Zombies

William Bailey tosses the dancer to the ground, and then dances on his back with the possessed person on top of him, theoretically. The dancer dances around the ring, head first on his or her back, with a jerky pulsating movement, propelling the body from the heels and the elbows, with the buttocks being raised and lowered.

Grace Bailey, or Gracie, calls for a black cloth around the waist and frock pulled up a bit so that it bags over. In the first phase of her dance, the possessed dancer whirls around the dancing ring, finally falling on her knees. The second phase of the dance is on the knees around the circle, singing "Too windee", a bilah song.

Under possession of *Manuka Vola* the dancer orders a towel placed about his neck, jumps and tosses his body around the ring in wide sweeps. The arms are raised up, always reaching for something, trying to pull some of the covering off the dancing booth, pulling at the colors on the center post, and so on. The head is turned up, the eyes staring up with a fixed gaze at the ceiling of the dancing booth.

The country song, "Ya Manuka, gala wat sa da matta, King Zombie Goo-Coo", is always sung during this dance.

Margaret Miller zombie calls for a piece of cloth tied very tightly around her waist, then begins to wheel with arms outstretched even with the shoulders. In the first phase of the dance, she wheels around the ring. Then, in the second phase, dashes at right angles from the center post, right out of the booth toward the place where the bodies of her family and her own remains are buried. If she is dancing in her own family's yard she goes directly to the graves and then returns. If in another yard she goes to the local grave area and then returns.

Revival Spirits

Shepherd Granville wheels and calls for a glass of water which is placed on his head and is never spilled. While he is wheeling, a special hymn, "While shepherds watch their flocks by night", is sung. He wears a white robe and is greatly revered.

When *Father Levas* comes, a chair is placed for him at the end of the table; here he sits and instructs. His special hymn is always sung, "The God of Abraham praise", and a black robe is placed upon the person possessed by him. Father Levas is impartial, coming as frequently to young initiates as to any other members of the band.

Shepherd Blair comes into the meeting in a great wheeling dance, wheeling around and around. He usually works with the wheeling shepherd in the ceremony, although he may come to other members of the band. Of him, it is said, "he likes a blue color, and usually you have to get a blue color to take care of him, but sometimes he will work in white."

Shepherd Bendigo, in life, was a wheeling shepherd with the gift of prophesy, especially as it related to the riddance of evil. Now, when he comes, he brings tremendous gifts for prophesy and his special power for cutting and clearing the most difficult of evils. He wheels, and sometimes breaks in his wheel toward the four corner posts. He never possesses anyone but a wheeling shepherd and he loves to wear red.

REFERENCES

CASSIDY, FREDERIC G.
   1961   *Jamaica talk*. New York: Macmillan.
HERSKOVITS, MELVILLE J.
   1941   *The myth of the Negro past*. New York: Harper and Brothers.
   1948   *Man and his works*. New York: Alfred A. Knopf.
KERR, MADELEINE
   1952   *Personality and conflict in Jamaica*. Liverpool: Liverpool University Press.
MOORE, JOSEPH G.
   1953   "Religion of Jamaican Negroes." Unpublished dissertation, Northwestern University. Evanston, Illinois.
SANKEY, IRA D.
   1878   *The enlarged songs and solos*. London: Morgan and Scott.

Space Rock: Music and Dance of the Electronic Era

GERTRUDE P. KURATH

The popular musical style known as "rock 'n' roll" has kept pace with the swift changes in the world around. Since 1956 it has split into many styles, and since 1968 a new trend has been developing — space music or space rock. This innovative style bases its techniques on several Western traditions: baroque, jazz, and rock. Its ideology breaks away from the contents of the still popular hard rock.

EQUIPMENT, TECHNIQUE, IDEOLOGY

The basic instruments used in space rock are acoustic or electric guitars and sets of drums. To these may be added wind and string instruments of European tradition, sometimes electrified; and also piano, harpsichord, and organ, and the electric vibraharp. At times composers reach into far-off lands, including India, the Near East, Africa, and Brazil, for strings and percussion instruments. The wide range of tone colors may be further expanded by electric amplification and distorting devices such as the *wah-wah*,[1]

I express my thanks to the Wenner-Gren Foundation for Anthropological Research, sponsor of this rock 'n' roll project; to my young collaborators, Roger Miller, musician, typist, and supplier of the explanations of the popular music terms; Larry Miller, musician; Susannah Juni, dancer; Steve Faigenbaum, video technician; to Reverend Richard Singleton, theologian; and to Gairt Mauerhof and the staff of the Liberty Music Shop, advisers in the selection of commercial albums.

[1] Wah-wah is an effect contained in a floor unit manipulated by the foot. It consists of a treble and a bass booster: the foot is pressed forward for a treble sound, backwards for a bass sound, so when rocked back and forth slowly or very fast (or anywhere in between), it can make an instrument sound like it is talking or crying or whatever you choose to imagine. It can be very expressive if used well.

fuzztone,[2] and *feedback*.[3] In studio recordings tapes can be manipulated for strange effects, and for the inclusion of sounds from nature. The human voice, amplified by a microphone, occasionally intones sounds or texts.

Like earlier acoustic jazz and electrified rock, space rock draws its tonal equipment from the basic scales and harmonies of European music. But, increasingly, the composers exploit other tonalities, liturgical or exotic, and atonality; and they experiment with unorthodox, dissonant chord progressions. The rhythms inherited from jazz and rock are bold and syncopated; the metric schemes are more irregular. The interweaving of instruments is ingenious, the structure is sophisticated. Repetition, variations on a theme, and the technique known as *riff*[4] prevail, but thematic developments may be complex.

Space rock often sounds like rock, due to the instruments and techniques, though the basic beat is not piston-heavy. It breaks away from previous popular music styles in its ideology, and in the instruments' function — to express the meaning. Briefly, this new ideology may be termed *mystical*[5] rather than realistic: its purpose and expression will become clearer in the description of examples from original and commercial recordings.

[2]   *Fuzztone* is a device usually contained in a unit on the floor with a "button" to turn it on or off, which is operated by pressure from the foot. It is stationed between the guitar and amplifier so that the signal from the guitar will go through it before reaching the amplifier. The guitar is plugged into the fuzztone by a connector cord, which in turn is plugged into the amplifier in like manner. Some types of fuzztones are hand-controlled, the units being plugged directly into the guitar input, using no more connector cords than without the fuzztone. Hand-controlled fuzztones have the definite disadvantage that for your hand to touch the switch, you have to stop playing the guitar temporarily.

The essence of the fuzztone is a small preamplifier, or preamp, which overamplifies the sound (the main amplifier is already amplifying the signal and the preamp amplifies it again) so that a fuzzy distortion sound is the result. With a fuzztone it is very easy to get feedback because the signal is overamplified and the sound coming from the amplifier is very loud. Two controls on the fuzztone allow for variability of volume and distortion.

[3]   Straight amplification starts at the microphone pickup on the guitar, which receives the sound of the guitar strings and sends a signal through the connector cord into the amplifier, which electronically amplifies the sound, sending it out through the speaker. *Feedback* occurs when the amplifier is turned up so loud that not only is the sound of the strings received by the microphone pickup, but also the sound from the amplifier. When the guitar plays a note the sound comes out of the amplifier almost instantly. When this sound is received through the pickup it is, in a sense, putting the sound it just sent through itself again and this is feedback. When a guitarist desires feedback, he will often hold the guitar so that the microphone pickup is extremely close to the sound source, the speakers of the amplifier unit, so the connection is more easily made and more easily sustained.

[4]   A *riff* is a series of notes put together, often repeated. If a song has a certain theme running through it, this is called the main riff. When a solo instrument is improvising and the other instruments are keeping a backup pattern, this is also a riff: in fact any series of notes is a riff, and often when musicians are referring to a particular passage in a solo, they will refer to segments of it as riffs.

[5]   *Mysticism* refers here to a state of mind resulting from an individual's direct communication with God or ultimate reality.

A taped recording by a young Ann Arbor composer, Roger Miller, can serve as a paradigm in the use of rock equipment, and in his statement of the philosophy of "man's growing awareness of his relationship and dependence on every living creature and the actions of every object and force in nature on earth and in space" (Miller and Kurath 1972), could be termed a religious attitude, except for the absence of systematized faith and ritual.[6] The music explores new paths for new thoughts.

EXAMPLES OF SPACE MUSIC

Miller's *With magnetic fields disrupted* (Miller and Kurath 1972) contains twelve episodes of destruction and of rebirth by a new sun. The instrumental equipment is a set of two electrical guitars, a trumpet, percussion, and vocals. This typical rock combination is played in rock manner, with a strong, basic beat and drum rolls at dramatic moments, diverse amplifications, and occasional improvisation. The innovative aspect is the employment of the chord progressions, dissonances, and electric devices for expression of the idea, rather than for display of effects. Some of his ideas grew out of "space jams" (group improvisations); some compositions developed from flashes of inspiration. The performance is always without a written score, but Miller prepared a written score, from a tape recording, which shows some of his expressiveness, especially in the use of electric devices. "In the sun" uses an intense fuzztone and vibrato dramatizing a girl's running into the sun, symbolic of destruction by new freedom. In "Nocturnal mission" the wah-wah gives the effect of planetary rotation. In "Point of view" the *reverb*[7] intensifies the dissonances and drum roll, before the return to the initial theme of responses. The roll is a typical rock device, as is the frequent syncopation.

The composer describes the instrumental devices for the expression of ideas. In "Point of view" the statement of a theme in the voice and the answering in the trumpet is symmetrical. From where the main verses stop the song becomes chaotic. The first part of this section (the main vocals) consists of visions flowing above chaos and out of this comes the statement ". . . and he will let you by!" The chaos disappears temporarily and heavy instrumental accents take over. Then a clear guitar note is

---

[6] *Religion* is defined here as man's attempt to adjust his life to the strongest and best power in the universe, usually called God, and to achieve the highest possible good. Most religions are organized systems of beliefs based on traditions and teachings. They include ethics, or codes of conduct.

[7] *Reverb* is an effect usually built into the amplifier unit by means of a coiled metal spring which vibrates and reverberates when the sound is run through it. The unit usually has a knob for controlling the intensity of the reverberation. Often, there is a foot switch connected to the amplifier so that the guitarist can turn on the reverb by foot pressure, allowing him more freedom of expression.

introduced and is disrupted twice by the chaos but triumphs over it. It slows down, then the guitar rushes back up into a main theme with the rest of the instruments.

The first part of "New air" floats in space and has wide intervals between notes. Percussion sounds are introduced sporadically, and although they are seemingly unrelated to the main musical line are actually an integral part of the music. The lyrics speak of a change of perception in reality and, with the music, create a feeling of spirits in another dimension.

The middle section of this piece is an improvisation on electric guitar with a repeating pattern in the other instruments built atonally. The solo includes the fuzztone, high volume on the amplifier, and feedback on certain notes. It is describing the previous lyrics as "Heading for the sun", and is a headlong rush in that direction. The solo ends (after the backup pattern has faded) and the bass and drums lead the song back to the "New air".

The coda to this song is a return of the floating feeling in the first part, but in a different way. The trumpet starts alone with the bass sliding in and down with the cymbals. At the end, the electric guitar, on reverb and tremolo, produces a strange sound, by use of a slide, which calls up an image of a spacecraft hovering above Earth's surface.

Two outstanding albums of space rock include an episode evoking the rhythm and majestic tempo of the ocean. *In the wake of Poseidon* (King Crimson 1970) creates this image with a rising and falling, harmonized melody on the legato melotron, against crisp syncopations and rolls on the snare drums, suggesting the swells and the frothy breakers. Spurts of flute, soft cymbals, and voice, enrich this nostalgic composition.

The track "Echoes" (Pink Floyd 1971) is stronger, even primordial. After bleeps like sparks of life comes the surging, pulsating rock beat of guitars and drums. Roger Miller says about this section: "[it] reminds me of being on the bottom of the sea, and as the guitars come in I feel like I'm rising upwards to the surface and finally break free and speed along at thousands of miles an hour about two feet above the ocean's surface" (personal communication). Cries of gulls intensify this sense of life on wings. A sunny joyous organ passage and occasional roars lead to tenderness. A combined surge and bleeping ends on a question mark. Miller, who witnessed a performance of this piece, describes the instrumentation:

Beginning throbs, by an acoustic grand piano on stage, run via microphone through a Leslie speaker.[8] Enter a floating electronic organ, guitar solos, and then

---

[8]   A *Leslie speaker* is a speaker which spins around in a motor very fast inside its cabinet to produce a strange whirling vibrato sound.

the full ensemble. A backup floating sound is often a slide guitar.[9] Vocal verses come in. Lyrics speak of "rolling waves" and "labyrinths of coral caves" connected with "strangers passing in the street" and "help me understand the best I can." These lyrics play well with the more cosmic passages to come connecting the high vision to human realities.

Funky[10] section, very earthy, has a backup by bass, drums, and organ while the lead guitar plays sharp leads with fuzztone, reverb, and often sustaining feedback during the solo. Sometimes the guitarist uses the vibrato tailpiece which rapidly changes the tension on the strings so that the strings become sharper and flatter in rapid motion.

The funky section fades out (live: musicians play softer and softer) with guitar on high feedback. An electronic prerecorded tape then fades in, in concert as well as on record. Pink Floyd have speakers set all the way around the auditoriums where they play. They'll often start a sound on stage and move it around the room or, if there are speakers placed in the balconies, create sounds falling from the sky or rising upwards. Through these speakers come the eerie sounds of the pre-recorded tape — a vast underwater hum with the cries of seagulls and strange sea creatures. The bass guitar quits the funky riff, and uses a slide to get a background hum from the amplifier. The drummer walks off the stage at this point for there is no beat in this next section. Floating organ notes with various hums form the background for a unique electronic guitar solo. The guitar player uses a wah-wah, but instead of "correctly" playing it as a wah-wah he plugs the amplifier cord into the guitar input and the guitar cord into the amplifier input thereby crossing the signal. Then, by manipulation of the volume control on the guitar, the guitarist creates a far-off whining wailing like underwater sounds bouncing off the ocean floor and searing through the depths.

This section then fades out. An organ chord fades in and the beginning piano throb through a Leslie speaker is heard. The rising from the depths of the ocean is about to begin. Light cymbal rhythms interwork with a guitar rhythm which plays inside of its own sound with an echo unit — it plays a note and on the echo of that note it plays again so that there is a note as well as an echo of the previous note. This produces a strange effect, somehow eliminating the percussive effect of hitting the string and turning the sound more into a pulsation.

A chord progression, started on the organ, spreads to the other instruments on the rhythm described above. An organ solo is played on top of that progression. The group rises in volume, nearing the surface after dwelling in the depths.

With a powerful burst, the guitar solos on a repeated cosmically victorious pattern, and the bass uses fuzztone for heavy effect. The beat is temporarily in the background for this majestic rush. Then the rhythm returns again, speeding along at thousands of miles an hour just above the ocean's surface. Then the bass (still on fuzztone) leads the ensemble up and out into a more earthbound vocal verse, tying the cosmic vision of the ocean to the human land dweller in a positive way.

A majestic chord progression follows this verse and gains power and more embellishments in rhythm and harmony as it progresses, fulfilling three cycles of the progression.

Then cosmic voices swiftly rise up into the sky and the mood becomes calmer. In performance, these cosmic voices (quite a large vocal ensemble, it seems) are

---

[9]   *Slide guitar* is a guitar played by the hand on the neck with a piece of rounded metal which bypasses the frets so that no definite division between notes is produced, all note changes sliding from one to the next.
[10]   *Funky* music is music with a lot of syncopations and a heavy beat, excellent for normal rock 'n' roll dancing.

played prerecorded on tape while the band improvises on the calmer progressions. After a short bit of this mellower mood, the cosmic voices rise again, this time more gradually and with more power, and the beginning piano note through the Leslie speaker returns. As they rise they fade away and the twenty-minute composition has reached its conclusion (Roger Miller, personal communication).

Other compositions rise to the sky and beyond. The track "Celestial voices" (Pink Floyd 1970) swells from an organ theme and drum rhapsody to a vocal and instrumental paean. Wayne Shorter's acoustic title track "Super nova" (1969) dispenses with an obvious beat. It suggests the flashing brilliance of a star with vertical cascades of a soprano saxophone on top of a restless bass and cymbal pattern. Larry Miller describes the roles of the instruments:

It starts out with the sax soloing, playing the theme, a short riff, spurts and runs going up in pitch and intensity. Then the guitars spurt around; in a little while they peak, and the sax comes in again. Then it simmers down and the drums bring it to a close (personal communication).

Similarly, in the tracks "Emergency!" and "Spectrum", Tony Williams (1969) creates eerie effects with a nervous beat and with atonal organ and guitar coloring. The "Visitor from Venus" by the Modern Jazz Quartet (1969) evokes space by an ethereal pulse that solidifies into the rhythm and harmonies of a piano, vibraharp, bass, and cymbals. The vibraharp plays the most prominent part in creating an eerie effect, with its prolonged pulsations.

Hubert Laws (1971) also exploits the dissolvent pulsations of the vibes in his rock version of Bach's *Passacaglia in C minor*. Though his treatment of the theme lacks Bach's grandeur, it spreads into outer realms of space, by means of an electric cello and flute as well as of the vibes and brushed cymbals. The first section clings to Bach's variations; the second becomes limpid and "spacy"; and the third consists of a jazzlike improvisation with percussion beat.

Some composers use themes from Christian and Asiatic music and thought. In their *Mass in F minor* the Electric Prunes (1967) combine liturgical and space music. Voices intone mass texts in plainsong modes — unfortunately with a catastrophic pronunciation of Greek and Latin. The instruments produce vigorous rock rhythms of guitars and percussion. Roger Miller finds the opening guitar feedback awesome, "because feedback transcends the normal note and vibrates on a higher plane." Reverend Richard Singleton (personal communication) interprets the mood of the part entitled "Kyrie eleison": "It proceeds from aggression to despair, as though beating against a wall, then giving up, in awe, interiorness, not hopefulness, but with some of the meaning of *kyrie* supplication," namely, mercy. Lalo Schifrin's *Jazz suite on Mass texts*

(1965) he considers "ethereal, pleading. It becomes rhythmic, dramatic, catches the meaning and structure of the *kyrie*. It creates a corporate and cosmic quality, as if God were high above a city, in the center of the universe, the world in travail, voices reaching to the center of the cosmos." In the ternary form, sopranos in free rhythm alternate with a conventional orchestra featuring Paul Horn's yearning flute.

With equal freedom, some composers seek inspiration from oriental religions. Pharaoh Sanders (1969) dilates on the theme of *Karma*, the path to God by way of action, in Hinduism. However, he features a nine-man ensemble of jazzwinds and percussion, plus maracas. Singer Leon Thomas interpolates vocals: "The Creator has a master plan/Peace and happiness for every man." He chants "Om!" After all, we are heading for unity of religions.

In his *Wailing dervishes* Herbie Mann (1967) used Near Eastern rhythms and instruments like the *oudh* and bagpipe, in strict hypnotic tempo. Like Sanders, this very modern composer reaches back to ancient trance inducement, the self-hypnotism of Siberian shamans.

These composers convey their mystical messages largely through the electronic manipulation of live instruments. Some technicians rely entirely on tape tricks. Perrey and Kingsley (n.d.) spent 275 hours in the preparation of *The in sound from way out*. They produced strange blurps for "Spooks in space." In general they devised comical, banal tunes, such as an "Electronic can-can." By contrast, James Peters combined the tape effects into an ultra-"spacy" *Noise for western dawn* (1972) with a floating beat (see appendix).

EXPRESSION THROUGH WORD AND MOTION

Poetry and dance can enhance the effect of recorded or live performances.

Sometimes, vocal texts underscore the ideology, as Roger Miller's "So far away it shimmers/The world softly glimmers" (Miller and Kurath 1972) and Pink Floyd's "Overhead the albatross hangs motionless upon the air, and deep beneath the rolling waves in labyrinths of coral caves, the echo of the distant tide comes billowing across the sand" (1971). Sometimes the vocals have no apparent connection with the music's meaning, or are vocables. They usually contrast with the despondent protest of eminent rock composers like the late Jimi Hendrix: "They're hoping soon my kind will drop and die/But I'm gonna wave my freak flag high, high" (quoted in Braun 1969:123). Hendrix, however, paved the way for space music by his use of experimental feedback and wah-wah.

Another art form has potentialities for intensifying the moods and patterns, namely, the dance. Much of this music is kinetic. It invites movement, visualization of the rhythms, spatial designs, and quality, for instance, by rotations to "Nocturnal mission", movement responses to "Point of view", or arm sweeps and hand flutters for *In the wake of Poseidon*.

Space music is suited to multimedia productions, as could be seen in an experimental performance of "Noise for western dawn" on November 16, 1972, before a receptive audience at the University of Michigan Union ballroom. Those present responded to the musical and kinetic message of expanded consciousness. Such sessions will probably never develop into a religious cult, but they can invigorate both the creators and recipients by the new sounds and optimistic vistas. Susannah Juni's choreographic notes for this music follow in the appendix.

APPENDIX: A MULTIMEDIA EVENT

Noise for western dawn was a multimedia event which began as a sound/visual poem by Jim Peters. This combined the sound piece (made by manually distorting the sounds on a tape recorder) and the *dawn* slides, which were shown on the screen directly behind the stage area. There were six slides, each with the word *dawn* written in different languages, starting in Sanskrit and ending with English. Other elements were added to this "poem":

Dancers wore white tank-style leotards and white tights. There was a corps of six dancers who appeared throughout the piece. Other dancers, forming a total cast of fourteen, joined for certain sections [see Table 1]. The plain white costumes were chosen for their simplicity and for showing the dancers as human bodies. It was hoped that the audience might identify with human forms. A very important reason for wearing white was its suitability for videotaping, which was done live during the event and projected simultaneously on the nine-by-twelve-foot screen opposite the front of the stage [see Figure 1]. There were three cameras taping at once. These images were then carried over to monitors where people viewed the images, put them through special effects generators, and chose which of them to show on the large screen visible to the audience. This was all done very quickly so that what was actually going on could be seen simultaneously on the screen but with special effects added.

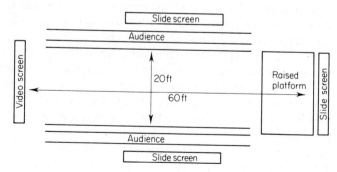

Figure 1.   Space for "Noise for western dawn"

Table 1.   Dance notes for "Noise for western dawn"

Tape numbering	Dawn slides, music	Technical dance data	Dance themes
000		six dancers enter, in blackout	
010			
020		lights	
	Slide 1 begins	*Static group improvisation* (forty-five seconds)	introduction
030		dancers stand in close group slow continuous sway shuffle: press parts of body and release with a shuffle	allows audience to settle themselves nonhuman, machine-like
040	rhythmic change	flicks: high energy, fast, with joints and appendages crouches, fast but relaxed	borderline between movement and silent stillness
050		strike unfocused shape minor switch in position *Transition: domino arm trick*	
060	musical tones louder, higher,	directional arms as a vehicle for focus	
070	faster	*School of fish improvisation* (forty-five seconds) breaking and forming a school of fish	first real movement in dance
		chaos versus group focus	intelligence has progressed but is still small
080		constant interdependence fast, simple, skittery shuffle lots of direction changes	be a fish, a stupid simpleton, a conformist fish
090	Slide 2 begins	on cue, converge sharply toward one of three points disperse in your own time	contrast: perfect focus, perfect chaos, yet keep
100	dying down to slow background	*Transition* convergence done slowly, not sharply	a sheeplike interdependence, even during chaos
110	rhythm— energy builds	change to slow sustained movement	
120	loud, clear	*Animal improvisation* (three minutes) move as an intelligent unit	marked increase in intelligence
130		remain integrated, sustained, close, focussed (e.g. with eyes), simple	animal sustained as a feline stalker
140	dying down to slow background		
150	rhythm— energy builds		each dancer is just a part of the body of the animal formed by all
160	loud, clear		
170			
180	dying down to slow background		
190	rhythm— energy builds		

Table 1.　(*continued*)

Tape numbering	Dawn slides, music	Technical dance data	Dance themes
200	loud, clear		
210			
	less sound, same energy	*Transition*: quick change to: *March dance* (thirty seconds)	first human element first comic element
220		choreographed	foreshadowing to circus
230			
	Slide 3 begins	*Refining dance* (one minute, fifty-five seconds)	
240		an energetic, precise, repeated phrase moves the group group is refined by throwing off dancers	shedding waste working for pure product
250		"waste" rolls into audience nine dancers move through mud, get stuck, but always move forward	evolution
260	brief pause	five dancers, then three, then solo: choreographed phrases each increasing in purity	
270	higher pitch swishing, blowing sound	*Transition* soloist exits stage left	
280	Slide 4 begins	entire cast enters right *Carpet dance* (two minutes) all dancers walk on and carpet	a pause, a moment to rest
290	a jab of sound electronics breaks background	stage with their bodies one by one	a time for video to be fancy, to take focus of audience
300			
310	break beginning of return to electronic		
320	activity		
330	pause in rhythm tones	*Transition* a close row of dancers forms downstage	
340	duck sounds Slide 5 begins	two dancers behind them *The breaking of dawn* (forty-five seconds) struggle: upstagers try to break	body parts peeking through line give
350	return to activity	through downstagers downstagers resist them	image of rays of sun
	energy–loudness increasing	finally there is a center-line breakthrough	first appearance of light in night sky
360	beeps, jabbing sounds	line turns inside out *Transition*	dawn has broken
370	Slide 6 begins	as line turns, dancers assume set circus roles	through the night
	band music enters	rest of cast rushes on	

Table 1. (*continued*)

Tape numbering	Dawn slides, music	Technical dance data	Dance themes
380	band alone	*Circus* (three minutes) much going on could extend onto aisle, audience-suggestions	a celebration, a festival of dawn like a circus fun
390			frivolous
	electronics enter	piston group moving simply, powerfully, up and down	a gay blast no need to be perfect
400	band alone electronics background	languid, glassy, dancy trio buffoons: boorish, sloppy, and taking too much space	
410		trio of chasers	
	electronics foreground	two groups demonstrate spectacular shows of energy	
420		body tower	
	band alone	line of dancers doing fly movements	
430		merry-go-round of bodies other preplanned activities	
440		many dancers are deceived as they rush to conquer a girl center aisle	
450			
460			
470			
	electronics enter	*Transition* on cue, dancers congregate	pure, serene, holy feeling
480	electronics alone	form tight, silent, but dynamic group	celebration may be a
	band alone	*Ending* (three minutes)	circus, but friends;
490	conflict	begin to move as a group out through aisle	dawn is not just a
	electronics alone silence	shed soloist center aisle group exits past video screen area as solo continues, be seated with the audience solo ends soloist sits in audience	joke

One of these special effects was a ten-second delay, so one could see on the screen what had happened ten seconds before.

An important feature was that several images could be "mixed" together on the screen. For instance, one could watch what was going on right then and what happened ten seconds before, all at the same time, on the video screen. One could, of course, also watch the live dancers. Video also produced other spectacular effects.

Another facet of the event was the projection of dance slides that had been taken beforehand. A "Kodalift" process left only black and white tones. Then solid colors were added to the pictures, making combinations of either black and red, black and yellow, or black and green. Throughout the piece different sets of these slides were projected simultaneously on the two slide screens behind the audience.

All the above-mentioned events were happening at once for the fifteen minutes' duration. The audience was presented with a "sensory overload" in that there were more things going on at once than they could possibly absorb.

REFERENCES

BRAUN, DUANE, *editor*
  1969   *The sociology and history of popular American music and dance, 1920–1968.* Ann Arbor, Michigan: Ann Arbor Publishers.
KURATH, GERTRUDE P., *editor*
  1971   *Radiant call.* Ann Arbor, Michigan: Ann Arbor Publishers.
MILLER, ROGER, GERTRUDE P. KURATH
  1972   *With magnetic fields disrupted,* score and tape recording. Ann Arbor, Michigan: Ann Arbor Publishers.
PETERS, JAMES
  1972   *Noise for western dawn,* poetry and tape recording. Ann Arbor, Michigan: James Peters.

Music
ELECTRIC PRUNES
  1967   *Mass in F minor.* Composed by David A. Axelrod. Reprise RS 6275.
KING CRIMSON
  1970   *In the wake of Poseidon.* Island 88024 ET.
LAWS, HUBERT
  1971   *Afro-classic.* CTI 6006.
MANN, HERBIE
  1967   *The wailing dervishes.* Atlantic
MODERN JAZZ QUARTET
  1969   *Space.* Apple STAO 3360.
PERREY, JEAN-JACQUES, GERSHON KINGSLEY
  n.d.   *The in sound from way out.* Vanguard.
PINK FLOYD
  1970   *Ummagumma,* two records. Harvest STBB 388.
  1971   "Echoes," on *Meddle.* Harvest SMAS 832.
SANDERS, PHARAOH
  1969   *Karma.* Impulse AS 9181.
SCHIFRIN, LALO
  1965   *Jazz suite on Mass texts.* RCA Victor LSP 3414.
SHORTER, WAYNE
  1969   *Super nova.* Blue Note BST 84 332.
WILLIAMS, TONY
  1969   *Emergency!* Polydor 2425 016.

Biographical Notes

MADELEINE V. ANDJELIĆ. No biographical data available.

JOHN BLACKING (1928–) is Professor and Head of the Department of Social Anthropology at Queen's University, Belfast, Northern Ireland. His interests include Venda music, ethnomusicology, cognitive anthropology, religion and education, music of the Gwembetonga and Nsenga, Zambia, and black power and white racist politics in white South Africa. His numerous publications include *How musical is man?*, *Process and product in human society*, "Tonal organization in the music of two Venda initiation schools," and *Music from Petauke* (2 long-playing records).

ANOOP C. CHANDOLA (1937–) is Professor of Linguistics and Oriental Studies, Oriental Studies Department, University of Arizona, Tucson. His main areas of interest are in evolutionary theory and method of language description, music and linguistics, Himalayan (Garhwali) folklore and linguistics, Hindi language and literature, Sanskrit, and Indic culture and civilization. His publications include *A systematic translation of Hindi-Urdu into English*, "Some systems of musical scales and linguistic principles," and "Metalinguistic structure of Indian drumming — a study in musicolinguistics."

EMILIA COMIŞEL (1913–) is a Professor at the Conservatorul "Ciprian Porumbescu" and Institut de studi sud-est europene in Bucharest. Her major interests are in the folk music and ethnology of Rumania, and comparative folk music and human geography. Her publications include "La forme architectonique de la musique populaire", "Les gueres de la musique populaire roumaine-Döuia," *The Roumanian popular ballade*, and *La musique de la ballade roumaine*.

JUDITH LYNNE HANNA (1936–   ) received her Ph.D. from Columbia University in 1976. She currently teaches in the Department of Family and Community Development, University of Maryland. She previously taught at University of Texas, Dallas and Fordham University, Lincoln Center Campus. Her main areas of interest are nonverbal communication, urban political behavior, education, arts and society, dance, and semiotics. Her publications include *To dance is human, Urban dynamics in black Africa, Dance and the social sciences*, and "The Dance-Plays of Biafra's Ubakala clan."

MIDORI HIMENO (1932–   ) is a Lecturer in Ethnomusicology at Shohwa Jr. College of Music, Japan. His main area of interest is in the ethnomusicology of Taiwan.

ROBERT KAUFFMAN. No biographical data available.

JOANN W. KEALIINOHOMOKU (1930–   ) is currently teaching at the University of Arizona, Tucson. She was previously Assistant Professor of Anthropology and Dance, World Campus Afloat, Chapman College, Orange, California. Her interests are dance ethnology, theory and methodology, especially non-European, Hopi Indian pottery, and affective culture, especially Hopi Indian and Hawai'ian. Her publications include "Folk dance," "Hopi and Polynesian dance: a study in cross-cultural comparisons," and "Dance and self-accompaniment."

GERHARD KUBIK (1934–   ) teaches at the Institut für Volkerkunde, Universität Wien. His special interests are boys' initiation schools, particularly in southeast Angola and northwest Zambia, court music, musical transcription from film, pattern perception and recognition in African music, and psychic projections in intercultural contact. His publications include *The Kachamba Brothers' band, Die Institution mukanda und assoziierte Einrichtungen bei den Vambwela/Vankangela in Südostangola*, and *Mehrstimmigkeit und Tonsysteme in Zentral-und Ostafrika*.

GERTRUDE KURATH. No biographical data available.

OLIVERA MLADENOVIĆ. No biographical data available.

JOSEPH G. MOORE (1904–   ) was formerly a Professor of Anthropology and Director of the Behavioral Sciences Division, Bridgewater State College, Massachusetts. His areas of interest are contemporary Jamaican and Cumina music and dance, contemporary Jamaican and Haitian social structure, contemporary Afro-American language structure, contemporary social organization, and contemporary spirit possession as cultural inheritance. His publications include "Religious syncretism in Jamaica," and *A comparative study of Acculturation in Morant Bay and West Kingston.*

CONG-HUYEN-TON-NU NA-TRANG. No biographical data available.

C. O. OKOREAFFIA (1926–) teaches at the Institute of African Studies, University of Nigeria, Nsukka. His special interests are in Igbo studies, language and culture, especially in eastern, central, and southern Nigeria, and Efik studies.

HEWITT PANTALEONI (1929–) is an Associate Professor of Music at the State University College, Oneonta, New York. His principal interest is ensemble drumming, its timing and structure. His publications include "Three principles of timing in A 1 dance drumming," "Toward understanding the play of Sego in Atsia," and "A possible notation for African dance drumming."

ANN M. PESCATELLO. No biographical data available.

E. KH. PETROSIAN. No biographical data available

B. N. PUTILOV. No biographical data available.

S. LEE SEATON (1943–) received his Ph.D. from the University of Hawaii. Until recently he was Assistant Professor of Anthropology at Bowling Green State University, Ohio. He is now Manager for Administrative Planning at Vydec Inc., New Jersey. His main publications include "The Hawaiian kapu abolition of 1819" in *American Ethnologist* (1974) and "The early State in Hawaii" in *The early state* (1978).

KSENIA SIKHARULIDZE. No biographical data available.

ELKIN THAMSANQA SITHOLE. No biographical data available.

GHIZELA SULIȚEANU. No biographical data available.

RURIKO UCHIDO (1920–) is a member of the staff of the Kunitachi Music College, Tokyo. His main interests are in the music of Japan, Amami Islands and South Korea, particularly in rice-planting music. His publications include "Uber das japanische Volkslied," and "The musical character of 'Taue-Baxashi,' a rice-planting music in Japan."

BONNIE C. WADE. No biographical data available.

KAREN ANN WATSON (1942–   ) has taught in the Department of Anthropology, California State University, Hayward. Her interests are in the areas of narrative patterns and creole speech of Hawaiian children, theoretical problems in narrative and myth, world song style, social context of speech behavior, and social context of speech behavior, narration, and conservation. Her publications include "A rhetorical and sociolinguistic model for the analysis of narrative" and "A proto-ethnosemantic differential for American cultural insignia: team totems in major league sports."

M. IA. ZHORNITSKAIA. No biographical data available.

Index of Names

Index of Subjects

Aboriginal song styles of Taiwan. *See* Taiwan music, aboriginal

Actresses: increasing freedom of in Spain, 127, 128; La Caramba, flamenco singer, 134; Maria Calderon, 129; Maria de Riquelme, 129; modern Indian film stars, 132, 133; modern Spanish, repertory, 132; participation limited in medieval Europe, 124, 124n, 125

"Affective culture": decline of in Hawaii, 58–59; a definition, 47–48; recent Hawaiian reinterpretations, 60–63; survival in Balinese dance, 53

African music, pattern perception and recognition in: abstract content of patterns, 231; Ambasa's tuning patterns, 238, 239, 240; choirs, tone and scale in, 246; conceptions of scale, 222; elementary and scanning patterns, 234, 235; film studies of motional patterns, Angola, 230–231; guitarists, Congo, 228, 229; harp tuning approximations, 245, 246; inherent patterns of textual phrases, 232, 233, 234, 235, 236; instrumental varieties, 235; Malawi multiple patterns, 227; melodic pitch layers, 233, 235; melodies, amadina and timbre, 235; patterns as source of pleasure, 228; rhythmic patterns, 223, 224, 226, 227, 228; rôle of the third musician, 236–237; scales, African and European, 242–244; sonic and non-sonic patterns, 230, 231; structured co-relation of patterns, 223–224; as a system of movement patterns, 227–231; tuning of the xylophone, 238–240; xylophone rhythmic patterns, 225–226, 232

African music, tactility and aesthetics in. *See* tactility and aesthetics in African music

Afro-American music, African influence in: asymmetrical timelines, 290; Anlo ensemble, Ghana, 287–290; Anlo rhythmic features, 288–289; drums, introduced and ancient, 287–288; notation problems, 288; pitch levels and timing, 289, 290

Armenia: dance styles of, 31, round dance studies in, 81, 84. *See also* Totemic Dances, Armenian

Balinese dance: Balinese self-awareness, 54; the *gamelán*, 49, 50–51; Hinduism and animism in, 52; ritual requirements of, 51; tradition common to all, 48–49, 52

Balkan tiered dance variations, 74, 76

Ballet: devices to convey meaning, 37; modern Spanish *Teatro Zarzuela*, 132

Boléro (Ravel), Lévi-Strauss' structural analysis of, 13

Bucharest Ethnological and Folklore Institute, 185n

Calendar of Rumanian feasts and customs, *See* Folklore calendar, Rumanian

California, Juanenno ritual round dancing, 75

Cantometrics, Lomax's project: circumplex interpretation, 97–99; clusters I-IV, 96–97, 102; clusters, I-VI, 104; cluster/model summary, 106; dendrogram, condensed, 104; ethnic units, rotated configuration, 100–101; grouped variables studied, 93–94; models for song styles, hypothesized, 95–97, 104, 105,